THE TURNING POINT

Roosevelt, Stalin, Churchill, and Chiang-Kai-Shek, 1943
The Moscow, Cairo, and Teheran Conferences

THE
TURNING POINT

———◆———

Roosevelt, Stalin, Churchill, and Chiang-Kai-Shek, 1943
The Moscow, Cairo, and Teheran Conferences

KEITH SAINSBURY

Oxford   New York
OXFORD UNIVERSITY PRESS
1985

Oxford University Press, Walton Street, Oxford OX2 6DP

London New York Toronto
Delhi Bombay Calcutta Madras Karachi
Kuala Lumpur Singapore Hong Kong Tokyo
Nairobi Dar es Salaam Cape Town
Melbourne Auckland

and associated companies in
Beirut Berlin Ibadan Mexico City Nicosia

Oxford is a trade mark of Oxford University Press

Published in the United States
by Oxford University Press, New York

British Library Cataloguing in Publication Data

Sainsbury, Keith
The turning point.
1. Teheran Conference
I. Title
940.53'14   D734.T4
ISBN 0-19-215858-9

Library of Congress Cataloging in Publication Data

Sainsbury, Keith.
The turning point.
Bibliography: p.
Includes index.
1. World War, 1939–1945—Diplomatic history.
2. Moscow Conference (1943)   3. Cairo Conference (1943)
4. Teheran Conference (1943)   I. Title
D749.S25   1985   940.53'2   84-12237
ISBN 0-19-215858-9

033588

24.95

Set by Getset (Bowden Typesetting Services) Ltd
Printed in Great Britain
at the University Press, Oxford
by David Stanford
Printer to the University

To
Geoffrey Warner
amicitiae causa

The Russians referred to the year that had passed (1943) as 'perelom'—the 'turning-point'.

Averell Harriman

The greatest tragedies of history have occurred not so much because of what was finally done, but because of what had earlier been foolishly left undone.

Robert McNamara

CONTENTS

INTRODUCTION AND
ACKNOWLEDGEMENTS

Much has been written about the Yalta and Potsdam conferences, but the first meeting between the three Allied leaders at Teheran has been somewhat neglected. It is time the omission was remedied, because the Teheran conference had its own importance. Militarily, it decided the main course of Allied strategy till the war's end. Politically, it paved the way for the Yalta division of Europe and much of the rest of the world into American and Soviet spheres of interest. There is also a particular interest in the fact that it was the first tripartite conference, and hence the first meeting of Roosevelt with Stalin.

The conference therefore was important in two different ways. Militarily, it marked the moment when American strategic ideas prevailed over the British plans which had dominated the first two years of the Anglo-American alliance. It came also at the moment when it became fully apparent that the USSR would almost certainly be militarily dominant in Eastern and perhaps in Central Europe after the war; and that the Western Allies would need to adjust themselves to this fact. At this conference Soviet pressures for a Cross-Channel Attack at the earliest possible moment, accompanied by a landing in the south of France, were supported by the Americans; and hence the mainly British and Empire forces in Italy and the Eastern Mediterranean were relegated to a supporting role. It has been suggested that, by pursuing a largely British strategy for the first two years of the alliance and a largely American strategy for the remainder of the war, the Western Powers missed the full benefit of either strategy; and that, because of this, Soviet armies reached Berlin, Vienna, and Prague first, and occupied the whole of Eastern Europe—with consequences which are still with us. I have argued in a previous book[1] that the pursuit of American strategic ideas in the first days of the alliance would have involved courses that were either militarily reckless or politically impossible. I examine the second possibility—the continuance of a Mediterranean strategy—in a purely tentative way at the end of this book. It would have involved a military gamble on campaigns across unpromising territory, and a political gamble on events in Western Europe. On the whole I can find no clear evidence that any feasible alternative strategy to that which was in fact pursued would have had better results. Others, of course, have concluded differently, and may still do so.

The Teheran conference was also far-reaching in its effects politically. The outline of a Soviet–American concordat on Europe and the Far East was sketched out by Roosevelt and Stalin, which looked ahead to future agreements at Yalta. The breaking up of Germany and control of its major industrial areas, the maintenance of a large number of small States in Central and Eastern Europe, the annexation of part of pre-war Poland by Russia, and of German territory by Russia and Poland, the permanent reduction of France to a minor power, and easy Soviet access to the Baltic and Mediterranean were indicated as part of the future pattern for Europe. Churchill and Eden, on the other hand, could not secure effective guarantees for Polish independence and self-determination, or the creation of larger and more viable States in Central and Eastern Europe. In the Far East the Roosevelt–Stalin *entente* envisaged the return to China of all her losses to Japan over the past fifty years and the acceptance of Chiang-Kai-Shek's Nationalist government as the legitimate government of China. The United States was to keep its captured Japanese island bases and become effective master of the Pacific: but Russia was to have privileged access to that ocean through a Chinese port or ports on the Yellow Sea. The need for assured communications with such ports seemed also to imply a Soviet 'sphere of influence' in Manchuria. It is clear that Stalin and Roosevelt did not intend that Britain would play any major role in the Far East after the war.

In short, in many important respects the understandings arrived at at Teheran—on Poland, Germany, China, and the Pacific—foreshadowed agreements at Yalta. Just as the military decisions reflected broad Soviet–American agreement and the growing Soviet–American military predominance at this stage of the war, so did the political understandings.

It became apparent at an early stage in the writing of this book that the four days' discussions at Teheran in November–December 1943 had to be seen in the light of previous negotiations at the Moscow Foreign Ministers' conference and the Anglo-American–Chinese conference at Cairo. The scope of this book therefore expanded to include a detailed account of both those conferences. The fact that most of the British documents, including the minutes of these conferences, are still unpublished made a narrative account seem desirable. This in turn ruled out certain other things, if the book was to remain a reasonable length. I have had largely to leave to other scholars the task of whatever fresh analysis of the consequences of

Teheran may seem desirable in the light of this account; and I have also had to eschew any detailed consideration of the origins and formulation of the political proposals which emerged at these conferences. There is still much to be done in this latter field, in the way of scrutiny of Foreign Office files particularly. As Professor Mark Stoler and others have pointed out, the sheer bulk of Second World War records imposes in any case the necessity of selectivity. Confronted with this overwhelming bulk, the scholar must often share the feelings of the Bishop of Barchester: 'In all these documents, there is a drift?' The foregoing will I hope explain the particular kind of selectivity I have chosen, both in materials and scope. To have enlarged either would have meant an even longer book, which would have taken even longer to write. Neither my publishers nor my constitution would have stood the strain. I regret, however, that I was unable to scrutinize the minutes of the US Joint Chiefs of Staff until the last stage of the writing. I have therefore been unable to give the same detailed account of their meetings as I have those of the British Chiefs.

On the vexed question of interpretation and bias, it may seem to some readers on the other side of the Atlantic that this account has an anti-American slant. I can only say that that was not my intention. I have allowed the records to take me in the direction they seem to lead. 'It is a capital error', as Holmes remarked, 'to theorize ahead of one's data.' I am not so foolish as to think this book will be read in the Soviet Union, but Soviet sympathizers on this side of the Iron Curtain may feel there is an anti-Soviet bias. Again, it is not intentional. I have tried to indicate that Soviet attitudes on political issues were usually understandable if not always justifiable; and that Soviet views on strategy, whatever political *arrière-pensée* there may have been, were based largely on rational, if over-simplified, military premisses.

Any historian of the Second World War must be immensely indebted to the official British and US historians. For this book the work of Ehrman, Howard, Matloff, Woodward, and the editors of *Foreign Relations of the United States, 1943*, has been particularly valuable. The first draft of the book was written entirely from documents, memoirs, and authorized biographies, such as those of Pogue, Sherwood, and Fraser. In revising, the works of many scholars who have touched on these conferences have been consulted. Inevitably one checks one's impressions particularly against the standard account, now twenty-five years old, of Herbert Feis. I have found Professor Stoler's *Politics of the Second Front* particularly suggestive among recent studies; and the work of Thorne, Barker, Carlton, and other historians who have quarried the British documents has been very helpful. I am grateful to the following for advice, help, or comments: Professor Elie Abel, Lio Barst, Robin Cecil, John Edmonds, Sir David Fraser, Lord Gladwyn, the Hon. Averell Harriman, Professor Michael Howard, Sir Frank Roberts, and Lord Sherfield. This book, like my previous one, has been written largely without the help of grants from foundations, but thanks are due to the Department of Politics and the Research Board of the University of Reading for assisting me from their slender resources, and to the Nuffield Foundation for help in the final stages of my work. None of the above is of course in any way responsible for any errors or shortcomings in this book. I am most grateful also to the staff of the Public Record Office, Kew, for their helpfulness; to my publishers for their patience; to my wife, Mary, and Mrs. E. Bridges, who have typed most of the manuscript; and to my old friend Professor Geoffrey Warner, who first gave me the idea for this book.

Keith Sainsbury
Caversham Heights—Emmer Green, 1979–83

ABBREVIATIONS

CBI	China/Burma/India Theatre
CCAC	Combined Civil Affairs Committee (in Washington)
CCS	Combined Chiefs of Staff
Cd	Command
CIGS	Chief of Imperial General Staff
C.-in-C.	Commander-in-Chief
C.o.S.	British Chiefs of Staff
COSSAC	Chief of Staff to the Supreme Allied Commander (Designate)
EAC	European Advisory Commission
FCNL	French Committee of National Liberation
FO	Foreign Office
IAC	Italian Advisory Council
JCS	American Joint Chiefs of Staff
LST	Landing Ship (Tanks)
OPD	Operations Planning Division, US War Department
SEAC	South East Asia Command
UK	United Kingdom
US	United States

THE C.C.S.

Routine meetings of the Combined Chiefs were held in Washington, and attended by the US Chiefs (General Marshall, Admiral Leahy, Admiral King, General Arnold) and representatives of the three British Chiefs. At international conferences the latter (General Brooke, Air Chief Marshal Portal, Admiral Cunningham, and General Ismay) replaced their Washington representatives. Exceptionally Brooke's Washington deputy, General Dill, also attended at international conferences. It is generally conceded that Marshall and Portal were exceptional in their ability to transcend national and service viewpoints, while King fell short in that respect.

CODE-NAMES

ANVIL, later DRAGOON   Landing in the south of France
BOLERO   Build up of US forces in UK prior to
                        invasion of Europe
BUCCANEER   Operation against the Andaman
                        Islands
CULVERIN   Operations against northern
                        Sumatra/Malaya
HERCULES   Operation against Rhodes
OVERLORD   Invasion of north-west Europe
QUADRANT   First Quebec Conference, 1943
RANKIN   Operations to exploit a German
                        collapse
SEXTANT   The Cairo Conference, 1943
SHINGLE   Landing at Anzio
TARZAN   Advance on Indaw/Katha area in
                        Burma
TRIDENT   Third Washington Conference, 1943

CHAPTER I

THE GENESIS OF THE TRIPARTITE MEETINGS

On an October morning in 1943 the US Secretary of State, Cordell Hull, boarded a plane in Washington on the first stage of the long journey to Moscow. It was an arduous journey in wartime conditions for a man in his seventies, who had never flown before; and partly for this reason there had been for some time considerable doubt whether the United States would be represented at the forthcoming Foreign Ministers' conference by its Secretary of State. Hull's chief, President Roosevelt, had for a time considered sending the Under-Secretary of State, Sumner Welles, and the Ambassador-Designate to the USSR, Averell Harriman, to meet the British and Soviet delegates. To both of these men he felt closer personally and to some extent in thought than he did towards Hull. Indeed, though he respected Hull's integrity, Roosevelt doubted the Secretary's diplomatic and intellectual capacity to deal with the complex issues which would be discussed.

It had become apparent, however, that there were compelling reasons for Hull to attend the conference. It was feared that if the United States did not send its Secretary of State, the Soviet Government would feel that America was not taking the conference seriously. There had been strong Soviet pressure for this, the first tripartite conference of the war, to be held in Moscow. The non-attendance of the American Foreign Minister would all the more seem like a snub to the Soviet government, which was always ready to take offence, and perpetually suspicious of Western intentions. Roosevelt at this stage of the war was particularly conscious of the need to break down this Soviet 'wall of suspicion', so that the United States and Russia should act together to settle the innumerable problems of the post-war world. In particular he was anxious to secure agreement on the setting up of an international peace-keeping organization in which Russian participation would be vital. Hull himself fully shared these views. It was, however, a matter of domestic politics which finally precipitated Hull's decision to go. The Secretary had long been jealous of Welles' influence with the President, and was aware that the younger man had frequently criticized him. The suggestion that his place might be taken, and his functions usurped, by a disloyal subordinate was too much for him. He insisted on going.

Roosevelt had then proposed to the Soviet government that, out of consideration for Hull, the conference should be shifted nearer to the United States, perhaps to the United Kingdom, or better still to Casablanca or Tunis. In North Africa there were large American forces under an American Supreme Commander. An American presence and American pressures would be more effectively felt there than in either Moscow or London. The British Premier, Winston Churchill, also weighed in with proposals which, oddly enough, tended to suggest a meeting in London or, failing that, some point in the Near East under British influence. But the Soviet Government was obdurate. Moscow it had to be. [1]

The proposed conference had originated in the first place as a by-product of Roosevelt's wish for a personal meeting with the Soviet leader Stalin. As early as December 1941 the President had proposed such a meeting to Stalin, and again in April and May 1942. At the end of 1942 he proposed Stalin should join Churchill and himself at the Casablanca meeting. Roosevelt was fully aware of the deep ideological gulf which separated his British ally, Churchill, the Tory imperialist, and Stalin, the Soviet Communist; he was also aware, as was Hull, that so long as Britain remained a world-wide imperial power, there would probably be a continuation of the conflict of interests between Russia and Britain in the Near and Middle East and the North-west Frontier of India which had existed since the nineteenth century. Roosevelt and Hull believed that provided the USSR was not deter-mined on either ideological or territorial expansion, particularly in the Far East, there was no such inevitable conflict of interests between the United States and the USSR. Granted the premisses, this was a reasonable assumption. The President also had great faith in his personal ability to charm and persuade, and saw it as his task to win over Stalin to the principles of international co-operation. At the same time he hoped to serve as a mediating influence between Stalin and Churchill. Hull agreed with this view of the United States as me-diator. In May 1943 he said to Anthony Eden, 'Let's talk Stalin out of his shell of suspicion and into practical international co-operation.' It was not to prove as easy as that. [2]

Two obstacles had long stood in the way of this meeting. The first was the difficulty of finding a meeting-place equally acceptable to Roosevelt and Stalin. There were genuine difficulties involved. Throughout 1942 Stalin had argued that his responsibilities as the effective supreme commander of armies bearing the full brunt of enemy attack on their own soil made it impossible for him to leave Moscow. Accepting this, Churchill had flown to Moscow for a personal meeting in August 1942. When Roosevelt had invited Stalin to the Anglo-American Conference at Casablanca in January 1943, the answer had been the same. But Roosevelt's constitutional position also presented difficulties. The President of the United States had to be able to receive bills from Congress and return them with his signature or veto within ten days. This made it difficult for him to go to Moscow or anywhere else in the USSR for a meeting.[3]

The second obstacle was Churchill's wish to be present at such a meeting. During the first two years of the tripartite alliance—from June 1941 to the summer of 1943—Churchill, the most mobile though the oldest of the three, had journeyed to the United States, to North Africa, and to Canada, whenever he thought a meeting with Roosevelt was necessary. He had also flown to Moscow to meet Stalin. Not unnaturally, this arrangement, by which he was the only one of the three in direct contact with the other two, suited him quite well. Moreover, believing as he did that the Anglo-American alliance was the basic and essential cornerstone of any future system of international peace and security, he had no particular desire to see Roosevelt and Stalin move closer together. He had been perturbed by Roosevelt's suggestion to Stalin, at the time of the Anglo-American conference at Washington in May 1943, that the American and Russian leaders should meet without the British. He felt it would be dangerous to let the two men get together without him. Stalin was hostile to British imperial interests, Roosevelt at best lukewarm. There was no saying what Roosevelt might agree to, at the expense of British interests, in his desire to win the Soviet leader's confidence and trust. Nor was he sure that Roosevelt could be trusted to stand up to Stalin on such questions as the future of Poland, already a source of contention between Britain and the USSR.[4]

This view had been confirmed by the events of May to August 1943. In the latter month Churchill and Roosevelt met again at Quebec. Churchill had stressed both publicly and to Roosevelt the importance of maintaining the Anglo-American alliance after the war. Roosevelt, however, considered that future peace and security depended far more on *four*-power co-operation in the future—that is, between the US, Britain, the Soviet Union, and China. The introduction of Chiang-Kai-Shek, the Chinese Nationalist leader, into the equation, as well as Russia, alarmed and annoyed Churchill. He had little faith in the capacity of the Chinese Nationalist government, either militarily or politically, and he regarded Chiang-Kai-Shek as quite as much an enemy of British imperial interests as Stalin.[5]

Since the Washington conference in May, moreover, relations between the Soviet Union and the Western Allies had deteriorated alarmingly. Stalin had reacted badly to the military decisions taken at the conference. Earlier in the year he had seemed to suggest that a meeting might be possible in 1943. But at the Washington meeting it had been decided to follow up the successful Mediterranean operations of the Anglo-American forces with attacks not only on Sicily, as already agreed, but probably on the Italian mainland. The long-promised Allied invasion of north-west Europe, which Stalin had been demanding since 1941, would not now take place till May 1944. Bitter reproaches followed from Moscow in personal messages from Stalin to Roosevelt and Churchill. Stalin particularly resented the fact that decisions vitally affecting Soviet interests had been taken by the British and Americans without consulting him. To signify his displeasure, he withdrew his tentative agreement to meet with Roosevelt in July or August. Stalin had also broken off relations with the London-based Polish government-in-exile in April, thus further exacerbating the already contentious problem of agreement on Poland's future. In addition there was bad feeling between London and Moscow on the subject of the costly and murderous Arctic convoys to Russia. Stalin regarded these as a binding commitment on the British government. Churchill did not accept this view. The convoys were one of the many commitments it was desirable to maintain if possible, but not in all possible circumstances and whatever the cost. Amid these mutual recriminations, relations between Russia and the Western Allies had reached a new low ebb, and were further exacerbated by Anglo-American negotiations for the surrender of Italy following the fall of Mussolini, about which Stalin said he was insufficiently informed.[6]

Roosevelt reacted to Stalin's displeasure by redoubling his efforts to bring about a personal meeting. Churchill for his part was rather less concerned. He was accustomed to Soviet reproaches, of which he had borne the brunt for the past two years. The fact that the USSR had stood aside from the conflict during the crucial year 1940–1, while Britain stood alone, made him less sympathetic than Roosevelt to Soviet pleas. Nevertheless, he felt the need to do something to restore a semblance of cordiality, and was urged to do so by his Ambassador in Moscow, Sir Archibald Clark Kerr. Churchill's first suggestion was that his Foreign Secretary, Anthony Eden, should go to Moscow, 'to smooth the bristles of the bear' as the latter put it. Stalin however saw no point in receiving a visitor who would merely repeat the unpleasant arguments about the Second Front and the convoys with which he was already familiar. If there was to be any kind of meeting, the Americans should also be there. On 8 August Stalin telegraphed to Roosevelt and Churchill, agreeing that a meeting of the three heads of government was 'desirable at the first opportunity' but reiterating that this would not be possible for him until the summer and autumn campaigning period was over. This pointed to late October or early November at the earliest. In the meantime, the Soviet leader proposed that a meeting of 'responsible representatives' of the Three Powers should take place to prepare the ground for the heads of government, and stressed the need for an agreed agenda and specific proposals beforehand.[7]

After consulting the War Cabinet, and in particular his Foreign Secretary, Churchill, who was with Roosevelt at the Quebec conference, conferred with the President. Roosevelt took a little while to make up his mind. A meeting of this kind was not quite what he had envisaged. Moreover the desirability of Cordell Hull attending such a meeting, probably in Moscow, raised all sorts of problems of the kind already enumerated. However, on 18 August he and Churchill telegraphed to Stalin accepting the idea of a meeting at 'Foreign Office level' in principle, but emphasizing that such a conference would be 'exploratory' in character, rather than one which would take decisions. Roosevelt was not minded to give too much scope to a conference at which he would not himself be present. It was to require two months' prolonged discussion and much argument about time, place, and personnel before the agreed meeting took place. Finally, however, all the loose ends were tied, and on 7 October Hull left on the first stage of his long journey. Two days later Eden left London for Cairo, Teheran, and Moscow.[8]

CHAPTER II

CONFLICTING AIMS AND OBJECTIVES

1. The US Approach to the Conference

The 'exploratory' meeting which Roosevelt and probably Churchill also envisaged was to turn out a much more elaborate and detailed affair than that description implied. It was indeed to produce more detailed agreements than any previous wartime conference. That this was so was due partly to the determination of Hull and Eden to achieve concrete results; and partly to the stipulation, which the Soviet government had made from the beginning, that the Western Allies should submit detailed agendas and proposals in advance of the conference. A formal, even bureaucratic approach was thus imposed on Britain and the United States from the outset, contrary to both Roosevelt's and Churchill's natural inclinations. Roosevelt indeed had added to his original insistence that the meeting should be 'exploratory' a further characteristic suggestion that there should be an 'informal list of subjects' and that the ministers should be free to 'discuss anything'. This preference for an informal meeting had to give way to the pressure for an orderly agenda. Hull's approach to the conference in fact, and particularly that of his State Department officials, was more systematic and orderly than that of his chief. His priorities, however, were not different from Roosevelt's. Both men regarded the agreement of Russia and Britain to the principle of post-war international co-operation as the first priority. This carried with it the necessity of securing also specific Soviet/British promises of participation in the international organizations which would be necessary to implement such co-operation. These objectives were not expected to be easy to obtain. In particular the suspicions and mistrust of the Soviet government, and its preferences for secretive and unilateral action had to be overcome. It was true Soviet experience of previous international organizations between the wars had not been encouraging for them. The League of Nations had singularly failed to halt the march of Nazi Germany, but had seemed only too ready to condemn Soviet actions. The USSR therefore would need some persuading to join a new international organization.

The problem with the British on the other hand was somewhat different. The Americans suspected that the traditionalists of the British Foreign Office had little faith in their idealistic proposals for international co-operation. The lukewarm attitude towards the League of most of the Foreign Office mandarins—and indeed of the Conservative governments—in the years between the wars certainly gave colour to this view. In addition Churchill had made it clear that he regarded the continuance of the Anglo-American alliance as a more important bulwark of post-war peace and security than any new international institution; and Eden's penchant for a revived France and perhaps, in some form, a revived Germany, together with plans he had put forward for the creation of larger federal states in Eastern Europe, seemed to point towards the kind of 'balance of power' approach to international policies which was anathema to liberal-minded Americans. It was not yet apparent to them, as it was later to be to their successors, that a defective system which works after a fashion is preferable to an ideal system which does not work at all. [1]

The American proposals for international co-operation had a further economic dimension, besides their ideas on peace-keeping and the peaceful settlement of disputes. Though neither was a profound economic thinker, both Roosevelt and Hull had been deeply impressed by the collapse of the international financial and commercial system in the early 1930s. The United States had suffered as much as any country from the internal economic depression which followed. They attributed these catastrophes firstly to the lack of international economic co-operation, particularly the failure to maintain international credit and liquidity: and secondly to the 'beggar your neighbour' policies of high tariffs, restricted markets, and other obstacles to the free flow of trade. The British Empire, with its network of preferential customs duties, had led the way along this, as the Americans saw it, destructive path. Russia, for its part, had pursued the goal of economic autarchy and rigorous State control of trade, eschewing any form of economic agreements other than bilateral ones with States which were prepared to trade with Russia on its own terms. It was important that both Britain and the USSR should commit themselves to future economic co-operation. [2]

Hull undoubtedly felt that he had considerable obstacles to overcome in the pursuit of his main objective; and it was this feeling no doubt which contributed to his euphoria when he returned from Moscow with that objective apparently accomplished. Before the conference Hull had already communicated his proposed 'Four-Power Declaration' on peace, security, and disarmament to both Russia and

Britain. This declaration constituted the main US proposal for the conference. Apart from this, the rest of the US contribution to the joint agenda for the conference also illustrated Hull's objectives, both positive and negative, and his priorities. It was relatively short. The proposed Four-Power Declaration came first. However, a Four-Power Declaration implied that the US wished China to be one of the signatories. The Soviet government immediately pointed out that this was to be a tripartite conference, in which China would not take part. Hull was already aware that it would be difficult to secure British and Soviet assent to Chinese participation in the Declaration. The British regarded China as too weak, politically and militarily, to rank as one of the 'Big Four', or as Roosevelt called them 'The Four Policemen'. The Russians for their part had no love for Chiang-Kai-Shek, shared the British view of China's weakness, and in any case did not want Far Eastern issues mixed up in the conference. They were not, as Stalin pointed out, involved in the war with Japan, and China was therefore not really an ally of theirs. Stalin professed to be afraid of provoking the Japanese into an attack on the USSR, if he seemed to be associating too closely with the Chinese Nationalists. It is unlikely, in fact, that at this stage of the war the Japanese would have wished to take on another opponent. None the less Stalin's fear may have been genuine, and was not entirely discounted by the Americans.[3]

Roosevelt and Hull, however, were determined that China's position as one of the four major Allies should be recognized. Looking to the future, they regarded China as a more suitable guardian of security in eastern Asia, and possibly a more manageable ally, than the British Empire. At the time this seemed unrealistic to Churchill and Eden and indeed to many other people. China was poor, economically backward, and riven by internal disorder and civil war. The Nationalist government controlled only about a third of the country, and that the remotest and most primitive part. The Japanese occupied about a half, including all the most advanced areas and the great commercial centres. The Chinese Communists controlled the rest. Yet twenty-five years later the British Empire in the Far East had ceased to exist, and China, united under one government for the first time since 1918, commanded enough muscle or at least enough self-confidence to defy first the United States and then the Soviet Union. Some of Cordell Hull's successors it is true might then have wished for the British Empire, with all its faults, in the place of the refractory Chinese Communists. Even Stalin's successors may sometimes have felt the same way. But these ironies of the future were mercifully hidden from Roosevelt and Hull, as indeed they were also from

Churchill and Stalin. Hull was determined that China should sign the declaration.[4]

For the rest, the US agenda recognized the need for at least some preliminary discussion of the treatment of Germany and other enemy States. Since the catastrophic German defeat at Stalingrad in February 1943 Soviet troops had driven the Germans further and further back towards the Polish frontiers: at the same time, the Western Allies' plans for the invasion of north-western Europe were already far advanced. Within a year at most, Soviet and Anglo-American troops might be approaching the frontiers of Germany from east and west—as indeed proved the case.

The Allies needed therefore to work out reasonably quickly some agreed policy in the short term for the occupation, administration, and government of a defeated Germany, and the surrender terms to be imposed upon her. It was desirable too that there should be some preliminary discussion of the long-term settlement for the German problem. Such questions as frontiers and reparations needed to be discussed, as well as the central question of whether a single unified German State should be permitted to exist. Germany was therefore the second item on the US agenda. Roosevelt and Hull had originally wanted the details of this long-term settlement, together with other territorial problems, to be left to a post-war peace conference: but they now recognized that some preliminary discussion of the issues was necessary.

Eden and Hull had already agreed that while it might be theoretically desirable to partition Germany, such a partition would be difficult to enforce on a strongly nationalist people indefinitely. It might be better to foster and encourage a decentralized federal State, which the German people might come to accept. Roosevelt and Churchill however leaned towards partition. Churchill for his part believed that Prussia, which he regarded as the root of all German evil, should be detached from the main body. The Ruhr perhaps might be internationalized; southern Germany should be united with Austria and perhaps Hungary in a federal State, which would take the place of the old Austro-Hungarian Empire, as an element in a new European balance of power. Eden however thought such a 'Danubian federation' should include only Austria and Hungary and possibly some Slav territories. Roosevelt for his part thought of a possible partition of Germany into perhaps three, four, or even five States. But he was inclined to feel that such issues should not be finally decided at this stage. Neither Roosevelt nor Hull was particularly attracted by the idea of a 'Danubian Federation'. Thus there were at least three different attitudes towards this central issue of Germany among the four main Western policy-makers, and it cannot be said that Eden and Hull had any clear and agreed long-term policy to present to the Russians. On the question of German reparations payments, Roosevelt had made it clear to Hull that he favoured payment by Germany in manpower—forced labour—and capital goods (machinery, machine tools, etc.), rather than money. He had not forgotten the lessons of reparations policies after the first World War, though he slightly misinterpreted some of them. Hull agreed with this view. Both the British and US governments were also agreed that Germany should be totally disarmed and that some form of Allied occupation would be necessary. But there were disagreements both between them and within each government as to the character and duration of the occupation.[5]

Roosevelt had indicated to Harriman, his new Ambassador to Moscow, that it might also be necessary to negotiate with Stalin and perhaps arrive at informal agreements on other territorial problems before the end of the war. Among such issues he undoubtedly included the question of German unity or partition and the disputed Polish frontiers with Russia and Germany. They might also include Russia's other territorial demands on Finland, on Romania, and in relation to the Baltic States. Roosevelt, however, intended to reserve such important matters to himself and Hull had no mandate to negotiate on them.[6]

The American leaders also recognized that, apart from long-term arrangements for international economic co-operation—on finance, trade, transport, labour, food, and agriculture—there would also need to be some short-term plans for economic reconstruction for those areas devastated by the war, particularly occupied Europe and the USSR itself. In these plans aid from the prosperous and undamaged US economy must play a key role. The United States had given generous military aid to both Britain and the Soviet Union during the war under the Lease-Lend programme. Among the inducements with which they hoped to persuade both countries to co-operate with them in the post-war era was the possibility that economic assistance would be continued in the form of grants and credits for reconstruction. These economic matters, therefore, were the third proposed item for discussion on the US agenda.[7]

The Americans also recognized the need to make some response to pressure from the Soviet and British governments for the creation of some interallied machinery for the current discussion of various European problems, which were either already causing difficulty or would soon be looming on the horizon. The problem of surrender terms and occupation arrangements for Germany was such a problem. The British government had put forward tentative proposals on this subject in July. Even more urgent was the question of the administration of liberated France, which involved the thorny problem of relations with General de Gaulle's Free French movement. De Gaulle, regarded by the Americans as a British protégé, was personally anathema to both Roosevelt and Hull. Neither had forgiven him for his characteristic brutal tactlessness in seizing two French islands off the coast of Canada in 1942 while the United States was still engaged in negotiations for their surrender. So far as possible they had excluded the Free French from the campaign to occupy French North Africa, and had only reluctantly agreed that the Gaullists should participate in its subsequent administration. That de Gaulle had thereafter easily outwitted and removed the American nominee, Giraud, was not calculated to endear him further to the Americans. Yet it was clear that the Free French leader already exercised great authority over the major part of the French resistance movement; and that when France was liberated, a substantial proportion of political leaders in occupied France would look to de Gaulle and the Free French as the natural heirs of French authority and government. Eden was well aware of this, and believed the time was coming when the Free French 'National Committee' should be recognized as the provisional government of France.[8]

A further problem which was already contributing to the unsatisfactory state of Soviet relations with the Allies was Italy. An armistice agreement with Italy had been hastily and secretly arrived at by the British and Americans after the overthrow of Mussolini in July 1943. At the beginning of September Anglo-American forces had invaded southern Italy and by October occupied about a third of the country. The Soviet government had resented the fact that it had not been adequately consulted on the armistice terms for Italy, and questioned the readiness of the Anglo-Americans to have dealings with and allow authority to such leading figures of the Fascist era as Marshal Badoglio, the Italian Prime Minister. Did the United States and Britain, they asked, really intend to dismantle the Fascist regime? In the circumstances it was not an unreasonable question. The Soviet leaders demanded that some interallied body should be created, with Soviet representation, which would ensure that in future the USSR knew what was going on in Italy, and could influence Allied policy there.[9]

In response to these British and Soviet pressures, the Americans thought it expedient to propose as a fourth main item for discussion 'Methods of dealing with current political and economic issues'. At the same time, however, they made it clear that they had doubts about the need for any new interallied bodies. Roosevelt had no enthusiasm for the creation of any organization which he could not directly control, either in Italy, as the Russians were demanding, or in London, as Eden was eventually to propose. Hull shared this view, and in addition had a foreign minister's normal preference for the negotiation of such matters through regular diplomatic channels. There might perhaps be issues which could be decided by one or the other of the foreign ministers meeting with the ambassadors of the other two. If any additional mechanism were required, it could be provided by further meetings of the foreign ministers themselves.[10] The Americans of course recognized that they would have to be ready to discuss such matters at the conference if either of the other two participants wished it; and the nature of the proposed British agenda soon made it clear that Eden and the British government did so wish. As for the Soviet demand for participation in some interallied body dealing with Italy, it was felt expedient to concede this in principle even before the conference began—with the important proviso that it should be 'advisory' and 'consultative' only, not decision-making. But the nature of the US agenda indicated that such matters were not high on their list of priorities.[11]

Indeed it was clear that the US stance in relation to this conference had as important a negative as a positive aspect. This took two forms. On political issues it was clear that Hull had no authority to endorse any general principles for a European settlement, such as Eden was proposing. The latter had put forward a proposal for a 'Declaration on Joint Allied responsibility', rather than 'Separate' responsibility for different areas of Europe. In effect Eden was inviting the United States and Russia to endorse the principle that none of the three States was seeking special 'spheres of influence' in any part of Europe. This would have given the United States and Britain an equal right with Russia to exert influence on the settlement in Eastern Europe; and of course also conferred on the USSR equal rights with Britain and the United States in relation to Italy and Western Europe. It is difficult to see how the United States could possibly have objected to such an un-exceptionable principle, particularly as it embodied Hull's deep-rooted objection to the whole idea of 'spheres of influence'. This he regarded as part and parcel of the bad old system of power politics, which the United States wished to sweep into the lumber room of history. Yet the US response to Eden's suggestion was extraordinarily cold and discouraging. Probably this was due to Eden's rather ill-advised inclusion in the declaration of a commitment to encourage 'federations' among the smaller States of Europe. The truth is that Roosevelt probably regarded the declaration as an attempt to embroil the United States prematurely in the contentious problems of Eastern Europe; especially the problem of Poland, where the US might seem to be participating in British support for the London Polish government-in-exile. The latter was regarded by the Soviet government as reactionary and hostile to the USSR. Roosevelt and Hull had no intention of antagonizing the USSR over a problem which they did not regard as a vital US interest, as Hull made clear to the Polish Ambassador in Washington. The British and American governments had already agreed at the Quebec conference on a draft 'Declaration on Liberated Territories' which bound the Allies to transfer power in the liberated countries of occupied Europe from military to local civilian authorities at the earliest possible moment. This declaration, which had been transmitted to the Soviet government, accepted the right of 'constituted governments' recognized by the Allies (that is, the European governments-in-exile) to share in this process of civil administration, pending the holding of free elections. Moscow however had objected, and the proposal was withdrawn. Roosevelt therefore proposed to choose his own moment to exert American influence on the Polish question and other problems arising from Soviet claims in Eastern Europe. Hull indicated as much to Eden, when the latter asked for US help to bring about a reconciliation between Russia and the London Poles. It was clear that on this issue Hull wished to hold a 'watching brief' at the Foreign Ministers' conference.

Eden had no more luck with his other proposal for Eastern Europe, mentioned above, which envisaged Allied encouragement of federal groupings of the smaller States of the region. There was much to be said for these proposals which, if successful, would have given Eastern Europe greater political and economic stability and contributed to its independence. The Soviet government, however, had already made it clear that it regarded these plans as an attempt to recreate, in a different, and more effective form, the so-called 'cordon sanitaire' of the inter-war years. This was the policy of establishing a network of alliances between the small States of the area and the West, which had been designed to exclude Soviet influence from Eastern Europe. Realistically the Soviet leaders saw no reason why they should agree to proposals which would be likely to strengthen anti-Soviet forces in that area and erect more effective obstacles to Soviet objectives. Roosevelt and Hull for their part regarded the Soviet veto as effectively aborting any such plans, since, if persevered with, they might antagonize the USSR. On this issue, too, therefore, Eden could expect little help from the United States. [12]

On military and strategic questions, the US approach was equally negative and here coincided with the British attitude. The important Anglo-American decisions in this field had, for better or worse, already been taken, particularly on Mediterranean operations and the timing and strength of the proposed Cross-Channel Attack in 1944. The British and Americans could do no more than elaborate the details for the benefit of their Soviet allies. Roosevelt and Churchill had made it clear to Stalin before the conference that they could not regard the meeting as primarily a military conference. Indeed the Foreign Ministers were not technically equipped to discuss such issues, as Hull pointed out to his Soviet counterpart. Nevertheless, the Americans, and more grudgingly the British, recognized that they could not avoid some discussion of these matters. The USSR made it clear that the Cross-Channel Attack was for them the most important item on any agenda. Moreover the Americans at least recognized that, after so many disappointments, the Russians could reasonably expect some reassurance that at last a Cross-Channel operation was definitely to take place. Two military representatives were therefore added to the US and British delegations. For the United States General John Dean, US Secretary of the Combined Chiefs of Staff was nominated to present the American view on military issues, and subsequently to take charge of a US military mission in Moscow. For the British, General Hastings Ismay was added to the delegation. As Churchill's Chief Staff Officer and representative on the British Chiefs of Staff, Ismay was fully informed on all military matters. Their brief was to inform the Russians of the details of forthcoming operations, answer questions, and indicate that, subject to certain conditions which were expected to be fulfilled, the vital Cross-Channel operation would definitely take place in May 1944. It was made clear, however, that they had no authority to alter decisions already taken.

The US approach then to the conference was clear and unequivocal. The three Allies should now agree on the broad principles of post-war international co-operation and take steps to implement them. On specific political issues relating to the enemy surrender-terms and peace-settlement, preliminary discussion might be valuable. Other European matters, East and West, should preferably not be discussed in much detail, though it was grudgingly recognized that some concession might have to be made to Britain on the role and status of the

Free French. The military part of the conference should be confined if possible to exposition of the Allies' respective plans. Such was the US stance at the outset of the conference.[13]

2. The British Approach

The British approach to the conference had some points in common with the US approach, but in most respects was widely different. Churchill certainly agreed with the Americans that the conference should be primarily exploratory rather than decision-making. Like Roosevelt, he felt that major decisions should be taken at the subsequent heads-of-government meeting, at which he himself would be present. However, he accepted the view of Eden and the Foreign Office that there should be a fairly exhaustive discussion of specific problems—mainly European—at the conference; and if possible some agreement, if only provisional. Some of the problems involved—Italy, Poland, Finland, Eastern Europe in general—were already a source of difficulty between Russia and the West. Others, for example the role of the Free French National Committee, were in contention between Britain and the United States. Like the Americans, Eden also wished to have a preliminary discussion and exchange of views on Germany, both the short-term problem of surrender-terms, occupation, and military government and the longer-term questions relating to a permanent peace-settlement with Germany. There were also various military problems connected with the Balkan countries, mainly concerning Allied relations with the various resistance movements. In Yugoslavia particularly the rival factions of Tito's Communist-led partisans and the pro-Royalist Chetniks were in conflict as much with each other as with Axis forces. It was a problem for the West whether to maintain existing support for the Royalists or switch to supporting Tito. These problems required discussion, since Soviet forces might soon enter these countries, and British missions were already active in Yugoslavia and Greece. Eden believed that continuous interallied discussion on many of these problems would be necessary after the conference and some machinery should be set up for this purpose. The Soviet-proposed political/military commission on Italy might prove a starting point, but Eden and the Foreign Office really hankered after some separate body, preferably located in London. It could reasonably be argued that London was a more convenient and suitable place for the discussion of many issues than Algiers or Italy, where the Soviet-sponsored commission would have to start its work. Then there was Eden's proposed declaration on joint rather than separate spheres of responsibility in Europe. Eden recognized that the unfavourable Soviet and American attitudes to this suggestion now made it probably a non-starter, but he had not quite given up.[14]

So far as Eden and his colleagues were concerned, agreement on the principles of future international co-operation did not figure quite as highly on the agenda as it did with the Americans. None the less Eden, with his pre-war background of support for the League of Nations, was more sympathetic to proposals for some new international organization than Churchill. In any case it was clear that the Americans wished to discuss it. Both Churchill and Eden were conscious of Britain's need for continued US aid both during and after the war. The US proposals included a discussion of assistance for post-war reconstruction, and this could form a useful starting point. Post-war international co-operation and the Four-Power Declaration therefore figured on the British agenda, though further down the list than on the US schedule.[15]

Two Middle-Eastern problems also appeared on the British agenda. The situation in Iran, under joint Soviet-British occupation, had for some time worried both the British and the Americans, who each had various missions in the country. The Russians and their Western Allies were not co-operating well, and often seemed to be at cross purposes, presaging on a small scale the difficulties that were to arise later in other countries occupied by both. Each suspected the other side, with some justice, of having its own post-war ends in view. The Americans also suspected Britain of imperialist aims. Eden had agreed with the Americans at their previous meetings that together they should press the Russians to adopt a more co-operative attitude; particularly as the Iranians themselves had expressed their concern and uneasiness about the future. The Western Powers also wanted the Soviet representatives at the conference to agree to a public declaration reaffirming an already agreed promise that the occupying powers would withdraw their forces six months after the end of the European hostilities. A public commitment of this kind would, they urged, reassure the Iranian people. It would also, of course, though it would have been tactless to say so, reassure the Western Allies that the Russians did indeed intend to withdraw.[16]

Turkey, which meant in fact the specific question of Turkish entry into the war, was also added to the agenda. As it turned out, the Soviet government, which had not hitherto shown much interest in the matter, also wished to discuss this. But the question of Turkish participation in the war had always been something of a King Charles's Head for Churchill. At an earlier stage of the war he had wished for it, as a possible base for future operations in the Balkans. Since the Americans had entered the war, however, they had firmly vetoed any such notion. Now, having at last pinned Churchill down to a Cross-Channel operation, after nearly two years of argument, they were even less inclined to countenance any Balkan or Aegean adventure. In the face of this Churchill had still persuaded his Commander-in-Chief Middle East, Maitland Wilson, to embark on limited operations against the German-held Greek islands off the Turkish coast. These operations were inadequately equipped, ill-conceived, and consequently going badly. Turkish assistance, particularly the use of Turkish air-bases, might tilt the balance. Eden however was less anxious to discuss the question. He was well aware, as indeed was Churchill, that the Turks had been remarkably cautious about committing themselves to war with Germany. This was not due to cowardice but for other reasons. The truth is, the Turks were more suspicious of Soviet intentions towards them than they were of German intentions. A long-standing Russian objective, dating back to the nineteenth century, had been to obtain control of the Black Sea, Constantinople, and the Dardanelles. Until the Russian Revolution there had been continuous pressure on Turkey from that quarter, which had resulted in the gradual loss of the greater part of the Turkish Empire in Europe. Only the defeat of Russia in 1917 had saved Constantinople and the Dardanelles. But the Turks had no illusions that the change of regime in Russia had affected the latter's objectives in this part of the world. As for the Western Allies, the Turks had not forgotten that in 1918 Britain had taken the lead in dismantling most of what was left of the Ottoman Empire, namely its possessions in the Levant and Middle East; and the United States had done little to obstruct the process. Not surprisingly the Turkish government, headed by Inönu who had fought in the First World War against Britain and Russia, regarded these potential allies with some caution. As a precaution against retaliation from Germany, but equally as a safeguard against Soviet intentions in the future, they demanded modern arms from the Western Allies, and particularly modern aircraft, as a condition of entering the war. At one stage the British government had indicated that in that event twenty-five aircraft squadrons might be made available. But since then the scale of Mediterranean operations had vastly expanded. With the Western Allies now heavily committed in Italy, and the Cross-Channel commitment looming up, it seemed unlikely that Britain could provide the twenty-five squadrons; and therefore equally unlikely that the Turkish Government would play. The Turks indeed proved to be for the Western Allies what Franco's Spain was to the Axis—an ally which was often wooed, but never won. Eden, however, was to be persuaded at Moscow to have one more try with the Turks, though probably without much optimism as to the result. [17]

As to Eastern Europe, it must have been already clear to Eden, in view of the Soviet and US attitude, that there was not much to be expected from the conference in that quarter. None the less, his agenda optimistically included the Eastern European 'package', including the proposal to eschew separate spheres of influence, and the question of possible confederations. It also included a general discussion of 'common policy for liberated territories' (that is, States occupied by the Axis but not at any time allied to them). Since France was to be discussed separately, this only left in Western Europe the smaller peripheral States—the Low Countries, Norway, and Denmark. This item, too, therefore seemed to the USSR and the USA to have a predominantly East-European slant. As had been indicated, the Americans were unwilling at this stage to enter into discussion of detailed commitments relating to Eastern Europe. Roosevelt like Churchill had already made up his mind that Soviet claims on Poland would probably have to be substantially conceded, and possibly the annexation to Russia of the Baltic States, too, subject perhaps to a plebiscite. But these were matters to be discussed between himself and Stalin. [18]

The problems of liberation in Eastern Europe had recently assumed a new urgency in British eyes as a result of Soviet negotiations with the head of the exiled government of Czechoslovakia, Edouard Benes. Although this government was located in London, negotiations for a Soviet-Czech treaty between Benes and the Soviet Ambassador in London had proceeded some way before Eden was informed. The proposed treaty was precisely the kind of 'special arrangement' between the USSR and a smaller State which could easily become the first foundation stone for the erection of a Soviet sphere of influence in Eastern Europe. The question was particularly delicate and urgent in view of the recent Soviet breach with the exiled Polish government, and the fact that Czechoslovakia, like the USSR, had a territorial dispute with Poland. Eden therefore had indicated to Benes and Maisky that he did not wish the negotiations to proceed until there had been an opportunity for Anglo-Soviet discussions at the Foreign Ministers' conference; and further, that the British Government would prefer a tripartite agreement between Russia, Poland, and Czechoslovakia. In other words, the proposed agreement should be dependent on the resolution of the Polish–Soviet dispute and the renewed recognition by the USSR of the Polish government in London. Moscow in turn had indicated its displeasure at this obstructive and 'unfriendly' attitude of the British government. They offered to make provision in the treaty for future Polish participation—which of course could be delayed indefinitely by Soviet obstruction, even if Polish–Soviet relations were resumed. This suggestion therefore was not sufficient to assuage British anxieties.

The Soviet government was in fact no more anxious to commit itself positively to general principles in relation to the 'liberation' of Eastern Europe than it was to commit itself negatively to a 'hands off' policy, or to specific (and unappealing) proposals for federations. Earlier in the war, in 1942, the USSR had appeared to be willing to accept something like a 'self-denying ordinance', at any rate so far as specific treaties or agreements with the smaller Allies, such as the proposed Czech treaty, were concerned. Eden's proposal at this time had been that neither Britain nor the USSR should conclude such agreements without first consulting each other. Now, however, the Soviet attitude on this, as on other matters, was less accommodating. They wished to go ahead with the Czech treaty; they did not wish to be hampered by obligations to consult their Allies in concluding similar agreements with other 'bordering States'. The latter term could include not only the Eastern European countries on which Russia had claims, such as Poland, Czechoslovakia, and Romania, but also Iran and China, as the British Foreign Office quickly realized. Eden therefore maintained his position on the matter and sent a formal draft proposal for a 'self-denying ordinance' to the Soviet government. But the omens for his policy on Eastern Europe were clearly not encouraging.[19]

Paradoxically, the Americans were prepared to make one exception to their general reluctance to discuss Eastern European issues in detail at the conference. It was partly for this reason that Finland appeared on the British agenda, though the question was later subsumed under the general heading of 'peace-feelers from Axis states'. If the problem of Turkey was to induce her to enter the war, the problem of Finland, from the US point of view, was to get her out of it as painlessly as possible. The advance of Soviet forces and the retreat of the German armies was already perilously exposing the Finns. They were in danger of being left isolated and exposed on the extreme north of the Russian front. Realistically the Finnish government recognized that it had backed a loser in adhering to the Axis camp, and now wished to sign an armistice. Feelers had already been put out by Finland to this end. The American government and people had much admired the dogged resistance of the Finns to Soviet attack in the 'Winter War' of

1939–40. They also had a soft spot for Finland because the Finns, unlike other countries, had not defaulted on their First World War debts to the United States. Churchill and Eden wished perhaps that the United States government would show less concern for an enemy state and more concern for the interests of staunch allies such as Poland and Greece. However, they were willing to discuss the question, and also the question of control over the Scandinavian entrances to the Baltic, which Eden anticipated the USSR would wish to discuss. [20]

It was therefore a long and detailed agenda, consisting of sixteen items, which Churchill communicated to Roosevelt at the beginning of September. It included all of the topics mentioned except the 'self-denying ordinance', which was added later. There followed a good deal of Anglo-American discussion of the various items, and some tidying-up of the British agenda as a result. It was clearly unnecessary for both the British and US agendas to contain the same items, so the Four-Power Declaration was removed from the British list. Eden also took the opportunity of suggesting various improvements in the language of the Declaration, designed to forestall possible objections from the Soviet government and other Allies. Thus it was suggested that it should be made clear that there was no intention of restoring Germany and other enemy States to the community of nations in the near future, a suggestion that the USSR would certainly have resisted; and also that there would be a definite role in the new international system for the middle-rank and smaller States. The shape of Roosevelt's ideas on a future international organization had already emerged. The four 'Great Powers' were to assume the major responsibility until such an organization was set up. Then they were to associate a few other States with their work in a small Executive Committee. There was also to be a general consultative body to which all eligible States would belong, to satisfy the smaller States. Churchill in general saw no objection to the broad outline of these proposals, though he favoured a separate committee for Europe. [21]

It seemed sensible also that all discussion on 'continuous machinery of consultation on common problems' should take place under one heading. The British suggestions to that end might therefore be combined with the item on the Soviet-inspired political/military commission. As a further recognition of and concession to US views, Eden also added 'other enemy states' to the item on the discussion of German surrender-terms, occupation arrangements, and long-term settlement; and included a reference to 'postwar economic cooperation with the USSR' in an item which called for the discussion of

Soviet participation in post-war international bodies. Further, the item on Finland was widened to embrace possible peace-feelers from other ex-enemy states—for example, Romania, Bulgaria, Hungary. Then there was the question of Austria, which had been absorbed by Germany in 1938. The US and British governments had already agreed that whatever else was decided for Germany and Central Europe, Austrian independence should be restored. They had agreed that a proposed declaration on this subject should be submitted to the conference. Reflecting US suspicions of British policies in Central and Eastern Europe, however, the US argued that there should be no commitment to encourage Austrian participation in any federation, as Eden and Churchill had wished.[22]

Finally, as a result of the arguments with Russia over the proposed Soviet-Czech treaty and his decision to propose a specific agreement on 'agreement with minor allies' (the 'self-denying ordinance') Eden also decided provisionally to add this item to the agenda. In the mean time there had been opportunity during September and early October for the British War Cabinet as a whole to discuss some of the major problems on the agenda, the discussion usually centring around a memorandum and/or proposals drafted by the Foreign Office and presented by Eden. The problems of Germany, both long-term and short-term, were discussed at length. These discussions revealed some of the differences within the British government on the future of Germany, particularly on the central question of whether or not a united Germany should be allowed to exist after the war. All were agreed, however, that Germany should be in any event much smaller after the war. Not only should Austria regain its independence; Alsace-Lorraine and the Sudetenland should be restored to France and Czechoslovakia respectively. Furthermore a substantial part of Upper Silesia and East Prussia, together with Danzig, should be ceded to Poland. This, it was envisaged, would probably be necessary as compensation for Polish territory in the east, which it was thought would almost certainly have to be ceded (or as the Soviet argument had it 'restored') to Russia. The Soviet argument was that these territories had been wrongly seized from her after the First World War. In addition the possible internationalization of the Ruhr and Kiel Canal was discussed. All this would clearly amount to a considerable 'slicing-up' of Germany as it then stood. Churchill again indicated his belief in the desirability of detaching the whole of Prussia from Germany and incorporating southern Germany in a federation with Austria, based on Vienna. With a prescient eye, and no great trust in Soviet good intentions, Churchill could already see that the successful conclusion of the war would probably leave the Soviet government in a position to detach much of east Germany permanently from the rest of Germany if she should so desire; and she might well so desire. In that event, particularly if the Ruhr were separately treated, what was left of Germany would not be a very formidable element in any Central European balance of power. Eden, however, repeated his doubts about the practicability of imposing dismemberment on Germany. A considerable degree of decentralization would probably work better. As to Churchill's pet project, of a 'Danubian federation' based on Vienna, Eden was all too conscious of the cool American response to the whole idea of encouraging federations in Central and Eastern Europe, and also of the probable Soviet objections. Not surprisingly it was agreed that the Cabinet did not wish to commit itself yet on this central issue of dismembering Germany. Both Churchill and Eden suggested they should avoid reaching definite conclusions for the present. They had better wait and see what concrete Soviet and US views or proposals emerged from the forthcoming tripartite meetings. There was general agreement, however, that Germany should be totally occupied and put under military government at the end of the war, and therefore no German central government should immediately be created to replace the Nazi regime, which it was taken for granted would be liquidated. It was also agreed that Germany should be totally disarmed and demilitarized; that the occupation should be based on separate zones, co-ordinated by an interallied Control Commission, rather than a mixing up of Allied troops all over Germany; and a majority view was in favour of a reasonably short occupation, of no more than two years, which meant a reasonably quick peace treaty, and perhaps, as Churchill clearly wished, the beginning of the period of German rehabilitation, or that of a German State of some kind, as a member of the European community. There were differences of view however in the War Cabinet on the desirability of 'rehabilitating' Germany quickly. It would certainly not be an idea which appealed to the Soviet government.[23]

There was also, as was to be expected, considerable discussion of the Polish imbroglio and the related East-European problems—the proposed Soviet-Czech treaty, Soviet claims on the Baltic States, Finland, and Romania, the 'self-denying ordinance'. Eden pointed out that it was essential to bring about a reconciliation between Russia and the London Poles, not only to safeguard the future status of that government and with it the ability of non-Communist, non Soviet-backed Poles to influence the future of Poland; but also in order to prevent conflict between the advancing Soviet armies and the Polish Underground resistance, which mostly looked to the London government for leadership. The London Poles, Eden argued, would have to be prepared to make territorial concessions in the east to achieve this: they must accept something less than the inflated Poland of the inter-war years—but not after all that much less, since they could expect to be compensated to some degree in the west. This was also broadly the view of the US, as expressed at Quebec. It would be to their advantage to accept this kind of bargain, since later on, if they were obdurate now, they would probably get worse terms from the USSR. The implication of this of course was that once the war was over, and the USSR less dependent on its Allies, the Western Powers might be unable to exert the same leverage on the Soviet government. This, Eden pointed out, was also the view of the US government. The London Poles admittedly had not made things easy for Britain to bring about a reconciliation with the USSR. Indeed they had tried to obtain a pledge from Eden that Polish frontiers should not be discussed at the Foreign Ministers' meetings; and in other ways had shown little willingness to contemplate surrendering any of the territory seized from Russia in 1922, though at the same time making large claims for the annexation to Poland of German territory. Nor on the other hand had the Soviet government responded positively to British efforts. With both sides to the dispute so intransigent, it was a hard case. None the less the War Cabinet agreed that Eden should continue his efforts for a solution on the lines he had indicated, and also that it would probably be necessary to agree to Soviet claims on Finland and Romania, as well as the reincorporation in the USSR of the Baltic States. Eden, however, was authorized only to give informal reassurances on this score, not to sign any formal agreement, still less make any public commitment at this stage; and in return the USSR should be expected to make some concessions, not only in relation to the renewed recognition of the Polish government, but also by giving some of the kind of assurances for the future independence of the East European States as were contemplated in Eden's 'self-denying ordinance' on 'separate agreements', or the proposed declaration on 'joint rather than separate responsibility' for Europe. The proposed Soviet-Czech treaty should be replaced by a tripartite treaty including Poland.[24]

Not unnaturally the Cabinet also gave its approval to Eden's proposal on machinery for continuous consultation on European problems—namely that there should be two bodies rather than one, the more important of the two to be located in London rather than the

Mediterranean. Eden's stated reason for this, for US and Soviet consumption, was the presence in London of so many of the exiled European governments. But clearly it would also be an advantage from the British point of view that Eden and the Foreign Office could in this way keep in close touch with its work. [25]

Finally, cautious approval was given to the idea of a new international peacekeeping organization, as envisaged in the Four-Power Declaration, though the Conservative members of the Cabinet probably agreed with the cynical remark of Richard Law, the Foreign Office Minister of State, that this was 'a public relations exercise'; also that Turkey should indeed be induced to enter the war, if her demands were not too high; and that efforts should be made to sort out the situation in Iran. In general, therefore, Eden's positive proposals were approved; and where, as in the case of Germany, no positive agreed policy could yet be seen for the long-term future, and indeed there were differences of view between the Prime Minister and the Foreign Secretary, it was agreed that a decent vagueness should be preserved. Eden was, of course, aware, as were his colleagues, that much would depend on how US and Soviet views were clarified at the conference and particularly on the degree of American support which was forthcoming for various aspects of British policy. Eden, like Churchill, desperately wished for such support. The omens, as we have seen, were not altogether encouraging. Eden hoped at least that the US Secretary of State would meet him in Cairo for preliminary talks. A greater degree of mutual agreement on the Anglo-American approach to the conference might then emerge than had so far been forthcoming. Hull, however, was cagey. Neither he nor Roosevelt was anxious to give the appearance of 'ganging up' with the British before the conference. One of their main priorities was to reduce Soviet suspicions, not increase them. Eden blandly agreed that 'formal' talks might arouse suspicion. But he proposed in any event to time his arrival in Cairo to coincide with Hull's, so no doubt there would be an opportunity for an 'informal exchange of views'. In the upshot, however, Hull made sure that he would not catch up with Eden until the two men reached Teheran the day before the conference. [26]

It was in this frame of mind, then, that Britain approached the meeting of Foreign Ministers. It was clearly, as one Foreign Office official put it, likely to be a 'difficult' conference. The lukewarm response of the US government to British proposals for Eastern Europe and the apparent hardening of the Soviet attitude precluded over-optimism, certainly, on these questions. But there was much to play for in Western and Central Europe and elsewhere besides.

Eden's bargaining position was the weakest of the three protagonists, but his diplomatic skill was considerable. He would have to make the most of it.

3. The Soviet Approach

Although the Soviet government had repeatedly pressed its Allies for a detailed agenda and specific proposals, and had received both, the Soviet agenda was the last to appear, at the end of September. Moreover it was extremely short. It consisted in fact of only one item— 'Measures to shorten the War'. To this end the Soviet government urged, in familiar tones, all measures should be taken in 1943 by the Western Allies to bring about the Cross-Channel Attack. To this item the USSR later added the proposal that Turkey and Sweden should be induced, blackmailed, or coerced into entering the war. At first the Western Allies could not believe that the Soviet government was serious. It had been made crystal clear that Britain and the United States did not envisage the Foreign Ministers' conference as in any sense a military conference. In any case the Foreign Ministers were not competent to discuss such matters; and the Western Allies had no intention of revising the military decisions made at Washington and Quebec. Had the Russians after all changed their minds? Were they still serious about the conference? However, those in London and Washington who were accustomed to interpreting signals from Moscow, which were often in a foreign language in more senses than one, quickly concluded this was not the case. What the Russians were saying, in effect, was that they were not prepared to give serious attention to anything the Western Allies wished to discuss until they had received absolute and foolproof assurances on the Cross-Channel Attack. Stalin had in fact already made it clear that he did not wish to limit the agenda simply to this; and Molotov had added to his message conveying the Soviet agenda the assurance that the USSR had no objection to discussing 'European Questions'. The latter phrase may or may not have been a sly thrust. No doubt the Soviet leaders reflected that the British in particular were very anxious to discuss Eastern Europe, which the USSR regarded as primarily its concern, but were not suggesting discussion of Africa, the Arab world, or India, where British interests were most involved. Nor for that matter was the United States proposing to discuss Latin America. However that might be, there was no reason to suppose the Soviet Government was not prepared to discuss European problems, subject to its main anxieties being satisfied on the military side. Indeed, the Soviet

Ambassador in London had told Eden that the USSR wished to discuss political as well as military issues, and had sounded Eden again about the British attitude to Soviet territorial claims. This of course was a hint that the Soviet attitude might be more forthcoming on other matters, if their territorial aims were conceded. For the moment Eden replied that agreement on the general principles of future co-operation should precede agreement on specific claims, but he got the message. He added that he recognized that a genuine concern for Soviet security was involved in the problem of future Soviet frontiers—a diplomatic way of saying that Britain did not regard the Soviet claims as wholly unreasonable, and in fact were sympathetic to them. The British and Americans further recognized that the Soviets were entitled to some further reassurances on the Cross-Channel Attack after so many disappointments. They therefore accepted this item without further demur, and reinforced their delegations accordingly. [27]

There was of course a further purpose behind the nature of the Soviet agenda, with its lack of reference to political problems (the Russians had already got their way on the question of a political/military commission for Italy, with Soviet participation). The USSR was indicating to the West that while it was prepared to discuss European and world-wide issues, if the US and Britain wished to, she herself had no urgent desire to do so. This had not always been the case. In 1941 and 1942, when things looked black for her, Russia had sought discussion on Soviet territorial claims, and asked for a definite recognition by the US and Britain of the 1941 frontiers of the USSR. At about the same time Maisky had assured Eden that Russia was not unsympathetic to the idea of a mutual 'self-denying ordinance' in relation to special arrangements with the smaller States of Europe. But this was when German armies were at the gates of Moscow and Leningrad. The USSR was desperately pleading for a 'Second Front in 1942' and very much in need of Western goodwill. Things were different now. The Soviet armies were rapidly advancing towards the disputed frontiers with Poland, Finland, and Romania, with the whole of Eastern Europe beyond. Allied approval of Soviet claims, while still desirable, would soon not be essential to their achievement. If, as now seemed possible, the West could be tied down to a major concentration of their military resources on operations in Western Europe, there was no real likelihood that Anglo-American armies would enter the Balkans, or any other part of Eastern Europe. There was therefore no reason why the Soviet government should tie its hands in that quarter by acceding to the proposed declarations on

'joint responsibility' and 'policy for the liberated territories', still less
to proposals for federations or any kind of 'self-denying ordinance'.
They wished to have a free hand. They had indeed long made it clear
that principles such as national sovereignty, territorial integrity, and
self-determination, to which the US attached so much importance,
would be subject to Soviet claims and Soviet interests in areas under
Soviet control. What had changed, as a result of Soviet efforts and the
strategic decisions of the Western Allies, was the extent of the area
which the USSR could hope to control at the end of the war.[28]

Until the Soviet archives are fully open to the West—if that ever
happens—it will not be possible to say precisely what induced Stalin
to put the question of Swedish and Turkish entry into the war on the
agenda. The military advantages were dubious in both cases. The
abandonment of Swedish neutrality could well provide Germany with
an excuse for a short sharp invasion of that country which the Allies
could do little to prevent. Stalin, however, had always been suspicious
of the Swedes, suspecting them of pro-German tendencies; no doubt
he saw some advantages in tying Sweden firmly to the Allied camp.
On the other hand, if Germany did occupy Sweden, while Finland
opted out of the war, the USSR would have every reason to move its
troops up to the Finnish frontier, and occupy the whole of Finland.
The inclusion of Turkey in the scenario was due partly to Soviet irritation at the apparent Turkish success in extracting arms from the
West, while giving little in return and indeed showing no eagerness to
use them against the Germans. The Turks should be told firmly that
they must either enter the war or expect no more assistance from the
West, and no future consideration for their interests. This was probably the main object of the exercise. The USSR had claims on Turkish
ports on the Black Sea and wanted, as she always had, to control the
Dardanelles. She did not wish to see Turkey strengthened to resist
these objectives.

The uncompromising nature of the Soviet approach was further
shown in her attitude to China. Molotov had early objected to the
inclusion of China in the Four-Power Declaration. Stalin went further
when on 6 October he telegraphed to Roosevelt that since it was to be
a Three-Power conference only 'he assumed that the declaration of
four nations is not included in the agenda of the conference'. This can
hardly have been intended seriously. The Soviets were well aware that
for the US, the declaration was the main objective of their attendance
at the conference. Roosevelt had indicated that at a pinch he would be
prepared to accept a Three-Power Declaration, to which other nations
including China could accede later: but this was a different matter to

withdrawing it from the agenda altogether. The Soviet attitude on this question, however, was a further indication that the USSR was little disposed to make concessions to Western views without some indication of a substantial quid pro quo.

It is tempting to regard the Soviet attitude merely as intransigent, suspicious, and self-centred. It was indeed all of these things. In order to be fair to the Soviet point of view, it is not necessary to hold the telescope the other way round, and look at all issues exclusively from the viewpoint of Moscow, as some of the more extreme revisionist historians tend to do. But in justice certain things have to be remembered. The Soviet Union had suffered a prolonged ordeal during the two years of the Nazi invasion—a nightmare of hardship, suffering, destruction, and death. Certainly the Western Allies had given generous assistance in military and other supplies. But whether because of genuine difficulties, or as the Soviet leaders suspected, because of lack of will, the Allies had not been able to launch the kind of operation—the invasion of Western Europe—which the Russians believed was most likely to help ease the pressure upon them. Instead the West had gone off to conquer North Africa and reopen the Mediterranean; in other words, as it seemed to Moscow, to pursue its own ends. Was this because the British, in their hearts, really wanted to see Russia as well as Germany weakened by a prolonged struggle on the Eastern Front? And had Roosevelt allowed himself to become Churchill's cat's paw? It was in many respects an unreasonable attitude, which ignored the Western expenditure of lives and effort on the bombing campaign, the war at sea, and the campaigns in the Pacific and South-east Asia. But in a nation fighting for its life, it was not altogether surprising. Looked at from Moscow, the British and Americans seemed to be engaged in a private war of their own and enjoying a cosy partnership, in whose discussions the USSR did not share. Moreover, the Western Powers had added to their lack of military co-operation an apparent unwillingness to concede Soviet territorial claims, claims which amounted in the Soviet view to little more than a restoration of the 1917 frontiers of Russia; frontiers which the Soviet government believed were necessary to safeguard Russia against the kind of attack she had suffered three times in the past thirty years. Eden was now apparently anxious to stop the USSR signing treaties with the East-European governments in furtherance of its interest: but the British government had already signed what agreements it wished with some of those governments. Why should the USSR be prevented from doing likewise? Well, perhaps there would soon be no need to seek Western goodwill in respect of Soviet claims: the Red Army would do all that was necessary. It was in such a mood, of wary suspicion, and stubborn determination to achieve its objectives, that the Soviet leaders approached the conference.

It is not difficult to see, and indeed was evident to Churchill and Eden, that Soviet and British objectives in Europe were in many ways antithetical, but most of all in Eastern Europe. The British objective was to restore the independence of the area, and of the individual States, but at the same time to strengthen them by voluntary associations which would enable the region to defend its independence against pressures from any quarter, including the USSR. The internecine feuds and animosities of the Eastern and Balkan States made this in any case a difficult objective to achieve. It required in the given circumstances both American support and a degree of Soviet acquiescence. But this was not a particularly appealing prospect for the USSR. A collection of small, weak, and squabbling States vulnerable to Soviet pressure and influence really suited the USSR much better, always provided there were no other powerful European State such as Germany in a position to take advantage of the situation. As for the Americans, they were suspicious of British motives and anxious not to be drawn into any deep involvement in the Eastern European problems, in which they might seem to be underwriting British aims and pulling British chestnuts out of the fire. They pinned their hopes to the creation of a better climate of future international relations and the creation of a world-wide system of guaranteed security which would mitigate Russian fears and induce her to deal fairly and mildly with her weaker neighbours. It is easy, so long after the event, to criticize this American approach as absurdly over-optimistic, as ignoring not only the long history of Russian expansionism and long-standing Russian objectives in Eastern Europe, but also the central fact that the Soviet leaders were committed to an ideology which embodied a deep hostility to American capitalism and Western political institutions. But the USSR had apparently modified its ideological zeal during the war. The international Communist bureau, the Comintern, controlled by the USSR, had been dissolved. In 1941 the USSR had signed the 'Atlantic Charter', embodying American ideals of political freedom, albeit with some reservations on the Soviet side. Given an assured and honourable role in the new international scene, perhaps the Soviet Union would now be willing to abandon its posture of hostility and suspicion, and begin to co-operate with the West for the common good. At all events, the attempt had to be made. If the Russians approached the tripartite meetings with wary suspicion, and the British with some uneasiness, the Americans approached them with a mood of cautious optimism.[29]

CHAPTER III

JOURNEY TO MOSCOW

1. Preliminaries

During the days Hull and Eden were *en route* to Moscow, the machinery of diplomacy did not come to a stop. Cables continued to flow between them and the State Department and Foreign Office: and between Washington, Moscow, and London. Meetings of the War Cabinet, the Politburo, and Roosevelt's circle of advisers continued to debate the issues. The question of the Soviet-inspired political/military commission exercised all the various parties. Its creation had been agreed in principle, but all else remained to be decided—its permanent location, its membership, its powers, the scope of its interests. The Soviet government naturally pressed for the widest possible scope and powers to be given to a body on which they would be represented—the first genuine tripartite body of its kind. The Commission would give the USSR for the first time some say in the conduct of affairs in the Mediterranean and Western Europe. They urged that it should deal with the problems arising from the ending of hostilities with *all* enemy states, not simply Italy. These would include armistice negotiations, surrender terms, occupation arrangements, and so forth. Eden however had now decided to press for a separate body in London to deal with these wider issues. Moreover, the Soviet government wished the commission immediately to have some power over the nascent military government in Italy—which neither Britain nor the United States wanted. The British preference for a separate body in London also inevitably meant some disagreement with the USSR, at any rate to begin with. A compromise solution had been floated in the Cabinet by Eden, by which the commission would begin its work in the Mediterranean—at Algiers first, then moving to Italy—and deal at first exclusively with Italian affairs. A little later it could move to London to take up the wider issues, leaving perhaps a subcommittee for Italy in the Mediterranean. But all this had still to be thrashed out between Hull, Molotov, and Eden. On the second point, the question of Allied military government in Italy, the Western view was totally at variance with that of the USSR. The British and Americans were not prepared to allow any tripartite body to interfere directly with General Eisenhower's military government, or Italian affairs generally, so long as active military operations were in progress in the area. It would complicate Eisenhower's job too much and also perhaps hamper the delicate negotiations to transform Italy from a defeated enemy into a co-belligerent. These negotiations involved some relaxation of the armistice terms for Italy, as an inducement to active co-operation. The Soviet government was known to look with disfavour on any leniency towards the Italians, while at the same time questioning the Anglo-American use of known supporters of Mussolini's regime. Once given the right to do so, the Soviet representative would probably veto the use of Marshal Badoglio, the Italian royal family, and others whom the Anglo-Americans found useful or necessary in winning over Italian public opinion. Churchill stated his position with characteristic forcefulness when he said the Allies could not tolerate a 'Soviet veto' on Eisenhower's control of 'minor matters', but he was expressing the general Anglo-American view. On this issue, then, there had to be, if possible, some agreed compromise.

The problem of the membership of the commissions on the other hand seemed more likely to cause variance between Britain and the United States, particularly on the question of whether French representatives should join the British, Americans, and Russians. French troops, controlled by de Gaulle's 'French Committee of National Liberation' (to give it its full title) had fought in the Middle East and North Africa, and were to make a substantial contribution to Allied forces in Italy. Moreover France by virtue of its geographical position had a major concern in the future of Italy. There was then a reasonable case for the British view that the Free French should be associated with, and ultimately full members of, the Italian Commission. This of course was difficult for the United States, in view of Roosevelt's and Hull's antipathy towards de Gaulle. It was a hostility which was fully reciprocated. De Gaulle trusted neither the United States nor for that matter Britain. He looked to a revival of pre-1914 Franco-Russian co-operation, as he was to tell Averell Harriman bluntly when the latter stopped at Algiers *en route* for Moscow. For its part Washington grudgingly conceded that the Free French position was stronger than in the early days of the war. The Gaullists now effectively controlled and administered French North Africa and, with minor exceptions, the rest of the French colonial empire. Free French forces, with considerable US help, had grown markedly and so consequently had their contribution to the war: the internal French Resistance movement, and Gaullist links with it, had also grown in strength. In addition the FNCL now had a more undisputed claim to represent France than in the early years of the war. Until 1942 there had been strong American links with the rival collaborationist French government at Vichy, which Washington believed commanded more support in metropolitan France than de Gaulle. The Vichy government had also controlled two priceless assets which it was essential should not fall into German hands or be put at Germany's disposal—the powerful French Fleet and French North Africa. But in November 1942 French North Africa had been invaded, and ultimately conquered, by the Western Allies: German forces had moved into what had previously been Vichy's domain—unoccupied France—and taken it over. On the orders of the Vichy government the fleet had been scuttled and now lay useless at the bottom of Toulon harbour. The Vichy government itself, under Marshal Pétain, had become a helpless puppet of the Germans. Aside from personal antipathy to de Gaulle—the latter's enemies differed as to whether the General was more likely to emerge as a semi-Fascist dictator of the Right or a tool of the Communist Left, but they were agreed on distrusting him—Roosevelt and Hull did not share British faith in the future of France, nor had they the same desire to restore France to a leading position in European and world affairs. But they conceded some concessions might have to be made, possibly on some association of the FNCL with the new commission and a future role in the administration of metropolitan France. But they still refused to consider recognition of that body as, in effect, the provisional government of France, as the British government increasingly felt would soon be appropriate. Roosevelt and Hull argued that the freedom of choice of the French people, when liberated, should not be so constrained or influenced. As a safeguard against undue Gaullist influence on the proposed commission, Washington proposed China and Brazil should also be members. To some extent this was probably a riposte not only to the suggestion of French membership but also the further British proposal that the Greek and Yugoslav exile governments should be specially involved with the work of the commission. The two cases however were widely different. Greece and Yugoslavia were near neighbours of Italy, had suffered much from pre-war Italian expansionist pressures and even more from Italy's wartime membership of the Axis. By contrast, the suggestion of Chinese membership of the commission was somewhat absurd. The Chinese played no part in the European war, certainly none in Italy. Nor were they at all knowledgeable or for that matter interested in Italian problems. Stalin indeed was later, at Teheran, to make what was possibly a sly thrust both at Anglo-American differences over Chinese status and at the past European record of freebooting in China. He observed that the European States would probably not relish Chinese interference, as a member of the new UN Council, in European affairs. This was undoubtedly true. Nor was the case for Brazilian membership much stronger. Brazilian forces certainly were ultimately to make a substantial contribution to Italian operations, but not for some time to come. No more than China could Brazil be said to have any great concern with, or knowledge of Italian problems. But the interchange is interesting as indicating both the strength of the American drive to elevate China to an equal position with the 'Big Three', and the wish to have reliable allies on the commission *vis-à-vis* the British as well as the Soviets. Clearly on these issues, too, much discussion would be required in Moscow.[1]

There was also time unfortunately during Eden's journey for a further cooling of Anglo-Soviet relations, the occasion being a particularly surly message from Stalin to Churchill on the vexed question of the Arctic convoys. Churchill's patience was frayed almost to the limit by what he regarded as an unjustified imputation of bad faith in this matter; at one point he refused to accept the message and returned it to the Soviet Ambassador. Eventually, however, it was agreed that Eden should try to settle the matter amicably at Moscow, rather than that it should be the subject of further angry exchanges by cable. Churchill's explosive reaction however probably did no harm. When Eden broached the subject in Moscow the Soviet reaction was much more reasonable. But this episode did not exactly improve the atmosphere for the impending conference.[2]

The British government for its part had made a gesture towards this end, by agreeing that the main Soviet item—the Cross-Channel Attack—and the main US item—the Three- or Four-Power Declaration—should be the first two items on the agenda. Eden perhaps had worked it out that the Western Powers would be able to give the Soviets the assurances they obviously needed that the operation would definitely take place; and then, given a little manœuvring on the difficult Chinese question, the Declaration would probably be accepted. This might put the Americans and Russians in a good mood for the discussion on some of the more contentious items on the long British agenda. In the event this gesture probably had little effect on the course of the conference; gratitude in politics is a very perishable commodity. But at least it helped to create a better atmosphere.

Eden and Hull also took advantage of opportunities *en route* to meet various people and obtain first-hand views of different problems. In

Algiers Eden talked to some of the Allied commanders and received discouraging reports of the progress of Italian operations. The German build-up before Rome had been quicker than expected. After the difficult and costly Allied landings in Salerno, Eisenhower was likely to have nothing to spare to send to the assistance of the hard-pressed British in the Dodecanese. In that case the remaining British-held islands might well fall to the Germans. In Cairo Eden had discussions with the exiled Greek ministers and King George of Greece and also with the Yugoslav government-in-exile. He questioned them about the schisms between Left and Right which were splitting resistance movements in occupied Greece and Yugoslavia. Eden had already recommended to his own government and the US that aid to the Yugoslav resistance should be stepped up if Tito's Communist partisans and the Royalist forces would stop fighting among themselves. In Greek politics the personality of the King, who like the Italian monarch had collaborated with a pre-war dictatorship, was particularly contentious. Eden discussed with the Greeks the possibility, which later came to fruition, that the Greek Orthodox Archbishop Damaskinos should become Regent temporarily when Greece was liberated and the King should not return until things had settled down. In this context it was presumed that the USSR, notwithstanding the dissolution of the Comintern, retained some influence over the Communist echelons of the Balkan resistance—Tito's partisans and the Greek underground army known as ELAS. This was one reason why Eden had wished these problems to be discussed at Moscow. The British Foreign Secretary was also informed *en route* of an approach to Washington by a dubious ex-Soviet diplomat, Helphand. Helphand's approach played on the Western Allies' fear that the USSR might, having cleared Russia of the enemy, sign a separate peace with Germany, in spite of mutual Allied promises not to do so. It was known that Germany had put out feelers to the USSR in Stockholm. Helphand pointed out that the Germans might offer Russia a similar bargain to that accepted by Stalin in the Soviet-German Non-Aggression Pact of 1939, conceding virtually all Soviet territorial claims and perhaps offering an undefined Soviet 'sphere of influence' in south-east Europe as well. He recommended that the Western Allies should get in first. The British Foreign Office's reaction to the proposal that the West should enter into a dubious competition with Germany for Soviet favours was sceptical. Helphand, it was argued, was no longer in close touch with Soviet policy, and might even be a 'double agent'. In general Foreign Office opinion was adverse. But as we have seen, Churchill and Roosevelt had already decided to go some way along this road by conceding most Soviet territorial claims. Churchill, in fact, was to go rather further than this later on, in his famous—some would say infamous—'percentages agreement' with Stalin in October 1944. But for the moment all this was in the future. It was, however, one of the anxieties in Eden's mind as he flew on to Teheran to discuss the tangled Iranian situation with the British Ambassador, Sir Reader Bullard. There were indeed many such anxieties: but certainly foremost in Eden's preoccupations was the crucial question of Poland and the associated problems of Eastern Europe; and secondly the task of trying to establish what he saw as the most suitable machinery for the continuing discussion of European problems.[3]

Following in Eden's footsteps, Hull at Algiers also talked to the Supreme Allied Commander, General Eisenhower, and other military men, and to the US political representative, Robert Murphy. He also met the discredited Giraud and the now triumphant de Gaulle for a brief discussion of French political problems. Hull reported to Washington that he found de Gaulle 'friendlier than expected'. The Free French leader must have been in an unusually tactful mood that day. He was to be much blunter with Averell Harriman a few days later, as has been noted. Hull then proceeded to Cairo where he, like Eden, met the Greeks and Yugoslavs, no doubt becoming a little better acquainted with the thorny tangle of Balkan politics as a result. Finally he caught up with Eden at Teheran. There was time only for a relatively short talk, contrary to Eden's wishes. Each man read into the discussion what he wished. Hull regarded it as the exchange of a 'few casual observations': Eden reported it as 'a useful discussion of tactics and attitudes on the chief items on the agenda'. Eden was probably deceiving himself. Hull was determined there should be no common Anglo-US 'front' at the conference. The British General Ismay for his part reported of this meeting that Hull looked 'old and frail'. Ismay felt the conference was 'getting off to a bad start'. Whether this judgement was true or not, the object of it all was about to begin. On 18 October the aircraft carrying the various members of the two missions touched down in Moscow, to be welcomed by Molotov, Maisky, Litvinov, and other members of the Soviet Foreign Ministry.[4]

2. The Leading Actors

Secretary Hull was over seventy at the time of the Moscow conference and had long experience of administering foreign policy. He had served as Secretary of State since the beginning of Roosevelt's first term. He was a Southerner and a former Democratic Congressman. Politically he belonged to the same school as his chief. In foreign affairs that meant the liberal internationalist tradition of Woodrow Wilson, with its emphasis on international covenants and institutions, common action for the maintenance of peace, and respect for national sovereignty and the independence of nations. 'Collective security' and 'national self-determination' were the watchwords of this school. Its members detested the old-fashioned European diplomacy with its balance of power and alliances, its 'spheres of influence' and 'buffer states', not only because it seemed to them devious and immoral but because in their judgement it did not work. In particular it had not prevented two destructive World Wars, into both of which the United States had been drawn, much against its will. Hull and those like him tended to distrust also the European practitioners of this school: they were afraid that simple old-fashioned moralists like Woodrow Wilson, like Hull himself, were apt to be outwitted by these clever diplomatists. That Churchill's views on international affairs leaned to the old-fashioned school of thought was pretty apparent. Roosevelt indeed, in a rare moment of exasperation, once said he was exhausted from 'years of dragging Winston' in the right direction. Eden, however, was known as a leader of the younger, more progressive Tories, who had supported the League of Nations before the war. It is unlikely that Eden and Hull would ever have become close personal friends. Eden was too vain, too mannered, too confident in his mastery of foreign affairs and diplomacy, in which he had specialized for most of his political career. But at least Hull felt that Eden was not too far away from his own conception of the proper organization for the post-war world. Hull himself was courteous and patient, though, like most such men, he could occasionally 'blow up'. He was not especially imaginative, rather inflexible, and not particularly knowledgeable about detailed European problems, which he regarded as minor compared with the great task of organizing world peace on the basis of Four-Power co-operation. His relationship with Roosevelt was an uncertain one, certainly less close than Eden's with Churchill. The President had appointed Hull in the first place mainly because of the latter's prestige and influence with Congress and the general respect which his integrity and high principles commanded. Roosevelt himself respected and quite liked the Secretary but did not set a very high store on his intellectual powers. Moreover, though the President trusted Hull and knew that the Secretary shared his general views on international politics, he did not trust the senior career men in the State

Department: he judged them to be mostly conservative in domestic politics and therefore hostile to his economic and social policies; and in foreign affairs he suspected them of being anti-Soviet and therefore unsuitable instruments for his policy of getting closer to the USSR. He had told Churchill some time before that he thought 'he could handle Stalin better than you or my State Department'. Roosevelt therefore tended to keep the State Department, and Hull with it, at arm's length, preferring to consult and use unofficial agents such as Harry Hopkins and Averell Harriman. Robert Murphy, the Department's representative in North Africa, was an exception, but Murphy had been told to report directly to the President and bypass the State Department. It was an extraordinary situation that the President of the United States should slight his principal adviser on foreign policy and his own Foreign Affairs Ministry, but Hull himself had contributed to it. Although not personally in awe of Roosevelt, he had a great respect, even veneration, for the office of President. He regarded himself as the principal executant of the President's foreign policy and his adviser, when his advice was requested. He did not feel that he should force himself on the President. In the jungle of Washington politics inevitably he was often elbowed aside. But his patience was not inexhaustible, as the episode of Sumner Welles, widely regarded as the President's agent in the Department, had demonstrated. Moreover he knew he was not without influence. Roosevelt's biographer, indeed, judged him in retrospect one of the two most influential members of Roosevelt's first two administrations, and in the wartime period, together with such men as Marshall, Byrnes, and Hopkins, as an 'assistant president'. This was probably to overstate the case. However, when Roosevelt was finally forced to choose between Hull and Welles, he chose Hull. Hull at any rate had never resigned, though he had sometimes threatened to do so.[5]

Anthony Eden was in 1943 at the height of his powers and prestige. He had made his political reputation as a champion of the League of Nations in the 1930s; and strengthened it when his opposition to Neville Chamberlain's policy of appeasing the dictators led to his resignation from the Foreign Office. There were those who felt he might have resigned earlier and opposed both Chamberlain and the dictators more vigorously. The historian A. J. P. Taylor, commenting on Eden's post-war book 'Facing the Dictators', remarked that Eden did not really 'face' Hitler and Mussolini, he only 'made faces' at them. But this was not the general view. The war had brought Eden back into the British government and Churchill had restored him to the Foreign Office in 1941. His political position at home was very strong. He had in general Churchill's regard and trust, and the Prime Minister had made it clear that he regarded him as his natural successor. His pre-war record had won him the support of the more progressive Conservatives and he was respected and liked by most of his Labour colleagues in the wartime coalition. To the wider British public he was better known than any other of Churchill's colleagues and already commanded great public prestige. Alone of the wartime ministers he had regularly accompanied Churchill to wartime conferences, besides leading missions himself on occasions, thus getting to know most of the Allied leaders. This was in fact his third visit to Moscow. No one questioned his grasp of foreign affairs or his skill and patience in negotiation. There were however flaws in his make-up. Hindsight of course often tempts the historian to make critical judgments in retrospect that were not made at the time. But even in the war years those who worked closely with Eden noted certain weaknesses. His vanity led him sometimes to overestimate the worth of agreements which he had been able to reach, and judge their real value too uncritically. He was sometimes indecisive. He was also apt to immerse himself too much in details, at the expense of the wider picture. He lacked the broad creative vision of Churchill: in a word, he lacked inspiration. None the less he was an able and well-informed minister, and his political base was at this time assured. This was as well, for Eden was aware that his negotiating strength *vis-à-vis* the United States and Russia was weak. Britain had been fighting for four years, had sustained many defeats, and lost vast territories in Asia to the Japanese after failing to halt the German tide in France and the Balkans. Recent victories at Alamein and Tunis could not wipe these defeats out, or entirely undo their effects. The British economic position had never been worse. To sustain the war effort, Britain had been obliged to expend most of its currency reserves, realize many of its overseas assets, and abandon most of its export markets. British shipping losses in the war at sea had been exceptionally heavy, her losses in men and materials in a dozen campaigns all over the world very considerable. The British Empire still had larger forces in the field than the United States, but the strain of maintaining a million men under arms plus a large navy and air force had become very great, in spite of generous assistance from the United States under Lend-Lease. The knowledge that the British war effort would collapse without this help clearly weakened her bargaining strength in any arguments with the Americans. Moreover, the American training and construction programme was beginning to have its effects and US forces would soon outstrip those of Britain. The USSR, too, with more than three times the population of Britain and several million men under arms bearing the brunt of the German war machine on the Eastern Front, was clearly in a stronger position. All this limited the possibilities for Eden. [6]

In his views on the wider aspect of foreign affairs, his reputation as a champion of internationalism notwithstanding, Eden largely held traditionalist and orthodox Foreign Office views. Even more than Churchill he wished to restore a working European community of States; and he was less inclined than his chief to kotow to US views, when those cut across that objective. He was inordinately patient with de Gaulle, whom he regarded as the best hope of providing the leadership which was necessary to restore France to her pre-war position and influence in Europe, an objective which Eden regarded as vital. He saw the necessity, too, for some powerful State to give stability in Central Europe, while not commanding all the resources which had enabled Nazi Germany to embark on a course of aggression. How precisely that was to be achieved was not yet clear to him, and he had tended to seem inconsistent and rather ambiguous in his various statements to the Cabinet and to his Allies on the future of Germany. But there was some excuse for fuzziness here. Much would depend on how American and Soviet views crystallized and neither had yet produced a formal plan, though both Roosevelt and Stalin clearly leaned to partition. Then, too, the Cabinet was divided on future policy towards Germany. As against Churchill's scheme for a Danubian federation involving South Germany, Eden as has been noted was inclined to think a decentralized, democratic Germany—somewhat diminished in size—the best solution. But he was clear that a satisfactory European balance of power required that there should not be a gaping hole in the heart of Europe, as Roosevelt and Stalin seemed to wish. The schemes for East-European federations, too, were designed to produce a more satisfactory balance and to strengthen the fabric of Europe, politically and economically. Not that Eden dissented from Churchill's view that the Anglo-American alliance would be a necessary part of any satisfactory system of world security for the foreseeable future: but undue subservience to the United States irked him. He had already tilted a lance more than once with Roosevelt and Hull over France and French affairs. He was to do so more dramatically over Germany in the future. He knew that the American view of future world security was in many ways very different from his. As far as the proposed new international organization was concerned, he was prepared like Churchill to give it his support, and hope that the Soviet Union might prove to be a co-operative and constructive member of it. But he did not quite share the roseate American view of its possibilities, or feel that no more need to be done to guarantee European security: and in the wider world he was prepared to fight for British imperial interests against Soviet or American attempts to ignore or diminish them. He had observed, moreover, that when it came to matters affecting US interests in the Far East or Latin America, his American Allies tended to be severely practical. Eden was not, like Churchill, a romantic and old-fashioned imperialist. He recognized that change must come in the Empire, particularly in India, but felt this should be gradual. The European colonial empires, most of all the British Empire, were a necessary element in world stability. Rapid dislocation of that system would only add to the world's problems, not help to solve them. Here again there was potential conflict with American views, which were hostile to European colonialism. [7]

The third principal at the conference, Soviet Foreign Minister Molotov, was an 'old Bolshevik', a veteran survivor of the Revolution. In Stalin's Russia of the 1930s, 'survival' had been the appropriate word. Molotov had achieved that feat, where others had gone to the wall, but he had known many anxious moments. Like every other Soviet minister he feared Stalin and knew that not merely his job but possibly his life depended on retaining the dictator's favour. Deep-rooted suspicion of his fellow men was almost inevitable after such a career, and was intensified with foreigners. Travelling to overseas countries, even allied ones, he slept with a revolver by his bedside. His view of foreign affairs and the outside world was further hardened by the Marxist-Leninist ideology to which he had been deeply committed all his life and which laid down that Western capitalism and Soviet Communism were inherent rivals and enemies. War had made the US and Britain allies perforce, but that was no reason to trust them. Historians sometimes speculate as to the conviction with which Soviet leaders believe in the faith. But there is no reason to suppose Stalin or Molotov seriously questioned its tenets. Their view of the capitalist West as unremittingly hostile to the USSR had certainly not been shaken by the policies of pre-war British and French governments which had, until the eleventh hour, in general shown more interest in establishing friendly relations with Nazi Germany than in constructing a viable alliance with the USSR. Britain and France had shown scant concern for Soviet interests in all this. Finally in 1939 the Soviet government had signed a Non-Agression Pact with Germany, making the best bargain it could and leaving the rest of Europe to its fate. This seemed to them a reasonable act of self-preservation at the time. The collapse of France in 1940, however, had been an unexpected blow to Russia almost as much as to Britain. The French army had been the best insurance against a Nazi attack on the USSR. But the Soviet leaders continued to hope that Hitler might hold his hand. When the blow fell in 1941 they accepted Britain and the United States as allies of necessity, but without changing their basic attitude towards them. That Churchill, an outspoken opponent of Soviet Communism for many years, was now Prime Minister of Britain was perhaps no great encouragement to do so, as far as Britain was concerned. Roosevelt and the Americans were more of an unknown factor. The United States had largely held aloof from European affairs in the inter-war years and therefore was not tarred in Soviet eyes with quite the same brush. If American policy had not helped the USSR, at least it had not actively worked against it. But the United States was after all the most powerful capitalist state in the world, and as such regarded with a wary and suspicious eye. The past two years as allies, with all the bitter arguments over the Second Front and Arctic convoys, had not helped to change the Soviet view of its Allies very much, in spite of the help in supplies and munitions the USSR had received.

As Soviet Prime Minister during the thirties, Molotov had been deeply involved in the formation of all Soviet policies. He had become Foreign Minister in 1939 and sponsored the policy of rapprochement with Nazi Germany which now lay in ruins. That Soviet policy was often opportunistic, sometimes brutally cynical, and on occasions more than reminiscent of old-fashioned imperialism does not, it must be added, necessarily disprove the basic ideological commitment of Stalin and Molotov to Marxism-Leninism. To them the interests of world Communism and of the USSR, as its homeland, were necessarily the same. In pursuit of those interests all methods were defensible. The end justified the means. The Soviet leaders suffered from none of the inhibitions which afflicted some American statesmen with regard to power politics. It was necessary to use the enemy's weapons against him.

As a diplomat and negotiator Molotov was stubborn, unyielding, patient, and humourless. His intransigence and unwillingness to compromise, even on small matters, without some definite quid pro quo —and not always then— could be attributed perhaps in Stalin's lifetime to a lack of freedom, and doubts as to whether any concessions he made would be acceptable to his chief. But Western negotiators formed the impression that it was not a role which was uncongenial to him. As it happened, the British and Americans on this occasion were to find him more affable and accommodating than on most future occasions. This perhaps may be attributed partly to the fact that Stalin was on the spot and could be consulted immediately about any doubtful point, and partly to the circumstance that the Russians were basking in the sunshine of a first major interallied conference in their own capital. The Foreign Ministers of Britain and the United States had come to them, to negotiate with the USSR on its own ground. It marked a change in status for the Soviet Union compared with the years of diplomatic isolation between the wars, and was appreciated as such.[8]

The remaining members of the US and British missions were for the most part officials drawn from the State Department and Foreign Office. No other prominent politicians were involved on the American side, with the exception perhaps of Averell Harriman. Harriman was to be active in Democratic politics after the war, and was not like the other US representatives a career service official. He was in fact a highly successful New York business man, who unlike most of his kind was a Democrat and Roosevelt supporter. He was also a family friend of Mrs. Roosevelt. As one of his fellow delegates judged it, he was not primarily a man of abstract ideas, but a practical, level-headed, clear-minded man of affairs—qualities which were to be valuable to many subsequent Presidents. He was trusted by Roosevelt, who had used him on Lend-Lease matters, including an important mission to Moscow in 1941, and then sent him to London as his special representative to Churchill, where to some degree he bypassed the US Ambassador. He was now to stay on after the conference as US Ambassador to Moscow. In Britain he had established good personal relations with Churchill, Eden, and other British leaders. His stay had given him a greater insight into the British view of foreign policy at the time than most other Americans, including Hull, possessed. This made his presence at the conference valuable to Eden, as someone who had a knowledgeable and sympathetic, though not uncritical understanding of his objectives. In particular, Harriman understood the significance of the Eastern European problems, including Poland. He judged in fact that Hull's priorities—the Four-Power Declaration and Chinese signature of it—were not entirely right; the Secretary should have given more weight to the desirability of extracting satisfactory assurances from the Soviets on Eastern Europe. At a time when US leverage with Russia was still considerable Hull should not, Harriman judged, have left Eden to battle more or less alone in Moscow on these matters. But Harriman was to Hull a somewhat suspect figure, a 'presidential representative', unlike the rest of the

US team who were responsible directly to the Secretary. Hull was jealous of his status as the leader of the US mission, and not inclined to share the role with anyone else; and he was not malleable on the issue of his priorities.[9]

The remainder of the US delegation were career foreign service men who belonged to what Roosevelt scoffingly described as the 'striped-pants boys' of the State Department. They included James Dunn, the Department's 'Political Adviser on European Affairs'. Dunn had worked with Hull on the initial US response to Soviet territorial demands in 1941–2. This response had been from the Soviet point of view negative, since the Department had urged Roosevelt to adhere to his previous view that detailed territorial adjustments should be worked out at a post-war peace conference rather than form a part of piecemeal interallied bargaining during the war. Furthermore, US pressure had been exerted on Churchill and Eden, who took a more favourable view of Russian claims. Dunn had also been concerned at the Quebec conference in the drafting of the proposed Anglo-American 'Declaration on Liberated Territories', parts of which would have restricted Soviet freedom to employ its forces in liberated Europe solely at its own discretion. Roosevelt was probably not wrong in thinking that men like Dunn, who had been closely associated with some of these aspects of American foreign policy, would not be particularly congenial to the Russians. Also in the party were G. L. Hackworth, the Department's Principal Legal Adviser, whose main concern was the legal and constitutional issues affecting the Four-Power Declaration and future US participation in international bodies, together with other issues of national or international law which might arise from agreements reached at the conference. One of these was a last-minute proposal by Churchill that the Three Powers might issue a solemn declaration from Moscow promising to bring German war criminals to book. It was hoped that this might restrain some Germans from committing the kind of atrocities which had marked German occupation of many European countries. The other American delegates were drawn from various divisions of the Department of State, including Information, Near Eastern Affairs, Commercial Policy, Political Studies, European Affairs (which provided several representatives), and Far Eastern Affairs. The delegation also included representatives of the US Embassies in Moscow and Teheran, and the Assistant to the Secretary of State, C. W. Gray. Of these men, one of the ablest was Bohlen of the European Affairs Division, trained as one of the few American 'Soviet experts' and Russian linguists. He was to act as US interpreter at the conference.

He was to be a major influence on US policy towards the USSR in the years of the 'cold war' and has been associated by some historians with the so-called 'Riga axioms', on which that policy was said to be based. Philip Moseley of the Political Studies Division on the other hand was to become an important member of the US delegation to the European Advisory Commission, which was to emerge from the Moscow conference as one positive result of Eden's labours. Hull had in general, it may be said, a strong and loyal team of experienced foreign service advisers. [10]

The Armed Service members of the US mission, added to it because of the Soviet insistence on discussing the Cross-Channel operation, formed a separate group. Hull was not very much concerned with them, and did not want to be. Apart from their chief, General Deane, *en route* to his new job as head of the US Military Mission in Moscow, they included two future members of his Moscow Mission and two representatives of the US War Department. All told, Hull led a mission of twenty delegates. There were also of course clerks, aides, and security men, plus two doctors.

Twenty was in fact the average size of the three delegations. Ismay was the most interesting of the other members of the British delegation, and much more experienced in straddling the fields of war and diplomacy than the American military men. For the past three years he had performed the difficult task of maintaining smoother relations between the volatile Churchill and the British Chiefs of Staff, including the CIGS Alan Brooke, an outstandingly able man who found it difficult always to be patient with Churchill's wilder flights of fancy. After this apprenticeship, even the prospect of negotiating with the Russians did not seem unduly forbidding. Ismay was a large genial man whose patience and good temper were invaluable in difficult moments, and whose conventional facade concealed an acute mind and great shrewdness. He had brought with him a strong contingent of five members of the military section of the War Cabinet office including one particularly gifted, like Ismay himself, in the high-level politics of war, Brigadier Leslie Hollis. Eden's party naturally also included a strong Foreign Office contingent, including the Assistant Under-Secretary of the Department, William Strang, later to join Moseley on the European Advisory Commission; the British Ambassador in Moscow, Archibald Clark Kerr; another senior Embassy member; senior representatives from the Southern, Central, Eastern, and Economic Departments of the Office; two members of the British Legation in Iran; and two of his private secretaries at the Foreign Office. [11]

The Soviet delegation included three members of particular note apart from Molotov. A. Y. Vyshinsky was a lawyer, whose performance as prosecutor in many of the treason trials of the thirties had earned him Stalin's favour and a reputation as one of the more sinister figures in the dictator's entourage. He was already nominated as the Soviet representative on the Italian Advisory Commission and had been held back to participate in the conference. He did not at any time in his life seem to regret his reputation or express any compunction for the part he had played in sending many men to their deaths. But his ability as an administrator and policy-maker was undoubted. Maxim Litvinov, Molotov's subordinate at the Foreign Ministry, was a former Foreign Minister himself, and a familiar figure at pre-war sessions of the League of Nations. He was remembered for a significant phrase 'peace is indivisible', a statement which he may well have recalled as he sat at the conference table with the representatives of three powerful States which had so singularly failed to unite to preserve peace while it still might have been possible to do so. He had been sacked and disgraced when his pre-war policy of collective security and alliances with the West was deemed to have failed. With the coming of new ties to the West in 1941 he had been hauled back out of oblivion, probably because it was thought that his knowledge of and contacts with the West—far greater than that of Molotov and Stalin—might now be valuable. He had recently served as Ambassador to the United States. The third figure of note was Marshal Voroshilov, a former War Minister and, like Molotov and Vyshinsky, a Vice-Premier. Voroshilov was also a survivor of the 'old Bolsheviks', Stalin's original inner circle at the time of the Revolution. His loyalty to Stalin was undoubted, and he was possibly one of the few men the dictator trusted. He had never been noted for his acuteness, and to say he was now past his prime is perhaps to put it kindly. One of the younger Soviet Generals, Major-General A. A. Gryzlov of the General Staff, attended the conference to keep an eye on Voroshilov and to help in the work on military matters. The remainder of the Soviet delegation, apart from a former Soviet Ambassador to Iran and one representative of the Foreign Trade Ministry, were drawn from the Foreign Ministry itself, and included five other deputy foreign ministers apart from Litvinov, together with representatives of the Legal Section, the American Section, the Second European Division, and the Near Eastern Section. The delegation also included Molotov's personal assistant and four secretaries. None of these diplomats were men of particular note except perhaps for Lozovsky, the former information chief. They were bureaucrats, trained to stand well back from the limelight.[12]

Most of these men, in fact, acting as advisers to their principals, did not attend plenary meetings of the conference regularly, some being summoned when they were particularly needed. Harriman, Deane, Hackworth and Dunn attended most often with Hull: Ismay, Clark Kerr, and Strang regularly came with Eden: Vyshinsky, Voroshilov, Litvinov, and an official named Saksin with Molotov.

These then were the representatives of the three states who between 19 and 30 October 1943 met daily to discuss the issues of war and peace.

CHAPTER IV

MOSCOW MEETING
THE SURRENDER OF EASTERN EUROPE

1. The Order of Business

To some of the participants, notably Eden, the Moscow conference seemed a slow and lengthy business. Yet in relation to the scope and complexity of the agenda twelve full days does not seem excessive. The Ministers themselves met in plenary session every afternoon, usually at four o'clock, in the Guest House of the Soviet Foreign Ministry. In addition to these formal sessions, there were less formal meetings between Hull and Molotov, Eden and Molotov, and Eden and Hull during the conference, as well as informal conversations in intervals between the sessions and at various luncheons, receptions, and banquets. Eden also had two private meetings and Hull one such meeting with Stalin. A drafting committee of six, two from each delegation, was set up, which held regular meetings between 23 and 29 October: towards the end of the conference this was reduced to a small committee of the three principal members, to expedite the business of the conference. In addition a tripartite subcommittee was created to consider ways of achieving more effective co-ordination of the policies of the Three Powers in Iran and the desirability or otherwise of issuing a public tripartite declaration on the subject: and an Anglo-Soviet subcommittee considered the question of agreements between major and minor Allies which Eden had put before the conference.

The conference had before it an agreed agenda of seventeen items, only one of which—'measures to shorten the war'—had been formally placed on the agenda by the Soviet government. The United States had proposed four items, two of them dealing primarily with post-war political and economic collaboration, one with 'methods for dealing with current problems' (on which the United States had in fact little new to propose): and only one item relating to a specific current problem, namely the question of Germany. The United Kingdom on the other hand had proposed fourteen items for discussion and added a further two during the conference. One of these fourteen, the proposal for improved machinery for consideration of 'questions requiring current and close collaboration', overlapped with both the American item on methods of dealing with current problems and the Soviet proposal for a political/military commission in the Mediterranean. It thus represented in effect a Soviet contribution to the agenda, as well as an Anglo-American one. Two other British items—on Germany and post-war economic collaboration—duplicated American proposals to some degree and were therefore combined with them on the agenda. Even so, those items which appeared solely on British initiative still constituted an extensive list, covering France, Italy, Poland, the Danubian and Balkan countries, 'other enemy countries in Europe', and 'liberated allied territory'—in short the whole of Western and Eastern Europe, in addition to the two Middle Eastern countries Turkey and Iran. The question of deterring and punishing German atrocities and the exchange of military information were also added to the agenda on British initiative. Thus the wide-ranging character of the agenda owed much to Eden's pressure, though it must be added that the question of Italian military government and future treatment was bound to come up, in view of Soviet uneasiness on this score and their proposals for a political/military commission. But certainly the USSR had shown no urgent desire to discuss other European issues, whether East or West.[1]

The conference also had before it a number of specific proposals or resolutions, as requested by the USSR. Three were Soviet proposals under Item 1, and were only formally tabled on the first full day of the conference. These proposals, it will be remembered, called for all possible measures in 1943 to bring about an Anglo-American invasion of France: and also for the Three Powers to demand of Turkey that she enter the war forthwith, and of Sweden that she permit Allied use of her air-bases. The USSR however put forward three further proposals during the conference, arising out of the agenda. Two of these concerned Italy. The Soviet government proposed a statement of principles for the treatment of that country (reflecting Soviet dissatisfaction with Anglo-American policy in this area), which the USSR suggested should be made public if agreed: and the Soviets also requested that a portion of the surrendered Italian battle-fleet and merchant marine should be handed over to Russia as reparations. In addition, the Soviet delegation proposed the creation of a tripartite commission to go into the details of creating a new post-war international body under the terms of the proposed Four-Power Declaration.[2]

The United States delegation put seven formal proposals to the conference, and added three more suggestions for improved military co-operation under Item 1. Apart from the proposed Four-Power Declaration, the Americans put forward a specific proposal on the handling of current political and economic issues, which amounted really to no more than the suggestion that all such issues should be handled through diplomatic channels, unless they warranted the holding of a special conference. A proposal to preserve the status quo is of course still a proposal, but this particular one ran counter to Eden's wish for new machinery. As it turned out, the US proposal was in effect pre-empted by the way the Soviet and British proposals in this field were handled by the conference, leaving Hull no option but to admit his proposal was now less important. That however was not to be the end of the story. The American attitude towards the new inter-allied bodies was to have inevitably a considerable bearing on the scope of the work they were ultimately to be allowed to perform (see p. 114 below). The US had also four proposals relating to economic co-operation and similar matters. Three of these related to immediate post-war problems, and dealt respectively with US aid to the USSR for reconstruction, joint action for assistance to other countries in need of relief and rehabilitation, and reparations. The first simply suggested that the US and USSR should initiate discussion on the subject: the second was not a definite proposal at all, but simply a statement of the problem and the suggestion that the work of the United Nations Relief and Rehabilitation Agency (UNRRA) might need to be supplemented by more long-range and permanent methods, including the establishment of an international lending agency. The third document stated a number of very considerable limitations with which the Americans wished to hedge the payment of reparations by Germany. These limitations reflected the US desire not to find itself in the position of subsidizing German reparations to its Allies through indirect means, and also its concern lest the complications of reparations payments and their effects on the German economy might hamper general European recovery. The US proposed that a special tripartite commission should be set up to deal with this problem. The fourth US proposal consisted of a lengthy statement of what was required for future economic co-operation, which included measures to promote expanded trade, stable exchange rates, investment for development, improved international transport and telecommunication, improved nutrition, and improved working conditions. It is difficult to extract definite proposals from the mass of verbiage surrounding this item but the main and immediate American objectives here were to encourage more discussion of these matters by the major powers, and particularly to encourage the USSR to play a larger part in them and in the planning of future measures along these lines. The germ of such future organizations as the World Bank, the International Monetary Fund, the International Transport Organization, the General Agreement on Tariffs and Trade, and the Food and Agriculture Organization lay in these proposals. They reflected the US concern with the need for international economic co-operation, particularly to avoid future world-wide depressions. finally there was an American memorandum on the principles to be applied in the surrender and post-war treatment of Germany. This is described in the United States minutes as 'a proposal', but was referred to by Hull, with perhaps unnecessary modesty, as 'an outline and framework which might form the basis for further study and discussion'. It was in fact a quite detailed programme for the treatment of Germany in the immediate post-war period, with specific recommendations for control, occupation, denazification, reparations, disarmament, and demilitarization: in the longer term it recommended the establishment of a decentralized and democratic form of government for Germany: it did not commit itself on the question of future German frontiers or on the question whether Germany should be dismembered. This document was treated by the conference as in effect a proposed programme for Germany 'as far as it went'—a significant qualification, so far as the USSR was concerned.[3]

The United States delegation also added to the Soviet proposals for shortening the war three specific but minor proposals for improving military co-operation between Russia and the Western Allies. These suggested the use by Allied air forces of Soviet bases for the purpose of 'shuttle-bombing'—that is, aircraft landing in Russia after the conclusion of certain missions, and returning after rearmament etc. from these bases to their home bases, perhaps carrying out further missions on the return journey. Secondly the Americans proposed the more effective interchange of weather information and the improvement of communications to this end; and thirdly that air communication between the two countries should be improved. For various reasons these proposals did not in general appeal very much to the Soviet government.[4]

The number of British resolutions before the conference was greater than those from Russia or the United States, reflecting the more extensive British contribution to the agenda. There were thirteen which were classified under the agenda as 'British', seven tabled before the conference and six during it. Two further resolutions were, in effect, joint British and American proposals. The majority of the proposals which were described as purely British reflected Eden's two main preoccupations—improved machinery for tripartite discussion of current European problems and the future arrangements for Eastern Europe. Under the first heading Eden had tabled initially a proposal in connection with the Soviet-inspired political/military commission which reflected the scheme discussed by the British cabinet before the conference. It envisaged a tripartite or possibly larger body which should be located to begin with in Algiers and concern itself with Italian problems; but which also looked to an extension of its terms of reference and a possible transfer of its headquarters at some future date. During the early stages of the conference Eden modified this proposal and specifically suggested the simultaneous creation of two separate bodies, one for Italy in Algiers and the other to deal with wider European problems in London. The British delegation produced two further proposals defining the terms of reference for these two bodies. On Eastern Europe, there was the proposal on agreements between major and minor powers: the proposed declaration on 'Joint responsibility for Europe' and the encouragement of confederations, already mentioned: and the proposed declaration on liberated territories which, it is suggested, had particular implications for Eastern Europe. Britain also put forward a proposed declaration guaranteeing the restoration of Austrian independence; this proposal hinted at the possible encouragement of Austrian participation in some kind of 'Danubian' federation, as Churchill desired, but about which the Americans had doubts.

The British proposals, however, were not limited to these two fields. Looking to the particular problems arising from the actual termination of hostilities, Eden had put forward two proposals, one suggesting certain principles to govern the conclusion of hostilities and the other concerned with the co-ordination of Allied responses to whatever 'peace-feelers' might be put out by enemy states. The first, dated the previous July, was concerned largely with the practical problems of surrender and its immediate aftermath. It recommended the imposition of terms agreed by all the Allies, the acceptance of surrender either from a government regarded as legitimate by the Allies, or else directly by enemy military commanders; the creation of tripartite armistice commissions to administer the terms: and the occupation of enemy countries under plans previously agreed by the Allies, under the control of the Allied Commander-in-Chief. This document also referred to a supervisory tripartite body to be called the 'United Nations Commission for Europe', a provision which caused some confusion at the conference, and led Eden to explain that in this respect these proposals, which had been formulated in July, had to some extent been superseded by the Soviet proposal for a political/military commission and the British elaborations of it: also by the specific American proposals for Germany.

The British proposal for a joint agreement on 'peace-feelers' reflected mainly the Anglo-American desire to avoid, in dealings with other enemy states, the kind of confusions and misunderstandings between the Allies which had caused Soviet resentment in the case of Italy. It also however reflected to some extent Anglo-American apprehensions about possible German approaches to Russia. This proposal called for the three governments to inform each other immediately of any 'peace-feelers' received from enemy countries and to consult together on their response.

The problem of achieving a greater degree of harmony on tripartite policy in Iran was a cause of concern to both the British and US governments. But it had been put on the agenda by Britain, and it was the British delegation which took the lead in formulating proposals for the tripartite subcommittee on Iran set up by the conference. Three such proposals were put forward; firstly for a declaration embodying the Allies' agreement to assist the Iranians to overcome the effects of the war on their economy and to work in harmony and in support of the various allied agencies involved in that task; secondly for a similar declaration reaffirming the allied commitment, under the 1942 Anglo-Soviet Treaty with Iran, to respect Iranian independence and to withdraw troops from Iran no more than six months after the end of the war; and thirdly for an agreement on the financial problems arising from the allied use of the Iranian railway system. These proposals reflected the Anglo-American desire to reassure the Iranians, and also their latent suspicion of Soviet intentions: they were clearly regarded by the latter as a reflection on their good faith and received a somewhat frosty reception.

Finally Britain proposed during the conference a resolution calling for an improvement in the exchange of allied information about Axis military forces. This was basically a response somewhat similar to the three US proposals on improved co-operation between the Allies under Item 1 of the agenda. The Soviets were in general cagey in their disclosures of any military information to their Allies, and this proposal was a gentle hint that more openness in this respect could also make a contribution to shortening the war. [5]

Two further proposals completed the list, but were classified as joint Anglo-American initiatives. The first of these laid down a joint scheme for the administration of liberated France. This scheme had been approved by Roosevelt and Churchill before the conference. It envisaged military government under the Allied C-in-C, but also the creation at the earliest date of a civil administration conducted mainly by French citizens, under the C-in-C's authority. Its most important immediate aspect was that it opened the door to the association of de Gaulle's Committee of National Liberation with the administration of France through the appointment of a 'Director of Civil Affairs' drawn from a military mission to the Allied Headquarters appointed by the committee. This represented a reluctant American capitulation to the realities of de Gaulle's prestige and influence in France. The insertion of a provision requiring the C-in-C to treat all political groups impartially was designed to lessen the impact of this concession, but was unlikely to do so in practice.

The second of the two joint resolutions was the declaration, proposed initially by Churchill but approved by Roosevelt, threatening retribution to any Germans who committed atrocities. It was intended to act as a deterrent for the future and caused little disagreement at the conference.[6]

The scope and complexity of the agenda as thus indicated and the number of proposals for discussion makes it hardly surprising that twelve days were required for the conference, as compared with the much shorter period of the actual heads-of-government meeting which followed. This makes it perhaps a little odd at first sight that Eden began to show signs of impatience when the conference had been in progress barely a week. On 24 October he sent Churchill a cable reporting that the conference was making 'fair progress' and that the prospects were good for agreement on his proposed London Commission, but 'the work is not very rapid'. Eden concedes in the same message that language difficulties and the amount of drafting and redrafting made this relative slowness almost inevitable. None the less he confided to Hull two days later that he was unhappy about the progress of the conference. 'The Conference', he records, 'was churning along ever more slowly, and I began to wonder whether anything would be finally settled'. Eden states that Hull agreed with him, and went along with his suggestion that Eden should ask for a meeting with Stalin immediately, to try to hurry things along. Molotov apparently was rattled by this request which no doubt struck him as a reflection on his efficiency as chairman. Whether Hull was in fact as impatient as Eden may be doubted. He does not seem to have complained about slow progress to Molotov, though there had been many opportunities to do so, nor to Stalin when the two had met for the first time on the 25th, the day before his conversation with Eden. He had the same day outlined to Molotov at the latter's request the subjects on which he hoped the conference would reach agreement. However, on the 27th Hull did give a hint to Molotov that speed might now be desirable, and this may have been partly prompted by Eden's representations. He then suggested a small subcommittee of the Drafting Committee 'to whip things into shape'; and reinforced it by the intimation that he would have to leave Moscow within the next three or four days. [7]

Eden's impatience at this stage may seem a little excessive, the more so since his private secretary was writing in his diary during this same period that 'the Soviets seem determined to make the conference a success' and 'the political side is going well'. The Drafting Committee had before it at this time the whole question of the composition, powers, and location of two new international bodies; also the Four-Power Declaration; the British resolution on 'peace-feelers'; a declaration on policy towards Italy; the declaration on Austria; and the declaration on German atrocities. Some of these emerged more or less as submitted by the various delegations, but on the London Commission, the Italian Advisory Council, and the Four-Power Declaration there were important differences which had to be ironed out; and the later British proposals had only been submitted after the conference began. In these meetings, as in plenary meetings, the necessity to translate every word spoken almost doubled the time required for every item of discussion. Eden was well aware of these difficulties and moreover could reflect that his most important proposal—that there should be separate bodies for Italy and for other European matters, and the latter body should be London-based—seemed at this stage of the conference likely to be accepted. His edginess and impatience were probably due partly to frustration over the rebuffs he was encountering on his East European policy; and partly to Winston Churchill, who chose this moment to question the absolute validity of the Allied commitment to the Anglo-American Cross-Channel Attack (Operation 'Overlord')—or at any rate the Quebec commitment to launch it in the spring of 1944 and no later. This news reached Eden at the precise moment when he and Ismay had assured Molotov that the commitment retained its full force, and when the success of the conference seemed to hang largely on whether the Soviets believed this assurance. Indeed the British delegation had always worked on the assumption that successful negotiations with Russia on other matters largely turned on this assurance being believed. Eden, it appears, was furious and felt that the ground might be cut from under his feet: he even talked of resignation. He felt he had no choice but to continue as though there had been no change in the British attitude, reflecting no doubt that the Americans might well deal with Churchill pretty firmly on this issue. Churchill however insisted that his doubts should be conveyed to Stalin, who, when it came to the point, took it surprisingly well. But all of this increased the strain which Eden felt, most of all perhaps from the consciousness of being, in more than one way, in the weakest position at the conference table. In point of fact Eden's representations to Stalin on the need to expedite decisions appear to have had no immediate effect. It was not until the 30th, as Eden records, that 'the atmosphere appeared to change', and Molotov by 'brisk and businesslike' methods brought the various issues to a conclusion. A day or two later Eden was reporting to Churchill that he had not realized earlier 'how much the Soviets wanted the conference to succeed', and 'there were of course checks and setbacks, but general progress was cumulative and we ended at the top'. Hull's reactions, as we shall see, were even more enthusiastic. [8]

2. The Conference Day by Day

19 October. Organizational arrangements

The conference convened for the first time, at Eden's suggestion, on the evening of the day the delegates arrived, but at this meeting little was discussed other than the procedure to be followed in regard to the time of the plenary meetings and the personnel to attend them. The first full session on the following day, October 19th, was likewise devoted mainly to business matters. Molotov was invited by the other two to take the chair, and after a suitable show of reluctance accepted the honour. It was in fact a sensible tactic to invite the Soviet Minister to preside over the conference. Apart from the implied compliment, it put the major responsibility for the success of the proceedings on Molotov's shoulders. It was agreed at this meeting that the Ministers could come to actual decisions on certain points, Hull pointing out that authorization could be obtained from their respective governments quite quickly where necessary. The meeting also accepted the agreed agenda prepared by the Soviets, the only point of debate being the question whether the US-proposed 'Four-Power Declaration on Security' should be included. Doubt on this point arose from correspondence between Roosevelt and Stalin, in which each revealed some of their characteristic traits. In response to the Soviet objection to Chinese participation in the Declaration, Roosevelt had thrown out the suggestion, in his offhand way, that 'the discussion should be limited to the future intentions of the three powers', with perhaps 'wider participation at some future date'. In his reply Stalin had said perhaps rather mischievously or at any rate legalistically, that he presumed therefore the Declaration would be dropped altogether from the agenda. It was up to Hull to disentangle the confusion and re-instate the Declaration on the conference's programme, which he proceeded to do with Eden's support. Molotov in fact made no objection and it was agreed that the Declaration should be the second item of discussion. Eden also suggested that his proposal for improved methods of discussing current questions (the main British proposal) should be Item 3, and 'Italy and the Balkans' should follow immediately as Item 4, followed by the US proposal on improved methods of discussing current issues as Item 5. Since the Soviet proposal for a political/military commission overlapped with the British and US proposals and had particular reference to Italy, this juxtaposition made sense, and was agreed. Molotov then distributed Soviet proposals under Item 1 'measures to shorten the war'. These, as already noted, included the additional proposals that Turkey should be 'invited' to enter the war and Sweden should be asked to provide air-bases for the Allies. Hull and Eden both intimated that they were prepared to discuss these two suggestions in a preliminary way, but final decisions would have to await their consultations with the British and US governments. The conference then adjourned until 3 o'clock the next day, when it was agreed they would meet in restricted numbers to discuss the military questions. The British and US delegations had already conferred that morning on their response on the Cross-Channel Attack and on other issues. At this meeting Eden had explained to Hull his ideas on the political/military commission and also made the first of his unsuccessful attempts during the conference to obtain Hull's support over Poland. Hull for his part spoke of his hopes for the conference and the need to overcome Soviet suspicions. Hull and Molotov had also had a brief preliminary interchange of courtesies, in which Hull had seized the opportunity to stress the importance of post-war co-operation between the Three Powers.[9]

20 October. The military issues: 'Overlord', Turkey and Sweden

The conference got down to serious business on the next day after a luncheon with many toasts, which, as Eden's secretary Oliver Harvey comments, was not the best preparation for a long and difficult meeting. He adds however that the ensuing discussion of the Cross-Channel Attack, which had caused so much bad feeling between Britain and the USSR in the past, was 'unexpectedly serene'. Eden too reported to Churchill that there had been no Soviet recriminations this time. Ismay and Deane gave the Russians the assurances that they were obviously seeking. The Quebec decisions remained unchanged. All preparations were going ahead on the basis of an invasion of north-west France in the spring of 1944. Eighteen Anglo-American divisions were to take part in the initial assault, to be reinforced by a further twelve within the first three months after the landings. Only three con-ditions had to be met: one, that German air strength should be much reduced; two, that the Germans should be able to bring no more than twelve divisions against the landings initially, and no more than fif-teen to reinforce them; and three, that the problem of supplying the troops over open beaches could be solved, it being assumed that the Germans would totally wreck any nearby ports. But Deane and Ismay stressed that these conditions were confidently expected to be met. During the six months before the planned invasion the Germans were to be weakened by sustained pressure on the Italian front and con-tinued air bombardment. A possible allied landing in the south of France, to coincide with the Cross-Channel Attack, was also men-tioned. Seven battle-tried divisions were to be brought back from Italy, together with landing-craft, to sustain the 'Overlord' operation.

As Ismay subsequently remarked, this statement of allied in-tentions to the Russians conveyed a decisive shift in the balance of Anglo-American strategy. During the first eighteen months of the Anglo-American alliance, British conceptions of strategy had in gen-eral prevailed. These had led the Allies into the invasion and conquest of French North Africa, the successful assault on Sicily, and most recently the landings in the south of Italy, reflecting the British belief in Mediterranean operations designed to threaten what Churchill called the 'underbelly' of Axis Europe. The American (and Soviet) belief in the superiority of a direct thrust across the Channel at the heart of Germany had had to give way to the British argument that sufficient Anglo-American forces for such an operation would not be available in 1942 or probably in 1943 either. Now, however, the grow-ing strength of the Americans had enabled them to insist that the Cross-Channel operation should definitely take place in 1944. Churchill had been obliged to accept this at Quebec. He had, as Harvey put it, 'sold the pass'. Churchill, as it turned out, was already having second thoughts; but at that moment these decisions represented agreed Anglo-American strategy. As Ismay comments, the 'peripheral strategy', as the Americans dubbed it (that is, Mediterranean operations), 'was buried': or was it?[10]

The Soviet delegates themselves were, in fact, wittingly or unwit-tingly, about to revive the corpse. For, combined with their insistence on the Cross-Channel Attack, they now brought forward the proposal that Turkey should be brought into the war. Up to this point the atmosphere had been reasonably cordial. The Russians had welcomed the Anglo-American assurances, as well they might. Things now became a little more sticky. For different reasons both the American and British delegations greeted the Turkish proposal with some reserve. The Americans were completely opposed to any diversion of resources from the main objective—'Overlord'. To stir the Turks into action might lead to precisely the sort of commitment in the Eastern Mediterranean they were most zealous to avoid. Eden for his part, with past experience of the Turkish attitude, knew that they would demand ample arms supplies, including the twenty-five fighter squadrons, which the Allies could no longer provide. Inducements, therefore, of the kind and in the quantity that would work, were not available. As for threats, Eden probably thought it unlikely that the Turks could be bullied by vague statements that their interests would not be heeded in the post-war settlement. The Turkish government was well aware that it would be a British interest, as it had always been, to prevent full Soviet control over the Dardanelles. Anyway, they would probably prefer a hypothetical risk in the future to the risk of war with Germany now. The Allies could hardly threaten Turkey with force, or try to invade and take over the country: those sort of measures, or the threat of them, would merely make Turkey an enemy rather than an ally. All in all the proposal must have seemed a blind alley to Eden. But what it might well do would be to revive and provide fresh arguments for Churchill's penchant for an 'Eastern Strategy', and this would probably lead to fresh and acrimonious arguments with the Americans. This was precisely what happened. Churchill had already wired to Eden a message which revealed his doubts about the Quebec commitment to 'Overlord' in the spring. He now instructed the Foreign Secretary to pursue the Turkish idea further with the Russians. The scope of Aegean operations might thus be sustained and expanded, British naval forces and shipping could make use of the Dardanelles, and perhaps ultimately Britain 'could give her right hand to (the Russians) on the Danube'. How would the Russians feel about that? They might not in fact, Churchill conceded, feel too happy about it: 'it may be that for political reasons the Russians would not want us to develop a large-scale Balkan strategy'. Still, the idea was worth pursuing.

Hot upon this message to Eden came further news from Italy. Allied operations were not going as well as had been hoped. This to Churchill was a reason for postponing 'Overlord' while the situation in Italy was stabilized and perhaps something could be done further

East. (To the Americans of course it was an additional reason for avoiding further commitments elsewhere.) Although Eden had reported the Soviets as 'blindly set' on 'Overlord', Churchill persisted. Turkey could not admittedly be given the inducements, in the form of air-strength, which would prompt her to enter the war now. But she might be persuaded to move gradually towards that point through a period of 'non-belligerency' which would include allowing 'full Allied use of the Dardanelles to aid Russia'. For good measure Churchill added that there was something also to be said for the Soviet proposal to bring Sweden more into the war. Indeed the Russians appeared to be reviving two earlier strategic conceptions of Churchill's which had seemed to have been finally shelved—an Eastern Mediterranean strategy and operations in the far north. finally, on 26 October Churchill instructed the hapless Eden to inform Stalin personally of the difficulties in Italy, and warn him of the possibility that the transfer of forces from Italy to the UK for 'Overlord' might have to be postponed; with the inevitable result that 'Overlord' itself might also have to be postponed. On the same day, however, Roosevelt wired Hull, as expected, that neither the Turkish nor the Swedish proposal appealed to the US Chiefs of Staff. Both might constitute a diversion from 'Overlord'. The most that should be done was to sound out the Turks on the possible use of their air-bases. This predictable American response made it unlikely that anything much would come of the Soviet suggestions, in spite of Churchill's more encouraging attitude.

For the moment, however, at this early stage of the conference, Eden obviously felt he must play for time on the Turkish proposal. He was uncomfortably aware that Britain had previously advocated Turkish entry into the war, indeed had twice invited it. To oppose it outright now, when the USSR was proposing it, might seem merely obstructive. He cautiously said that 'in principle' Britain favoured the idea, pointed out the difficulty of giving the Turks what they would ask for, and indicated that the matter could be further considered. On the Swedish proposal he was similarly non-committal, but took the opportunity to say that the Swedes would probably be more receptive if the USSR would indicate its willingness to respect the independence of Finland; a remark which elicited the frosty reply from Molotov that they should stick to the point, which clearly, in his opinion, was not Soviet intentions towards Finland. Hull for his part fell back on the safe ground that he was not a military man, and would have to refer these questions elsewhere: but he thought American views were similar to Mr. Eden's. It was left that the British and Americans

would consult their governments and Chiefs of Staff, and the conference would return to these matters later on. As for the Russians, the
present writer has already given his opinion that the object of this
exercise was perhaps at least partly to bring pressure to bear on the
British to halt all arms supplies to the Turks, since they were not using
them against Germany. There seemed otherwise no logic in the Soviet
posture of simultaneously demanding 'Overlord', the whole 'Overlord', and nothing but 'Overlord', yet at the same time starting hares
which might encourage Churchill, particularly, to go off in other
directions. But perhaps one is inclined sometimes to overestimate
both the Machiavellian qualities and the foresight of Stalin and
Molotov. The Soviet leaders were in any case always inclined to overestimate what the British and Americans could do, if they really set
their minds to it: quite possibly they did not see the full implications
and consequences of their proposals. Further reflection led them at
Teheran to be much more decisive in demanding 'Overlord', at the
expense if necessary of Mediterranean diversions. [11]

21 October. The Four-Power Declaration: Arctic convoys

The first full day of the talks, however, had gone fairly well. On the
following day the conference turned to the main US proposal, the
Four-Power Declaration on Security. Prior to this plenary meeting
Harriman and Deane had met with Molotov, primarily to discuss the
perennial topic of the locale for the hoped-for heads-of-government
meeting, which was still not settled. The discussion did not get very
far. Harriman's reactions and comments however are always interesting and at this early stage he was cautiously optimistic. He was
throughout the conference less inclined than Hull to be swept away by
the hospitality and cordiality of their Russian hosts. Thus he reported
cautiously to Roosevelt 'there may be difficulties ahead', but none the
less it seemed that the Soviets were persuaded of the genuine
American desire to co-operate with them, and for their part seemed to
'have made up their minds they want to do business with us'.

At the plenary session this was Hull's day. To the previous day's
meeting he had made little contribution, leaving it to the military representatives and Eden to do most of the talking on the military questions. Now, however, he was involved with a proposal in which his
heart and mind were deeply engaged. Hull put the Four-Power
Declaration to his colleagues as an indication to the world that the
Three Powers were determined to act together in the future, not only
in the immediate post-hostilities period to deal with the defeated
enemy countries, but to preserve peace and security in the long-term

future. To revert to isolationism, which had characterized both the United States and Russia in the past, would be disastrous. The three countries must seize the favourable tide of public opinion, which might not long outlive the war, and commit themselves now. The Declaration asked them to make such commitments, firstly to the continuance of co-operation for peace and security after the war, secondly to the creation of an international organization with armed forces at its disposal, and thirdly to try to bring about general disarmament. This latter was an old and favourite cause for liberal internationalists of the pre-war era. If it could be achieved, it would clearly strengthen the position of an international body which, it was envisaged, would itself have armed forces which it could use. The contrast was with the pre-war League of Nations, unarmed and impotent in a world of fully-armed nation States.

The discussion which followed was amicable but not without substance. For Hull it was a great point gained when both Eden and Molotov accepted the general principles of the Declaration, especially when the latter stated that the Soviet government was unequivocally in favour of them. The position of China however inevitably caused some difficulty. Molotov repeated the Soviet objection to the drafting of a *Four*-Power Declaration in the absence of China. When it was suggested that the Declaration should be drafted and Chinese authorization to adhere to it could be sought and gained while the conference was still sitting, he queried if that would be possible. After Hull had urged the psychological importance for the unity of the alliance of not excluding China, Eden again proposed the obvious compromise of going ahead with the formulation of a declaration and then asking the Chinese government to approve and sign it. Thereupon Molotov gracefully gave way. After Hull had seized the opportunity of an intermission to reiterate to Molotov that the Chinese should not be given a slap in the face over this issue, the conference proceeded to more detailed consideration of the draft. Eden made his suggestions for alterations in the wording which were designed to achieve two objectives: firstly to make it plain to the Soviets that the British and Americans had no intention of immediately converting their recent enemies the Germans into respectable members of the international community, as the Russians were inclined to suspect. The Axis powers were to be described as 'their enemies' simply, not 'their present enemies'. The new international organization was to be open only to 'peace-loving' States—a categorization which Germany and its allies would clearly have to earn over an extended period of time. These changes were obviously welcome to the Russians and in the absence of any US objection were agreed. Secondly, Eden's changes, prompted in this instance partly by pressure from British Commonwealth States such as Australia and Canada, and the smaller European States, were designed to reassure the smaller powers that they were not proposing to create a 'Four-Power dictatorship'. Accordingly a provision for some form of consultation with the smaller States was included in Article 5, which envisaged Four-Power action to maintain peace in whatever period was needed for the creation of the new organization. This amendment too was accepted without argument. Molotov then proposed changes which were more fundamental; and it became clear to Eden probably, if not to Hull, that the USSR was not disposed to accept any limitations imposed by its Allies to Soviet freedom of action in the immediate post-war period, particularly in territories occupied by the Soviet armies—which would of course be mainly in Eastern Europe. The Soviet government was prepared to pledge itself under Article 2 of the Declaration to 'joint action in imposing surrender terms' on the enemy States, but not to 'subsequent joint action' in territories occupied by its armies. Under Article 7 of the Declaration there was equal Soviet objection to a provision which bound them, in the post-war period, not to use their forces within the territory of other States without 'joint consultation and agreement' with their Allies. Molotov had of course some reasonable or apparently reasonable grounds for his objections. Article 2 as drafted, he argued, might be held to make the conduct of military operations against enemy States not yet defeated dependent on Allied agreement; Article 7 as drafted might limit the freedom of all of them to enter into agreements with other States to station forces at bases within occupied or liberated States. Both Russia and Britain, he pointed out, already had some treaties of this kind. Eden could not deny the force of this objection and the provision requiring 'agreement' as well as 'consultation' was dropped from Article 7. Article 2 was deferred for further consideration and the Anglo-American delegations promised to consider a new formula. But at the end of the session Hull could feel that his proposal had been agreed, so far as the general principle and most of the details went, while on the vexed question of Chinese participation he seemed likely to get his way. No doubt he was well satisfied with the day's work.[12]

Eden possibly felt a little less satisfied. He had developed sensitive antennae to the nuances implied by drafting amendments to international agreements, and probably had picked up those implied by the Soviet stance. In the evening of that same day (21 October) he had another engagement which he probably was not looking forward to

with great enthusiasm. Before the conference it had been agreed that
he should see Stalin to discuss the contentious question of the Arctic
convoys and to try to smooth down the acrimonious feelings engendered by the Churchill–Stalin exchanges. It was to this meeting that
he set out, in the bullet-proof limousine which Molotov had thought-
fully provided, at 10 o'clock that evening. Not surprisingly, the meeting was, as he records, 'rather sticky' at first. Stalin complained that
Churchill evidently 'no longer wished to correspond with him'.
Moved no doubt by this remark, Eden intimated that Mr. Churchill
had thought the tone of Stalin's last communication unnecessarily
abrupt, but he hoped they could now discuss the matter further. The
atmosphere then improved, and Stalin listened patiently to Eden's
explanation of the difficulties involved in running the convoys and his
request that more British naval personnel be allowed to go to
Murmansk to service the British ships as they came in. Interestingly,
Stalin complained that the British sailors did not always treat Russian
sailors 'as equals', a remark which again reveals a certain Soviet
'chip-on-the-shoulder' attitude towards its Allies. Eden probably
thought that the British seamen had more cause for complaint. It is
likely, however, that when insular Russian sailors met equally insular
British sailors, both sides sometimes behaved badly. However, this
part of the discussion had gone better than Eden or his companion
Clark Kerr had expected, and Stalin now expanded further. In discussing military operations he conceded that the Italian campaign was
tying down the equivalent of about forty German divisions in Italy
and the Balkans and preventing their use, therefore, on the Russian
front. This was an unusually generous admission, indeed virtually the
first time the Russians had conceded that the Italian campaign had
any value to them. The conversation concluded with a further discussion of the perennial topic of where the heads of government might
meet but Eden, like Harriman earlier, got no further on this subject.
None the less the meeting had passed off unexpectedly well, and it was
with a sense of relief that Eden reported to Churchill, after a meeting
with Molotov to clear up the details the next morning, that they
seemed to be in 'unexpectedly smooth waters' on the convoy issue.[13]

*22 October. The European Advisory Commission and the
Italian Advisory Council: Italian Government: the Italian navy*

Eden needed all the self-confidence and optimism he could muster for
the next day's proceedings. The conference turned to the main British
proposal for improved machinery for continued tripartite discussion
of current problems (Item 3). At this juncture, it will be remembered,

the British proposal took the form simply of an extension of the scope of the Soviet 'political/military commission' and the possible eventual division of the body into two—one for Italy and the second, more important, for other European questions. But Eden had already determined to propose that *two* separate bodies should be created *now*, and the British delegation was preparing new proposals for this. Eden was aware that the Americans had no great enthusiasm for the creation of a tripartite body with an extensive scope in London—or in fact anywhere but in Washington. Indeed, the main American proposal (Item 5) ran directly counter to any such idea, since it recommended continued reliance on normal diplomatic processes, supplemented where necessary by further high-level tripartite conferences. Eden was already worried about the lack of a common Anglo-American front on so many of the issues before the conference. He was afraid the afternoon's proceedings might open up the cracks further for Molotov's probable edification. However, a preliminary discussion of these issues with Hull during their talk on the 19th had given him some reason to hope that the US attitude might not be too unhelpful, though Hull had not in any way committed himself. What the Soviet attitude would be he could not foresee, but it might well be adverse. Admittedly Molotov would probably welcome the idea of a wider field of activity for a body on which Russia would be represented. On the other hand Eden had to make it plain that the Italian body would not have any immediate direct control over Italian military government, as the Russians wished. This would probably provoke some Soviet acrimony. Then there was the awkward question of French participation on these bodies. Eden probably hoped that his support the previous day for Hull's position on Chinese participation in the Four-Power Declaration might induce the Secretary to take a liberal view on the question; particularly as Roosevelt had apparently conceded the general principle of French representation on the commission (the then-proposed 'Mediterranean' body) as early as 10 September. However, Roosevelt had modified this by a message to Stalin and Churchill at the last moment suggesting that French participation in the commission should be limited and they should have nothing to do with 'the occupation of Italy'. This left the whole question somewhat uncertain. Then there was the further complication of US support for Brazilian and Chinese representation, which Eden regarded as not only inappropriate, but as opening the door to requests from all the Allied nations. Eden decided he would press for full French representation on the Italian body, but perhaps be more cautious about the London Commission membership.

The Foreign Secretary also had the tricky task of disentangling himself from previous British proposals on these subjects, particularly that of 1 July for a 'United Nations Commission for Europe' and that of 12 October for a political/military commission which might *ultimately* split into two. He had to explain why the British government had twice changed its mind; and clear up the confusion that these changes had created. It was altogether a difficult brief.

Eden began by stressing the wide scope that his proposed additional commission would have, a point which he thought would appeal to the Soviets. For the reasons already given he suggested that it should meet in one of the three capitals, and proposed London. This in turn made a separate body desirable to deal with Italian occupation policy. On the latter subject he went on to say what he knew would be less palatable to the USSR, that during actual military operations in Italy this body would have only 'consultative' and 'advisory' functions. It would not have executive powers over the government of Italy, which would be the responsibility of the Allied (that is, Anglo-American) C-in-C. Turning to the question of composition, he mentioned the possibility of French, Greek, and Yugoslav delegates joining the Three Powers on this body, but added tactfully the phrase 'if desired'. Neither Hull nor Molotov commented on the last point, but Molotov's initial reaction to the general proposal seemed to show for the first time slight traces of irritation. No doubt this was caused partly by the clear intention of the British and Americans to limit the ability of the USSR to interfere directly in the government of Italy (though Eden had added that the C-in-C might at his discretion place areas, presumably well away from the fighting, under the direct supervision of the tripartite body). Perhaps also Molotov was slightly nettled by the way the British had taken over a Soviet proposal, adapted it to British objectives, and somewhat confused matters in the process. What was the relationship to the British proposals of 1 July, with its 'United Nations Commission'? he enquired. Those proposals had been acceptable to the Soviet government. The point, of course, was that the 1 July proposal had envisaged a body which would have considerable supervisory powers over the military government of occupied enemy territory. Eden answered evasively. The UN Commission had been envisaged specifically to deal with Germany's surrender and occupation. Britain now thought a 'wider planning body' was necessary. Molotov did not press the point but raised the further question of the US proposals under Item 5. How did they fit in? In any case, he suggested, they should return to the subject tomorrow when there had been time for the new British proposals to be translated. Hull at this point intervened in a way helpful to Eden's case. He not only said that the US proposals under Item 5 did *not* imply opposition to Eden's purposes, but added that his own suggestion was now 'less important'. Regular diplomatic methods would 'supplement' the work of the two proposed bodies. This was a welcome assurance from the British point of view. Molotov's enquiry at this point whether the work of the commissions would prevent matters from being dealt with in the regular way is perhaps indicative of a Soviet disposition not to hand over too much to a London-based body. It was agreed however that the conference should take up the subject again next day: but that the whole matter, together with the British proposals (including that of 1 July) and the US proposal under Item 5, would need to be considered by the Drafting Committee, which the conference had on Eden's suggestion agreed to create at the beginning of the session. Dunn, Vyshinsky, and Strang were to be the principal members of this committee. [14]

The conference then turned to Item 4 on the agenda, under which the British government had proposed 'an exchange of views' on Italy and the Balkans. Molotov opened the discussion and spoke of Soviet dissatisfaction over Italy. This, he said, was due to their lack of information about what was going on and, he implied, doubts as to the strict enforcement of the armistice terms, since the British and Americans had now accepted the Italians as 'co-belligerents'. Eden replied that the setting-up of the Italian Commission would deal with the Soviet desire for information. As to the terms, circumstances had changed somewhat when the Italian government had agreed to become a 'co-belligerent', and in effect asked to change sides. But the Italians would get no remission, he added, which they did not earn by making a positive contribution to the war. On the political side, Fascism and the Fascist structure of government were being rooted out: the British and Americans hoped to bring more liberal and socialist figures into the Italian government, but it was difficult, after twenty years of Fascism, to find enough suitable and 'authoritative' people. Molotov then made more concrete the obvious Soviet feeling that something should be done to hasten the process of destroying Fascism. He proposed a public declaration, which would commit the Allies to 'democratization' of the Italian government; the establishment of democratic freedoms; liquidation of all Fascist organizations; and the arrest of war criminals. Eden, with Hull's assent, commented mildly that these were much the instructions under which Allied military government was operating, but agreed to study the Soviet proposal. Finally, both men offered to furnish documents outlining Allied policies so far. Hull added that they all wanted to destroy Fascism, but these things took time. Molotov responded amicably and then brought up the suggestion that part of the surrendered Italian navy and merchant marine should be allocated to the USSR as reparations. Soviet forces had not, he conceded, played a very large part in the war against Italy, but Italian participation in the war had certainly done harm to Russia. The USSR suggested that one battleship, one cruiser, eight destroyers, four submarines, and forty thousand tons of merchant shipping would be an appropriate Soviet share—about a seventh of the Italian navy and a quarter of the merchant fleet. Both Eden and Hull were probably a little taken aback by a suggestion they had not been prepared for. Britain particularly had regarded the Italian naval booty, particularly the merchant ships, as a welcome addition to resources much strained by the heavy losses sustained in four years of war. However both men agreed to submit the Soviet request to their governments, Molotov remarking that he did not expect an 'immediate' decision.

So far so good, Eden may have reflected. On the main British proposals, Hull had been positively helpful: possibly Eden's support on the priority to be given to the Four-Power Declaration had borne fruit in this regard. Molotov had been, for his part, less difficult than might have been expected. But they were not over the hump yet, since the conference was to return to the matter of the commissions the next day; and then the question of composition and terms of reference of the two bodies would still have to be hammered out in the Drafting Committee. Eden knew very well that Hull was not especially keen on the proposed London Commission, and it was evident Molotov, too, had his reservations about it. On Italy, the discussion had not gone too badly. Eden had made his point, and there had been no Soviet outburst. As for the proposed principles in the Soviet 'declaration', these were unexceptionable from the Western point of view. One wonders whether Eden, if not Hull, reflected at all cynically on the expressed Soviet enthusiasm for Western democratic forms and freedoms—in countries other than the USSR. All three delegations were apparently content to accept the unexpressed assumption that they all meant the same thing by 'democracy'. This perhaps deserves to be recorded as an early illustration of the way in which the exigencies of the wartime alliance were to lead to the tacit acceptance of very dubious assumptions, and the sweeping under the carpet of fundamental differences of ideology and objectives which it might have been healthier to bring out into the open. Churchill perhaps recognized this more fully than the other Western leaders and recognized also that the logic of this unpalatable fact was that the USSR had either to be treated as a future enemy—a posture almost impossible to combine with a wartime alliance—or else some *modus vivendi* would have to be looked for which involved not shared ideals but simply a mutual respect for each other's vital interests. For the moment, however, the West was set on the course of seeking full Soviet co-operation on a world plane, a policy which the Americans were determined to pursue and which the British felt obliged to go along with.[15]

That Eden felt obliged to go along with this policy and not 'rock the boat' on relations with the USSR is shown perhaps most clearly in his attitude to the proposed Soviet-Czech treaty. A little later, during the sixth session of the conference, Molotov pressed him on this point and asked for a decision. The treaty was ready for signature: why should the two parties not go ahead and sign it? Britain and the USSR might then be able to work out something to cover such problems in the future. Eden thereupon withdrew his opposition to the treaty. In London this news was greeted with consternation by Cadogan, the permanent head of the Foreign Office: the War Cabinet, he pointed out, had not authorized a 'total surrender' to the Soviet point of view, but had envisaged some real concession on the resumption of Soviet relations with the London Poles. The provisions of the treaty carried no such assurance, in spite of Eden's soothing report that 'Molotov had gone some way to meet us'. Certainly the USSR had added a provision allowing other nations to participate, but that might mean anything or nothing. Cadogan recognized, however, that Eden had been influenced by 'wider considerations'. Those wider considerations were of course Eden's wish that the conference should be a success, and particularly that the London Commission should be set up. With the main British proposal in the balance as was still the case as late as the 26th, it must have seemed politic to Eden to make a graceful concession on this and some of the related East-European issues, where he sensed he was likely to lose anyway. The real point of the British objection to the Soviet-Czech treaty had been the exclusion of Poland, specifically of the London Polish government. On this matter a combination of Soviet intransigence, American detachment, and Polish obstinacy had left him, as Cadogan admitted, 'without any cards to play' at this conference. Better not to continue thwarting the USSR on a matter where they had a reasonable case, and to address the Polish problem directly in some hoped-for more favourable context. Eden also had to remember Hull's position and known views. Hull had made it clear that he regarded Eastern European problems as subordinate to the great task of securing Soviet post-war co-operation, as exemplified by the Four-Power Declaration. He would have been very resentful if Eden had soured the atmosphere and perhaps thwarted his main objective—which the USSR could still have found ways of obstructing if they wished. So Eden gave way.[16]

23 October. Yugoslavia: the EAC and IAC

The next day Hull had a private meeting with Molotov before the plenary session at which he further underlined his priorities. In his single-minded way he took the opportunity of again urging on the Soviet Minister the necessity of trust and mutual confidence, and the desirability of Soviet participation in all Anglo-American discussions on post-war policy. He particularly mentioned the discussions going on in Washington on post-war economic co-operation; and again urged that now was the time to act, since after the war unity and support for international co-operation might soon evaporate. Hull of course recalled very well how this had happened in the US after the First World War. He mentioned the kind of adverse factors of which isolationists in the United States could make use—the fear of Soviet-backed Communist infiltration, the treatment of religious bodies in the USSR, the sparring between the press of the two countries on such issues. Molotov naturally made soothing noises on these two points, but gave Hull no particular encouragement on the question of economic co-operation. Again one is struck in this interchange by Hull's apparent assumption that any future difficulty in economic co-operation would arise from an unwillingness to do so rather than from the objective difficulties of co-operation between the two different economic systems and the differing aims the two States might have. Molotov at least must have been well aware of this, and probably thought simply in terms of a bilateral deal with the United States for some form of economic aid to the USSR.

So the two men went on to the fifth plenary session of the conference. Eden had noted in his report to Churchill that the conference still had to deal with some of the most contentious issues, in which he included Yugoslavia and Poland. 'An exchange of views on the Balkans' was the second part of the Item 4 on the agenda. Molotov remarked that a discussion on Yugoslavia was specifically provided for under a separate item of the agenda, and reserved his comment. But Eden took advantage of the item to outline the difficulties the British were encountering because of the rivalries between Communist and non-Communist resistance movements in Yugoslavia; and the desirability of getting them to work together. Soviet assistance to this end, he implied, through the use of their influence with the Communist-led movements, would be valuable. In Yugoslavia this referred to Tito's partisans and the political structures they were creating, as opposed to the forces led by Mihailovich which owed allegiance to the royalist government-in-exile in Cairo. In Greece it applied to the Communist-led armed force ELAS and its political wing EAM. Molotov was non-committal and professed ignorance of what was going on. This was probably partly genuine. The USSR had no military mission in either country at this time and only a tenuous radio contact with Tito. Missions were not in fact exchanged by the USSR and the Yugoslav partisans until six months later, whereas the British had sent missions the previous March and were supplying both groups with arms and supplies. The British problem was that Mihailovich's forces did not seem very active in fighting the Germans, while Tito's partisans seemed to divide their time between fighting the Germans and fighting Mihailovich. A similar situation was developing in Greece. The Soviet attitude to these Communist-led forces was one of ignorance compounded with suspicion, as tended to be the case with any movement not directly under their control. As Milovan Djilas complains in his account of the early contacts between the Yugoslav partisans and the Soviets, the latter felt no great interest in or enthusiasm for the revolution which the Yugoslavs were making. Hull's attitude to the whole question was again negative, as was to be the case whenever Eastern European questions came up. Since this could be considered primarily a military matter, he asked General Deane to speak for the US. He himself had 'nothing to add'. Hull could hardly have made his lack of interest more apparent to Molotov. Deane enthusiastically supported a programme of Allied-encouraged sabotage in the Balkans, but on Molotov's suggestion the subject was then postponed to a later date, and Eden promised to supply information on British sabotage activities in the area.

Eden had not got very much change out of either of his colleagues on these matters, but for the moment he was probably quite content to let the matter drop. It really suited him better to get the difficult London Commission issue out of the way first before tackling the even more difficult Eastern European issues. Tactically also he may well have thought that with Churchill and the War Cabinet waiting for results it might be as well, if possible, to report a success before going on to issues where it already seemed that success would be hard to come by.[17]

The conference then returned to Eden's immediate preoccupation, the two commissions. Up to a point matters went well for Eden.

Molotov accepted the idea of two commissions of the kind Eden proposed and made no difficulties about the limitations to be imposed on the Italian body's powers. It was agreed that the Italian Commission should be set up at once and the matter was referred to the Drafting Committee for action, on the basis of Eden's proposal. When discussion turned to the 'European' Commission, however, things were less satisfactory from the British viewpoint. Molotov accepted that it should be in London—a satisfactory point for Eden—but made it clear that he did not wish for this London body to have a wide remit to consider current questions; he proposed the Drafting Committee should act on the basis of Eden's 1 July proposal which envisaged a body concerned only with the end of hostilities and the post-hostilities period. Moreover, that proposal had envisaged a body which would have vast powers of supervision over Allied enforcement of armistice terms—presumably therefore over occupation policy. Eden again stressed that he thought a body was needed which would have wide powers to consider *current* European questions—he instanced 'peace-feelers' from enemy States. At the previous meeting he had instanced also such long-range questions as the future of Germany and 'general policy for the liberated areas'. Molotov's response to this was chilly. If the terms of reference for the London Commission were made too broad, he remarked, there would be little left for the foreign ministers themselves to do using the regular diplomatic machinery. Hull's proposal (that many issues could be handled by tripartite meetings between the foreign minister of each State and the ambassadors of the other two) had in the Soviet view much to be said for it. The London Commission should start by considering armistice terms for the enemy States, as envisaged by Eden's July proposal. As to other matters to be submitted to it, perhaps some combination of Hull's and Eden's proposals could be worked out. This was not at all what Eden wanted. Moreover he had obviously had second thoughts since July about the desirability of setting up a supervisory body which would give the Soviets a permanent power of control—and presumably of veto—over Allied occupation policy in every enemy country. However, for the moment he had to be content with this state of affairs. But he did not propose to let the matter go by default. By the next day (24 October) detailed British proposals for the terms of reference of both bodies had been deposited with the Drafting Committee. Those for the London Commission—now called 'The European Advisory Commission' made some concessions to both Molotov's and Hull's views. They proposed that the commission should address itself first to 'the principles to govern the conclusion of hostilities', and mentioned that other methods of consultation, including the tripartite meetings between each foreign minister and ambassadors suggested by Hull, would still be required for some issues. As a further sop to Hull, whose support was vital, it did not specify French representation, only that 'other members of the UN' might sometimes be invited to attend. But it also specifically envisaged wider terms of reference. The commission would take into account 'any European question' the Three Powers agreed to refer to it. [18]

However, this attempt to restore the position, at least partially, did not emerge unscathed from the Drafting Committee. In the terms finally agreed, it was made clear that the London Commission would concern itself primarily with 'questions connected with the termination of hostilities', which were spelt out as 'the terms of surrender' and the machinery to enforce them. All that was left of the 'wide-ranging forum' desired by Eden was a grudging reference, in one of the later clauses of the agreement, to the possibility that the Three Powers might review the 'competence' of the Commission, if circumstances should call for it. Eden in fact sustained a defeat; and he was defeated primarily because the United States did not support him.

In relation to the proposed Italian body—now referred to as the 'Advisory Council for Italy'—the proposed British terms fared better in the Drafting Committee; for here they had the general support of the Americans. The Italian Council was only to 'advise' their respective governments and the Allied C-in-C on the problems of Italian government: it could make recommendations to the Allied governments, but, like the European Advisory Commission, it could not take 'final decisions'. The Allied C-in-C would continue to operate Italian military government under the orders of the British and US governments, and it would be up to him to decide when the Italian Advisory Council could be allowed to play a more direct executive role in the government of Italy—which meant that Washington and London would decide when this would happen, or if it would happen at all. These terms of reference emerged from the Drafting Committee with no fundamental change, partly no doubt because the USSR really wanted this body to be established urgently. But on this issue it was Molotov who accepted partial defeat. The idea that the Council should 'direct' the Allied military government, as the Soviet Union had originally proposed, had been relegated to the Greek Kalends. The Americans, too, after further discussions in plenary session, made concessions to the British view. Not only did they accept the principle of French representation on the council without the last-minute qualifications suggested by Roosevelt, but the cautious ref-

erence to possible Greek and Yugoslav membership in the British proposal was considerably strengthened. The Greeks and Yugoslavs were
now to become full members 'as soon as possible'. The question of
Chinese or Brazilian membership had been tacitly allowed to drop.
On the outcome of this matter, therefore, Eden could eventually feel
some satisfaction.[19]

All this, however, still lay in the future. On the 23rd Eden could
only feel that he had made some progress, but there was difficult going
ahead of him in relation to the European Advisory Commission.
Another difficulty was Turkey. He had received an encouraging
message from Churchill on the Soviet proposals regarding Turkish
and Swedish participation in the war, which would give him some leeway in adopting a reasonably forthcoming attitude on that issue—but
he was not sure it was leeway he really wanted. The most difficult and
unpromising part of the conference from his point of view was still to
come. On the next day (24 October) the conference was due to tackle
Eastern European questions, including Poland, and the question of
federations. Meanwhile, Hull for his part was reasonably satisfied.
Not only had he won approval for his Four-Power Declaration and,
with Eden's support, probably on the issue of Chinese participation
too, but Molotov had proved so far very amenable on the question of
Soviet participation in Italian government. Moreover it was clear that
the Soviet Foreign Minister shared Hull's desire to limit the scope of
the European Advisory Commission, so this question was also likely
to come out more or less as the United States wished. Molotov's generally friendly attitude also encouraged the American in his hopes for
future post-war co-operation and made him the more anxious not to
antagonize the USSR by probing too much on Eastern European
problems. The Secretary believed that a satisfactory outcome on these
issues depended in any case on Soviet goodwill and their general feeling of security. The important thing then, at this stage, was to win the
former and contribute to the latter. It seemed to most Americans at
the time a very tenable viewpoint.[20]

From the Soviet point of view at this stage the results of the conference had been mixed. They had secured assurances on 'Overlord'
which seemed pretty foolproof; and it must have been encouraging to
Molotov to note not only the US agreement with them on overall
strategy, but also Hull's evident lack of interest in Eastern Europe,
and his attitude to British proposals generally. There were more
cracks in the Anglo-American front, evidently, than had been
imagined—or at any rate really believed. On the other hand the
Americans particularly had not been very forthcoming as yet in

relation to Soviet proposals for Turkey and Sweden, or on the request for Italian shipping; and the USSR had had to accept a partial rebuff on the control of Italian affairs. This may or may not have made Molotov and Stalin the less disposed to be accommodating on East European matters.

24 October. Poland: Iran: Eastern Europe: the 'self-denying ordinance': 'spheres of influence' and federations: the Soviet-Czech treaty

With these difficulties in mind, Eden took another opportunity on the morning of the 24th to seek Hull's support in bringing pressure to bear on the USSR over resumption of Soviet relations with the London Poles. He proposed they should tackle this difficult issue at a small meeting later in the conference, which meant shifting the matter lower than its agreed place on the agenda at no. 11. Hull agreed to defer the matter, but his response to Eden's request for support was disappointing. He would only tell Molotov that the US hoped to see this breach in the alliance repaired. In other words it was an appeal, not pressure, which was promised. Hull added 'it was more of a British problem' than an American one. Eden no doubt gathered from this that the London Poles had somewhat exaggerated the degree of US support they could expect. At any rate he felt he had to accept this rather unsatisfactory assurance. During this same meeting the two men expanded their general agreement on the objectives they would pursue in regard to Iran. The United States had already agreed with Eden's proposal that the conference should issue some reassuring declaration of Allied good intentions towards Iran. It was agreed that the declaration might reiterate the Allied intention to withdraw their forces after the end of hostilities, and include an undertaking that the Three Powers would 'support' the foreign advisers at work in Iran. In other words, they should try to obtain a Soviet undertaking to co-operate fully with its Allies in this area. Hull also suggested that their general response to the proposed Soviet declaration on Italy should be one of acceptance (on the ground that these principles were already the basis of Allied policy in Italy) but qualified by insistence on the overriding importance of military considerations and the practical problems of reforming a twenty-year-old system of government overnight. Both of these factors, it should be pointed out to the USSR, might impose delays in the actual carrying out of the programme for the complete destruction of Fascism in Italy.[21] When the conference reconvened at three o'clock that afternoon it was agreed, on Molotov's request, that the question of Germany (Item 7 on the agenda) should be postponed for the moment. It had already been agreed that Item 6, on France, should be taken later. Hull had only handed the US proposals for Germany to Molotov the day before, and the Soviet Minister needed more time to study them and no doubt confer with Stalin and others. However, according to Hull's account, Molotov had already indicated that Stalin's first reaction to the US suggestions for Germany had been 'enthusiastic'.

The next item on the agenda was Eden's proposal on 'agreements between the major and minor powers' (Item 8). Eden had already made up his mind that he would have to give way gracefully on the specific question of the Soviet-Czech treaty (see above, pp. 74–5), but still hoped for some agreed formula to cover future agreements of this kind—the 'self-denying ordinance' which the Russians themselves had seemed willing to accept the year before. Feeling his way cautiously, he said that the real objective here was to avoid 'a competitive scramble to secure the allegiance of the smaller powers' and the formation of 'spheres of influence' in Europe. He wanted to ensure Anglo-Soviet consultation and agreement on such matters: but the British government had no objection to the Soviet-Czech treaty itself. Eden was making a gesture to the USSR, but he was also giving Hull the opportunity to express support for the principle of 'no spheres of influence'. In view of Roosevelt's adverse reaction to this British proposal when it had been first mooted, Eden cannot have hoped for much assistance from Hull. But a general statement of US opposition to 'spheres of influence' would have been helpful at this point, and would have been in keeping with Hull's (and Roosevelt's) professed views. But Hull was not to be drawn. In response to Molotov's query he made it clear that the US did not want to become involved in the matter, and that he regarded it as an Anglo-Soviet affair. At this point Eden, accepting that Hull was determined not to become involved, and that his presence at any further discussions was likely to be more unhelpful than helpful, agreed that the question of a possible agreement on this matter should be referred to an Anglo-Soviet subcommittee of one member from each delegation. Molotov then read a statement on the question. In this it was made fairly clear (though the actual language of the statement is somewhat self-contradictory) that the USSR would only consider an Anglo-Soviet agreement which did not limit Soviet freedom of action to conclude agreements 'with bordering States' on matters affecting 'the direct security of their boundaries'. This was a pretty elastic definition, which would cover almost any agreement with Poland, Finland, Czechoslovakia, or Romania which the USSR was likely to make: and indeed would extend over a wide area of States south and east of the USSR from

Turkey to China. Incidentally it also prejudged the issue of the disputed Polish–Soviet frontier by defining Czechoslovakia as 'a bordering State'. It did not require much further discussion in the Anglo-Soviet subcommittee to ram this point home; what was left of Eden's proposal by that time could just as easily be turned against Britain, for example in relation to British agreements with Greece, which, after all, was by no stretch of imagination 'a bordering State' with the United Kingdom. Eden therefore eventually dropped the proposal, Molotov underlining the point that this left the USSR with complete freedom of action over such agreements. In short, the 'self-denying ordinance' sank without a trace. [22]

Eden had sustained a major defeat and, in spite of his putting the best face on it in his report to London, knew that he had. British policy for Eastern Europe had sustained a check. There was worse to come.

The next item on the agenda was Turkey, but this, it had been decided, should be discussed in relation to Item 1 when the conference returned to the Soviet proposals under that heading. The question had of course already been discussed in a preliminary way at the beginning of the conference, and awaited the considered views of the British and US governments on Turkish participation in the war. After an intermission, therefore, the conference turned to Item 10 'Common Policy towards Iran'. Molotov immediately revealed the lack of Soviet enthusiasm for such a discussion by raising the legalistic point that under the Anglo-Soviet-Iranian treaty of 1942 Iranian participation in any such discussion was required. Possibly it may have occurred to Eden and Hull that the discussion of other countries' affairs in their absence only seemed to worry Molotov when he had other reasons to raise objections, as in the previous case of China and the Four-Power Declaration. However Molotov graciously withdrew his objection, on being pressed, and suggested a small sub-committee on the matter. This was duly constituted, with two representatives of each delegation, including some of the diplomats who had served or were serving in Iran. The subcommittee met for the first time on 26 October, when the proposed British declarations were tabled together with agreed American amendments, and further British proposals for the harmonization of Allied policies in Iran were made. In the absence of Russian translations of the proposals, however, the Soviet delegation had no difficulty in preventing any further progress that day. Subsequent meetings of the subcommittee, it may be said, brought little further agreement. [23]

After this brief interlude on the Middle East, the conference proper had returned to Eastern Europe, inaugurating another difficult phase

in the discussions for Eden. Item 12 on the agenda, dealing with possible confederations in the Danubian and Balkan areas, had been
merged with Item 17, Eden's proposed declaration on 'joint rather
than separate spheres of responsibility in Europe'. The remainder of
Eden's Eastern European policy was now to be debated. It was a
policy which had three aspects: on the one hand it asked the Three
Powers—and in this case more importantly the USSR—to renounce
unilateral action (such as the Soviet-Czech treaty) in any part of
Europe. In a different guise therefore it revived the spirit of the 'self-
denying ordinance'—though it is fair to say explicitly for Western as
well as Eastern Europe. On the other hand it invited the Three Powers
to give positive encouragement to the merger of the smaller States of
Europe in larger, federal units. Although this too could have implications for Western Europe—for example the Low Countries—it had
particular implications for Eastern Europe. At the same time, Eden's
declaration envisaged a positive commitment to respect the
independence and rights of self-determination of the smaller nations
of Europe. On this at least he might expect some support from the
United States. Soviet intentions, however, he already suspected
would run counter to these proposals. It seemed that the USSR was
much more set on a policy of 'divide and rule' in Eastern Europe—a
policy which was hardly likely to be favourable to the independence of
these States, let alone the creation of larger and stronger units.

The policy of encouraging federations in Eastern Europe had been
sponsored by Britain for some time previously. It represented an
attempt to undo some of the political and economic damage to Eastern
Europe which it was now realized had been wrought by the break-up
of the great empires of Austro-Hungary, Tsarist Russia, and
Ottoman Turkey after the First World War. The Foreign Office had
taken advantage of the presence in London of several exiled governments from Eastern Europe to encourage negotiations on these lines
among them, particularly between Poland and Czechoslovakia.
Yugoslavia and Greece were other possible candidates, and Churchill,
as we have seen, had added a further possible grouping. If as seemed
quite likely the Allies decided to break up Germany, part of south
Germany might then be encouraged to federate with Austria and
Hungary—Austro-Hungary in fact recreated without the turbulent
Slavs. Obviously the USSR might well have doubts about a powerful
and largely Germanic State of this kind, and therefore might well
resist the latter proposal. But on the other proposed federations the
Soviet attitude had earlier been surprisingly forthcoming. Eden well
knew that, apart from the Soviet attitude, the internecine feuds

between the various races of Eastern Europe would make these object-tives hard to attain. But in the early stages progress was being made and a post-war Polish/Czech federation was certainly on the cards. Then, however, circumstances changed. The Soviet government had begun to suspect a sinister motive—the creation of a belt of States hostile to the USSR. It had happened before. These doubts were fed by some unwise remarks by some of the exiled Polish and Yugoslav leaders. In 1943 the USSR, as Eden put it, had begun to 'pour cold water' on the Polish–Czech negotiations. There followed the open breach between the London Poles and the USSR over the 'Katyn murders'. Seeing this, the Czech leader Benes had decided to seek the best bargain he could with the Soviets and had negotiated the Soviet-Czech treaty. Thus, by the time the conference met, Eden's policy had already encountered heavy weather, and the United States' attitude, when sounded, had proved to be negative and discouraging. The US had no objection to federations *per se*, Hull had intimated, but all this should come later when the basic foundations of tripartite post-war co-operation had been laid. Eden therefore approached his task at the conference table with very little optimism about the result. Perhaps, however, if the USSR was not too obstructive and Hull not too nega-tive, something might be salvaged from the wreck. The brief dis-cussion which followed, however, and even more that which followed two days later, justified his worst fears. Hull made it clear that he had not really considered Eden's proposals very carefully. (The US minutes tactfully omit Eden's slightly acid remark that the Secretary had had the documents for three weeks.) Molotov merely proposed that in that case they should take up the matter again later, but Eden already had a pretty good idea what the Soviet reaction was likely to be. Without positive US support he was again unlikely to make much progress. Hull then indicated what was most in his thoughts by asking if the Drafting Committee was ready to report on the Four-Power Declaration or at least some of its articles; and it was agreed that the conference should take this first thing next day, followed by the ques-tion of Germany.[24]

Thus ended a day which was considerably more satisfactory to Molotov and Hull than to Eden. The Soviets had got their way over the Soviet-Czech treaty and, encouraged by Hull's lack of interest, could clearly see their way to spiking Eden's guns on the other 'dangerous' aspects of his East-European policy. Hull for his part had avoided being drawn into the unwelcome toils of East-European commitments. The Soviet attitude continued to be friendly towards him and the Drafting Committee was making good progress with the

Four-Power Declaration. He was further encouraged in his hopes when the Soviet representative on the Drafting Committee, Vyshinsky, took the opportunity to say to some members of the US and British delegations that evening at the ballet that the USSR saw 'no real obstacle' to the closest kind of co-operation.[25]

25 October. Germany: dismemberment: Austria: 'peace-feelers': post-war co-operation

As it turned out the Drafting Committee had not quite finished with the Four-Power Declaration though it was evident, when Vyshinsky reported, that agreement was very near. The conference therefore proceeded on the next day directly to the question of Germany. Molotov had already intimated to Hull the previous day that the Russians welcomed the US proposals on this subject. These it will be remembered called for unconditional surrender, the total disarmament of Germany, tripartite occupation under an Allied Control Commission, a Three-Power Commission for reparations, total control of German economic and political life, and the institution of democratic government. It recommended also that the German State should be 'decentralized'. It did not, however, commit the Allies to the dismemberment of Germany, and made no specific recommendations on frontiers. This document had been exhaustively discussed between London and Washington and there were no substantial Anglo-American differences—at least between Eden and Hull. (Roosevelt had, as has been noted, a harsher view on such questions as dismemberment.) Eden opened the discussion by saying cautiously that while the British government was attracted by the idea of dividing Germany into separate States, it was uncertain whether such a separation could be imposed and maintained by force. The discussion proceeded amicably, but it soon became apparent that the Soviets regarded the proposals as not too bad so far as they went, but not going far enough. Molotov emphasized that Germany must be totally stripped of war materials and rendered quite harmless for the future. He made it clear that the USSR would probably press for the dismemberment of Germany. In what may or may not have been a slightly malicious attempt to open up cracks in the apparent Anglo-American agreement on the matter, he twitted Eden, who had expressed himself non-committally on dismemberment, as being perhaps 'less resolute' towards Germany than the US. (In this Molotov was perhaps misled by a knowledge of Roosevelt's views.) Hull hastened to correct the impression: if anything, he said, the US was now slightly less in favour of dismemberment than it had been. The Soviet Minister was clearly nettled by this rebuff and remarked that the Anglo-Americans were obviously ahead of the USSR in their study of this subject, but that was due to Soviet 'preoccupation with the conduct of the war'. Recovering himself, he added that Soviet opinion certainly tended to favour the dismemberment of Germany, and he did not wish to rule out 'forcible' dismemberment: and certainly Germany should not keep any of her conquests. On this point Eden and Hull expressed full agreement. Germany must at least revert to its 1937 frontiers. This led naturally to the British proposal that Austrian independence should be restored. There was no disagreement here and it was agreed without demur that the Austrian question should be referred directly to the Drafting Committee. On Eden's suggestion it was also agreed that the proposals for Germany should be referred to the new London Commission.[26]

There was time to consider one more item, namely the question of peace-feelers from enemy countries (Item 13), on which there was a British resolution committing the Three Powers to report any approaches they received and to consult together on their replies. This proposal was also referred to the Drafting Committee, from which it emerged virtually unchanged, thanks perhaps partly to the conciliatory attitude Eden now adopted over approaches which had already been received from the Eastern European Axis countries. Molotov had evidently not fully recovered from his annoyance, and commented on the approaches from various groups in Hungary and Romania in his most glacial manner. The USSR, he said, was only interested in unconditional surrender as far as these countries were concerned, and had no interest in negotiating with them on any other basis. The same applied to Finland. He implied that he doubted if any of the various groups which had made overtures would 'work their passage' by encouraging positive action against the German war effort, such as sabotage. Molotov's attitude was prompted by the fact that there had been various approaches by the leaders of such groups to the British and United States governments, sometimes in association with governments which were still collaborating with the Axis. Most of these groups were of the centre or right, and the Soviet government viewed them without enthusiasm. These people had done little to oppose Germany when the latter's star was in the ascendant, and now were clearly seeking to enlist the sympathy and support of the Western Allies to save them and their countries from the consequences of their actions. Although Britain and the United States had acted quite properly, informing the USSR of these approaches, and giving their interlocutors scant encouragement, Russia viewed the whole business with deep suspicion; suspicion which had been increased by allied policy in Italy, where the West was consorting with Fascists and clearly set on allowing the Italians an easy way out of the difficulties into which their Axis alliance had led them. The Soviet government was not prepared to let that sort of thing happen in any country within its sphere of operations.

These suspicions may have have been excessive; but in all the circumstances they were not entirely unnatural. In his reply Eden was at his most conciliatory, and set himself to dissipate Soviet doubts. The West recognized that these were matters primarily for the Soviet government, he said. Eden was intimating to the Russians that while the Western Allies reserved to themselves the primary say in Italian policy during the actual course of military operations, they were prepared to concede the same degree of primacy to the Soviet Union in areas where its armed forces would soon be operating. As usual when Eastern European matters were under discussion, Hull played no part, and Eden now proposed that these questions, together with the problems of the Yugoslav resistance (Item 16 on the agenda), should be pursued in bilateral talks, outside the conference. It was a further indication that Eden felt the presence of the US Secretary on these occasions was if anything an embarrassment. He might get further with Molotov on his own. [27]

It is possible to see in Eden's attitude the germ of that judgement which led the British government during the following year to open up the possibility of a division of south-eastern Europe into *de facto* 'spheres of interest', at any rate while hostilities continued. If the US government was not prepared to use its influence in this area, then this might be the best strategy to explore. Was that what the Soviet government would really like? He would know more clearly where the Soviets stood perhaps after the following day's discussion on 'joint versus separate areas of responsibility' which was the next item on the agenda. In fact when the idea of the division of the Balkans into temporary spheres of interest was mooted by the British the following year, the US Secretary held up his hands in pious horror. Moral indignation is all very well, but it is difficult not to feel, when one reads in Hull's memoirs the flat statement that, with the entry of Soviet armies into Romania in April 1944, 'the relationship between the USSR and the Balkans came to the forefront of our diplomacy', that the Secretary might have allowed it to come to the forefront of his own preoccupations a little earlier. [28]

During this same day (25 October) Hull had had the opportunity to understand a little more clearly the nature at least of Soviet preoccupations. He had met Stalin for the first time in the afternoon, and had had a brief personal talk with Molotov in the customary interval for refreshments during the plenary session. Hull had used both opportunities to press his view that the conference should seize the opportunity to lay the foundations of post-war political and economic co-operation. In this connection he emphasized the political significance that would be given to a meeting of the heads of government as soon as possible. He had got little encouragement from Stalin on the latter—the place of the meeting was still a stumbling-block—but Molotov had spoken encouragingly of the good prospects for agreement on post-war co-operation and the German settlement, the main issues which the US had raised. Eastern Europe of course was not mentioned. Molotov had himself taken the opportunity to press the Secretary on Turkish participation in the war, making it clearer than he had before that what the Soviet government really objected to was the continued supply of arms to Turkey while the Turks still made no contribution to the war against Germany. The Soviet Foreign Minister got little satisfaction for his pains, however. Hull merely repeated that it was a military matter; he had referred it to his government; and they would have to wait for the US Chiefs of Staff's reaction.[29]

26 October. Eastern Europe: 'spheres of influence' and federations: the Four-Power Declaration

On 26 October the conference finally disposed of Eden's Eastern European policy—that is to say Molotov and Hull between them did so. Under Items 11 and 12 the three men returned to Eden's proposed declaration on 'spheres of influence' and federations. This declaration it will be remembered committed the signatories to three main principles: firstly the restoration of freedom and self-determination to the enslaved peoples of Europe: secondly the encouragement of larger associations and groupings of States provided they were not directed 'at other States': and thirdly the renunciation by the Three Powers of any intention to create 'separate areas of responsibility' (that is, spheres of influence) in Europe. It was a document which would have been approved by Woodrow Wilson at his most demanding, since it included two principles which figured most prominently in the Wilsonian canon of good international behaviour—respect for self-determination and opposition to 'spheres of influence'. It also recommended unions of States in the form of federations, a suggestion which should have been acceptable to the United States, which could be said to have invented the federal idea. It might have seemed logical therefore for the United States to welcome Eden's plan. But Hull was still the prisoner of his two major articles of faith, firstly that the broad principles of Three-Power co-operation should be agreed upon first, specific questions later; and secondly that the United States government should not become embroiled in any British schemes for Eastern Europe, especially if they seemed likely to antagonize the USSR. The Secretary dilated at some length on the first of these two propositions (it would have been maladroit to mention the second). He intimated he had little to add, and left the matter to the other two. Hull had given Molotov all the encouragement he needed to administer the *coup de grâce*, but the Soviet minister was in something of a dilemma. He would have been pleased from one point of view to see the offending document disposed of there and then, but in point of fact the Soviet government had something to say on the subject of confederations, was determined to say it, and wanted it put on the record. Did Hull mean, he asked, that they should not even discuss Eden's proposal? The Soviet government was willing to do so. Hull, feeling perhaps some qualms of conscience, added that the United States hoped that the conference would not declare itself 'in favour' of spheres of influence. This curiously negative way of putting it was satisfactory from Eden's point of view as far as it went, but was not too difficult for Molotov to deal with. Of course, he protested, the Soviet government had no intention of dividing Europe into separate zones: but Eden, he pointed out, had intimated that he regarded the declaration against spheres of interest and the commitment to respect self-determination as more important than any positive encouragement of federations. If these first two principles were of general application, argued Molotov, they might as well go into the Four-Power Declaration, thus giving them world-wide application. This was a reasonable point and Eden could not but agree, though a slightly awkward one for Britain and the United States, since such a procedure might raise the uncomfortable question of how such principles related to the Monroe Doctrine and the British Empire. It was adroit of Molotov to adopt this line, and he may have foreseen that Eden, faced with this dilemma, and not wishing to complicate or obstruct Hull's task in getting the Declaration through, might prefer to let the matter drop.

The Soviet Minister then turned to his main theme—the proposed federations in Eastern Europe. The Soviet government had grave doubts about the desirability or propriety of encouraging federations in Europe at this stage. Not unreasonably he argued that it was doubtful how far the present governments-in-exile—most of them non-elected and of a very provisional character—had the authority to pursue such schemes. Moreover, if Axis States, such as Hungary, Bulgaria or Romania, were included in some new grouping, the Allies might be tempted to treat them better than other ex-enemy States— which would be unfair. The real core of Molotov's objection, how- ever, was the suspicion that the object of this whole policy was to build up a bloc of States in Eastern Europe hostile to the USSR—a second 'cordon sanitaire' on the lines of the French-inspired alliances of the inter-war years, but more effective because made up of larger group- ings. Eden, recognizing a lost cause, admitted in his reply that Molotov's arguments 'had some force'. He intimated that Britain would not press the point about encouraging federations at this stage. So the policy of federation in Eastern Europe, which Britain had been encouraging and working on for the past two or three years, received its death-blow on 21 October 1943. Together with the other elements of Eden's policy—'joint rather than separate spheres of responsibility' and 'the self-denying ordinance'—it disappeared from view, and with it British attempts to limit or constrain a free hand for the USSR in Eastern Europe. Hull had pinned his hopes to the belief that the USSR was more likely to behave well, in Eastern Europe as else- where, if her confidence was first won and her assent secured to the principle of post-war co-operation. By his lack of support for Eden, he had ensured that his policy would prevail.[30]

It was to Hull's major proposal, the Four-Power Declaration, that the conference then turned its attention. After Vyshinsky and Hackworth had reported on some minor differences on the wording, which were settled without difficulty, the question of Chinese partici- pation was reopened. Molotov again rehearsed his doubts about the practicability of obtaining the Chinese government's authorization for the Ambassador's signature in time, and Hull repeated his re- assurances. It was evident that Molotov's queries were merely pro forma, and that the Soviet Union was prepared to concede this point. Hull for his part was intending to make full use of American diplo- matic channels to ensure the necessary authorization was achieved in time. It was again evident in the ensuing discussion that Molotov's main concern was with the possible effects of what was now Article 6, limiting the use of 'military forces within the territory of other States except for the purposes envisaged in the declaration'. The United States had already modified this article to make it refer only to the post-hostilities period, in the light of suggestions that otherwise it might be taken to limit the conduct of military operations. The US had also removed the requirement of general Allied 'agreement' to the use of forces by any one of them after the end of the war. 'Consultation' only was now required. These changes had already made the article more palatable to the Soviet government, but Molotov was anxious to make the point quite clear. Having fended off British attempts to limit Soviet freedom of action in Eastern Europe, he was not minded to commit the USSR to any American proposals that might have a similar effect, especially in regard to Soviet treaties with those States. Hull then made a strong appeal to the USSR to take the article in the general spirit of the declaration, which was directed basically to ensuring Three-Power co-operation in the surrender and disarmament of the enemy and subsequent maintenance of peace and security. Molotov, reflecting no doubt that the phrase in the article 'for the purposes envisaged in this declaration' could be widely interpreted, made no further demur on this point, but added a doubt about a further article in the declaration which was designed simply to make it clear that it did not affect relations between the Allies and countries with whom they were not at war. (In the case of the USSR, such countries included Bulgaria, Sweden, and of course Japan.) Molotov appears to have thought the article might limit Soviet actions in regard to some of these states. Hull thereupon agreed to remove this article altogether. On this, Molotov said they were now all agreed on the Declaration and suggested the creation of a tripartite commission under Article 4 to begin discussions on the setting-up of an international organization. Hull naturally welcomed this suggestion, as evidence of Soviet commitment and even enthusiasm in regard to the proposed organization, but added the proviso that such discussions should in the early stages be informal and confidential. On this note the eighth session concluded, and Hull immediately proceeded to seek, by cable, the necessary US and Chinese authorization to sign the Declaration.[31]

26 October was, in many respects, the decisive day of the Foreign Ministers' conference. It was a day of achievement for Hull and Molotov, and of total defeat for Eden. Molotov had, with Hull's co-operation, thwarted Eden's Eastern European policies and secured to a large extent a free hand for Russia in that region. He had also 'watered down' the Four-Power Declaration, wherever it might be interpreted as limiting Soviet freedom of action in Eastern Europe. Hull for his part had secured two of his main objects—Soviet/British participation in the US plan for post-war security, and the recognition of China as one of the 'Big Four'. He was a happy man. Eden had to take whatever comfort he could from the fact that his 'London Commission' might still come to fruition, albeit with more limited powers than he had originally hoped. He might perhaps have persisted

more strongly than he did on the Eastern European proposals, but the 'wider considerations' to which Cagodan had referred had prevailed. However, one can now see Eden's state of frustration and impatience at this stage of the conference in its full context. It is evident from his private secretary's diary references (at this stage Harvey was writing that 'the political side of the conference is going well') that Eden did not reveal his full dissatisfaction to his associates. Nor indeed did he reveal it fully in his reports to Churchill and the War Cabinet. But it was on this day, according to his own account, that he communicated his dissatisfaction to Hull during the adjournment for refreshments. Whether or not Eden exaggerates Hull's own dissatisfaction—and there is no reference to the conversation in Hull's own memoirs—it appears that the Secretary agreed that Eden should communicate his uneasiness on the progress of the conference to Stalin. On the same day Eden received Churchill's message on the unsatisfactory situation in Italy, and the latter's determination not to let the campaign 'go to ruin' for the sake of 'lawyer's arguments' on the date of the Cross-Channel operation. Stalin had better be informed that 'Overlord' might have to be postponed by a month or two. This added to Eden's worries, but at least it provided a reason for asking to see Stalin. He had also heard that the Soviet delegates had successfully stalled any progress on his proposed declarations on Iran in the sub-committee's meeting that day. He asked Molotov to arrange a meeting with Stalin as soon as possible, to which the Soviet Foreign Minister, apparently with some reluctance, assented.

27 October. Italian policy: Italian shipping: declaration on liberated territories: French civil administration: date of 'Overlord'

On the following day the conference was due to return to the question of military measures to hasten the winning of the war, under Item 1. Eden had asked for a day's further delay on this topic, in view of the fact that he had to see Stalin in connection with Churchill's intimation of the possible delay to 'Overlord'; the meeting had been arranged for that evening. Eden clearly thought it advisable to ascertain Stalin's reaction to this unwelcome news before tackling the subject again at the conference. The Foreign Ministers therefore reverted to the question of Italian policy and the proposed Soviet seven-point declaration on this subject under Item 4. Since the subject had been first discussed, at the fourth meeting on 22 October, Eden and Hull had communicated to Molotov Eisenhower's instructions on the principles to govern occupation in Italy, which they argued 'largely gave effect' to the principles advocated in the Soviet declaration—that is to say, the liquidation of the Fascist system and government, the restoration of democratic freedom, release of political prisoners, and the arrest of war criminals. At the same time, they pointed out, the pace of change, and the degree of freedom of speech, the press, etc. would necessarily have to be subject to the overriding dictates of military operations. This also applied to the transformation of the Badoglio government into a more broadly representative body through the introduction of more liberal and left-wing members. The Anglo-American memorandum went on to suggest that the Soviet proposals and their own memorandum should be referred to the Drafting Committee, to see if an agreed resolution on Italy could be worked out. When the conference actually took the matter up, however, Hull was extremely cautious in his approach, although he had received Roosevelt's general approval of the Soviet principles. Roosevelt had concurred with the view that these principles were in general conformity with allied policy in Italy, but had agreed with the Secretary's caveat that military needs must govern their application and that the Allied C-in-C's decision must prevail on such matters. When Hull made a somewhat inconclusive opening statement, Molotov sensed the feeling that his proposed declaration might be seen as a reflection on allied policy up to that time. While clearly not agreeing that Anglo-American policy could be described as 'largely' in accord with the proposed declaration, he affirmed diplomatically, though perhaps with a trace of sarcasm, that there was no intention of 'evaluating' existing policy. A simple resolution on the subject of agreed principles was all that was proposed. Eden and Hull then agreed that the documents should be sent to the Drafting Committee as their memorandum indeed had suggested. If an agreed resolution could be worked out, it was implied, it could then be published.

Molotov then turned to the Soviet government's request for a portion of the surrendered Italian fleet and merchant marine. Again Hull temporized. In this case there was some excuse. He had received a cable from Roosevelt indicating a rather non-committal attitude, and Hull was probably not too sure what the President's ultimate view was going to be. Personally he, like Eden, was sympathetic to the Soviet government's request. Indeed Eden that same day cabled the War Cabinet asking for some sympathetic gesture on this matter, which would be helpful to him in his negotiations with the USSR. When the British reply came, it was not in fact particularly helpful. There was opposition in the War Cabinet, mainly from ministers who wished to keep as much as possible of the Italian shipping at the service of the Western Allies—who admittedly badly needed it—and

Churchill was asked to send a temporizing reply, suggesting the matter should be discussed by the heads of government. For the moment Eden, like Hull, felt obliged to say that he had as yet no firm instructions. Molotov may have felt at this point that the Western Foreign Ministers were very ready to press for progress on their own proposals, but less forthcoming in dealing with Soviet suggestions. Indeed his disappointment at the negative response to this request so far was to become apparent at a later stage. However he passed on without comment to the question of Balkan resistance to the Axis, which also came under Item 4, and distributed a document containing such information as the USSR had—or thought it politic to divulge— about the situation in Bulgaria. The general tone of this document was to the effect that, while the Bulgarians clearly wished to get out of the war (in their case not against Russia but only the Western Allies) the existing political groups were not prepared to take any risks to do so. The Soviet view, it was clear, was that, as in Romania and Hungary, the Allies could not look to Conservative or the so-called 'moderate' or 'parliamentary' opposition for any useful action. They would continue to collaborate tamely with the Germans, as in the past, while attempting to take out reinsurance policies by assuring the Allies that this collaboration was forced upon them, and their hearts were not in it. There was an implied reflection here on allied policy in Italy. How much real practical help had the Badoglios and the like been able to induce the Italian people to give to the Allies, for example in the landings in Italy? Not a great deal, it was implied, and with some justice.

However, there was no discussion of this document, and the ministers proceeded immediately to consider Item 14, which was Eden's proposed declaration on allied policy in the liberated territories. This was a further attempt by Eden to pin the Soviet government down to the acceptance of some principles to govern policy in the areas occupied by Soviet armies—though naturally it did not spell out that implication in precise terms. But it was obvious enough. The conference already had before it a document specifically committing the Allies to the restoration of democracy and self-determination in France, the most important State in Western Europe to be liberated; and the Allies were undertaking to pursue similar principles in the major Axis States (Germany and Italy). It was fairly clear therefore that the thrust of this particular proposal applied to the smaller countries in both Western and Eastern Europe. A declaration of this kind had already, it will be remembered, been agreed by the US and British governments, only to be withdrawn in the face of Soviet opposition. Eden's proposal asked the Three Powers to accept that they should in general restore 'allied governments': but where no such government existed (or perhaps, by implication, there was no allied agreement on an 'acceptable' government), at least there should be a general commitment to hold 'free elections' as soon as possible, as a basis for such a government. Eden tactfully referred to the governments of the smaller Western countries, Norway, Holland, and Belgium, but he clearly had in mind the potentially difficult cases of Poland, Yugoslavia, and perhaps Czechoslovakia. However, knowing that he would get little support from Hull, Eden now recognized that there was little chance of an agreed declaration issuing from the conference, and proposed merely that, after an exchange of views, the British proposal should be referred to the European Advisory Commission. Hull's subsequent observations indeed could hardly have been less helpful to Eden's case. The Secretary cast as much doubt as even Molotov could have wished on the credentials of some of the allied governments and dragged in his *bête noire* the French Committee, which was due to be discussed under another item on the agenda. However he accepted Eden's suggestion that the whole matter should be turned over to the EAC. The conference, Hull argued, had not 'had time to work this out', implying that it had more important things on its mind. Eden again could not resist commenting that the British proposal had been in since 15 September, underlining the fact that the Secretary had had plenty of time to 'work it out' if he had wished to do so. However there was clearly no profit in pursuing the subject, and Eden accepted Molotov's formal proposal that the question be referred to the EAC. It was a further defeat, if only a partial one, and a further breach in the Anglo-American alliance.[33]

During the intermission Hull and Molotov chatted amicably together. The Secretary recorded that Molotov was 'even more friendly' than before, as indeed he had every reason to be. It was during this conversation that Hull intimated to the Soviet Minister that he would probably have to leave in about four days' time, a remark which may have been prompted by his conversation with Eden the previous day. It was agreed that a small drafting sub-committee, consisting of Hackworth, Vyshinsky, and Strang, should be constituted to hurry things along.

In the final session that day, the conference took up again briefly the position of the French Committee of National Liberation, and the agreed Anglo-American document on civil administration in Liberated France. Eden, recognizing the Americans had made considerable concessions on the issue of the committee's projected part in French administration, was notably conciliatory and diplomatic in his remarks. He stressed that the French Committee was not 'a recognized French government' and that the document committed the Allies ultimately to a 'democratically constituted authority' elected by 'the free choice of the French people'. Hull said virtually nothing, but simply signified his agreement. However, Molotov, perhaps unintentionally, probed the wound by asking a number of pertinent questions, which made it clear that French civil administration would largely consist of nominees of the Free French, admittedly under the authority of the Allied C-in-C. Naturally Molotov approved the Allies' expressed determination to have nothing to do with the Vichy regime other than to liquidate it, but exactly what, he asked, would be the proposed 'balance' which the Allied C-in-C was directed to maintain between all pro-Allied political groups? This, of course, put the finger on an anomaly in the document, which represented an attempt to save Hull's face. Eden diplomatically replied that it would be the 'best balance they could get' and the subject was allowed to drop. It was agreed that the European Advisory body would be the appropriate body to negotiate the details with the FNCL and the matter was referred to it. Perhaps naturally, the US minutes condense and gloss over this part of the discussion as though drawing a veil over an unfortunate episode. This was probably the best moment of the day's proceedings for Eden. It represented the successful culmination of years of patient work on de Gaulle's behalf in the face of persistent American opposition. One could wish that it had been more appreciated by its beneficiary.[34]

Eden's work for the day was not yet over. In the evening he set forth with Ismay for his second meeting with Stalin, which both expected to be as difficult as the first. It turned out surprisingly well. Stalin was patient and even amiable as the two men explained the difficulties the Allies had run into in Italy, and the possible consequences for 'Overlord'. He remarked reasonably enough that the Western Allies had to choose between 'Overlord' and an all-out attempt to break through in Italy and make the main assault on Germany from that quarter: but that would bring them up against the Alps, which hardly seemed the best route. It would make more sense to pursue limited objectives in Italy, then go on the defensive and concentrate on 'Overlord'. But he conceded again that the Italian campaign was valuable in locking up about forty German divisions in Italy and the Balkans. Eden hastened to say that a limited objective was precisely the Allies' strategy—their objective was the Pisa–Rimini line, north of Rome but well short of the Po valley. As to the delay to 'Overlord' it was impossible to be precise as to one month or two (in fact it turned out to be one month). But

Eden assured Stalin it would be as short a delay as they could possibly make it. The subject was concluded amicably. Eden then turned to the heads-of-government meeting, and another inconclusive discussion of possible meeting-places followed, which was notable only for Stalin's suggestion that Molotov go in his place, in terms that suggested that he regarded the latter as his deputy and *alter ego*. This agrees with the judgement of the US Embassy in Moscow a little earlier that the burden of supervising large-scale military operations had compelled Stalin to delegate much of his work as Prime Minister to Molotov.

At the end of their meeting the two men touched on the progress of the conference, and Eden expressed his view that things had rather bogged down and that he would like to see some decisions on subjects they 'had been discussing for a week'. Stalin received this request courteously enough and promised to discuss it with Molotov. On this note the two men parted, though in fact there was little sign of a difference in the pace of the proceedings for the next day or two.

Eden's sense of relief at the lack of acrimony, and perhaps too his satisfaction with the probable outcome of events in relation to the French Committee and the European Advisory Commission, is reflected in his report to Churchill the following day. Evidently basing himself on Eden's reports, Churchill records that the Russians had seemed to want a 'permanent friendship' with the West, and 'had met us on a number of points' (presumably including the Italian Advisory Council and its limited powers, the European Advisory Commission, and the understanding attitude on the 'Overlord' problem). It was in view of the harmonious atmosphere which had been created that Eden had suggested that he would like to make a gesture on the Soviet requests for Italian ships, and particularly requested authority at least to say that Britain agreed 'in principle' even if the details would have to be worked out later. As has been noted, he got little satisfaction on this. It is typical of one side of Eden's character that in spite of the setbacks he had sustained, he should have reported in this relatively satisfied and confident tone to London.[35]

28 October. The military questions again: 'Overlord', Turkey and Sweden

The following day—the tenth day of the conference—the ministers returned at last to the military questions raised under Item 1. In view of Edens *démarche* the previous evening the Russians were concerned to establish again that the Quebec decision on 'Overlord' still stood and that the limiting conditions as to the number of German divisions would not be too rigidly observed. Reassured on both of these points,

Molotov obviously felt there was little more to be said, but asked that the statements of the Western military representatives be included in the protocol of the conference together with 'stated decisions'. Eden said he was sure they could agree on a statement of the decisions for the record, and the ministers then passed on to the other Soviet proposals for 'shortening the war'. It is evident the discussions left the Soviet delegation still unsatisfied.

In the light of Eden's and perhaps Hull's impatience with the slow progress on matters with which they were most concerned, it is perhaps pertinent to note that the Russians had had to wait a full week for the Anglo-American reply to their suggestion that Turkey should be coerced into the war. When it came, it was disappointing. The US reply was the most negative. As always the US Chiefs of Staff would not countenance any further diversion from 'Overlord', and they feared that this, and the Swedish proposal also, might lead to such diversions. Eden's reply, reflecting Churchill's encouraging messages, was more sympathetic and constructive. He listed the advantages that might follow from Turkish entry—the opening of the Dardanelles to allied shipping, the additional diversion of German forces to the Turkish frontier, and the usefulness of Turkish bases to Aegean operations. But he felt bound to say that the Turks would probably demand immediately more in the way of additional weapons than the Allies felt able to give. However perhaps they could be induced to move through a gradual phase of 'non-belligerency', which would permit the use of Turkish airbases, towards full participation in the war at a later stage. This might gain some of the advantages of the Soviet proposal without leading to the kind of diversion of resources which the Americans feared. Hull concurred with this and suggested that the Turks could be asked at once to provide air-bases, while remaining technically neutral: in other words Turkey should take on a similar status in the war to that of Egypt, which had been highly advantageous to the Allies. Later on, when it became 'militarily possible', Turkey might be induced to enter the war.

Molotov was obviously put out by this reply to his proposal, particularly as Eden's response on the suggested request to Sweden for air-bases was as negative as that of the US. These bases, the Foreign Secretary argued, would not add much of value to the Allied air-effort. Hull reported Roosevelt's and the US Chiefs' equally negative reaction. Molotov remarked that in the Soviet view Turkey could be coerced into the war by joint pressure from the Three Powers, and this would be in the interests of the Allies *and* of Turkey: but clearly the British and Americans did not agree, either on this matter or on the

Swedish proposal. At any rate, he said, the Turks should be sent no more arms. Against whom would they be used, since evidently they were not going to be used against Germany? This was an awkward question, which Eden evaded by saying the West was in fact well behindhand with existing promises of supplies for Turkey. Molotov then asked if the British and Americans had any other proposals for shortening the war, since the Soviet proposals did not appeal to them. Hull replied by reiterating the US proposals for improved co-operation in military matters, with reference to such topics as shuttle-bombing and the exchange of meteorological information, improved communication, etc. Closer co-operation between the general staffs and the Allied governments could certainly shorten the war. Molotov remarked rather ungraciously that this was all very well, but not really the point at issue. Obviously concluding that the discussion had become unprofitable he then suggested they let the matter drop and adjourn until the next day.

It may be remarked that even if Molotov himself did not appreciate the fact, the US Chiefs of Staff were really aiding rather than thwarting Soviet objectives by their opposition to Turkish entry into the war. It was in the Soviet interest, both from the political and the military point of view, that the Western Allies should concentrate their efforts on 'Overlord' and Italy. This was of far more use to the USSR than venting their spite on Turkey. On reflection Stalin and Molotov may have realized this. At all events, the Soviet delegation turned out in force for the dinner at the British Embassy that evening and a reception at the US Embassy the following evening. The British occasion was notable mainly for an outburst by Litvinov to some of his British and American colleagues, which revealed the depths of Soviet animosity towards the London Poles and indeed the Polish people generally. The Poles, he said, were antagonistic to the USSR and cherished the delusion that Poland was a great power. Litvinov implied that there would have to be a change of heart on both those points before the USSR would alter its attitude to them.[36]

29 October. Terms of reference and membership of EAC and IAC: postwar economic co-operation and Reconstruction: reparations: dependent territories: Poland: the Four-Power Declaration: Italian shipping

Litvinov's tirade was hardly a promising prologue to the discussion of Soviet–Polish relations which was due to take place the following day, having been postponed from its original place on the agenda. Before coming to that difficult question, however, the Ministers took up first on the 29th the reports from the Drafting Committee on the differences which had emerged over the composition of the two proposed 'political and military' commissions and the terms of reference of the London body. On these issues Eden once again found himself playing a lone hand against the combined Soviet and American view. Part of the difficulty over the membership of the IAC arose, he suggested, from a confusion over the originally suggested 'political/military commission' and the body now proposed. Eden himself of course was largely responsible for this confusion through his successive proposals on the subject. Roosevelt's last-minute objections to full French membership of the commission, he suggested, should really be taken to apply to the London body. As for the Greeks and Yugoslavs, their suffering at the hands of the Italians and their contribution to the war against Italy entitled them to a place on the Italian commission. Hull could not but agree that Roosevelt's messages on the subject had referred to the single body originally planned, but added, unhelpfully to Eden's case, that the US Chiefs of Staff had since made it clear that the objection applied equally to the membership of the Italian Advisory Council. To this Eden retorted that the Allied C-in-C General Eisenhower (who was of course closer to the issues involved than the US Chiefs) had agreed to French, Greek, and Yugoslav membership. Molotov, who had no enthusiasm for the participation of the right-wing Greek and Yugoslav governments, was quite content to let the US Secretary argue the case and merely suggested that the question would have to go back to the Drafting Committee.

On the London commission's membership, which was next discussed, the Soviet and British positions were reversed. The British position, agreeing in this case with the United States' view, was that the London body should for the moment be tripartite only. Otherwise every government-in-exile would want to be on it. This contrasted with Eden's support for French, Greek, and Yugoslav membership of the Italian commission. Molotov did not fail to point out that the British government's original proposal for a United Nations Commission for Europe (of 1 July) had not excluded the smaller allies. Turning to the terms of reference for the London body and reverting to his earlier objection which had clearly been reiterated by Vyshinsky on the Drafting Committee, he argued that these should not be so broad as to make its scope boundless. Here Eden was on stronger ground, and made the effective point that the conference itself had already referred such questions as policy towards the liberated territories, the administration of France, and policy for Germany to the

Commission. These questions went beyond 'the ending of hostilities and the armistice terms' to which the USSR wished to limit the London commission's terms. Moreover the British proposal required the assent of all three governments before any matter other than the surrender terms and the enforcement of them could be referred to it: the USSR therefore could prevent its scope from being unnecessarily widened. However he indicated that he was prepared to accept some formula which focussed the commission's work more specifically on 'questions connected with the ending of the war'. (This, Molotov had pointed out, had been the original British proposal of 1 July.) Accepting the spirit of Eden's concession, Molotov then proposed that these questions should be referred back to the Drafting Committee, obviously with a view to some compromise being worked out. (At this point it may be said that such a compromise was arrived at: the British representatives accepted that other Allied governments might be invited to discussions of the London commission on matters that particularly concerned them. The Soviet members for their part agreed that while the first order of business for the commission should be the enemy surrender terms, its scope might be widened to consider other matters.)

During the interval for refreshments which on this occasion was probably welcome, Eden could reflect that his head was in Henley's words 'bloody but unbowed'. He had been hard pressed, but had for the most part maintained his position. There was still a chance that his views on the composition and terms of reference of both bodies would in general prevail. He had demonstrated the quality which one of his War Cabinet colleagues was to describe later as 'the ability to fight his corner'. Hull and Molotov for their part probably reflected with some satisfaction, though perhaps for different reasons, that on this, as on some other points, Soviet and American views coincided to a considerable degree, leaving the British as 'odd man out'. [37]

After the interval the conference turned to Item 15 which covered all the questions related to post-war economic co-operation and reconstruction raised by both the American and British governments. Hull outlined the various US suggestions in this field afresh—economic assistance for reconstruction, financial and commercial collaboration, the proposals for reparations—and urged his two colleagues to commit their governments to action. It was a cause dear to the Secretary's heart and on this as on other occasions he pointed to the failures of the past and their consequences, particularly after the First World War, as a warning against failure to tackle these problems in time. He emphasized that the United States was not making formal and specific proposals for the most part, but suggesting that serious discussion should begin, and indicating the general principles which might apply to any future action. The discussion which followed was amicable but not perhaps as fruitful as Hull would have wished. As was to be expected, Molotov was most forthcoming on the question of US assistance to the Soviet Union for reconstruction, and agreed that negotiations would eventually be desirable on the question of longer-term assistance to other countries. On the suggestion that some international Lending Agency might be established for this purpose, he was slightly less encouraging. The USSR was prepared to accept the 'general principles' indicated in this document, he said, and those which recommended the creation of other specialized organs of international co-operation, but did not favour immediate negotiations on them. Their governments would need to give those questions 'further study'. However he accepted Hull's suggestion that their governments might consider the holding of an international conference to develop these ideas. There is an interesting difference in the emphasis in the British and US accounts of this part of the discussion, the US record suggesting a slightly more encouraging response than does the British. In particular the US minutes omit Molotov's discouraging remark on the proposal for joint assistance to other countries, that 'the time for detailed negotiations was not yet'. There seems to have been some editing of the minutes here. However that may be, Hull had probably elicited as much as he expected. But the Soviet response on suggested principles for reparations foreshadowed rather more disagreement. One would have had to be very insensitive not to appreciate that a country which had suffered as much as the USSR at the hands of the Germans was likely to take a harsher view on the question of what the Germans should pay than those whose countries had not been invaded and ravaged. Nor was it surprising that the USSR should find it more difficult to look at the problem in the objective way recommended by the Americans, whose memorandum stressed that reparations should not be allowed to impede European recovery or permanently lower the German standard of living. The USSR could not agree that any commissions should be set up, as the American proposal recommended, until the Three Powers had agreed on the general principles. The subject was allowed to drop. Again the US records, wittingly or unwittingly, condense this part of the discussion in a way which minimizes the extent of the Soviet disagreement, referring simply to 'certain Soviet objections'. The British account indicates that Molotov specifically indicated that the living standards and general interests of Germany's victims should be regarded as equally important to those of the Germans, and, with Italy in mind, no doubt, as well as the East-European Axis countries, that German allies should also be made to pay. Hull assured him that the US had accepted the general importance of both of these considerations and with that the conference passed on to other business.[38]

At this point Hull disturbed the harmony of the proceedings somewhat by referring to something which was not on the agenda—an American memorandum on the principles which should govern the administration of 'dependent' (that is, colonial) territories. This document called for an Allied declaration that it was the duty of the administering authorities of such territories to prepare them for self-government, to fix the dates for their independence 'at the earliest practicable moment', and to pursue commercial policies in these territories which were in the interests of their peoples and of the world as a whole. These were principles to which many British politicians of the left subscribed and with which Eden himself may up to a point have had some sympathy, but its introduction at this moment was tactless. When the memorandum had been communicated to Eden back in March he had indicated that it was 'unacceptable to the British government in its present form'. In spite of this Hull had communicated the memorandum to the Soviet government on 24 October, apparently without consulting Eden beforehand, whereupon the British Foreign Secretary had reminded him of their opposition to it. Yet Hull still insisted on dragging it in. Eden was understandably annoyed by this disregard of his views, and no doubt also by the 'finger-wagging' attitude of the memorandum, which was aimed at the European colonial powers and particularly at the British system of Imperial Preference. He replied shortly that he was not prepared to discuss the matter except to say that his government was not in agreement with the Secretary's paper. Eden felt obviously that Hull's remarks were out of order, since the subject was not on the agenda. Molotov cautiously—and tactfully—remarked that the subject 'should receive further study' and passed on to the next item on the agenda. After all, Eden might suggest that the Letts, or the Estonians—or even the Tartars or Kazakhs—were as much 'dependent peoples' as the Indians or Nigerians. It was a subject on which neither man wished to dwell at that moment. Eden could already imagine the explosive cable which Churchill would dispatch to Washington if the subject were taken any further.

Unless Hull deliberately wished to snub and infuriate Eden, which seems unlikely, this was his most ham-handed action of the conference. The cause of anti-colonialism was an old and in many respects honourable one with American liberal internationalists, but to raise it in this way and at this time was tactless and could achieve no useful results. Moreover it weakened the force of Eden's position on Poland, the next item on the agenda (where Hull had promised qualified support), by pointing the finger at the British attitude to subject peoples. [39]

When this subject was taken up at last, under the item on the agenda which dealt with Soviet–Polish relations, Eden did his best, but probably without much hope of any result. He urged that the split between the USSR and the London Poles constituted for Britain an embarrassing breach in the Alliance. The British government was left uncertain how to treat the Polish government in London or what attitude to adopt to the Polish resistance, which largely looked to that government. Fortified by the previous exchange Molotov replied in his most negative vein. Poland was largely a Soviet concern; as for the Polish resistance, he did not favour helping 'unreliable elements'. Russia wanted an 'independent Poland', but under a government 'friendly to Russia'. This was perhaps the first time, but not the last, when this useful phrase was produced by one side or the other in the argument. Unfortunately it does not seem to have been fully realized by the Western leaders, though one suspects that it was by the Russians, that it was close to being a contradiction in terms. In view of the past history of Polish–Russian relations, it was unlikely that any genuinely independent Polish government would be particularly friendly to Russia. Hull intervened with some anodyne platitudes on the importance of restoring good-neighbourly relations, which must have struck both his listeners as inappropriate to the two States under discussion. Eden suggested that some members of the London government, notably Prime Minister Micolajczik and Foreign Minister Romer, were friendly to the Soviet Union: but elicited no response from Molotov, who clearly doubted their ability to prevail over the more right-wing members of that government. Eden obviously felt at this stage there was no point in pursuing the subject further and said dismissively that he had expressed his views and still hoped that relations would somehow be restored. His concession over the Soviet-Czech treaty had no effect in softening the Soviet stance. It was Eden's final defeat on Eastern Europe. [40]

The conference then returned briefly to the Four-Power Declaration, now agreed and ready for signature. Chinese authorization having been received, it was agreed the declaration should be signed the next day. All the phrases in Hull's original draft which might have

limited Soviet action in its own sphere to policies agreed with its allies
had now been removed. The Four Powers were not now committed to
'act together in all matters relating to the occupation of enemy territory and of territory of other States held by that enemy' as Hull's
original draft had proposed. Nor were they committed to 'act jointly'
for the maintenance of international peace and security, but only to
'consult with one another with a view to joint action'. Finally they
were required only to 'consult jointly' before employing their military
forces within the territory of other States, not to consult *and agree* on
such action. Whether Hull was fully aware of the significance of these
changes may be doubted. Probably he would have replied that it was
the spirit and not the letter of the Declaration which was important.
Molotov at least was quite satisfied. He now made a final enquiry
about the Soviet request for Italian warships, to which Roosevelt had
returned a rather non-committal though not completely negative
reply. This was naturally unsatisfactory to the USSR, which had had
to wait a week for an answer, and had now been told by the Americans
that the matter could be further discussed at the heads-of-government
meeting. Hull replied that he had no final decision as yet, but had
urged his government to give the request 'favourable consideration'.
Eden for his part had not yet received Churchill's cable of that date,
which was more positive than the initial US reaction, though it reflected the divisions within the War Cabinet on the use to which these
ships should be put. It listed certain technical difficulties in handing
over ships to Russia, and the probable claims of other Allies, and for
this reason suggested there would need to be further discussion on the
Soviet request, preferably at the heads-of-government meeting. However, Eden was told that he could, if the US agreed, inform the
Russians that their claim was accepted in principle and that the proportion asked was not unreasonable. Hull also said that he had urged
a speedy decision on the question on his government, and did in fact
cable Roosevelt the next day urging him to accept the Soviet request
in principle. This elicited a favourable response from Roosevelt
which, when conveyed to the Russians the following day, together
with Churchill's messsages, much improved the atmosphere. For the
moment, however, Molotov allowed his irritation to show and remarked that he could not understand the delay in deciding such a
simple question, or why it should be referred to heads of government
whose meeting had yet to be arranged. Eden and Hull, as has been
noted, were both conscious of the desirability of making some concession to the USSR on this point, but were handicapped by the lack

of positive response by their governments and could therefore give Molotov no satisfaction. The session thus ended on a rather inharmonious note.[41]

By this time the Ministers had been meeting for eleven successive days, and their patience was perhaps becoming a little frayed by the long hours of discussion. The interchanges between Hull and Eden on dependent territories no less than Molotov's remarks on Italian shipping illustrated the fact. On the previous day also, when Hull had once again invoked the heads-of-government meeting to decide the matter of Turkish entry into the war, Molotov had remarked abruptly that the heads of government had surely more important things to consider. It was perhaps a consciousness that tempers on all sides were getting a little short, and the knowledge of Eden's expressed impatience two days earlier, which led Molotov to seek out Hull that evening in his rooms, during a reception at the US Embassy. The Secretary had stipulated that he would not attend social functions in the evening, but he readily received the Soviet Minister. During their conversation Hull relieved any anxiety Molotov may have felt by praising the accomplishments of the conference under the latter's chairmanship. He urged Molotov not to allow unfriendly comment in the Soviet press, for example on the Cross-Channel operation, to mar the accomplishments of the conference. The Secretary suggested that if Stalin would publicly approve the work of the conference and at the same time indicate that he personally favoured a heads-of-government meeting as soon as military operations allowed, the effect would be very beneficial. Molotov agreed to convey this to Stalin, and clearly did so.[42]

30 October. The conference concludes

The following morning Eden called on the Secretary, and the two men agreed that some positive response to the Soviet request for Italian ships would help to sweeten the atmosphere. Eden communicated Churchill's favourable response which he had just received, and Hull promised that he would further urge a favourable response on Roosevelt. Before this meeting Hull had already dispatched his message to the President along these lines. Eden also suggested, rather surprisingly in view of Churchill's known opinion, that a Russian representative should be invited to the next Anglo-American military conference. Thus all three ministers were obviously conscious of the need to wind things up harmoniously at this stage.[43]

Molotov's intentions were shown at the plenary session, at which Eden recorded 'a complete change of atmosphere', due to Molotov's 'business-like approach', which resulted in the successful winding up of all their business at that session. Molotov opened by saying that they only now needed to finish with the Drafting Committee's work, implying that they had reached the stage where any remaining unsettled issues on the various documents and proposals were sufficiently few and minor to make this possible at that session. Apart from this there was the question of signing the Secret Protocol of the Conference, embodying all their various agreements and decisions; and the decision on which of these agreements and decisions should be made public in a press communiqué. There was also the matter of the report from the subcommittee on Iran. Before they came to the work of the Drafting Committee, however, Eden for the last time raised his proposal for a declaration of some kind in favour of democracy and independence in Europe and against 'spheres of influence'. Litvinov this time replied for the USSR but employed the adroit arguments already used by Molotov. The Allies, he reminded them, were already committed to democracy and independence by the Atlantic Charter and other documents. As to spheres of influence, none of them had any desire for such things. Eden's proposal therefore was surely superfluous. In any case, why should the principle only be confined to Europe? Defeated on points, Eden withdrew.[44]

Molotov's assurance that there was little left to argue about proved perfectly valid when the Ministers came to the final report of the Drafting Committee. There were in fact only three points of substance remaining. Eden pointed out that the declaration on policy towards Italy still referred to some Fascist institutions which had not been liquidated, and this might be held to reflect on Anglo-American policy up to this date—a point on which the British and Americans had always been sensitive. Molotov remarked, reasonably enough, that the reference only stated the facts, but in the spirit of give and take which now prevailed, agreed to withdraw the references.

The second point of difference concerned the resolution on peace-feelers, and the applicability of the principle of 'unconditional surrender' to all the enemy States, including the 'odd men out' who were not at war with all three of the Allies. These were Bulgaria, with whom the USSR was not at war; and Finland, with whom the US was not at war, and whom the Americans had always wished to spare the full rigours of defeat. Not unnaturally this was a less appealing proposition to the USSR, against whom the Finns had fought hard; the Soviet delegation indeed had made it obvious throughout the conference that they wished to make no exceptions in favour of any of the states of Eastern Europe. However Molotov merely observed moderately that the USSR took the phrase to mean simply that the three powers would give each other 'moral support' against all their enemies. In the same spirit of accommodation as before he suggested that if the Drafting Committee could not quickly find an agreed form of words (it was implied that same day, since Hull was due to leave on the morrow), the whole passage should be dropped, as in the upshot it was.

Finally there was a further brief discussion on the Soviet proposal to set up a Three-Power commission to discuss the creation of a new international organization. Hull had displayed some uneasiness the previous day about this proposal. His concern seems mainly to have been prompted by the use American isolationists might make of any public announcement along these lines, and also by a desire to prepare the ground thoroughly before formal machinery was created. Molotov again made a concession to the US point of view and it was agreed there should be further diplomatic exchanges on the matter before action was taken. The subcommittee on Iran then reported that there had been no agreement between them, and it was decided to refer the question for further diplomatic discussion.

On all other issues agreement was complete, though in some cases it amounted to agreement to differ, and/or to take no action. None the less, the agreed decisions and resolutions were impressive. They included the Four-Power Declaration, where Hull had preserved the main outlines of his proposal while accepting some 'watering-down' of those clauses which might have been held to limit Allied freedom of action in their own sphere of operations to agreed tripartite policies: the creation of the Italian Advisory Council, where the Americans had made concessions on the membership and the Soviets on the terms of reference: the European Advisory Commission (now officially so designated) where the British had compromised on the desire for very wide terms of reference and the American and Soviet delegates had gone a little way to meet them: the declarations on Italian policy and 'peace-feelers' where both sides had made concessions: the declarations on German atrocities and Austrian independence where there had been little difference of opinion: the memoranda on French policy which had been referred to the EAC for action, with no real difference of opinion, and on Germany, which had been similarly referred, with apparently a substantial measure of agreement: and the question of general policy towards the liberated areas, where the British proposal had also been referred to the EAC, though on the basis of little real agreement. On the military issues also there had been broad agreement on the overriding importance of the Cross-Channel Attack, though somewhat weakened by Churchill's reservations. Here, too, the USSR had as yet not got very far with its proposals for Turkey and Sweden. The 'gaping void' in all this harmony was, as Eden stresses in his memoirs, the lack of any agreed policy for Poland and the rest of Eastern Europe, at a time when the Soviet armies were rapidly advancing, and the Russian position therefore becoming steadily stronger. But this had come about fundamentally because neither the United States nor the USSR wished the issue to be tackled at the conference, and Eden therefore, in a minority of one, could not hope to prevail.[45]

However, at this moment, as the conference ended, all was sweetness and light. The delegates duly signed the Four-Power Declaration at a public ceremony, the Chinese Ambassador signing for his government. A press communiqué was then approved on the recommendation of the Drafting Committee. It had been agreed that the Four-Power Declaration, the creation of the Italian Advisory Council and the European Advisory Commission, the declaration of policy for Italy, the agreement on Austrian independence, and the declaratory warning on German atrocities should all be made public: a general reference was also made to the discussions of military operations, closer military co-operation, and the 'taking of decisions' in this field. The Drafting Committee had also agreed on the wording of the more detailed Protocol (see Appendix A) and Most Secret (Military) Protocol, incorporating the full results of the conference, the agreed decisions, the matters referred to the EAC, and the extent of agreement or disagreement on matters referred back to governments for further discussion. The three Foreign Ministers duly signed the documents and, after Molotov had thanked them for their co-operation, Eden and Hull complimented Molotov on his chairmanship. On this note, as the US minutes put it, 'the conference ended'.[46]

CHAPTER V

MOSCOW TO CAIRO—
AND CHIANG-KAI-SHEK

1. The Aftermath of Moscow

The Moscow conference ended in an atmosphere of euphoria and mutual esteem. At a farewell banquet on the evening of the 30th, attended by Molotov, Eden, and Hull, Stalin's presence signified his approval of the conference and its results. Hull was seated next to Stalin and had further cause for pleasure. Not only did the Soviet dictator congratulate him on 'a successful conference', but he further emphasized Soviet willingness to 'co-operate for peace' and to bring to an end Soviet isolationism. Stalin also reaffirmed Molotov's earlier assurance that Russia had no intention of signing a separate peace with Germany. The peace-feelers which Berlin had been putting out in Stockholm would be ignored. 'A separate peace', Stalin assured him, 'was impossible.' Even more important, because completely unexpected, Stalin gratuitously informed Hull that the USSR would enter the war against Japan once Germany was defeated. Molotov subsequently gave Eden a hint along these lines, but this was the first time an explicit assurance had been given of Soviet intentions. Knowing how much Roosevelt and General Marshall, the US Chief of Staff, had wished for this assurance, Hull was delighted. In reporting the news to Roosevelt, Hull stressed that the assurance had been unsolicited and that Stalin had stated no conditions or price for Soviet entry into the Far Eastern War. As was to be later apparent, there is a difference between assurances given in the unbuttoned atmosphere of a banquet, and hard bargaining round a conference table. Roosevelt clearly had anticipated this, and was not unduly perturbed to discover that there was a price to be paid. However that might be, Hull could reasonably feel that Stalin's promise had set the seal on his achievements in Moscow.[1]

As it happened, Hull was not able to depart as quickly from Moscow as he had wished. Bad flying conditions delayed his departure and Eden's until 3 November. This delay enabled Eden and Molotov to tie up some loose ends relating to Turkey. The negative American response to Soviet proposals, contrasted with Churchill's more enthusiastic reaction, had led to this matter being relegated to bilateral Anglo-Soviet talks. Eden had somehow to reconcile the Soviet wish for strong pressure to be exerted on Turkey with the American desire to avoid any allied commitments in that quarter and Churchill's enthusiasm for anything which promised further support for operations in the Eastern Mediterranean. It was the last of the many difficult briefs which Eden had been obliged to handle at the conference. Churchill's suggestion that the Turks should be asked in the first instance to permit allied use of their air-bases and to open the Dardanelles to allied shipping, as a step from 'neutrality' to 'non-belligerency', provided a possible compromise, if Russia and the United States could be persuaded to accept it.

When Eden discussed a possible approach to Molotov along these lines with Hull on the 31st, prior to a meeting with Molotov, the Secretary gave his cautious approval. Roosevelt's telegram of 26 October had stated that there were no resources to spare from 'Overlord' for Turkish, or for that matter Swedish, adventures. However, Hull agreed that it was desirable not to spoil the harmonious atmosphere created by the conference by seeming to be 'merely negative'—though it is difficult to see how Eden could represent the US attitude as anything else. Eden said that he would press the British proposals on Molotov, though he added that the Russians would probably regard this solution as 'too mild'.

The meeting with Molotov later that day proved, as Eden had anticipated, a difficult one. The Soviet Foreign Minister was surly. Britain and the United States, he complained, had turned down every Soviet proposal aimed at shortening the war, but had produced no proposals of their own. Eden may have reflected that it was not easy to do business with someone who could switch affability on and off like a table-lamp, but he persisted. Resisting the temptation to remind Molotov that the Western Allies had never intended the Moscow conference to be a military one, he suggested he should put the British proposal to the Turks. To this Molotov grudgingly agreed, subject to the proviso that Eden would also try to persuade the Turks to enter the war fully at an early date. He added ungraciously that he would leave the negotiations to Eden. The USSR did not wish to participate. But he agreed Eden should also try to get Hull to agree that it should be a Three-Power request to Turkey.

Returning to Hull the next day, Eden found his colleague no more forthcoming than before. Hull took the view that he had no authority to agree to a Three-Power approach. Eden was therefore obliged to sign a bilateral agreement with Molotov. However, the representations which Hull made to Washington during and after the conference on the desirability of not returning a completely negative attitude to Soviet suggestions did eventually bear fruit. On 4 November Roosevelt intimated that the approach to the Turks could be a Three-Power affair, but at the same time made it clear again that the United States would oppose any diversion of resources from 'Overlord' and Italy to operations further east. Thus Eden, who had left Moscow for Cairo on 3 November, had on the one hand a mandate to press the Turks to enter the war, and on the other a firm indication that he could offer them no inducements to do so. A meeting at Cairo with the Turkish Foreign Minister, Menemencoglu, had already been arranged. In view of the unpromising nature of his mission, Eden probably looked forward to it with no great enthusiasm. Indeed he had only agreed to it at a late stage in the conference.[2]

The tale of Eden's talks with the Turkish delegation can be briefly told. As he expected, the Turks turned a deaf ear to his blandishments. The provision of air-bases, they argued, would be a stepping-stone to full participation in the war. Eden could hardly challenge them on this point, since this was what was intended. Moreover, the Turks argued, Germany was in a position to react strongly and the Allies could promise little help. Indeed, the British had not been able to help their own garrisons on the Dodecanese. Menemencoglu would do no more than put the proposal to his government. It was what Eden had expected. He turned his attention to a discussion of the Greek situation with the Middle East service chiefs. The Communist-led ELAS forces were now openly flouting the authority of the Greek government-in-exile and the Commander-in-Chief, Middle East, General Wilson. It was agreed they ought to be disavowed and British aid concentrated on the non-Communist elements in the Greek resistance. In view of the fact that the Communists were making capital of the Greek king's unpopularity to widen their support, it was also agreed that it would be politic for George II to create a Regency at the moment of liberation, and not to enter Greece with the Allies. Later a plebiscite on the monarchy might be held. Satisfied at any rate with that part of his work, Eden left for home, determined to recommend these policies to the Cabinet.[3]

Eden reached London on 10 November. During his journey the preparations for a conference of heads of government had been substantially advanced. As will be seen, Churchill was on the point of setting off for the Middle East, and Eden was required to join him there in the last week of November. In the week or two that elapsed before that time, Eden, as he recounts, devoted himself largely to some of the issues left over from Moscow, one of which—Poland—would certainly come up again in any conference of the heads of governments. The London Poles had been intransigent before Moscow, refusing to contemplate any surrender of territory to Russia. Eden now found them alarmed by the harshness of the Soviet attitude in Moscow and the lack of American concern, and consequently in a more accommodating mood. They told Eden that they now hoped the heads of government *would* discuss Poland, and assured him that if Britain and the United States agreed on a plan which Poland must accept 'to safeguard its future', then the London government would agree, provided there was an Anglo-American guarantee of the settlement. Eden warned them that the Americans did not seem disposed to give a very high priority to the question, but asked the Foreign Office for the outline of a territorial settlement. In the light of the Soviet attitude, and the certainty that the Western Allies would have little power to influence the outcome, this followed predictable lines. Russia would insist on the Curzon Line, though she might be persuaded to make some concessions to Poland. Possibly the largely Polish city of Lwów might be left inside the Polish frontier. Anyway Poland should be amply compensated by an allocation of German territory, including East Prussia, Upper Silesia, and Danzig. In return for this complete acceptance of Soviet demands, the Foreign Office plan recommended that Russia should be asked to resume relations with the London government, allow that government to return to Poland in the wake of the Soviet armies, and undertake to hold free elections. None of these reciprocal concessions was in fact to materialize though some were promised. For the moment, however, Eden could at least feel that the London Poles had given him some cards to play in the next round of discussions with the Russians.[4]

In Washington Cordell Hull, whose leisurely journey by sea had brought him home on the same day as Eden, also took up, perhaps rather belatedly, the Polish problem. Concerned by the criticism of the failure to reach any agreement over Poland at Moscow which was appearing in the Polish press in America, Hull endeavoured to soothe away these fears in an interview with the London government's ambassador Ciechanowski, but without much success. Ciechanowski warned Hull that the London government and the Polish underground army might well make trouble for the Soviet armies unless a satisfactory settlement was reached. He asked that the London government's Prime Minister, Micolaijczyk, should meet Roosevelt and Churchill before any discussion took place with the Russians.

Hull transmitted these warnings to Roosevelt, who had already left to join Churchill in the Middle East: but the plight and the fears of the London Poles were not high on the President's agenda. Nor does it seem that this foretaste of many difficulties to come convinced Hull that he might have given more attention to the Polish problem in Moscow.[5]

Hull in fact was still preoccupied with plans for the post-war world and the reaction of the American people and Congress to them. He and Roosevelt found time, however, to begin circumventing Eden's wishes for the future role of the European Advisory Commission. He had already appointed Robert Murphy to the Italian Advisory Council. He now appointed the US Ambassador in Britain, John Winant, to the European body in London. These appointments demonstrated the American attitude to the two bodies, and effectively withdrew some of the support Hull had appeared to offer Eden in Moscow. Murphy was a senior State Department official who had the ear of the President and the President's Chief of Staff, Admiral Leahy. His was to be a full-time job. Winant, on the other hand, was not close to the President, and had the normal duties of an Ambassador to attend to. True his position had become more important as the result of the withdrawal from London of the President's special representative, Averell Harriman, but this also added to the other calls on Winant's time. Russia also appointed a high-ranking official, Vyshinsky, to the Italian body, while giving the London Commission job to its ambassador, Feodor Gusev. In effect Hull and Molotov were converting the London body to the 'meetings of a Foreign Minister with the Ambassadors of the other two governments' which both had advocated in Moscow instead of the highpowered tripartite body Eden had wished for. It was a demonstration on a small scale of the Soviet-American axis which was to dominate allied diplomacy during the next few months.[6]

Eden could do little about it. He was concerned at that moment with the problems of the Balkans and the obstreperous French. On Yugoslavia and Greece he had come to opposite and at first sight contradictory conclusions. In Yugoslavia he had decided that Tito, with twenty times as many men in the field against the Germans as Mihailovich and far more popular support, represented the future. This augured ill for the prospects of the Yugoslav government-in-exile and the exiled King Peter. But Eden had little of Churchill's romantic sentiment for Balkan royalties, though he was prepared to make an effort to bring about a *rapprochement* between the government and Tito. In Greece on the other hand it seemed that the Communist-led EAM were more concerned with preparing to seize power after a German withdrawal than actually fighting the Germans. Moreover it appeared that they did not have the same support as Tito. Furthermore Greece was more vital to Britain's future position in the Mediterranean than Yugoslavia. Therefore support for EAM should be withdrawn. Eden had some difficulty in getting these two opposed lines of policy through the War Cabinet, but eventually his wishes prevailed. [7]

Eden's other problem was with de Gaulle and the Free French. This came at a particularly inopportune moment, since Eden was still hoping to obtain allied recognition of the French Committee as a provisional government and also a Free French representative on the European Commission. De Gaulle, however, now proceeded characteristically to infuriate both Roosevelt and Churchill. In Algiers he ousted the American nominee General Giraud from the Committee, and in the Middle East his representative arrested the members of the Lebanese government, who had demanded immediate independence, and dissolved the newly elected Lebanese Parliament. Churchill fired off indignant cables to Roosevelt, threatening, not for the first time, to disavow de Gaulle. In London the War Cabinet authorized an ultimatum to the French over the Lebanon. Eden, Massigli, de Gaulle's Foreign Affairs Commissioner, and Harold Macmillan, the British ministerial representative in Algiers, worked manfully to damp down the crisis: but it was not until 23 November, the day Eden left for the Middle East, that the Lebanese ministers were reinstated and the crisis past. Eden must have reflected as he boarded his aircraft that a war is easier to conduct without allies. [8]

2. Reactions to the Moscow Conference

Reflecting the attitude of the administration, American reaction to the conference was enthusiastic. Hull personally was highly satisfied with his achievements. The main American objectives had been achieved. The USSR had undertaken to co-operate in a new world order and participate in an international peacekeeping organization. She had publicly committed herself through the signature of the Four-Power Declaration. China's status as one of the 'Big Four' had also been publicly acknowledged through her signature of the document. Moreover the apparent Soviet mood of friendship and warmth gave promise that the detailed European issues to which Eden attached so much importance would be solved in the spirit of friendly compromise. The welcome which the USSR had given to the American proposals for Germany, though tempered by demands for greater severity, was encouraging in this context, as were the Soviet proposals for Italy, with their emphasis on democracy. True, he had not been able to make much progress on future international economic co-operation, to which he attached much importance: but given the apparent Soviet willingness to embark on a new and more constructive path in the world, that must surely follow. In the negative sense, too, Hull could feel pretty satisfied with his work. He had avoided being drawn into premature commitments in Eastern Europe. He had felt obliged to concede the setting-up of the European Advisory Commission but felt sure that the USSR would join him in restricting this, in his view, superfluous body to a relatively limited role. He had conceded the substance of the Soviet request for more information on Italy, but staved off the awkward demand for active participation in Italian affairs. Eden had done the dirty work for him, and the Russians had shown surprisingly little resentment. On the military side he had had no difficulty in maintaining top priority for 'Overlord' and could feel fairly sure that the rigid restrictions imposed on Eden's mission to Turkey and the obvious caution of the Turkish government would ensure that that particular invitation would come to nothing. Moreover he had emerged from the conference with one totally unexpected gain—Stalin's personal assurance that the USSR would eventually enter the war against Japan. Hull probably really regretted only one aspect of the conference—that in relation to the Italian Commission and the scheme for the administration of France he had felt obliged to move closer to some recognition of de Gaulle and his detestable Committee. In the expressive American phrase he had been forced to 'eat crow'. But this was after all merely the continuation of the gradual change in United States policy towards France which had been taking place, albeit with the utmost reluctance, ever since the effective demise of the Vichy government at the end of 1942. As an experienced politican Hull no doubt reflected philosophically that in politics one could not hope to win them all.

These judgements were reflected in Hull's interviews with the Press and his speech when he was invited to address Congress—the first US Cabinet Minister to be so honoured. He painted a glowing picture of a new and happier chapter in world politics. The conference, he said, 'had launched a forward movement' and been characterized by 'an atmosphere of mutual understanding and confidence'. He emphasized that boundaries and territorial questions had in general been left to a post-war peace conference. There had been no secret territorial agreements and disgraceful bargains, such as had marred the end of the First World War. There had therefore been no detailed discussion of the smaller European countries; but democratic principles had been agreed with Britain and Russia for the government of Italy, and it could be taken that these would be generally applied. He sounded, however, a warning note on Eastern Europe, to the effect that 'there was no guarantee that the exiled governments would necessarily be restored'. This had general application, but clearly was intended particularly as a warning to the Polish government-in-exile. The Poles had shown a disposition to question the results of the conference and were being, as Hull (and for that matter Churchill) thought, unnecessarily intransigent on the matter of territorial 'adjustments' with the USSR.

Roosevelt shared Hull's satisfaction with the results of the conference. He had met Hull at the airport to mark his approval, and telegraphed warmly to Stalin on the 'excellent feeling' engendered by the conference. The greater part of American press comment followed his lead. The dean of Washington commentators, Walter Lippmann, judged the outcome 'constructive beyond his fairest hopes'. Only one or two commentators expressed reservations, pointing to the lack of Soviet reassurances on Poland, the Baltic States, and Eastern Europe generally. One left-wing commentator went so far as to say that the United States had 'underwritten' Soviet expansion in that area. But these were in the minority. A famous phrase of Hull's has been often quoted and is worth quoting again, for it exactly summarizes the general American mood, and at the same time encapsulates the American liberal's dislike of certain devices of the 'old diplomacy'. 'As the provisions of the Four Nation declaration are carried into effect', he declared to Congress, 'there will no longer be need for spheres of influence, for alliances, for balances of power, or any other of the special arrangements through which, in the unhappy past, nations strove to safeguard their security or to promote their interests'. Hull was to live long enough to see a Soviet sphere of influence in Eastern Europe become an accepted fact of international life; and also to see the United States put together a great multinational alliance in order to restore an effective balance of power in Europe. His words seem today like a commentary on the vanity of human wishes.[9]

One or two Americans who had participated in the conference were a little more cautious in their assessments. Harriman, now US Ambassador to Moscow, was particularly dubious about the generally euphoric attitude. The USSR, he felt, had been allowed to 'get away with it' on Poland and Eastern Europe. They had not been obliged to state their specific demands because Hull's silence and generally uninterested attitude had made it unnecessary. But the Soviet opposition to Eden's constructive suggestions on federation in Eastern Europe, taken together with their attitude on Eden's other proposals, Harriman subsequently stated, looked like the first trace of a design for 'Soviet hegemony'. He wondered if Stalin wanted 'a pulverized Europe' which he could more easily control. He regretted Hull's lack of support for Eden on these issues and on Poland. This assessment of Soviet intentions strikingly resembles the better-known Bohlen judgement on the results of the Teheran conference, where Roosevelt carried the logic of Hull's approach a stage further. Bohlen judged that the overall effect of the Teheran blueprint for Europe, if carried into effect, would ensure Soviet domination of the sub-continent. In his memoirs Bohlen cynically but perhaps realistically adds that the unexpected Soviet adhesion to the Four-Power Declaration and their willingness to join in the new international organization probably represented only a desire to be in on Anglo-American activities in this field so as to keep an eye on them and make sure they were not turned against the USSR.

There is little doubt that Harriman did feel some of the misgivings to which he alludes in his memoirs. It is perhaps unfortunate that he did not express them even more openly to Roosevelt in his post-conference report, where they are a little muted, and criticism of Hull is tactfully suppressed. On the other hand, Harriman's report does emphasize his belief that the Russians would stand firm on their territorial claims, would probably insist on the dismemberment of Germany, and would also insist on their right to act unilaterally in Eastern Europe; moreover the Soviet leaders detested the London Poles. His report also includes the significant remark that he 'took with some reservation' Soviet statements that they 'were willing to have a strong, independent Poland' and were not 'interested in the extension of the Soviet system'. Apart from that one sentence, however, Harriman seems to have relied too much on Roosevelt's ability to read between the lines and to draw the same conclusions as he himself had done.

It has been argued that, while Hull's (and Roosevelt's) hopes for future Soviet co-operation and an end to old-style diplomacy have proved to have been wildly optimistic, none the less Hull was right not to support Eden on Eastern Europe. The Soviet leaders were clearly unwilling to enter into agreements limiting their freedom of action; and therefore to insist on them might have wrecked the conference. It could of course be asked, since the results Hull achieved were to prove of such little permanent value, whether this would have been a great tragedy. But there was obviously more at stake than the Four-Power Declaration and the other agreements reached at the conference. The future of the wartime alliance, and therefore the future conduct of the war also depended to some extent on a successful outcome.

Nevertheless it is difficult not to feel that Hull might have fired a more obvious warning shot or two across Soviet bows on such points as 'spheres of influence', without any risk of wrecking the conference. His silence on these matters, as Harriman points out, was taken as consent to the Soviet plans for Eastern Europe.[10]

In Britain the public reactions were much the same, though the government in its official statements naturally made more of the creation of the two new commissions (Eden's particular achievement) than Hull had done. In their statements to Parliament Eden and his second in command at the Foreign Office, Cranborne, stressed the significance of the creation of these two bodies, which would enable the Three Powers to 'continue working together to concert their views on political problems arising from the war' and 'co-ordinate policy in Italy'. They also dutifully lauded the agreement on the Four-Power Declaration as 'a strong foundation for future world peace'. Not unnaturally Eden drew a veil over the less successful aspects of the conference from the British point of view. But some members of Parliament unkindly drew attention to the omissions, particularly the lack of reference to Poland, or to the recognition of the French National Committee as a provisional government. One left-wing member put his finger on Eden's anxieties when he pointed out that after the war Russia would be the greatest military power in Europe. A strong prosperous Germany and also a revived Austro-Hungary would be desirable. The same member also drew attention to British embarrassments over Greece, and suggested that a plebiscite on the monarchy would undoubtedly be necessary. This remark elicited from a Conservative member the acid observation that perhaps one should not stop at Greece. Why not plebiscites in the Baltic States and the Ukraine also? Needless to say, Eden did not comment on this embarrassing suggestion, and in general the parliamentary and press reaction was, as in the United States, overwhelmingly favourable.[11]

Privately, however, Eden may have pondered on one perceptive observation in the House of Commons debate, namely that 'the different social and political philosophies [of the USSR and the West] will make postwar co-operation difficult'. Eden was aware of this, if Hull was not. He was also aware of how far the results of the conference fell short of what he would have wished. Although in his first report to the War Cabinet and Churchill he had put the best complexion on affairs, as was his custom, he had an accurate idea of the gains and losses. So far as Western Europe was concerned, and Italy, he had got for the most part what he had wanted. The EAC had been set up and was to operate in London. The Soviet-desired Italian Commission had been neutralized, and a place had been found not only for the French, but for the Greeks and Yugoslavs also. Very probably the French would eventually take their place on the EAC as well. The terms of reference for that body were more limited than he had wished, but there was the possibility of enlarging them in the future. On Germany the outlook was more dubious and it was clear that a struggle lay ahead on this issue, particularly as one alternative solution—the creation in its place of a powerful Central European Confederation—had been effectively turned down. On Poland and Eastern Europe his policy lay in ruins. From the British point of view the results of the conference here were worse than negative. Not only had the Russians shown no willingness to make any kind of concession on Poland, and resisted firmly any proposals that might limit their complete freedom in Eastern Europe, but Hull's obvious unwillingness to associate the United States with British initiatives had made it clear to the Russians, or so they must have thought, that they had nothing to fear from that quarter. The United States was apparently willing to give the Russians *carte blanche* in that area. On the other hand, the USSR had accepted gracefully the clear intimation that Anglo-American policy would prevail in Italy, had accepted without demur Western proposals for France, and had said nothing to embarrass the British either on the difficult question of Greece, or for that matter on Yugoslavia. Genuine Four-Power co-operation over the whole European scene seemed to be ruled out; but perhaps an understanding on the alternative though less satisfactory basis of *de facto* spheres of influence might be possible?

Churchill's reactions were somewhat similar. Both in his summing-up to the War Cabinet and later in his memoirs he stressed the practical value of the additional interallied machinery which had been set up, in the shape of the European and Italian Commissions, and the useful agreements on Italy, Austria, 'peace-feelers', and German atrocities. He, too, paid lip-service to the value of the Four-Power Declaration and the generally harmonious atmosphere of the conference, which led Eden to call it subsequently 'the high tide of tolerable relations'. But Churchill, like Eden, was aware of what the latter called 'an ominous void' on Poland, and on Eastern Europe generally.[12]

Eden's tendency to put the best face on things is shown not only in his reports at the time of the conference, but also characteristically in his memoirs, where he says only that 'the search for a common policy in the Balkans was one of the issues on which uneven progress was made'. On this and on Eastern Europe generally, 'little progress and many setbacks' would have been more accurate. Nevertheless it must be said that even experienced hands like Clark Kerr and Ismay seem to have been influenced by the affability and hospitality they encountered in Moscow. Kerr described the conference as 'an outstanding success' and Ismay records that for the first time he was optimistic about relations with Russia. [13]

In the recesses of the Foreign Office, however, the permanent officials surveyed the results of the conference from the British angle somewhat more coolly. An official summary of the conference noted the general achievement of British objectives in relation to the EAC, Italy, and France, but on the other hand that the proposed declarations on spheres of influence, liberated territories, and confederations had got nowhere and indeed had encountered strong Soviet opposition; while on the Balkans and Poland there had been no more than some inconclusive discussions, together with a minimal exchange of information. Nor had there been much progress on the harmonization of policies towards Iran, which had been referred to the three ambassadors in that country. On minor matters—the convoy question, the declarations on 'peace-feelers' and German atrocities—there had been some gains, but the general tone of the document is not over-enthusiastic. [14]

A later Foreign Office appreciation had commented on Hull's speech to Congress that the Secretary had clearly been interested solely in obtaining Congressional approval for his proposed new international organization. Hull's remarks on the end of such old-fashioned devices as balance of power, spheres of influence, and alliances were merely 'wishful thinking'. Noting caustically that the Secretary had not said that the Monroe Doctrine was out of date, the memorandum remarked that Hull would soon have to face some of the other practical facts of life, such as the Soviet intention to hold on to the Baltic States. Another official added that Hull's dislike of some of the exiled refugee governments was evident from his remarks, which were in keeping with the US unwillingness at the conference to support Eden's proposal that these governments should in general be regarded as the legitimate holders of political power. But at least this might serve, the writer commented, to show the intransigent Poles that they could expect little practical support from Washington. [15]

The Soviet government's reactions to the conference are as usual more difficult to assess, but can be guessed. Publicly, Soviet press and diplomatic response followed the official line in hailing the conference as a success and stressing particularly the priority given to 'measures to shorten the war'—primarily 'Overlord'. It can be assumed that the Soviet leaders took considerable satisfaction not only from the clear Anglo-American commitment, but also from the unmistakable indications that the United States was likely to side with Russia in any strategic arguments with Britain. Clearly the full weight of Anglo-American military power would shortly be diverted well away from Eastern Europe and the Eastern Mediterranean. The US reaction to the proposal to bring Turkey into the war, whether welcome or not *per se* to the USSR, served to confirm this. On the political matters discussed, the Soviet leaders could reflect that they had stood firm on their determination to have a free hand in Eastern Europe, but had made no progress in obtaining an immediate right to influence Italian affairs; and no doubt the same would apply to France and other parts of Western Europe. On the other hand the Americans had shown a gratifying willingness to deal unsentimentally with Germany and had seemed to share none of the obvious British anxieties about the balance of power in Europe. Putting these facts together with the apparent unwillingness of the Americans to become involved in Eastern European problems, it must have seemed to the Soviet leaders that there was a basis for the division of Europe into *de-facto* spheres of influence; and, given a satisfactory solution for Germany, which reduced it to a political and military nullity, this might not be a bad thing from the Soviet point of view, at any rate in the short run.

Speaking to the Soviet and Allied press in Moscow on 10 November, Litvinov, as the spokesman for the Soviet government, underlined the Soviet point of view. After referring to the setting up of the new tripartite bodies for Italy and Europe generally, he mentioned the agreement on 'peace-feelers' which he linked with the principle of 'unconditional surrender'. This was a clear indication that in relation to the lesser Axis states such as Finland and Hungary, and of course even more Germany, the USSR would tolerate none of the fudging of the principle or modification of surrender terms such as had occurred in Italy. Then, turning to Eastern Europe, he made the Soviet position crystal clear. The USSR desired 'friendly relations' with the London Polish government, he said, but saw little chance of this in existing conditions. Also the USSR was unalterably opposed to artificial confederations in Eastern Europe and, he implied, the conference had accepted this view. As for 'Soviet frontiers' (that is, the 1941 frontiers with Poland and the inclusion of the Baltic States) these had not been discussed by the conference, but the USSR regarded them as inviolable. Harriman found this last remark unnecessarily bellicose, and the general tenor of Litvinov's remarks must have reinforced his conviction as to the intransigence of Soviet attitudes over Eastern Europe. It would be necessary to make US views clear without any further delay, unless Roosevelt was prepared to let the whole question of the future settlement there go by default. However that might be, the Russians had left no room for doubt as to their determination to get their own way in that part of Europe which their armies were to occupy, and which they regarded as their own preserve.[16]

It has been argued, particularly by some revisionist historians, that since the United States and Britain were imposing policies of their choice in Western Europe, the USSR had the right to do the same in that part of Europe which was of vital concern to their security and which would be freed of Nazi occupation largely by Soviet military operations. How far the first of these statements is true can perhaps be judged from the preceding account of the Moscow conference. The Western Powers had submitted to the USSR for approval their proposed policies for France and Germany, and accepted for Italy a statement of principles which the USSR had proposed. The Soviet Union, on the other hand, had neither explained its policy for Eastern Europe, nor sought Western approval. Both premise and conclusion are therefore equally dubious.

3. Anglo-American Political and Military Preoccupations: the Decision for Teheran and Cairo

During the Moscow conference little progress had been made towards resolving the one issue which still stood between Roosevelt and his long-desired objective—a personal meeting with Stalin. The Soviet leader had already agreed—on 8 September—to a meeting of the three heads of government at the end of November or beginning of December, preceded by a 'preparatory' meeting of the Foreign Ministers in Moscow. In the same message to Roosevelt he had proposed Iran as the place for their meeting, which meant in effect the capital, Teheran. Churchill had immediately agreed, but Roosevelt had raised the constitutional difficulties of his position (see above, p. 9), and in mid-September had suggested various alternatives to Stalin. For the next two months the issue was batted backwards and forwards between Moscow, Washington, and London with, in the later stages, Hull, Eden, Molotov and Harriman all joining in the argument in Moscow. In the end, however, the position adopted by Stalin at the outset had to be accepted in every detail. The Foreign Ministers met in Moscow from 19 to 30 October: the three heads of government assembled in Teheran for a three-day conference on 27 November. It was an object-lesson of the advantage in negotiation of standing pat on all points of detail, when the other side wants the main objective much more than you do. It was a lesson the Russians learnt rather too well, and tended to apply in circumstances not always so favourable.

Since the protracted argument over the meeting-place achieved no result whatever, there is no need to rehearse its course in any detail. After Roosevelt and Churchill had suggested almost every possible and impossible alternative, ranging from Cairo to Basra and Asmara to Beirut, Roosevelt was finally convinced by Hull's report from Moscow that the Soviet leader would not go any further afield than Teheran. Stalin's professed reason was that the German summer offensive had merged without pause into a Russian counter-offensive, and he could not therefore go beyond the range of rapid and easy communication with the front. No doubt this had considerable weight, but it is probable that Stalin also preferred to meet with the other two in a country where there was a Russian military presence, and where there was a Soviet Embassy where his security could be more effectively guaranteed. Stalin made this point obliquely when in one message to Roosevelt he mentioned the desirability of meeting somewhere where they all three had 'diplomatic representation' which as far as the USSR was concerned was not the case in most of the other suggested venues. Deadlock therefore appeared to have been reached. On 5 November, after the conclusion of the Moscow conference, Stalin reiterated to Roosevelt that he could not go beyond Teheran, but repeated a suggestion he had already made to Hull in Moscow that he should send Molotov (whom he described as his 'first deputy Prime Minister in the government') with full powers to meet Roosevelt and Churchill. [17]

Meanwhile, however, further complications to the schedule had been introduced by Churchill and Roosevelt, leading ultimately to another international conference at Cairo being inserted in the period between the Foreign Ministers' meeting and the proposed Roosevelt-Churchill rendezvous with the Russians. This development sprang in equal parts from Churchill's desire to persuade Roosevelt to revise in important respects the Quebec timetable for 'Overlord', and from Roosevelt's desire to have a personal meeting with the leader of the other great allied State, China's Generalissimo Chiang-Kai-Shek.

Simultaneously therefore with the final stages of negotiations with Stalin over the Teheran meeting, an involved though largely unacknowledged diplomatic contest was being waged between Churchill and Roosevelt on the question of whether they should first meet separately and if so where, when, and with whom. It was a bout between political heavyweights, but Roosevelt's superior ring-craft assured him in the end of victory on most points, though not on all.

Churchill wished primarily to meet with Roosevelt and the American Chiefs to persuade them to relax the rigorous Quebec schedule of troop transfers from the Mediterranean theatre for the Cross-Channel Attack. The movement of seven divisions and most of the heavy landing-craft from the Mediterranean before November would, he believed, fatally cripple the Allied 'build-up' in Italy, and even make it possible perhaps for the German forces there to launch a counter-attack and drive the Allies out of the peninsula. These transfers, as he had indicated to Stalin during the Moscow conference, should be delayed, even though the scheduled date for 'Overlord'—1 May 1944—might then have to be postponed for a month or two. He thought it essential to straighten these matters out with the Americans before committing themselves further to Stalin. On the other hand, Churchill had no desire to meet with Chiang-Kai-Shek, or to spend hours discussing potential allied operations in Burma to help the Chinese. He had no enthusiasm for such operations in jungle conditions favourable to the Japanese, preferring to wait until allied naval power could be used in the Indian ocean (as it was already being used in the Pacific) in amphibious operations on the Burmese Coast or the Dutch East Indies. In any case he regarded the Burma theatre and the Chinese as of minor importance compared with the great issues to be decided in Europe, or for that matter compared with the vast operations already being launched in the Pacific and New Guinea by the American commanders Admiral Nimitz and General MacArthur.

Roosevelt and the US Chiefs of Staff, however, regarded the whole issue of European strategy for 1944 as settled by the Quebec decisions, and were alarmed and irritated by Churchill's apparent wish to back away once again from an agreed plan to cross the Channel. He had already done that once successfully in 1942 and diverted the weight of Anglo-American military power to operations in North Africa, Sicily, and Italy during the year that followed. The US Chiefs were determined not to be outmanœuvred again. However they did want to prevail upon the British Chiefs and Churchill to embark on operations in Upper Burma to help the hard-pressed Chinese. Roosevelt, who had allowed himself to be persuaded to adopt the British strategy for Europe a year earlier, was this time determined to stick to the agreed plan and support his Chiefs of Staff. Furthermore he had two political ends in view. He wished to capitalize on the apparently favourable mood of the Russians, as demonstrated at Moscow, by establishing a cordial personal relationship with Stalin, as a firm basis for future Soviet-American co-operation. Such a relationship might well be jeopardized if the Americans seemed to be 'ganging up' with the British and again concerting operations with them before meeting Stalin. The Russians had shown often enough during the past year that they were highly suspicious of these regular and intimate Anglo-American meetings which always seemed to end with the British view prevailing and decisions for Mediterranean operations rather than the long-desired assault on Western Europe across the Channel. Roosevelt was anxious not to reawaken these suspicions.[18]

On the other hand, the President did wish to meet Chiang-Kai-Shek. China was to be, in Roosevelt's conception, the fourth main element in the post-war organization for international security. But in order to fulfil that role China had first to be strengthened militarily and politically. She had to be enabled to play a major part if possible in winning the war, and helped to regain her lost territories; and her status had to be recognized by Britain and, even more important, by Russia. A beginning had been made in Moscow with the Chinese signature of the Four-Power Declaration. Roosevelt wanted to follow this up by discussing China's future with Stalin. The Soviet leader's indication at Moscow that Russia would eventually enter the Far Eastern War, though welcome from the military point of view, added urgency to the matter. If Soviet military power was brought to bear in that conflict, it could only effectively be done in Manchuria and North China. But once established militarily in these areas, the USSR would probably seek to gain advantages, both military and political, at the expense of its weaker neighbour. The long-standing Russian desire for warm-water, ice-free ports in the Pacific might lead to a demand for a resumption of the privileged position that Russia had once enjoyed in the use of Port Arthur as a naval base and for rights in other ports as well. If so, to secure communications with its base or bases in that area, Russia might then wish to exercise some sort of permanent control over Manchuria. It was desirable, therefore, that before a possible discussion of all these issues with Stalin, Roosevelt should meet with the Chinese as well as the British, both to concert military operations and to discuss the whole question of China's role in the post-war world and the possible complications with Russia. As early as the previous June, when all these problems were beginning to loom on the horizon, Roosevelt had cabled Chiang-Kai-Shek suggesting a meeting in the autumn, which the Chinese leader, conscious both of his military weakness and political isolation, had gladly accepted. Now Roosevelt was determined that this meeting should take place, and that Far Eastern rather than European operations and political questions should be the subject of any immediate discussions with the British. There was still of course the problem of Soviet suspicions of any Anglo-American meeting. In order to overcome this problem, Roosevelt conceived the idea of inviting a Soviet military representative to attend any joint meeting of the Anglo-American Chiefs of Staff which might be arranged. The idea was warmly supported by Cordell Hull and Averell Harriman from Moscow, and also more suprisingly by Eden, as a firm indication of willingness to admit the USSR to the inner councils of the Anglo-American alliance; the US Chiefs of Staff, after some hesitation, had concurred. [19]

Roosevelt therefore had a complicated hand to play, and played it with considerable skill, if with some artfulness. He was assisted by Churchill's relatively trustful and deferential attitude, and also by the latter's errors of judgement. The immediate cause of the train of events which led to the decision to hold an Anglo-American meeting in Cairo sometime in November was a cable from Churchill to Roosevelt on 20 October, just as the Moscow conference was beginning. This message was prompted by the unsatisfactory state of the campaign in Italy and the Eastern Mediterranean and the anxiety which was felt by Churchill and the British Chiefs of Staff on that score. On the surrender of Italy on 3 September, Allied forces had crossed the Straits of Messina from Sicily to the 'toe' of Italy and a week or so later an amphibious landing had been made at Salerno on the west coast of Italy south of Naples. Further west the island of Sardinia was also occupied. In the Eastern Mediterranean lay the Italian-held Greek islands of the Dodecanese off the coast of Turkey. At Washington and Quebec it had been agreed that, given favourable circumstances, an attempt should be made to occupy these islands; but at the same time decisions had been made which contradicted that assumption, since it had also been agreed that some of the landing craft and troops which would have made effective operations possible were to be transferred from the Middle East to other theatres by the end of August. This latter decision was duly carried out just before the surrender of Italy. General Wilson therefore found himself at the beginning of September with inadequate resources for the Dodecanese operation. In all this the Allies in Europe were paying the price for the attitude of the US Naval Chief, Admiral King. King had virtually monopolized the supply of landing craft for his cherished operations in the Pacific, releasing a bare two thousand or so for all European operations. It was this shortage of landing craft in the European theatre which both restricted the scale of allied operations against Italy and imposed the rigid timetable for the return of these craft to the UK for 'Overlord'.

Meanwhile Kesselring, the German commander in Italy, had re-acted quickly to the Italian surrender. Italian troops in the north were quickly disarmed. German formations were rushed southwards and were able to take control of Rome before the Allies could move in. The bridgehead at Salerno was rapidly encircled and the allied landings held. By the time the Salerno forces were able to break out and link up with Montgomery's troops advancing from the south, German control of north and central Italy had been effectively established. A substantial build-up of German divisions south of Rome allowed Kesselring to withdraw slowly to a defensible winter line protecting the capital. Allied hopes of capturing Rome in October were dashed. In the Eastern Mediterranean also the Germans, at Hitler's direct orders, had acted quickly. They had taken control of Rhodes, the largest island in the Dodecanese, and begun operations against the small detachments which Wilson, at Churchill's prompting, had landed further north on the Islands of Cos, Leros, and Samos. Cos was retaken by the Germans on 3 October, depriving Wilson of his one usable air-base on the islands. Churchill unsuccessfully brought pressure to bear on Eisenhower, commanding in Italy, to help with landing-craft and air forces; and appealed directly to Roosevelt for help. Eisenhower was not unsympathetic, but his own problems were daily increasing. Roosevelt and the US Chiefs, suspicious as always of Churchill's plans in the Eastern Mediterranean, returned a frigid 'No'. Churchill was forced to submit, to cancel plans for an attack on Rhodes, and effectively to leave the remaining British forces on the Dodecanese to their fate.

By mid-October, therefore, the Mediterranean position was far less favourable than had been hoped. Not only were operations in the Dodecanese moving towards catastrophe, but in Italy Eisenhower, with eleven divisions, was confronted south of Rome with a German force of nineteen divisions. Only in the air did the Anglo-American forces enjoy superiority. Stalemate and a long winter campaign loomed ahead, and the only way in which the balance could be altered was by the use of allied naval power to launch amphibious attacks against the German flanks and rear. But such operations would require the very landing-craft scheduled to return to the UK in November for use in the Cross-Channel Attack.[20]

On 19 October the British Chiefs of Staff had considered this dire situation. On the 20th Churchill sent his cable to Roosevelt, in which he noted that tremendous changes had occurred in the war situation since the Quebec decisions had been taken, and asked for 'a full conference of the Combined Chiefs of Staff in North Africa', preferably not later than 10 November. On the 21st General Alexander, commanding the Allied Armies in Italy under Eisenhower, submitted a depressing report on the prospects there, further increasing the anxiety felt by Churchill and Alan Brooke, the British Army Chief of Staff. Roosevelt, however, was in no very accommodating mood. As Brooke for one had foreseen, Churchill's frantic efforts first to launch, and then to rescue the Eastern Mediterranean operations, had aroused Roosevelt's worst fears and those of his military advisers. Nevertheless Roosevelt had his own reasons for thinking a staff meeting with the British might be necessary, connected more with the Far East than with Europe. On the 22nd therefore he returned a temporizing reply. There could perhaps be a Combined Chiefs meeting, but not until the results of the Moscow conference had been analysed and the US military planners had finished their current appraisal of allied strategy. As the Moscow meeting was due to end two days before the US planners reported on 1 November, this would just, but only just, make it possible for a Combined Chiefs meeting to take place in the second week of November. The American President could not resist a jab at Churchill's (in his view) exaggerated hopes of the possible damage to the German hold on the Balkans from the activities of the Greek and Yugoslav guerillas. The Balkans, he observed, seemed to be in a chaotic state, with Greeks and Yugoslavs spending more time fighting each other than fighting the Germans. Perhaps an American general should be sent there to pull things together? As the Eastern Mediterranean had always been regarded as primarily a British sphere of operations, and there were many British missions operating there, this was a nasty thrust. Roosevelt then went on to reveal at least one of his preoccupations. The Combined Chiefs meeting should take place *after* their meeting with the Russians, he suggested: a meeting beforehand might 'prejudice relations'. Almost every line of this message was a red rag to Churchill. Always less inclined than Roosevelt to be tender of Soviet susceptibilities, he was less so than usual at this moment, after Stalin's offensive message on the Arctic convoys, received only a week before. In his reply he pointed out to Roosevelt that Russian troops were not involved in any of the Anglo-

American operations to be discussed, emphasized his view that they should concert their strategic plans before meeting the Russians, and asked that the Staffs should meet on 15 November. He could then meet the President a few days later, and if the difficulties with Stalin were sorted out, they could go on to meet him. As for the Balkans, he pointed out that guerilla operations, plus the threat of Turkey entering the war, were keeping twenty-five German divisions in the Balkan area, and so helping to create the conditions which would make 'Overlord' possible. He might have added that if Roosevelt was concerned about Russian susceptibilities, he should have done more to gratify the Soviet desire for Turkey to enter the war, instead of making it virtually impossible. He told Roosevelt frankly that he was deeply anxious, both about the Italian campaign, and the success of 'Overlord'. In neither case did the forces seem adequate. The Anglo-American planners had allocated 25–30 British and US divisions to 'Overlord' and 22 to Italy for 1943–4. The Germans had 30 or so divisions in France and the Low Countries already, and more than 20 in Italy. By retreating from the Balkans to a shorter line, they could withdraw sufficient troops from that area to bring an overwhelming force of 40 or so divisions to bear in either theatre. In Italy this would make it hard for the allied armies to hold their ground, let alone advance. In France it might prejudice the success of the whole Cross-Channel operation.[21]

Roosevelt appears to have recognized that Churchill was genuinely anxious. On 25 October he replied that it seemed from Stalin's attitude that no meeting with him would be possible, but he and Churchill could certainly meet in North Africa or Cairo with their staffs. Less palatable to Churchill was Roosevelt's accompanying suggestion that Chiang-Kai-Shek should join the two leaders, and Molotov also, as a substitute for the meeting with Stalin. Roosevelt, however, lulled Churchill's suspicious by implying that there would be time for Anglo-American consultations first, before the Chinese and Russians joined the talks—which was what Churchill wanted. Churchill was not to know that the idea of inviting not only Molotov but a Russian general to 'sit in' on the Anglo-American staff meetings was being actively canvassed in Washington. Indeed, on that same day General Marshall had written to Roosevelt's Chief of Staff, Admiral Leahy, that he had come round to the idea of having the Russians participate.

For the moment, however, Churchill must have felt relieved. The meeting with Stalin was still in doubt but it looked as though a fruitful Anglo-American discussion would take place. Although the opportunity of bringing real pressure to bear on the enemy in the Eastern

Mediterranean and the Balkans had probably now been lost, at least it might be possible to persuade the Americans to modify the absurd rigidity of their timetable for 'Overlord' so that pressure could be sustained in Italy through the winter and spring. On the 26th he telegraphed to Roosevelt enthusiastically that he would 'meet him anywhere' but hoped it could be before Roosevelt's proposed date of the 20 November. They could meet at Casablanca, he suggested, and then go on to Cairo later to meet Chiang and Molotov. Roosevelt, however, now dropped his bombshell. On the 26th he wired Churchill that in view of the happy atmosphere at the Moscow conference which could be 'the beginning of genuine tripartite co-operation', it was important to stimulate this mood and increase Stalin's confidence. He therefore proposed they should invite Stalin to send a Russian military representative to sit in on meetings of the Anglo-American Chiefs of Staff. The next day Roosevelt put the other part of his plan for circumventing Churchill into operation. To Chiang-Kai-Shek he suggested they should meet in Egypt 'between the 20th and the 25th November'. Since he had proposed 20 November to Churchill, the prolonged and leisurely consultations over European strategy which the latter looked forward to were clearly not likely to take place. The President in fact was determined not to expose himself to Churchill's blandishments *à deux* if he could help it. He had good reasons—or reasons which seemed good—for wishing to meet the Russians and the Chinese, quite apart from this, but there was the additional advantage that their presence would put an effective stopper on Churchill's plans. As Brooke had foreseen, the furore over the Dodecanese operations, and Churchill's readiness to fall in with the Soviet suggestion about Turkey, had aroused all the latent American suspicions as to Churchill's real commitment to 'Overlord', as opposed to what they saw as the pursuit of purely British objectives in the Eastern Mediterranean and the Balkans. Although Churchill had assured Roosevelt as recently as 7 October that he did not wish to commit large allied forces to the Balkans, his actions seemed to belie this assurance.

Were American suspicions entirely unjustified? Not entirely, perhaps. Certainly neither Churchill nor the British Chiefs ever put up a serious plan for the invasion of the Balkans, and Churchill always accepted that eventually the Channel would have to be crossed in order to win the war. Yet even British commentators such as Sir Arthur Bryant concede that Churchill was haunted by the possibility of a bloodbath on the assault beaches of France, or a subsequent stalemate and prolonged wasting carnage like that of the Western Front in the First World War. The longer the German strength could be wasted away by prolonged but relatively inexpensive operations at the periphery of Europe, and the more German divisions could be drawn away from the west into Italy and the Balkans, as well as Russia, the less likely his fears were to be realized. Probably in his heart of hearts, Churchill always hoped that if the day of the great gamble were postponed long enough and the war of attrition in the Mediterranean pursued vigorously enough, the Cross-Channel Attack might eventually prove relatively easy, and the final campaign in the West mercifully short. [22]

However that may be, by his persistence over Turkey and the Dodecanese Churchill had now set all the alarm bells ringing in the United States. Stimson, the US Secretary of War, had earlier concluded that 'Overlord' would never stand a chance of success under a British commander, since the British did not really believe in the operation. He was now using all his influence to persuade Roosevelt, Hopkins, and the US Chiefs to stick to their intention to appoint General Marshall to the command. Only Marshall in his view had the prestige to overawe Churchill and the British and the steadfastness of character to force the operation through at the agreed time against whatever obstacles or blandishments might be offered. The US Chiefs themselves were on the point of recommending to the President that the 'Overlord' commander should be in charge of all operations against Germany—in other words should be supreme over Mediterranean operations as well as those in North-west Europe—in order to ensure that 'Overlord' should maintain its agreed priority in resources. [23]

It is against this background that one must judge Roosevelt's slightly devious handling of the arrangements for the forthcoming conference. It was to his interest to postpone the date for his meeting with Churchill as much as possible. He was now given an additional excuse to do so by the news that Hull was not likely to be back from Moscow until 10 November. Roosevelt could reasonably argue that he needed to talk to Hull personally about the results of the Moscow conference, and therefore could not himself leave the United States until then. He proposed, like Hull, to travel in a leisurely way by sea to North Africa, and wished to spend a few days there discussing the situation with his Mediterranean commanders. Therefore the meeting with Churchill and the Combined Staffs conference could obviously not take place before 20 November, instead of the 10th or 15th as Churchill still hoped. Meanwhile the latter had reacted explosively to the suggestion that the Russians should join in Anglo-American military planning. This was simply going to be a one-way bargain, he argued, since the Russians had not invited Anglo-American representatives to participate in their planning, and indeed were always very secretive about the details of their plans. A Soviet general would have no real authority to discuss anything freely. He would merely sit there and, as Churchill colourfully put it, 'bay for the Second Front'. Moreover the need for translation would impose intolerable delays. Surely he and Roosevelt could meet together with their Staffs before the 20th, and before meeting the others, if only for two days? Roosevelt replied uncompromisingly that he could not guarantee to be there till 20 November—in fact, since Hull's departure from Moscow had been further delayed, possibly not until the 22nd. However, he told Churchill that Chiang, and by implication the Russians, would not be arriving until the 25th, leaving the British Premier with the impression that there would still be time for a private Anglo-American conference of two or three days first. Nevertheless Churchill was still uneasy. Surely, he asked, Hull could wait for Roosevelt in Egypt or North Africa, thus enabling the President to start earlier and meet Churchill in Gibraltar or North Africa, perhaps on the 15th? They could then go on to Cairo to meet Chiang, Molotov, and the Russians from the 24th to the 28th. Perhaps they could go on from there to meet Stalin at Teheran if only for a day. Roosevelt, however, had no desire to meet Churchill privately in North Africa or anywhere else. On 3 November Churchill grudgingly agreed to meet him in Cairo on the 22nd, but reiterated that they must consult together before the Russians joined them. [24]

Churchill had now been forced to abandon his hopes for prolonged Anglo-American discussion of the 'Overlord' versus Mediterranean question before the meeting at Cairo; and had felt obliged to agree that the Russians should at some stage join in the discussions, as well as the Chinese. He still, however, expected there to be a few days for private Anglo-American talks at Cairo before the Russians arrived. Roosevelt reinforced this impression rather disingenuously by assuring Churchill on the 5th that 'the Combined Chiefs would have many meetings' before the Russians or Chinese joined them. At the same time he dangled the possibility of a prior meeting at Oran before the Prime Minister's eyes. On the assumption that the two men would meet at Oran on the 19th Churchill agreed to Roosevelt's suggestion that Chiang should be invited to Cairo on the 22nd—three days earlier than previously agreed. [25]

In the mean time Stalin had made it plain beyond any doubt that he would not go further than Teheran. Churchill however had taken the practical step of asking General Ismay to find out authoritatively if it was really the case that communications from Teheran to the outside world were so liable to be interrupted as to make Roosevelt's hesitation in going there justifiable. On the 6th he transmitted Ismay's report to the effect that this was not in fact the case, and the following day Averell Harriman reported from Moscow that his own investigations supported this. Harriman urged Roosevelt to go to Teheran, if only for a day or so, since it was of such importance that he should meet Stalin. This evidently decided Roosevelt and on 8 November he telegraphed to Stalin that he would after all be prepared to go to Teheran, and suggesting they meet there between 26 and 30 November. He then proceeded to dash Churchill's remaining hopes by telling Stalin that he hoped the Anglo-American Staffs would begin work on the 22nd and that the Russian representatives would come there *at that time*. To make assurance doubly sure he then invited Chiang-Kai-Shek to come on the same day (that is, four days earlier than had been previously arranged). [26]

Churchill of course still expected a gap of about three days between the Anglo-American meeting and the advent of the Russians and the Chinese, while Stalin was unaware that the Chinese were also coming to Cairo. This latter omission was a major error on Roosevelt's part since Stalin was at least as determined that no official Russian representative should meet publicly with Chiang-Kai-Shek as Roosevelt was not to meet privately with Churchill. Quite apart from the fact that Stalin, like Churchill, had his doubts about the Chinese claim to rank as one of the 'Big Four', there was the fact that Russia was not, unlike Britain and the United States, either at war with Japan or allied to China. Chinese military operations were an irrelevancy as far as the Russians were concerned; moreover Stalin was not yet ready to take on the Japanese, and had no desire to antagonize them at this juncture, or to give them such a clear indication of his future intentions. On 10 November Churchill gave the show away to Stalin by mentioning in a message to him that the Chinese would be at Cairo. By return he heard from Moscow that Molotov and the Russians had been invited to Cairo on the 22nd, and also, for the first time, that Roosevelt had decided to go to Teheran.

Roosevelt's chickens now came home to roost, in the shape of a reproachful note from Churchill and a stiff message from Stalin. Churchill, feeling that he had been hoodwinked, complained that he had been given to believe that the British and American staffs would have 'many meetings' before being joined by the Russians and Chinese. He asked that the arrival of Molotov and the Russians should be delayed until the 25th.

Roosevelt, who was just about to leave Washington to embark on the battleship *Iowa* was forced to reveal his true preoccupations. 'I have held all along', he wired to Churchill on the 11th, 'that it would be a terrible mistake if Uncle Joe (Stalin) thought we had ganged up on him on military action . . . it will not hurt if Molotov and the Russian military representative are in Cairo too.' For good measure he added that the Russians should not only be at the Cairo conference before the Teheran meeting, but should also return with them to Cairo for any subsequent discussions. Churchill knew he was beaten, and subsided into intermittent grumblings about the difficulties which Roosevelt's 'arrangements for the military conversations' would cause. One part of Roosevelt's plans, however, was about to come unstuck. On the 12th Stalin informed both men that Molotov would not after all come to Cairo. Subsequently the reason was given that Stalin had an attack of illness, and therefore Molotov, his 'first deputy in the government' could not be spared from Moscow. One may suspect that it was a diplomatic illness. Stalin made the real reason clear in his customary oblique fashion when he added to Churchill that 'in Teheran a meeting of only three heads of the governments is to take place . . . the participation of any other countries must be absolutely excluded', adding drily 'I wish success to your conference with the Chinese on Far Eastern Affairs'. Churchill could not resist replying 'I understand your position and am in full accord with your wishes' (that is, the exclusion of the Chinese from Teheran), and repeating the message to Roosevelt. The plan therefore which Roosevelt and the US Chiefs of Staff had laid to have the Russians present at Cairo to help circumvent any British proposal to tamper with 'Overlord' came to nothing. But Roosevelt could still reflect, as the *Iowa* carried him towards North Africa, that his timetable of talks with the Chinese would probably take care of that problem.[28]

The above episode, comic in many ways, yet a little tragic, too, in view of the gravity of the issues involved, reveals how much the Anglo-American partnership had changed from the cosy intimacies of the early days, when the Americans were very much the newcomers in the war. Now their self-confidence had grown with their resources and experience of war. They were conscious that they had become the senior partner in the alliance, and were no longer prepared to be so receptive to British wishes, or tender of Churchill's susceptibilities. Their priorities too had changed. Russia was now considered more important. At the time of the Quebec conference military planners had prepared for Harry Hopkins, Roosevelt's closest adviser, an estimate of Russia's future position which was in most respects very prescient. 'Russia's post-war position in Europe', it read, 'will be a dominant one. . . . There will be no power to oppose her tremendous military forces . . . Britain is building up a position in the Mediterranean *vis-à-vis* Russia, but even here she may not be able to oppose Russia unless she is otherwise supported. . . . Since Russia is the decisive factor in the war, she must be given every assistance and every effort must be made to obtain her friendship. . . . Since she will dominate Europe [after the war] it is essential to develop and maintain the most friendly relations with Russia.' Finally the paper had added that Russian support in the war against Japan would make that war shorter and less costly for the US. These then were the considerations which governed Roosevelt's thinking and that of his military advisers, as they approached the Cairo and Teheran conferences. It was Russian friendship, trust, and goodwill which was now more important to them than that of Britain.[29]

All this was apparent to Churchill. But he had done all he could. So on 11 November, nearly two years after Roosevelt had first suggested a meeting to Stalin, and three months after Stalin had suggested Teheran, the question of the Three-Power meeting was finally settled. On that same day Roosevelt embarked on the first stage of the journey. He was accompanied by Harry Hopkins, by his personal Chief of Staff, Admiral Leahy, and the other members of the US Chiefs of Staff, General Marshall, Admiral King, and Air Force General Arnold; as well as his aides and doctors and a strong team of advisers from all three services. The following day Churchill embarked on the battleship *Renown* with two members of the British Chiefs of Staff, the First Sea Lord, Admiral Cunningham, and Churchill's own Chief Staff Officer and representative on the Chiefs of Staff, General Ismay. The US Ambassador to Britain, John Winant, also travelled with him. The two other members of the British Chiefs of Staff, General Alan Brooke and Air Chief Marshal Portal, followed later, as did Eden and his permanent head at the Foreign Office, Cadogan. In Moscow Ambassador Harriman, Bohlen, now attached to the US Embassy, and General Deane of the military mission, prepared to leave for Cairo; in Algiers Harold Macmillan, and in Ankara Lawrence Steinhardt, the American Ambassador, made similar preparations. In far-off Chungking Chiang-Kai-Shek and his American Chief of Staff, Stilwell, also prepared to leave. The most important and certainly the most high-powered allied meetings of the war so far were about to begin.

CHAPTER VI

THE BIG FOUR AND
THE CAIRO AGENDA

1. The Allied Leaders

Much has been written during the past forty years about the four statesmen who met at Cairo and Teheran. It is hard to find much to add to the picture. In 1943 Franklin Roosevelt enjoyed enormous power and prestige, both nationally and internationally. He had held the highest office in the United States for over ten years and had twice been re-elected, breaking the long-established American convention that a president should serve no more than two terms. He had rescued the United States from the worst economic crisis in its history, brought his country gradually from its isolationist position to full participation in the Allied Coalition, and was now the unchallenged leader of his country. Congress, which had often thwarted him in the past, was not inclined to challenge or hinder the country's wartime leader. The majority of the American people had always supported him and now more than ever were solidly behind his leadership. He knew that he could probably, if he wished, secure election for a fourth term, which would keep him in office until 1948. Personally he was a man of great charm and vitality, which was in no way diminished by his crippled condition. He had great confidence in his persuasive powers, both in domestic politics, and in his dealings with foreign statesmen. Inevitably long years of power and the isolation of the presidential office had somewhat corroded his judgement and character, increasing both his vanity and his self-confidence. Fortunately, the effects of a democratic political system and the constraints it imposes, even in wartime, safeguarded him against the complete megalomania to which dictators tend to succumb. There were still voices that he would listen to, even when they uttered unwelcome truths. In military matters the US Army Chief of Staff, George Marshall, was his guide: in international politics he paid some attention to Cordell Hull and one or two others, but his principal counsellor was his close confidant and aide—regarded by some Congressional critics as his evil genius—Harry Hopkins. On both domestic and

international matters his wife, Eleanor Roosevelt, could still sometimes serve as the voice of his radical conscience.[1]

Roosevelt's approach to the problems of international diplomacy,
as to the problems of domestic political administration, was neither
orderly nor systematic but basically intuitive and pragmatic. He was
wary of formal blueprints, elaborate plans, and detailed agendas,
especially in foreign affairs, where so much depended on the decisions
of others and situations could change rapidly. His policy, particularly
when disagreements threatened, was to keep things fluid, if necessary
postpone the moment of decision, and then seize a favourable opportunity and use his powers of persuasion to win acceptance of his
policies. Undoubtedly Roosevelt's intentions were good. He wished
to see a world of peace and prosperity, in which men and women
should be free to live under a government of their choice, free from the
threat of war and if possible free from want and the threat of economic
depression. He rightly saw that the former would require an effective
international peace-keeping body and the latter a more effective
system for the management of world trade and the world's economic
resources. But the realities of international politics and the exigencies
of the wartime alliance both posed problems in relation to these objectives. Roosevelt had retained his broad commitment to the principles
of Wilsonian internationalism but he also had a firm grip on the facts
of international power. No international system would work if it
lacked the support of the world's most powerful states. In the event of
allied victory these would be the United States, Russia, and Britain.
China was a special case. For the moment she might be economically
backward, politically divided, and militarily weak, as Russia too had
been twenty years earlier; but her potential was enormous. It was on
grounds of potential rather than actual power that Roosevelt based his
argument for the acceptance of China as a fourth member of the allied
'Great Power Club'. The President had used this argument to Eden
amongst others during the latter's Washington visit earlier in 1943,
together with the contention that a strong and united China would be
a useful counterpoise to Russia in the Far East. On both counts it
could be argued Roosevelt showed considerable prescience. But this
view had both military and political implications. The purpose of the
projected campaign to reconquer Burma, which the Americans had
been urging on the reluctant British for some time, was not only to
reopen a channel for supplies to the Chinese and so enable China to
play a more effective military role against Japan; it was also to give the
war-weary Chinese renewed hope and confidence in the goodwill of
their allies and in their future role in the world. Roosevelt further

intended to bolster Chinese morale, and the position of the Chinese leader, Chiang-Kai-Shek, with assurances of generous treatment after the war. China was to regain all the territories she had lost to the Japanese, including Formosa, which had been Japanese territory for nearly fifty years.[2]

Roosevelt's view of China and its future role was essentially, then, a long-range one. In the immediate future Russia and the British Empire were more important considerations, both in winning the war and for the post-war ordering of the world. Since allied victory was the prerequisite for the implementation of Roosevelt's policies, the first essential was to keep the Allied Coalition together and the second to strengthen it with bonds of mutual confidence, so that it would continue to function in peace. In order to achieve this, some compromises in basic Wilsonian principles might have to be accepted. In particular the principle of self-determination, restated in allied declarations during the war, might have to be watered down a little. Soviet territorial demands—for the annexation of the Baltic States, for cessions of Polish, Finnish, and Romanian territory—might have to be conceded, without too nice a regard for the letter of the Wilsonian law. In the Far East, too, the USSR might seek extensions of territory or influence which would involve concessions by China. If in return, however, Soviet and American support were guaranteed for a settlement which included the restoration of all its lost territory to China, and a place for China in the supreme international decision-making body, this should not be a bad bargain from the Chinese point of view. The British Empire and the other European colonial empires also presented a problem. Viewed in the light of the principle of self-determination they were indefensible, a view which was certainly accepted by Roosevelt and most of his circle. Moreover British power was clearly on the decline, while the other European colonial powers had been defeated and occupied. France, in Roosevelt's view, could not hope to regain its position as a Great Power in less than twenty-five years, if then. Even if the colonial possessions lost to the Japanese were regained, Roosevelt doubted if the European hold over them could be maintained for very long. A graceful concession to the demands for national independence in the not too distant future would be the best policy for the colonial powers. In taking this view it could be argued that Roosevelt again showed considerable prescience, though perhaps it should be added that American policies then and since have contributed something to the fulfilment of these prophecies. However, a few discussions with Churchill over India had convinced him that the British leader was beyond the reach of reasoned argument on this issue. Roosevelt continued to bring pressure to bear on Churchill through third parties from time to time, but in their personal discussions he let the matter drop. He was not prepared to imperil present or future co-operation with Britain in order to win his point: he was content by and large to leave the process to the inexorable logic of history.

It would be easy to stigmatize the President's willingness to accept some compromises on matters of principle as cynical opportunism. Some critics have done so. But it was not wrong or foolish for Roosevelt to have accepted that politics—and particularly international politics—is the art of the possible. To gain the major objective—an effective Four-Power partnership in the post-war world—was a worthwhile objective, for which some sacrifices of principle could reasonably be made. The question was, of course, was such a partnership—at any rate between Russia and the Western Powers—attainable? It seemed to Roosevelt that he had to assume that it was. The alternative was to envisage a world of continuing international tension and the ultimate prospect of a Third World War. Experience of such a world for the past forty years makes it difficult to criticize Roosevelt for seeking to avoid it. Even Churchill and Eden, who were less inclined than Roosevelt to take an optimistic view of relations with Russia, recognized this unpalatable logic. As Eden had acknowledged to Roosevelt during their talks in March 1943, 'it is better in any event to be on good terms with the Russians than not'. Both Eden and Churchill were in fact equally prepared to contemplate compromises and bargains with the Russians over territorial and other matters in order to win Soviet goodwill. From Roosevelt's point of view, of course, the logic applied as much in relation to the unpalatable fact of the British Empire as in relation to Soviet territorial claims, though British dependence on the US made it less necessary to be tender of British susceptibilities. [3]

Roosevelt's realism and grasp of the facts of power are also evident in his approach to the precise nature of the organization for future international peace-keeping. The experience of the pre-war League of Nations had demonstrated that no such organization could work without the support of all the major Great Powers and equally that the structure of peace-keeping had to recognize the facts of international power. Wilsonian internationalism paid lip-service to the principle of equality between nations, but it was clear that the responsibility for actual peace-keeping operations would fall on the Great Powers; therefore the rules of the organization must recognize this. Roosevelt envisaged a Four-Power Council as the main peace-keeping organ in the immediate post-war world, to which might be added eventually elected representatives of the principal regions of the world, as a token recognition of the rights of other states. Embryonically therefore Roosevelt's thoughts foreshadowed the Security Council of the United Nations. By proposing this elevated position for the major war-time allies, Roosevelt hoped to guarantee Soviet and British support.

In their proposals for economic co-operation also the Americans recognized the need for some dilution of the pure milk of Wilsonian internationalism, which theoretically favoured unrestricted inter-national Free Trade. Hull's proposals at Moscow had recognized the need for some regulation of international trade, to control fluctuations in commodity prices and currency values and so limit the worst effects of the international trade cycle. Roosevelt and Hull hoped that effec-tive international controls in this area might induce other States, par-ticularly Britain, to abandon or reduce their national protective measures, and also encourage the Russians to liberalize their trade practices. [4]

In pursuing his objectives Roosevelt had of course to make use, as far as he could, of the human instruments he found to hand. The most prominent of these were the three other Allied leaders. Roosevelt's feelings for Churchill were compounded of admiration for the Englishman's courage and leadership, an affection that was some-times a little patronizing, and from time to time an exasperation he found it difficult to conceal. The two men corresponded regularly and frankly throughout the war. Roosevelt once cabled Churchill 'It is fun to be in the same decade with you' and much of the time it probably was. But inevitably the two sometimes disagreed. The long-drawn arguments over allied strategy, relations with Russia, France, and China, the post-war future, sometimes wore Roosevelt down. He thought Churchill's old-fashioned Conservatism and dogged imperi-alism hopelessly antediluvian. Sometimes he felt he was almost drag-ging Churchill into the twentieth century very much against the latter's wishes. In one respect Churchill's leadership of wartime Britain was unfortunate, in that it gave Roosevelt and the Americans generally a slightly lopsided view of British attitudes. Many of his Conservative colleagues, including Eden, were less reactionary than Churchill; and the views of his Labour colleagues in the government, particularly Attlee and Cripps, were much more progressive on India and imperial questions generally than Churchill's. But when Americans looked at Britain and thought about British policy, they tended to see just Churchill. This probably helped to increase

American suspicions of British policy which were in any case deep-seated, not only with Roosevelt but with most of his circle. As liberals and anti-imperialists they had lived all their lives in a political world where the British Empire stood for much that was reactionary and objectionable. They were convinced that the main British objective was the restoration of that Empire in full and that this governed every British move in allied diplomacy. This made it difficult for Americans to judge even British strategic proposals objectively. If Churchill and the British Chiefs preferred a Mediterranean to a Cross-Channel strategy it was because they wished to restore the British position in the Mediterranean and the Middle East: if they hankered after amphibious operations on the Sumatran or Malayan coast rather than a land campaign in Burma, it was due to a similar preoccupation with the recovery of Singapore, as opposed to aiding the hard-pressed Chinese. Their suggestions about Balkan operations, even their plans for the occupation of Germany, had the sinister motive of involving the Americans more deeply in Europe's post-war problems. Many of these suspicions were voiced in Roosevelt's confidential talks with his advisers, as the *Iowa* made its way towards Cairo. In addition the British were suspected of lukewarmness towards Roosevelt's 'new thinking' on international problems and plans for a new international order. Churchill's vigorous anti-Communism was certainly no help in the difficult task of inveigling the Russians into the fold; and for Cordell Hull the British Empire with its system of preferential tariffs was a major obstacle to his plans for a new international economic order.

Churchill's attitude to Roosevelt was less complicated, and more trustful. He had watched with admiration Roosevelt's gradual conquest of the deep-seated American isolationist tradition, and remembered with gratitude the successive acts of practical assistance—the Destroyers-Bases deal, Lend-Lease, the increasing participation in the Atlantic battle—which Roosevelt had coaxed out of a reluctant Congress, even before Pearl Harbour brought the United States into the war. His attitude to Roosevelt personally was cordial, loyal, and understanding and he showed uncharacteristic patience, for the most part, with what he regarded as Roosevelt's sometimes uninformed comments·and proposals for Europe and the Empire. Privately he thought that Roosevelt and the Americans generally knew very little and understood less about India and other imperial problems: nor did he think the President particularly knowledgeable about Europe. Eden too was dubious about F. D. R.'s knowledge and judgement in international affairs. Still Churchill was conscious that he had much to be thankful for. Without the Americans Britain could not have hoped to emerge victorious against Germany, let alone Germany and Japan combined; and Roosevelt above all men had brought the Anglo-American alliance about. That alliance was going to be as vital in shaping the peace settlement as it had been in war, and Churchill regarded it as paramount.[5]

Churchill himself, like Roosevelt, was at the height of his power and reputation in 1943. The British people might have their reservations about Churchill as a post-war Prime Minister and even more reservations about the Conservative party he led, as was soon to be apparent: but they whole-heartedly supported him as the only possible wartime leader. In the House of Commons his position was overwhelmingly strong: even in the darkest moments of the war, after the collapse of the British Empire in South-East Asia and the defeat at Tobruk, his critics had never been able to muster more than twenty or so votes against him in a vote of censure. Now that the tide of war had turned, his critics in parliament could do no more than indulge in occasional sniping. His coalition government represented the whole spectrum of the major political parties and therefore guaranteed parliamentary support. His Labour colleagues in the government, led by Clement Attlee, were both efficient and loyal. Former critics in his own party who had supported Neville Chamberlain were silenced. The most prominent of them indeed were either dead or had been exiled to various diplomatic posts abroad. But if his position at home was strong, Churchill was well aware that Britain's international position, especially *vis-à-vis* the Americans, was weak. American troops in the European theatre now nearly equalled the number of British troops. The United States' productive machine had outstripped the British contribution to the war. Britain's need for US financial aid added a further dimension to a relationship which was coming to be one of dependency rather than equal partnership. Already the Americans had begun to take a tougher tone with their British allies. At the Washington and Quebec conferences Churchill had felt obliged to agree to a definite date for the Cross-Channel Attack, which he had resisted for over a year. In addition Churchill was deeply concerned about the growing American flirtation with Russia. Hull's lack of support for Eden in Moscow and Roosevelt's unwillingness to meet Churchill privately before the Three-Power conference were ominous signs. Though his regard for Roosevelt and his general confidence in the President's goodwill remained largely undiminished, Churchill was worried. The intrusion of Chiang-Kai-Shek into the scene further disturbed him.[6]

Neither Roosevelt nor Churchill had met Chiang-Kai-Shek before. The Chinese leader had spent most of his life fighting to unify his country. A professional soldier trained in Japan, a Christian and something of an ascetic in his personal life, Chiang, like most army officers everywhere, was deeply conservative in his political outlook. He regarded the powerful Chinese Communist Party with its half-a-million guerilla troops as quite as much an enemy of China—the China he wished to see—as the Japanese. In the thirties he had been criticized for devoting more of his energies to fighting his internal enemies than to resisting the Japanese invaders, who had seized Manchuria at the beginning of the decade and occupied most of the Northern provinces, including the old capital, Peking, in 1937. Shanghai, Nanking, and Canton in the South had followed, together with a good part of the fertile Yangtze valley. The Japanese now controlled most of the north and centre of the country. Chiang and his Nationalist forces had been driven into the remote and backward provinces of the south-west, losing control of most of the industry and commerce of the country. The effects of this withdrawal were not only military and economic but also political and psychological. Chiang and his Kuomintang party were isolated from the intellectual and liberal elements in Chinese politics. His wartime capital of Chungking was in the most backward part of China, dominated by feudal warlords and landlords. There were few liberal influences to offset the General's conservative, or as some called it, 'Fascist', tendencies. Nationalist China was, in fact, effectively a one-party State, with Chiang as dictator. The Communists in the areas they controlled had won the allegiance or at least the passive support of the peasants, by carrying out drastic reforms to curb the power of the landlord class and hold down rents. This Chiang was unable or unwilling to do, and as a result his popular support was ebbing away.

After twenty years of war and civil war, the plight of Nationalist China was desperate. The economy was in ruins, inflation rampant and uncontrolled. The administration was inefficient and corrupt, the people war-weary. Famine was endemic. The Nationalist armies were demoralized, ill-equipped, often unpaid. Although nominally consisting of over three hundred divisions, it was estimated by US experts that only about sixty of these were capable of even sustained defensive action: less than thirty divisions, mostly US-trained, could be expected to carry out offensive operations. The US air forces in China, led by General Chennault, were the Nationalists' only other effective weapon. The Nationalist armies had virtually ceased to conduct aggressive operations against the Japanese.[7]

Theoretically Chiang's power as President, head of government, and Commander-in-Chief of the armies was absolute. In fact he was in the hands of the warlords, the rich landlords, and corrupt financial cliques, centred round the finance minister, H. H. Kung, who was also the Generalissimo's brother-in-law. The Chinese leader also depended heavily on his wife, the formidable Madame Chiang-Kai-Shek, whose relatives and friends dominated the Nationalist administration. The General himself was vain, obstinate, isolated from criticism and in any case very unwilling to listen to it. So bad was the Chinese situation, it is true, that even the most efficient, able, and honest administration would have been hard put to cope with it. The Nationalist administration, which was none of these, had ceased to try. It looked to its allies, particularly the United States, to win the war and rescue China from its plight. In the mean time the Nationalists expected the United States to increase its supplies by air and, as an earnest of future intentions, demanded that Britain and the United States should mount large-scale military operations in South-east Asia. These operations should have the objective first of opening a land route for supplies to China, and secondly clearing the whole of Burma of the Japanese. Politically, Chiang was prepared to follow the US lead, and he trusted Roosevelt. But he was equally suspicious of 'the Imperialists' (Britain) and 'the Communists' (Russia). [8]

Churchill, Eden, and the British Chiefs of Staff regarded Chiang and the Nationalists with disfavour politically, and had a low opinion of their military abilities. The Nationalist leaders were known to be bitterly opposed to European imperialism; it was indeed almost the only point on which Chiang agreed with the Communists. As a result of considerable pressure Chiang had already that year induced Britain to abandon the extraterritorial rights which British subjects had long enjoyed in China. The next step would probably be a demand for the return of the great port and naval base of Hong Kong, now occupied by the Japanese. In spite of Chinese denials, the British Foreign Office also suspected Chiang of further expansionist aims, threatening possibly British possessions in South-east Asia and even India itself. Churchill regarded it as particularly sinister that Chiang had shown a marked sympathy for the aspiration of the Indian nationalist leaders, most of whom had been jailed for the duration of the war.

It was hardly likely therefore that Churchill would welcome any proposal to elevate the Nationalist regime to a higher place in the councils of the Allies. But quite apart from their suspicion of Chiang, the British view was that the Americans grossly exaggerated the importance of China's contribution to the war effort, and overestimated her ability to play a major role in the world after the war. All the evidence they had suggested that the Nationalists were doing very little fighting and were unlikely to do much in the future. It was questionable how far operations designed primarily to help them were really worthwhile, especially as the main operation suggested was a land campaign in Burma, for which Churchill and the British Chiefs had little enthusiasm. To commit British troops to the swamps of Burma was, they felt, to meet the Japanese in the conditions which most favoured them. In any case, the course of the war towards the end of 1943 suggested that such a campaign might be unnecessary. The great sweep of American naval and military operations across the Pacific, already begun, supplemented perhaps by similar British operations against Malaya and the Dutch East Indies, might make it possible to bypass the Japanese forces in Burma altogether. Cut off eventually from their supplies, they would then be forced to surrender. As for the post-war international organization, in any Council of the Big Four China could not pull her weight, and would simply join the United States and Russia in opposing British imperial interests. 'It is an affectation to pretend China is a Great Power', Churchill minuted to Eden in October 1942. In a Big Four Council, China would merely constitute a 'faggot vote' for the United States. Eden agreed that the American view of China's potential future role was 'unreal' but felt Britain had to accept this unreality for the sake of the Anglo-American alliance. Churchill was not really convinced, but tended in practice to fall in with this view. He had agreed at Quebec that the British Chiefs and the newly constituted South-east Asia Command under Mountbatten should examine the possibility of land operations in Burma and amphibious operations in the Indian Ocean. But Churchill and the British Chiefs were agreed that any such projects must rank well below Cross-Channel and Mediterranean operations in any order of priorities. [9]

Roosevelt however 'continued to cling', as his biographer puts it, 'to his high hopes for China's postwar greatness'. By November 1943, however, his view of the Nationalists and of Chiang was not quite as roseate as it had been. A string of reports from his representatives on the spot had cast doubts both on China's military contribution and on the Nationalists' competence, political strength, and commitment to democracy. General Stilwell, who somehow managed to combine the posts of Chief of Staff to Chiang, Commander of US troops in the China/India/Burma theatre, and deputy to Mountbatten, described the Chinese armies as 'underfed, untrained, and neglected'. Chiang he described as 'inactive yet grasping'. Gauss, the US Ambassador, was equally scathing. 'Chiang', he informed his government, was only a 'minor asset'. China, he thought, was too war-worn and ill-equipped to do much fighting. The Nationalists felt they had done their bit by resisting the Japanese when the latter were at their strongest, and could now sit back. Moreover Gauss doubted the Nationalists' commitment to the political values enshrined in the Atlantic Charter. The Kuomintang, he thought, was more concerned with holding power after the war than creating a democracy; indeed the Nationalist government in his view displayed unmistakable 'Fascist-like tendencies'. Other US representatives supported these views: one of them described Chiang as 'an Emperor in all but name'. Some Americans, however, thought differently. Hornbeck, the State Department's Adviser on Political Relations, still judged the Nationalists to be the 'strongest power in China' and believed that Chiang's regime was supported by the Chinese people. Patrick Hurley, whom Roosevelt had dispatched to report on the Chinese situation, conceded that little could be expected militarily from the Nationalists and agreed that they wanted to reserve their forces for a future internal struggle with the Communists: politically, however, he thought Chiang 'opposed to imperialism and communism, but in favour of democracy'—a view which Chiang himself did his best to reinforce.

Roosevelt, therefore, was exposed to conflicting reports. He was inclined to accept the growing view that not much could be expected of China militarily. The case for military operations in Burma and nearby areas could no longer be held to rest on any immediate military dividend that support for Chiang was likely to bring. It rested rather on the need to bolster up China and Chiang's regime against the danger of complete collapse. As for Chiang himself, there seemed no real alternative to continuing support for him. The Americans were stuck with the Generalissimo. Moreover Roosevelt was aware that the Americans were to some extent caught in a propaganda trap of their own making. China, as Gauss remarked, had been long 'over-praised'. For years the American public had been fed on a diet of uncritical praise of China's war effort and the towering quality of Chiang's leadership. To cast doubts on these cherished beliefs now would administer too great a psychological shock. So far as support for Chiang was concerned Roosevelt felt it was too late to draw back; at the same time he remained firmly convinced that it was essential to build China up as a future bastion of his projected new international order. [10]

Whatever their differences of view over Chiang-Kai-Shek,

Churchill and Roosevelt had no doubts about the importance of the fourth allied leader—Joseph Stalin. The latter had been the leading figure in the Soviet system since the death of Lenin twenty years earlier. For the past decade he had exercised almost absolute power. Those leaders of the Revolution who had the character and stature to oppose him had been eliminated. Western observers, including Churchill, sometimes postulated a degree of control over Stalin exercised by the shadowy figures of the Soviet Communist Party's policy-making body, the Politburo; but there was in fact little evidence for this. Stalin seems to have regarded his associates Molotov, Voroshilov, Mikoyan, and Kaganovitch as servants and instruments rather than colleagues. Their advice might be useful on tactics and methods, but their influence on decisions of strategy and high policy was questionable. Stalin in any event held the ultimate strings of political and military power in his hands, since he combined the posts of party boss, head of government, and Commander-in-Chief. The Soviet dictator's dominant characteristics were ruthlessness, cunning, patience, and suspiciousness. It was these characteristics which had enabled him to survive the years of revolutionary conspiracy and struggle for political power, and he carried them into his dealings with the West, reinforced by the ideological doctrines which depicted all capitalists as enemies. But even without the added stimulus of Marxism-Leninism, his attitude would probably have been the same. Suspiciousness was his ruling characteristic, though it had not yet degenerated into complete paranoia. As Milovan Djilas put it, 'he trusted nothing he did not hold in his fist'. His suspicions of Western policy, as we have seen, were not entirely without cause: British and French policies in the inter-war years had often seemed to favour Nazi Germany and Fascist Italy, while attitudes to Russia had been wary or openly hostile. The wartime alliance had in some ways reinforced these attitudes. In particular Stalin suspected Churchill of delaying the invasion of wartime Europe as much from a desire to see Russia and Germany exhaust each other, as from purely strategic motives. Equally, of course, Churchill had not forgotten the unofficial Soviet-German alliance of 1939–41, and the fact that Stalin had been quite prepared to see France go down to defeat and Britain in mortal peril without lifting a finger. Stalin for his part, according to Djilas, regarded Churchill as 'a far-sighted and dangerous bourgeois statesman'. Yet, if the same authority is to be believed, he compared Churchill to a petty thief. Churchill and Eden in return oscillated between hope and fear in their attitude to Stalin. They respected his abilities but loathed his cruelties—a point of view which was shared by their Labour colleagues Attlee and Bevin. At times Churchill thought he was making some progress in establishing some sort of normal relationship with Stalin: at other times he was infuriated by the dictator's rudeness, surliness, and overbearing demands, and despaired of him. Eden, too, swung between these poles. In March 1943 he had told Roosevelt that he did not think Stalin 'wanted to communize Europe'. At the time of the Moscow conference he had even cabled Churchill that the Russians 'were in a mood to move with us in all matters if they are accepted as equals'. Stalin he thought was 'oriental and a hard bargainer, but more reasonable than Molotov'. Neither of the British leaders wanted to abandon completely the hope of tolerable relations with Russia after the war. But at the same time they viewed the prospect of Soviet post-war power with increasing dread. In the end Soviet policy remained something of a mystery to them, as Stalin no doubt intended. Churchill described it, in a famous phrase as 'a mystery, wrapped in an enigma'. Eden's feelings on Stalin personally were probably summed up in a cable to Churchill from the Moscow conference—'Joe is unaccountable'. None the less Russia had sustained the bulk of land operations against Germany for two years and would continue to be a crucial member of the Alliance until the war was won: and after it was won Russia would be the dominant power in Europe. The effort to reach agreement had to be continued.[11]

Stalin's attitude to Roosevelt before the Teheran conference probably included a large element of curiosity. As a 'bourgeois statesman', the leader of the wealthiest capitalist country in the world, Roosevelt could hardly be trustworthy. But could he perhaps be as naïve as he seemed? However that might be, the inherent conflicts of capitalism made it inevitable that there should be divergences between US and British interests in many areas. The Moscow conference indeed had made it evident that the two differed both on questions of strategy and on European questions. There could be nothing but profit for Russia in exploiting and widening these differences, especially if Roosevelt were so obliging as to co-operate. Meanwhile the latter alone among the three leaders approached the meeting with unreserved feelings of cordiality and optimism. He knew little of Stalin, or indeed of Russia and the Soviet system, but he had confidence in his ability to establish a good personal relationship. His confident judgement to Churchill earlier, 'I think I can handle Stalin better than your Foreign Office or my State Department', was now about to be tested. To the US ambassador to Russia he had earlier expressed the view that Stalin did not want anything but security, and that if the United States adopted an open-handed attitude to Soviet demands, the Soviet leader would be won over, and 'would work for democracy and peace'. As the Americans saw it, this hopeful attitude was not unwarranted. Soviet territorial demands did not seem to them totally unreasonable. They amounted, after all, at this stage, to little more than a demand for the restoration of Russia's 1917 frontiers. The Soviet government had disclaimed any desire to impose its system on other states, and had given some proof of this by its dissolution of the Comintern, the international Communist bureau, through which Moscow had often dictated the policies of other Communist parties. The Soviet reluctance to commit themselves to any specific principles for an Eastern European settlement did not seem to the Americans to be necessarily sinister, or as ominous as it seemed to Eden and Churchill. Indeed at that juncture it had suited American tactics very well. The general Soviet posture of goodwill and cordiality at the Moscow conference had seemed to the Americans most encouraging. The apparent Soviet acceptance of Western principles for the treatment of Italy, Germany, and France, and Soviet willingness to consider future economic co-operation were other good auguries. Moreover the abolition of the Comintern and the apparent restoration of a degree of religious freedom gave promise of removing two of the major causes of Soviet–American friction and suspicion.[12]

2. The Allied Delegations to Cairo

The American and British leaders both took large delegations to the Cairo conference. The American delegation was particularly large—over fifty in number—and particularly strong, if anything over-weighted, on the military side. The Americans had sometimes felt at previous conferences that they were 'out-gunned' by the British and that this had contributed to the fact that they had been outmanœuvred. They were determined this should not happen again. Their delegation included not only the three Chiefs of Staff and the President's personal representative on the Chiefs of Staff Committee, Admiral Leahy, but also a large number of senior and junior staff officers and planners from the War and Navy Departments. A number of serving officers from the Far East were also summoned to Cairo at the outset of the conference—Stilwell, Chennault, Wedemeyer (Mountbatten's American Deputy Chief of Staff), and Merrill (Assistant Chief of Staff to US forces in the China/Burma theatre). Also present were General Somervell, Commander of the US Army Service Forces, and General Deane of the US Military Mission in

Moscow. Significantly General Eisenhower, commanding in the Western Mediterranean, was not summoned to give his views until late in the conference.

By contrast Roosevelt took only a few political advisers, and his choice of these was eclectic. Hull was left behind, together with his entire State Department team, on the face of it an extraordinary state of affairs. For political advice Roosevelt relied on his confidants and close associates, Hopkins, Harriman, and Leahy, together with various US ambassadors summoned from their posts—Steinhardt (Turkey), Kirk (Egypt), Winant (Britain), and of course Harriman from Moscow. It was the advice of the men on the spot rather than the State Department planners that Roosevelt wished to have available. He had however brought two civilian advisers from the Washington government, neither of them State Department men or government career officers. John McCloy attended in his capacity as Assistant Secretary of War, and Lewis Douglas as Deputy Administrator of the War Shipping Administration. Both of these, however, were concerned with the war effort rather than diplomatic or foreign policy matters.

Two of those mentioned above—Harriman and Deane—were at the Moscow conference and have been discussed earlier. Much the most interesting and important of the large contingent who had not been with Hull at Moscow were Marshall and Hopkins. General George Marshall was the outstanding American soldier of his generation. He had been selected for the post of US Army Chief of Staff in 1939 over the heads of many men senior to him. In Washington—a city not noted for its veneration of public men—his unquestioned integrity, as much as his ability, commanded respect from politicians and servicemen alike. Roosevelt relied on his judgement implicitly. Indeed part of the reason for the delay in appointing a Supreme Commander for 'Overlord', about which Churchill had been complaining for some time, was that it had been tentatively agreed that the command should go to Marshall. When it came to the point however, neither Roosevelt nor the other Chiefs of Staff wished to lose Marshall from his key position in Allied strategic decision-making. Certainly Marshall's withdrawal from Washington and the Chiefs of Staff would have been much felt, not least because of his colleagues' deficiencies. Admiral Ernest King, the Chief of Naval Operations, was a tough and indefatigable naval officer, of great ability: he was also crotchety, hot-tempered, and narrow. As an ally he was, as one British colleague put it, 'not a good co-operator'. Nor was Dill's judgement that 'King's war is in the Pacific' entirely unfair. The great naval and amphibious sweep across the Pacific towards Japan was, save for MacArthur's South-west Pacific operations, largely an American Navy campaign. A war without either Allies or Army participation was very much to King's taste. Consequently, on the Chiefs of Staff Committee he paid lip-service to the accepted Allied doctrine that European operations should have priority, while often undermining it in practice. In addition his First-World-War service in London had given him a distrust of the British. The third member of the US Chiefs was Arnold, the Chief of Army Air Forces, an able man in his own sphere and easy to work with, but lacking in any profound strategic appreciation. Outside air matters he had little to offer. Nor was the defect remedied by Admiral Leahy. Leahy had been a reasonably competent Chief of Naval Operations and made a tactful chairman of the Chiefs of Staff but like the others had no profound contribution to make to allied strategy. He owed his position as Roosevelt's personal Chief of Staff to the friendship they had established in pre-war days, rather than to commanding abilities. Because he had served in Europe, as Ambassador to the Vichy government from 1940 to 1942, Roosevelt sometimes discussed political matters with him. In this sphere, however, his principal contribution was to add to the anti-Gaullist atmosphere which surrounded Roosevelt. But the responsibility of taking an overall view of Allied Grand Strategy and achieving co-ordination with allies largely fell to Marshall.

Among the other military men, the Far Eastern commanders included two colourful personalities, Stilwell and Chennault. Stilwell was a soldier of great talents and a fine trainer and leader of troops, but a bitter rancorous malcontent who found little good in most of his fellow human beings. His nickname 'Vinegar Joe' aptly described him. Few men could have been less suited to posts which required him to co-operate not with one ally only but two. He habitually referred to Chiang as 'Peanut' and had a low view of most of the Chinese leaders, military and political. His opinion of most British leaders in his area was not much higher. He liked Mountbatten at first but soon became critical of him, as he did of most people. Chiang and other Chinese leaders had more than once intimated to Roosevelt that Stilwell was unsuited to posts requiring diplomatic as well as military abilities: but both Roosevelt and Marshall had faith in Stilwell and it was not until the end of the following year that they were induced to remove him. Chennault, on the other hand, the dashing commander of the US Air Forces in China, had one quality that Stilwell lacked. He was able to get on with Chiang-Kai-Shek. Consequently, he was often able to get what he wanted where Stilwell could not. What Chennault, a devotee of the air arm, wanted was more planes and bases to pursue his aim of defeating the Japanese by strategic bombing. Hurley, Roosevelt's roving Ambassador in the Middle East, and later Ambassador to China, was another colourful figure. A conservative lawyer and business man and a former Secretary of War under Hoover, he was like many of those round Roosevelt deeply suspicious and critical of British imperialist aims. Though devoted to US interests himself, he felt it was 'un-allied' of British representatives to show the same assiduity in pursuing their country's interests. Wedemeyer, Mountbatten's Deputy Chief of Staff, was another American with a rather similar outlook, though he mellowed somewhat during his association with Mountbatten.[13]

Of the civilians in the US party Harry Hopkins was undoubtedly the most influential. Until the war Hopkins had had no experience of foreign affairs, still less of military problems. His career had been an entirely civilian one, first as an administrator of one of Roosevelt's 'New Deal' agencies, later as Secretary for Commerce. But he had taken to diplomacy and global war as a duck takes to water. He possessed an almost unique ability to read his chief's mind, and could be trusted to convey Roosevelt's wishes to others with absolute fidelity. It was these qualities and Hopkins's patent and disinterested devotion to Roosevelt's interests which inspired the President's trust. Others in turn came to realize that Hopkins could always gain Roosevelt's ear and could sometimes influence him—and moreover knew when to try. The war revealed other qualities no less valuable, most importantly a mental toughness and determination which more than compensated for his ailing physique; and an instinct for essentials and getting to the heart of the problem. Like most liberal Democrats he was anti-imperialist, but this did not as a rule affect his relations with his British allies. He liked and got on well with Churchill and was more concerned to win the war than to outsmart his allies or avoid being outsmarted by them. The same can be said of Averell Harriman, who also had the ear of the President, the more so because of his recent experience of both London and Moscow.[14]

The British delegation was more evenly balanced than the American. Churchill brought to Cairo not only the Foreign Secretary Eden, but the permanent head of the Foreign Office Sir Alexander Cadogan, as well as other Foreign Office officials. His delegation also included Harold Macmillan, the British Minister attached to Eisenhower's HQ, and Knatchbull-Hugesson the British Ambassador to Turkey, together with the British Minister Resident in the Middle East, R. G. Casey, and the British Ambassador to Egypt, who were of course on the spot. Churchill also brought with him one other member of his government, the Minister of War Transport, Lord Leathers, to discuss supply and shipping problems with the Americans. With Eden and Cadogan by his side Churchill was not so cut off from expert diplomatic advice or dependent on his own intuitions as Roosevelt. Cadogan's qualities supplemented Eden's. He was a calm, experienced, and shrewd diplomat and administrator, whose published diaries reveal also a shade of that slightly patronizing self-assurance which has not always contributed to the popularity of British diplomats.

The British military delegation was also naturally a strong one. It included from the Far East Mountbatten himself and General Carton de Wiart, Churchill's personal representative with Chiang-Kai-Shek. Mountbatten had been appointed to South-east Asia with the task of instilling new life and energy in a theatre where morale was low and which had become sluggish and inactive. He was well fitted for the task. Bursting with energy, enthusiasm, and enormous self-confidence, full of ideas, he had the quality of drive to an almost excessive degree and wore out people even more quickly than Churchill. But he also had charm and the ability to get on with his allies. He went down well on the whole with the Americans, most of whom, including Marshall, thought well of him. Churchill was also able to consult his Middle East Commanders, General Maitland Wilson, Admiral John Cunningham, and Air Chief Marshal Douglas, who were all on the spot, together with Naval Commander-in-Chief Levant, Admiral Willis and the Air Commander-in-Chief Mediterranean, Air Chief Marshal Tedder, who had been summoned from their posts.

Churchill and the British Chiefs of Staff were therefore in a position to draw on enough sources of information to give them a reasonably comprehensive picture of the situation over the whole Mediterranean theatre as well as the South-east Asia/China/India theatre. The Chiefs of Staff themselves of course, as with the Americans, were the heart of the military delegation. Of these, Admiral Andrew Cunningham, the First Sea Lord, was more of a fighting sailor than a strategist. He had in any case only recently joined the Chiefs of Staff, though he had served briefly as British representative to the Combined Chiefs in Washington. He was content on the whole to speak up for the Navy, and leave the strategic direction of the war to his (in this field) more experienced colleagues. Air Chief Marshal Sir Charles Portal, the Chief of Air Staff, was a highly experienced staff officer of outstanding ability and considerable intellectual quality, whose even temper and

patience often made him a good mediator when disagreements between the British and American Chiefs became acute. Some
Americans thought more highly of him than his colleagues. But the
outstanding figure on the British as on the American side was the
Army Chief of Staff, General Alan Brooke. Brooke had held his
position for just two years, during which the Allies had climbed from
the pit of defeat to a point when victory in the war could be glimpsed.
Like Marshall among the Americans he was generally acknowledged
to be the most able British soldier of his generation—which has not
always been the case with holders of his post. His obvious ability and
decisive, rather forbidding manner enabled him to command the
respect of all his military subordinates, including the difficult and obstreperous Montgomery. He was not afraid to stand up to Churchill,
and frequently did so. On Brooke, indeed, fell the principal burden of
checking the Prime Minister's wilder flights of fancy, aided by the
invaluable Ismay, who formed the link between the Prime Minister
and the Chiefs of Staff. Impatient and quick-thinking, Brooke found
it difficult to work with slower minds and was often forced to keep a
tight rein on his temper in his discussions with Allies. He concealed a
sensitive and emotional nature under a controlled mask, drove himself
relentlessly, and was often desperately tired. Opinions differ as to
whether Brooke or Marshall had the most profound grasp of strategy.
But that they were both men of outstanding character and ability cannot be questioned. The two men had inevitably many differences of
opinion over three and a half years of partnership in global war, but
came eventually to respect and admire each other's qualities.

One other member of the British delegation must be mentioned,
since his role in the higher direction of the war was crucial. Field
Marshal Sir John Dill, Brooke's predecessor as Chief of Staff, was the
British Army representative on the Combined Chiefs of Staff, in effect
Brooke's deputy in Washington. Normally when the British Chiefs
met directly with their American counterparts their deputies were
naturally not required. Dill, however, had obtained a special position
in Washington through his relationship with General Marshall.
Marshall eventually came to respect Brooke, but he had from the
beginning of their relationship both respect and affection for Dill, who
possessed personal charm and integrity as well as professional ability.
Having the confidence of both Marshall and Brooke, Dill was an
invaluable link and interpreter between the two. It was taken for
granted that he should be at the conference. [15]

The Chinese delegation, which was small, can be more briefly
summarized. It consisted essentially of Chiang, though the secretary-

general of the Chinese National Defence Council and a number of Chinese generals and representatives of other services came with them. The Chinese generals made a poor impression on their British and American allies, but it is difficult not to sympathize with them. With no experience of such meetings, a record of defeat, and almost completely isolated from other theatres of war, it is not surprising they had little to offer to the deliberations on strategy. Madame Chiang however was a different proposition. A member of the powerful Soong family which dominated Chinese politics, she was an exceptionally strong-willed and forceful character, egotistic and intolerant of opposition. Western observers frequently judged that she dominated her husband, and certainly Chiang had complete trust in his wife: it also seemed to some observers at Cairo that, since Madame Chiang customarily interpreted for her husband, it was not always clear whose opinions they were listening to. But, if the British at Cairo were beginning to feel that they had declined from the position of an equal partner, the Chinese were on the face of it at an even greater disadvantage; for with little to offer they had much to ask. This disadvantage, however, was offset by Roosevelt's willingness to give.[16]

3. The Cairo Agenda

So far as the British were concerned the purpose of the Cairo conference was, and always had been, primarily military. Its prime function was to provide Churchill and the British Chiefs of Staff with the opportunity to persuade the Americans that the date for 'Overlord' should not be regarded as governing all other factors to the extent of imposing a rigid strait-jacket on Mediterranean operations. In particular it should not be allowed to dictate an absolutely rigid timetable for the return of troops and landing-craft to the United Kingdom. As Churchill had pointed out to Roosevelt, these troops and craft would be effectively withdrawn from the combat against the enemy for perhaps six months, which would be a wasteful misuse of resources. Meanwhile the Italian campaign would be prejudiced: all hopes of taking Rome and advancing north to the Pisa–Rimini line would have to be abandoned. In addition opportunities further east—of bringing Turkey into the war or opening the Dardanelles—would be lost. Already in his view a valuable opportunity of exploiting German weakness had been missed through the failure to support the Dodecanese operations.

In their final memorandum for the Cairo conference, drawn up at a Chiefs of Staff meeting on 10 November and approved by Churchill, the British Chiefs repeated the arguments used by Churchill to Roosevelt in his messages of 20 and 23 October. Much had changed since the Quebec conference. Italy had been invaded and knocked out of the war, the Russians had made sweeping advances on their front, there was a greater possibility of bringing Turkey into the war. The memorandum hammered on two themes: (1) that it was essential to keep up pressure on the Germans all through the coming winter and spring in order to weaken them as much as possible by the date of 'Overlord'; (2) that the British in no way departed from their commitment to 'Overlord', and fully expected it to take place 'next summer'. But they attached no particular importance to any given date (that is, to 1 May 1944). The memorandum therefore recommended (1) that all necessary measures should be taken to sustain the Italian offensive at least until Rome had been taken and the advance made to the Pisa–Rimini line; (2) that the guerilla forces of the resistance in Yugoslavia, Greece, and Albania should be nourished with supplies as much as possible and every effort made to stir up trouble through sabotage etc. in the Balkan satellites Romania and Bulgaria; (3) that the attempt to bring Turkey into the war immediately and to open the Dardanelles to allied shipping should be continued. The memorandum also repeated a proposal for a unified command in the Mediterranean which had already been put to the Americans but had been sidetracked by the US proposal for an overall European Command, to which Churchill had returned a dusty answer two days earlier. The British Chiefs wished to see the British Middle East Command, covering the Eastern Mediterranean, unified with Eisenhower's North African/Italian Command, covering the Western Mediterranean. The purpose of this proposal was to avoid the kind of fruitless appeals for help from one theatre commander in the Mediterranean to the other which had characterized the Dodecanese fiasco. [17]

By presenting the arguments in this way, Churchill and his advisers sought to reassure the Americans that their hearts were still with 'Overlord' and their proposals were not intended to substitute priority for Mediterranean operations for the agreed strategic priority of Cross-Channel operations. But to minds as suspicious of British intentions as the Americans', the references to Turkey and the Dardanelles, Balkan resistance, and the importance of Italian operations were quite enough to keep suspicion alive. They could see the date of 'Overlord' receding in the distance once again. Once weaken the stranglehold of the fixed date and absolute priority for 'Overlord', and Mediterranean operations might get out of hand, swallowing up resources intended for that purpose. The Americans feared the 'suction-pump' effect of such operations. They had already, under great pressure, made one concession on the 'Overlord' timetable by agreeing to postpone by six weeks the departure of sixty-eight landing-craft from the Mediterranean. They did not wish to be led further along that path. The proposal for a unified command in the Mediterranean also had its sinister side: it would make it easier for a Mediterranean commander to switch resources—American resources—from agreed and limited operations in Italy to unforeseen and possibly unlimited operations in the Balkans and Eastern Mediterranean. As it had been agreed at Quebec that the principal Mediterranean command should go to a Briton, in return for the appointment of a US Commander to 'Overlord', this was a worrying thought for the Americans. The British proposals were not likely therefore to reassure. Brooke was not mistaken when he wrote in his diary 'I feel that we shall have a pretty serious set-to, which may strain our relations with the Americans'.

The British Chiefs had no intention of laying any special stress on South-east Asian operations at the conference, though they knew that the Americans would wish to discuss them, and Mountbatten and Stilwell would be there to report on their plans. Something would have to be done in Burma certainly. But the British view was that any decision on these operations should await a firm agreement on plans for the European theatre and the information on Russian intentions which they expected to get from Stalin. Any discussions with Chiang-Kai-Shek and the Chinese at Cairo could at best be provisional. After the meeting with Stalin they could return to Cairo to put their European plans into final shape and then see what would be left over for South-east Asia.

Similarly, Churchill had no intention of being drawn into any political discussions with Chiang-Kai-Shek over British imperial possessions in South-east Asia. He continued to view the President's plans for China's future with considerable scepticism. Certainly if Roosevelt chose to discuss the future settlement in the Far East, he could not stop him. He might even have to go along with any political commitments the latter made to Chiang, for the sake of the Anglo-American alliance, provided they did not tread on British interests: but that was not the purpose for which he himself had come to Cairo. [17]

The American approach to the conference was very different. On the military side they were determined to pin down the British firmly to their Quebec commitment to 'Overlord'—both its strategic priority and its timetable. As a guarantee of this they desired British agreement to command arrangements which would ensure that the use of troops and resources everywhere throughout the European theatre would be geared to helping the Cross-Channel operation and prevent any unnecessary diversion of resources to the Mediterranean. Their final recommendations to the President therefore, submitted during the *Iowa*'s voyage, were that 'Overlord' on the agreed date should remain the primary ground and air effort for 1944; that strategic bombing from the UK and Italy should be primarily aimed at helping this objective; that 'Overlord' should have priority in resources over the Mediterranean, and that the latter theatre should do the best it could with the resources already allocated to it; that subject to these limitations the allied forces in Italy should continue to exert 'maximum pressure' on the Germans, but with the object of aiding 'Overlord' rather than in pursuit of any specific objective such as Rome or the Pisa–Rimini line; that eventually substantial forces from Italy should be diverted to a landing in the south of France, thus further shifting the axis of operations away from the Mediterranean; and finally that the US delegation should make it absolutely clear to the British that the United States would have no part of any Balkan campaign. Operations in the Balkans should be limited to commando raids, strategic bombing (presumably with what was left over after the diversion of most strategic bombing resources to 'Overlord') and supplies to the guerillas. Efforts should continue to be made to bring Turkey into the war, but it should be made quite clear to the Turks that little US aid would be available for them (thus ensuring the unlikelihood of such efforts prevailing).

To guarantee the sanctity of this order of priorities, the US Chiefs again proposed that a Supreme Commander (it was assumed it would be Marshall) should be appointed to take charge of all Anglo-American operations against Germany, that is, both 'Overlord' and the Mediterranean. This Supreme or Overall Commander would be responsible for supervising these operations and allocating resources between them. Subordinate to him would be not only the North-west Europe and the Mediterranean Commanders-in-Chief, but also a strategic bombing 'supremo' who should control American bombers in the United Kingdom and Italy as well as British Bomber Command. In effect this new Overall Commander would take over most of the functions of the Combined Chiefs of Staff in Europe. With such vast powers, and especially with the prestige of Mashall invested in the office, the Supreme Commander would be virtually invulnerable to pressure from Churchill or the British Chiefs of Staff. Subject to these proposals the US Chiefs agreed that the British recommendation of a unified command for the whole Mediterranean should be accepted.[19]

There was never any possibility that Churchill and the British Chiefs would accept these command proposals, which would have almost completely removed their power to influence the higher direction of the war in Europe. The US Chiefs themselves recognized that their plan would encounter strong British opposition. To counter this opposition they suggested that in the last resort the Americans should be prepared to accept a British Overall Commander for Europe instead of Marshall—provided it were Dill. Marshall had complete faith in Dill's integrity, and believed that he had served long enough in Washington to have imbibed correct (that is, American) notions of strategy. Unlike other British generals Dill could be trusted to maintain priority for 'Overlord'. Roosevelt, too, though he naturally favoured the Overall Commander plan, was doubtful if the British would accept it, and was not sure that it would be a good thing to accept a British Supreme Commander—even Dill—as a quid pro quo for British acceptance. No doubt he foresaw that American public opinion would object to a British Supreme Commander for European operations in which American troops would ultimately outnumber the British. However it was agreed that the proposal should be formally submitted to the British at Cairo and that, if it failed, they should none the less accept the British plan for a unified command in the Mediterranean. Marshall, with characteristic fairness, pointed out that the Americans had consistently recommended the concentration of authority in the hands of one Supreme Commander for each theatre, and even if their more sweeping plan was not accepted, it would be illogical not to go this far. With equal fairness, he added that the British had some reason to feel sore over Eisenhower's refusal to help at the time of the Dodecanese operations. A single Mediterranean theatre commander might have taken a different view. Theatre commanders, he added drily, were never keen to spare resources from their own theatre. In any case, the Americans agreed, they should go ahead and unify all American strategic bombing forces, UK and Mediterranean, under one commander. It would be a step in the right direction.

On operations in South-east Asia the American Chiefs contented themselves with the recommendation that a limited amphibious operation should be conducted to recapture the Andaman islands, supported perhaps by a British/Indian movement down the South

Burma coast towards Akyab and Ramree, with Rangoon, the Burmese capital, as the immediate objective. No specific mention was made in their memorandum on South-east Asia of the major land campaign in Upper Burma to open land communications with China, which had figured largely in previous discussions with the British. It was assumed that something would be done, but the truth was the American planners had begun to have doubts about the contribution towards winning the war which might be expected from China, whose maximum contribution to any offensive land operations might be no more than the equivalent of nine or ten US divisions, if that; and these would have to be equipped and supplied from US resources. For any more Chinese divisions to be brought up to concert pitch intensive training under US supervision would be required, and this would take time. By the time larger Chinese forces were available, the US amphibious attack across the Central Pacific and from New Guinea would very likely have brought the Japanese to the point of capitulation. Therefore all perhaps that was needed to be done was to send the Chinese enough supplies to enable them to maintain their defensive operations and continue holding down the Japanese forces in China. That objective could probably be achieved by stepping up existing airborne supplies over the High Himalayas, without opening up a land route for supplies via Upper Burma. In that case, the US planners asked themselves, was a land campaign in Central and Upper Burma really necessary? Could the Japanese army in those areas be bypassed and left to wither on the vine? The snag was, of course, that Chiang was insisting on a campaign to free Burma as well as amphibious operations in the Bay of Bengal; and without the encouragement supplied by some military activity of this kind, Chinese morale might finally crack altogether. Roosevelt himself attached great importance to this argument, and Marshall was more inclined than his colleagues to believe China might still play a useful military role in the war. For the moment however, the US Chiefs were content to let the issue be thrashed out in the coming staff conferences with the British and Chinese, and to see what Mountbatten and Stilwell came up with; and also what Chiang thought he could do and what he would demand. The precise nature of the campaign for Burma therefore, and the role of China in that campaign, remained uncertain.

Finally therefore the US Chiefs proposed that in his first meeting with Chiang-Kai-Shek Roosevelt's agenda should consist of a request to Chiang to outline the Chinese situation; Chinese views on possible Soviet entry into the war; a progress report on operations against

Japan; an enquiry into what assistance precisely the Chinese could furnish in a possible campaign in North Burma; a discussion of additional air bases in China for Chennault's proposed strategic bombing operations; and a discussion of US supplies and training of Chinese forces. In addition the President should also be ready to discuss, if the Chinese initiated discussion, US forces and command arrangements in the China/India/Burma theatre (the vexed question of General Stilwell's position); and certain post-war problems that the Chinese might wish to raise. Prominent among these might well be Chinese participation in the occupation of Japan and future security arrangements in the Far East. A Sino-American treaty of alliance and the provision of bases in China for the US would probably be involved in any such arrangements, as the discussions on board the *Iowa* indicated. Roosevelt also made it plain that he was already thinking of the post-war settlement in China and the difficulties which might exist between China and Russia. Marshall and King raised the point that the USSR would probably seek access to a warm-water port in North China and might wish to control communications to it—which would run through Manchuria. As Roosevelt pointed out, however, the Chinese themselves would want to regain Manchuria, once the Japanese had been evicted, and also wanted some say in Outer Mongolia, which the USSR had detached from China in the 1920s. This discussion no doubt confirmed Roosevelt's decision to take these matters up with Chiang and Stalin. The President also no doubt took note of Marshall's rather depressing estimate of the condition of even the best Chinese troops (the US-trained ones); and of the US Chiefs' general view that the British felt that only minor amphibious operations could be undertaken in the South-east Asian theatre unless more extensive US help were offered them. As neither King was prepared to spare such additional resources from the Pacific nor Marshall from 'Overlord', there were going to be obvious difficulties here.[20]

For his initial meeting with Churchill, the US Chiefs proposed that Roosevelt should concentrate on Europe: firstly he should discuss command arrangements and seek to persuade the Prime Minister of the merits of the US proposals; secondly he should make it crystal clear that the United States would have nothing to do with any Balkan operations; and thirdly he should discuss possible arrangements for a quick occupation of Germany in the event of a sudden German collapse. This involved the consideration of the precise areas which should be occupied by US, British, and Soviet forces. A plan had been prepared by the allied planners in London under General Morgan, the Chief of Staff designate to the eventual Supreme Commander

(COSSAC). This plan envisaged a US zone in south-west Germany and a British zone in the north-west of the country. It became evident in the discussions on the *Iowa* that Roosevelt did not like this plan. He suspected it was a British plot to involve the Americans in the problems of post-war France, across which US lines of communication from South Germany would have to go. At one point, according to the US records, Roosevelt made the startling observation that the British would 'undercut every move the US made in the southern zone'. Quite what the President meant by this extraordinary remark about an ally is difficult to say. It was too much for General Marshall, who pointed out that the proposed zones were the logical outcome of the existing plans for 'Overlord' and the axis of advance of the British and US armies into Germany, which would follow from the fact that the Americans would be on the right of the advance and the British on the left. With that the subject was allowed to drop, leaving the US Chiefs perhaps a little bewildered.

The US Chiefs had also put on the agenda for the President's first meeting with Churchill questions arising in relation to Russia, particularly the Soviet proposals for involving Turkey and Sweden in the war. If the President did not raise Turkey, Churchill himself probably would. Their specific recommendations, however, had made it clear that the Turks could expect little help from them. If Churchill could persuade the Turks to enter the war and perhaps fight a campaign with what help the British could provide, well and good. As the Turkish government had just finally rejected Eden's limited proposals for the use of air-bases as too dangerous, it did not seem very likely that Churchill would be successful. [21]

The discussions on board the *Iowa* were discursive and covered a wide range, as discussions with Roosevelt, and indeed with Churchill also, were apt to be. The Italian political situation, the numerical balance of British and American military forces, the European Advisory Commission, the arming of French troops, the Italian navy all came up. What emerged most strikingly from Roosevelt's *obiter dicta* on these and other topics was twofold. Firstly the President was clearly determined to steer clear of direct involvement in European political problems after the war as far as possible. US troops were to be withdrawn from every part of Europe except occupied Germany as soon as possible; and even in Germany Roosevelt hoped to withdraw the US occupation forces in 'one year or two'. Armed action by ground troops in the event of civil disturbance or a threat to peace would be up to Russia and Britain. Any US contribution he hoped to limit to naval and air forces.

Secondly the President had become deeply suspicious of British intentions and motives, to an extent which would have shocked Churchill had he been privy to the conversations on the *Iowa*. Roosevelt's remarks about Morgan's proposals for occupation zones were the most striking evidence of this, but he also seems to have regarded Eden's European Advisory Commission and British policy in relation to Italian affairs with some suspicion. Nor, as we have seen, was he happy about a British unified command in the Mediterranean. By contrast neither Roosevelt nor indeed his Chiefs of Staff expressed any doubts about Soviet motives or intentions in Eastern Europe. All this was not a happy augury for the kind of Anglo-American rapport which Churchill still hoped could be maintained.

It was also clear that the President intended to have political as well as military discussions with Chiang-Kai-Shek. It is not possible to be as precise about Roosevelt's plans for these as it is in the case of US military plans for the conference. The President had discussed Far Eastern problems in a general way with Cordell Hull before the Moscow conference but apparently made no attempt to get a more definite view, still less a specific 'position paper', from the State Department between then and the departure for Cairo. Possibly he discussed what he might say to Chiang and what proposals he might make with Hopkins on the journey out, but there is no record of this. But it seems clear from what he actually did at Cairo that he had decided to hold out to the Chinese leader glowing prospects for the future: and that this decision was made to some extent as a part of his general plan to elevate China to world status in the post-war international order: and partly as an inducement to the Chinese to hold on, even if the military discussions did not give them what they wished.

Whatever may be the case, Roosevelt had a full schedule ahead of him in Cairo. It was equally clear that Churchill and the British delegation were likely to experience much frustration and many disappointments. [22]

CHAPTER VII

THE FIRST CAIRO CONFERENCE:
PROBLEMS WITHOUT SOLUTIONS

1. Preliminaries

Chiang-Kai-Shek was the first of the three leaders to reach Cairo.
When Churchill and his party arrived in the *Renown* on the morning
of 21 November, they found Chiang and his wife already installed in
a villa half a mile from Churchill's. The conference was to take place
in the residential suburb of Mena some miles west of the centre of
Cairo, and close to the Pyramids. Full-scale plenary meetings of the
staffs were to be held in the Mena House Hotel. For the President's
convenience it had been arranged that plenary meetings of the three
leaders and other meetings involving Roosevelt should normally be
held at his villa, which the US Ambassador, Kirk, had vacated for the
occasion. Churchill's villa, three miles west of Roosevelt's, had been
made available by the British Minister-Resident in the Middle East,
R. G. Casey. The British and US Chiefs of Staff were similarly
accommodated in separate villas, as were other members of the
various delegations. The strictest security measures were in operation: troops and anti-aircraft guns surrounded the conference area,
which had been cordoned off from the rest of Cairo.

Needless to say, Churchill had not been idle on the voyage out. Not
only had he conferred with his colleagues on the *Renown* but he had
taken advantage of a stop at Algiers on 16 November to inspect the
Free French situation at first hand. After a day at Algiers, Churchill
and his party had proceeded to Malta, where they were joined by the
other members of the British Chiefs of Staff, Brooke and Portal.
Although Churchill was unwell with a heavy cold and temperature, he
had called the Chiefs of Staff together on 18 November for a final discussion before Cairo. The meeting seems to have been used by
Churchill mainly as a dress-rehearsal for the arguments he intended to
deploy at the conference and which he had already expounded in fact
both to Roosevelt by cable and to the British War Cabinet. In what
Brooke describes as a 'long tirade' he repeated his regrets about the
lost opportunities in Italy, the Balkans, and the Dodecanese, the need
to get things going again on all these fronts, and the desirability of

bringing Turkey into the war. The British General Alexander, commanding the Allied Armies in Italy, was present at the meeting and had assured the Chiefs of Staff that if the Americans would agree to leave their precious landing craft in the Mediterranean till mid January, he could carry out an amphibious operation on the Italian west coast which would give them the great prize—Rome. The Americans, Churchill argued, must be made to see sense about the delay to 'Overlord'.

Brooke for his part did not disagree with Churchill's general line. Indeed he was writing gloomily in his diary at this time that the United States was 'a drag on our Mediterranean strategy' and 'I despair of getting the Americans to have strategic vision'. He felt he should have resigned rather than agreed to a fixed date for 'Overlord' at Quebec. Brooke, like Churchill, considered that the only chance of a successful 'Overlord' in 1944 was to further weaken the Germans by maintaining unremitting pressure on the only active front—the Mediterranean—during the next six months. Like Churchill, too, he seems to have also retained a faint hope that such pressure, combined with the forward movement of the Russian armies, might so weaken Germany as to make 'Overlord', when it came, comparatively easy. None the less, Brooke was worried about his chief's mood. He felt that Churchill's frustration over the Dodecanese failure, reinforced by what he diagnosed as a hankering after a 'purely British theatre' in the face of growing US military superiority, might lead the Prime Minister to overplay his hand. He feared Churchill might retaliate for American unhelpfulness over the Dodecanese by threatening non-co-operation with the Americans in 'Overlord', which would merely increase US obstinacy. These fears were not unreasonable. Churchill had already antagonized Roosevelt, Marshall, and the US Secretary for War, Stimson, by his persistence over the Dodecanese business, and also by his ready response to the Soviet suggestion that Turkey should be brought into the war. He had added fuel to the flames by using General Alexander's pessimistic report of the situation in Italy to suggest a postponement of 'Overlord' to Stalin. By so doing he had fatally weakened his purchase with Roosevelt and the US Chiefs of Staff, as Brooke had feared.[1]

It is true that Brooke himself was not always the ideal advocate to present a case to the Americans. One American historian indeed, citing Brooke's often critical diary assessments of Marshall and Eisenhower as strategists, has described him as 'anti-American'. This was not so: it would be possible to find in Brooke's diaries equally critical judgements of almost every leading British general, including

Alexander and Montgomery. Brooke was both impatient and self-confident and his standards were of the highest, which meant that at the highest level of command he tended to be hypercritical in his judgements. But tiredness and frustration sometimes led him to exaggerate differences of opinion, as his biographer concedes. The gulf between what he wanted and what the Americans were prepared to agree to was wide enough, but not quite as wide as Brooke in his more sombre moments imagined: and as Dill had pointed out to him, the Americans had made many concessions to British strategic ideas in the past. Even from their present position of strength they were in fact to make some at Cairo. But Churchill and Brooke were not perhaps the ideal men to extract these concessions from them.

Eisenhower, summoned from his Allied Command in the Western Mediterranean to Malta, was also the recipient of Churchill's views on the necessity of keeping up the pressure in Italy, and even extending its scope eastwards to the Balkans. As one of the early proponents of the 'Overlord' strategy, Eisenhower was as unresponsive as other Americans. His view, which he was later to expound at Cairo, was that Mediterranean operations should be judged solely by their contribution to 'Overlord'; and no more resources should be diverted to that theatre than were necessary to ensure holding the position and keeping a sizeable number of German troops occupied. This to his mind ruled out Aegean and Balkan operations in the immediate future; and in Italy even the advance to the Po valley might have to wait on a favourable opportunity. This reaction, coming from an American who was still a Mediterranean commander, was not encouraging. [2]

Roosevelt meanwhile was making his way in a leisurely fashion towards Cairo. The *Iowa* arrived at Oran on the morning of 20 November, two days before the conference was due to begin. He could have been in Cairo the next morning, the 21st. However, quite apart from his desire not to be inveigled into a premature conclave with Churchill, Roosevelt had also determined to find time for discussion with his North African commanders, more particularly perhaps because Eisenhower was already in his mind as a possible 'Overlord' commander, if it was decided that Marshall was indispensable in Washington. Eisenhower, just back from Malta, met the President at Oran, and travelled with him by plane to Carthage, just north of Tunis. After settling in Eisenhower's villa, Roosevelt spent the afternoon visiting his son's photo-reconnaissance air squadron; and the evening with Eisenhower, Spaatz, the US theatre air commander, and Tedder, the British air commander. The following day

Roosevelt dallied further, spending the afternoon in a tour of the Tunisian battlefields with Eisenhower. He did not leave for Cairo until late on the evening of the 21st. He would get to Cairo punctually for the start of the conference and not before.

During his talks with Eisenhower it became clear that Roosevelt's doubts about parting with Marshall had increased. Eisenhower, however, was still put on notice that he would probably return to Washington as 'Acting Chief of Staff': but he was also made aware that Admiral King and others wished Marshall to remain at his post, and incidentally that Churchill would accept either man for the 'Overlord' command. He must have felt that his future was still uncertain. Much clearly depended on whether the British continued to resist the appointment of an 'Overall' commander for all European operations. The intensity of the American Chiefs' commitment to this concept can be judged from the fact that they were prepared to accept Dill's appointment instead of Marshall, as the price for British acceptance. Equally they would have agreed, if Marshall had become 'Overall' European Commander, to Montgomery's appointment to the actual command of the 'Overlord' operation. It is interesting to speculate on the results of such a combination. Marshall, like Brooke, might well have been able to overawe Montgomery by sheer force of character. There were not many who could.

Be that as it may, it is clear that the Americans regarded the acceptance by the British of the concept of an 'Overall' European Commander as one of the major objectives of the conference, second only in importance to the maintenance of priority and a fixed date for 'Overlord'. As was predictable, they were to fail in this first objective, together with its subsidiary requirement of a European air 'Supremo'. The second objective—priority for 'Overlord'—they were able to attain with only minor concessions. So far as the Far East was concerned, and the role of China in the war, the Americans were to be partially successful. Their objectives here were an amphibious operation in the Indian Ocean, the development of strategic 'shuttle-bombing' of Japan via Indian and Chinese air-bases, the 'stepping-up' of supplies over the 'Hump' to China, and, with rather less conviction, a land campaign in Burma to open the Burma road. The paradoxical result of the negotiations here was ultimately that they failed to get the operation in which they most believed ('Buccaneer'), but did get the Burma campaign about which they were beginning to have doubts, and which neither the British Chiefs, nor Churchill, nor the SEAC commander Mountbatten believed to be strategically sound.[3]

This mixed bag of results no doubt accounts for the generally luke-warm American reaction to the conference, to which I shall revert later. It must be said, however, that it was Roosevelt's wishes which really shaped the course of the conference. By ensuring that the Chinese were present from the beginning, and by delaying his own arrival, he achieved his two main objects: firstly that the conference should not be the Anglo-American 'get-together' before Teheran and, in particular, not the private conclave with Churchill that the latter had wished: and secondly that Far Eastern problems should dominate the agenda and permit the British relatively little time to press their case on 'Overlord' and the Mediterranean. In the upshot, South-east Asia provided nine of the items on the agenda for the Combined Chiefs, and 'Overlord'/Mediterranean operations only four. Roosevelt was also determined that he should win Chiang-Kai-Shek's confidence and trust by ensuring that the latter returned from Cairo with something substantial, both militarily and politically. In the up-shot, Chiang did not obtain militarily all of his large and often un-reasonable demands: but the undertakings on Burma and allied promises on supplies were sufficient for Roosevelt's purposes. Politi-cally, moreover, Roosevelt felt able to give Chiang large assurances as to the return of lost territories, and subsequently obtain Churchill's and Stalin's support for them; which ensured that Chiang would not only remain in the war, but would continue to be pro-American. Not surprisingly Roosevelt, almost alone among American participants, considered that the conference had been on the whole a successful one for the United States.

Conversely, for the British the Cairo conference was to be an uphill fight. They had lost the main battle before it had begun, when the Chinese were invited, and so were not able to go to Teheran with the broad Anglo-American agreement on European and Far Eastern strategy for which they had hoped. The most they were able to get the Americans to agree to was that the British case should continue to be put at Teheran. British successes at Cairo in fact were largely of a negative kind. They succeeded in finally laying to rest the American proposal for an 'Overall' European commander, together with any notion that Russian and Chinese representatives should permanently figure in the operations of the Combined Chiefs of Staff. They were able also to postpone a final decision on 'Overlord' versus the Mediterranean (and also the Mediterranean versus the Pacific) until after Teheran. In the mean time Brooke and his colleagues had to spend much (as they considered) wasted time on Chinese matters, while Churchill, with increasing frustration, had to sit by while the

President was closeted with Chiang and his wife. It was not a happy conference for the British.

2. The Conference Day by Day

Although the Cairo conference lasted only five full days, compared with the twelve days of the Moscow conference, a great deal of activity was packed into it. Two tripartite plenary meetings were held, one with the military staffs and their political chiefs present and one with only the three heads of government and their political advisers. In addition there were three meetings of the Anglo-American military staffs (the Combined Chiefs) without the politicians, at two of which the Chinese military representatives were present for part of the time. The US and British Chiefs of Staff also had separate daily meetings during the five days of the conference. There were, too, many encounters of a less formal kind. Churchill and Roosevelt lunched or dined together three times. The British Chiefs gave a dinner for their US counterparts and vice versa. Churchill met Marshall for lunch on one occasion. The Americans, however, devoted more personal attention to the Chinese than the British. Roosevelt had separate conversations with Chiang on several occasions during the conference; Marshall and Hopkins each had one formal meeting with the Generalissimo. Generals Arnold and Somervell had a special meeting with the Chinese staff representatives to discuss supply. Nor did the British entirely neglect the Chinese. Churchill met the Generalissimo separately on three occasions, and Eden also conferred with Wang-Chung-Lui, the Secretary-General of the Chinese National Defence Council. There were many other informal talks, most of them not formally recorded. Churchill and Brooke in particular had made use of the twenty-four hours spent waiting for Roosevelt to confer with their Middle East commanders and Mountbatten. They had also met formally to consider the wealth of American documents and proposals which had emerged from the *Iowa*'s voyage. These included the US Chiefs' proposals for the conference agenda, to which the British submitted an alternative (and simplified) agenda: the US proposals for operations in SEAC, on future boundaries of this Command and on the development of long-range strategic bombing of Japan from India and China: and the American estimates of the current military position of Germany and Japan, both of which, it was concluded, were now forced on the 'strategic defensive', though capable of isolated offensive moves. The British Chiefs had plenty of work to do. It was perhaps as well they had an extra day to do it in. Finally however all the participants were assembled. On Monday 22 November the conference began its work.[4]

22 November. The conference agenda: priority for SE Asia operations: the 'Overlord' timetable and the East Mediterranean: 'Buccaneer' and the Burma campaign

Roosevelt's plane landed at 9.35 a.m. at Cairo West. He was met by Churchill and escorted to his villa, where Hopkins and Leahy were also to stay, and where he conferred with the US Ambassador Kirk and with Averell Harriman. The staffs immediately got to work. The US Chiefs met at eleven o'clock at Mena House Hotel with Leahy in the chair: the British Chiefs, presided over by Brooke, were already in session. Since both Marshall and Brooke had orderly minds, the military discussions at Cairo followed an agreed agenda and proceeded in an orderly fashion, save when they were interrupted, much to Brooke's annoyance, by attempts to grapple with the Chinese. The political talks, however, proceeded in a more irregular and informal manner, in accordance with Roosevelt's custom. The US Chiefs had prepared a provisional agenda for Roosevelt's talks with Chiang-Kai-Shek and Churchill, but it does not seem that he adhered to it very systematically. It is difficult to be precise about this, since many of the conversations were not minuted or officially recorded. This informal method suited Roosevelt's style: he preferred to try to control the course of a discussion, rather than be bound to a fixed agenda; and a discussion which was not officially recorded could not easily be used afterwards as evidence of a binding commitment. This too suited Roosevelt, since he was often using such conversations as a means of clarifying his mind and feeling his way towards an eventual decision. There was method in the President's madness, though that method often drove others to madness. Even Churchill, who was not noted for his punctiliousness in sticking to a timetable or agreed procedures, complained to Eden that 'the President was a charming country gentleman but his business methods were non-existent'. But Roosevelt was not to be disturbed from the accustomed tenor of his ways.

Sensibly, the British and US Chiefs took as their first priority the business of getting an up-to-date picture of each other's minds. While Field Marshal Dill was reporting to the British Chiefs on American attitudes, Winant was explaining to the American Chiefs the major British preoccupations, as he saw them. Both men did a faithful and accurate job. Fresh from his regular meetings with the American

Chiefs, Dill reported that the latter were highly suspicious of British intentions on 'Overlord', largely as a result of Churchill's activities. They believed that the British still regarded the Mediterranean as the primary target, in spite of the Quebec agreement to make the Cross-Channel Attack the priority for the future. They themselves were determined to stick to 'Overlord', though they might be willing to show some flexibility on the precise date. They were also interested in operations in South-east Asia, and wished to discuss them. As for the Eastern Mediterranean, they had been prepared to accept a purely British attempt to 'rush' the Dodecanese, but this had not come off. They were afraid any further operations in that area might constitute a serious drain on 'Overlord' resources. The Americans, Dill went on, were still very much interested in their project for an Overall European Commander and a strategic air 'supremo', and intended to press these. Brooke's response to all this was predictably stiff. The Americans, he implied, were wilfully misunderstanding the British position. The point of maintaining pressure in the Mediterranean was to further weaken the Germans and so make 'Overlord' more practicable. If the Soviet armies could maintain their offensive, the combined effect of simultaneous pressure from the east, south, and south-east might compel so great a withdrawal of German troops from the west as to make 'Overlord' comparatively easy. As for South-east Asia, this was a British command, and the Americans were no more entitled to be consulted about specific operations there than the British were about specific operations in the Pacific. This was an unwise attitude to adopt, as Dill pointed out. The Americans were more likely to be forthcoming with supplies and equipment for operations they had approved. This of course applied to landing craft amongst other requisites. Brooke might have retorted that Admiral King had shown no particular willingness to supply the landing craft required for the proposed attack on Sumatra (Operation 'Culverin') from his own vast Pacific resources. However the CIGS contented himself with saying dismissively that they had the American paper on operations in South-east Asia and could discuss them at their next meeting. There was apparently no discussion of the US Command proposals at this meeting, though the British Chiefs were forced to return to them later to administer the *coup-de-grâce*. But Brooke knew already that so far as they were concerned, the US proposals on this subject were a 'non-starter'. The British Chiefs agreed to look at the South-east Asia proposals next day and passed on to consider the agenda for their discussions proposed by the Americans. The latter had proposed a rather elaborate agenda, in which the Combined Chiefs would begin by reaffirming the 'Over-all strategic concept for the prosecution of the war and basic undertakings in support of it' (that is, the defeat of Germany *first* and priority for 'Overlord'): continue with the general subject of what other European operations (primarily, what Mediterranean operations) could be fitted into this general strategic pattern, but first discussing the US estimate of the German situation, and com-manders' reports on the strategic bombing offensive and the Battle of the Atlantic; and including also a discussion of the state of readiness on 'Overlord' and various other projected operations, and the plans for US/British/Soviet collaboration. Then they should proceed to the war against Japan and similarly consider the general 'enemy situ-ation', the overall strategic plan for the defeat of Japan, reports on South-east Asia, China, and the Pacific, the programme for transfer of resources to the Far East after the defeat of Germany, and specific operations for the defeat of Japan. Then they should proceed to the allocation of resources, prepare their final report for the President and Prime Minister, approve any necessary directives, and discuss the forthcoming Teheran conference.

Interestingly enough the American agenda had put the 'Overlord'/Mediterranean topic ahead of the Far Eastern theatre on the agenda. They clearly wished to confront their British colleagues with the basic Quebec agreement on 'Overlord' priority and to embed any discussion of Mediterranean operations firmly within the framework of this prior strategic agreement. The British Secretariat, however, no doubt after consulting Brooke, had concluded that this agenda was unnecessarily long-winded and elaborate, and would lead to discussing the same subjects under more than one heading. General Hollis, therefore, as head of the British Secretariat, had produced a simplified agenda, in which the Combined Chiefs would reaffirm the 'basic agreements', and then discuss Overlord and the Mediter-ranean: then the war against Japan: then hear progress reports etc. This, it was pointed out, would cover most of the points on the US agenda in a simpler way. Hollis's accompanying memo argued that the Combined Chiefs must first settle the contentious question of the lack of flexibility in regard to the 'Overlord' date, since this governed the practicability of other amphibious operations both in the Mediterranean and the Far East: then they should settle command arrangements for all European operations and consider whether a landing in the south of France would be practicable, and if so when: then move on to South-east Asia and hear Mountbatten's and Stilwell's proposals (and presumably the Chinese): and finally deal with other progress reports.

Brooke expatiated on the rationale behind this alternative proposal. Dismissing US fears about the British attachment to the 'basic strategy' ('Overlord'), he remarked that all this had been agreed at Quebec. Therefore little discussion on the first item would be necessary. Clearly progress reports, 'situation' and operational readiness reports should come last, or they would get bogged down in the discussion of too much detail. In one respect, however, they would have to alter the Secretariat's proposal. Propelled, though no doubt reluctantly, by his orderly and methodical mind, Brooke pointed out the logic of the situation in which they found themselves, a logic imposed by Roosevelt's arrangements for the conference. Since Chiang-Kai-Shek, Stilwell, and Mountbatten were already on the premises, and could not be detained from their far-off responsibilities any longer than was necessary, they had to consider South-east Asia operations early in the conference. That subject, therefore, must be considered before European/Mediterranean operations. The British Chiefs accepted the unpalatable logic, and it was agreed that with this alteration Hollis's paper should be transmitted to the US Chiefs.

Then the British Chiefs turned to the *aide-mémoire* which Churchill proposed to use at the conference, based on the discussions between Churchill, the War Cabinet, and the C.o.S. themselves. This dwelt dolefully on the well-worn theme of the setbacks sustained in the Mediterranean during the last few months. The Italian campaign had bogged down; Rome had not fallen in the autumn campaign as had been hoped. They had failed to give adequate supplies, particularly by sea, to the Yugoslav and Albanian partisans; consequently the latter had failed to retain control of some of the Adriatic ports they had occupied, and the Germans were regaining control in the Balkans. Worst of all was the setback in the Dodecanese, where the Germans had also regained control. The effect of these setbacks on the attitudes of Turkey, Bulgaria, and Romania had been disastrous. The cause of all this, Churchill's paper argued, was twofold: the 'rigidity' of the Quebec timetable which dictated the withdrawal of resources from the Mediterranean while they were still needed there, and long before they could be used across the Channel: and secondly the 'artificial line' dividing the Western Mediterranean from the Middle East Command, which had prevented the transfer of resources to the latter commensurate with its responsibilities in the Eastern Mediterranean. Churchill proposed therefore that the withdrawal of troops and landing-craft from the Mediterranean should stop for the time being: the Allies should press on to Rome, step up supplies to the Balkan guerillas, seize a bridgehead on the Dalmatian coast and bring Turkey into the war: and finally, prepare to resume the Dodecanese offensive with an attack on Rhodes by January 1944.

The C.o.S. agreed with the general line of Churchill's argument, but, as often, thought that he might spoil a good case by overstating it. Cunningham felt that a look at the actual work of the Royal Navy would probably show some considerable seaborne transport of supplies to the Balkan guerillas. Brooke agreed. Churchill's paper had also asserted that the Germans had withdrawn seven divisions from Italy. This was not at all certain, and anyway, it was unwise to say so when their thesis was that the Italian campaign was forcing the Germans to send resources there! It was agreed that the C.o.S. would consider the *aide-mémoire* further at their next meeting.

The British Chiefs now felt they were ready to meet their American colleagues that afternoon. After a brief discussion of the administration of civil affairs in Europe, in which Brooke argued (along Eden's lines) that most of this business should be transferred from Washington to London, where the Supreme Commander for 'Overlord' and most of the exiled governments concerned would be, the C.o.S. adjourned.

Meanwhile Winant had been giving the US Chiefs an accurate view of the British Chiefs' state of mind—their wish to take advantage of the Italian situation, the desire to stimulate Balkan resistance, and the need to involve Turkey in the war, without being hampered by a fixed date for 'Overlord' which bore no relation to a changing situation. Winant gave it as his opinion that in Italy the British regarded Rome as the main prize, and were not set on advancing as far north as the Po valley: and that the British commitment to 'Overlord' still remained, though they felt that the date for the operation should be related to the 'right moment' in terms of German morale and resources in the west, rather than a pre-arranged fixed timetable. In response to a question from Admiral King, Winant touched on an aspect of the forthcoming Teheran conference which had been worrying the Americans. They had been receiving for some time reports from General Deane and Ambassador Harriman in Moscow of Russian pressure to maintain the offensive in the Mediterranean. Linking this development with the Soviet demand for Turkey to be brought into the war, and Stalin's unexpectedly mild reaction to Churchill's *démarche* during the Moscow conference, the Americans wondered if perhaps the Russians were becoming less keen on the Cross-Channel Attack than they once had been. Possibly the successes of the Soviet summer and autumn offensive, following the massive victory at Stalingrad, had altered their views on the necessity of this operation. It might be that Stalin now considered the maintenance of unremitting pressure on the Eastern front and in the Mediterranean would be sufficient to bring the Nazi regime down. At Algiers Harry Hopkins had confided to Eisenhower's aide his fears that the whole 'Overlord' strategy was very much open for reconsideration at Cairo and furthermore that the Russians might team up with the British at Teheran in favour of Balkan and Mediterranean operations rather than 'Overlord'. In fact the fear proved groundless, and General Deane afterwards conceded that he had worried the US Chiefs unnecessarily. In his reply to King's question Winant, who had no direct means of assessing Soviet opinion, said cautiously that certainly the British thought the Russians less interested in the Cross-Channel Attack than they had been, and very anxious to get Turkey into the war. General Arnold, harping on the old American fear of 'a Balkan campaign', asked whether the British thought that Balkan operations could be undertaken without interfering with 'scheduled operations' (that is, 'Overlord'). Winant replied, in effect, that the British felt an inexpensive programme of raids, supplies to the resistance, sabotage, and the like would be sufficient in the Balkan area.

It is doubtful if the US Chiefs paid much attention to Winant's soothing assurances on the British commitment to 'Overlord', and lack of commitment to a 'Balkan strategy'. Their fears were too deep rooted. As for the Soviet commitment to 'Overlord', they had, as we have seen, some anxieties. But it is probable they attached more importance to the warning messages from Deane and Harriman, than the opinions of Churchill and the British, who had an obvious axe to grind and might be the victims of wishful thinking. However, Winant's general thesis accorded very much with their own picture of British thinking. It confirmed them in their determination to resist it. They agreed to meet the British at three o'clock that afternoon for a Combined Chiefs of Staff meeting, and see what happened.[5]

That same morning, while Churchill was paying a courtesy call on Chiang-Kai-Shek, Roosevelt had drafted a message to Stalin suggesting that the Americans should arrive at Teheran on 29 November and stay for 'two to four days'. He had also mentioned the fact that the US Embassy in Teheran was some distance from the British and Soviet embassies, and the consequent security risk involved in travelling between the two. In so doing Roosevelt opened the way for a competition between Stalin and Churchill for the privilege of accommodating the President. Roosevelt, concerned about offending either man by a decision to stay with the other, was at first inclined to stay at the US Embassy; but as was usually the case at this period of the Alliance it was Churchill's feelings which the President decided to hurt in the end.

Churchill's visit to Chiang-Kai-Shek passed off quite well. Always intrigued by new and colourful figures, the Prime Minister's first reactions to the Chinese leader were favourable. He found Chiang 'calm, reserved, and efficient', a judgement that those Westerners more continuously in contact with Chiang would have questioned, though they might have agreed with Churchill's opinion that Madame Chiang was 'charming and remarkable'. However the favourable personal impression did not alter Churchill's judgement that the Americans much overestimated the potential Chinese contribution to the war against Japan.

In the afternoon Churchill also paid a courtesy call on Roosevelt, prior to Roosevelt's first meeting with Chiang-Kai-Shek. No doubt the Prime Minister tried to get Roosevelt to discuss the serious business of the conference with him; but judging by Churchill's disgruntled references to the attention Roosevelt devoted at Cairo to the Chinese rather than to him, it does not seem likely that he succeeded to any great extent, either on this or on later occasions. Roosevelt was an artist in avoiding discussion of issues he did not want to discuss. On the other hand he was affable enough to make Churchill reasonably optimistic about the conference.

After Churchill's visit the President had what was probably a longer meeting with Chiang-Kai-Shek and his wife, together with Marshall and Hopkins; and it is quite probable that while they took tea together Roosevelt did begin the discussions with Chiang of Chinese military and political requirements, which occupied so much of his time at Cairo.

In the afternoon, while the political leaders were still exchanging their first courtesies, the British and American staffs gathered at Mena House for their first meeting. On Leahy's suggestion Brooke was voted into the chair. This proved to be something of a doubtful honour, since the Combined Chiefs' meetings at Cairo were to be lengthy, overcrowded, and sometimes bad-tempered. Their first meeting, however, was to be none of these things, since it was devoted mainly to the organization and agenda of the conference. It was agreed without dissent, in the light of Chiang's presence, that Far Eastern business should take priority, as the British had reluctantly accepted at their meeting that morning. In fact, Ismay pointed out, Roosevelt and Churchill had already agreed to hold a plenary meeting with Chiang-Kai-Shek and the military staffs the following day. Taking advantage of the situation, Marshall produced a paper from

Stilwell on China's role in the war, which he suggested the British and US Chiefs should consider at their separate meetings early next morning, and jointly consider when they met later in the day. In the light of the imminent meeting with Chiang-Kai-Shek and the Chinese, there was nothing for the British to do but to fall in with this suggestion. No doubt surprised but pleased to find things going their way, the Americans then made no difficulty about dropping their rather cumbersome agenda in favour of the simplified British proposals. Agreement on the basic strategy was to come first, then Southeast Asia operations, the subject of most concern to the Chinese: only then were they to turn to European strategy. Other Far Eastern operations and the general conduct of the war against Japan would come next and finally the CCS would hear progress reports from the various commanders.

After a brief discussion of the arrangements for the Teheran meeting, Marshall then raised the general question of future Soviet/Chinese relations with Anglo-American Combined Chiefs, in the light of Soviet dissatisfaction with their previous absence from these conclaves, and indications that the Chinese felt the same way. It might be necessary, Marshall suggested, to make some provision for a more permanent arrangement. Since Churchill and the British Chiefs had agreed to the Chinese and Soviet invitations to Cairo with ill-concealed reluctance, this proposal for a permanent complication along these lines found little favour with the British. Ismay indeed doubted whether the Russians wanted anything more than to be invited to full-scale Anglo-American conferences. The Soviet military men had not fully realized, he said, until quite recently, that the Combined Chiefs was a *permanent* body meeting regularly in Washington, and not simply a meeting of the British and US Chiefs at full-scale conferences. Marshall's US colleagues, Leahy and King, also expressed doubts about the practicability of such an expansion of the CCS, the latter pointing out that the Soviet and Chinese representatives could not attend the same meetings, since they were not at war with the same enemy. It was agreed, however, that the Russian and Chinese might be invited to attend selected meetings of the CCS at which their interests were particularly at stake; and that at Teheran at least the Russians must be invited to attend any meetings that were held. Subject to possible further consideration, the matter was then allowed to drop for the time being. There was just time for Brooke as chairman to see to it that they wasted no time going over the agreement on broad strategic objectives and priorities arrived at in Quebec. It was agreed, obviously on his suggestion, that under Item one, the

Quebec formula ('Germany First' and priority for 'Overlord') should simply be restated without discussion. It was a minor victory for Brooke's chairmanship.[6]

The business of the day was not finished however. After Roosevelt had entertained Churchill and Mountbatten to dinner—which seems to have been mainly a social occasion—the two leaders were joined by their Chiefs of Staff for an informal discussion. Like so many of the meetings with which Roosevelt was concerned, there seems to be no formal record. But Brooke and Leahy agree that the main subject of conversation, in keeping with the decision to give priority to South-east Asia, was Mountbatten's projected operations in that theatre, particularly the Burma campaign. Mountbatten presumably outlined the resources, particularly in landing-craft, which would be required for such potential operations as 'Culverin' (an attack on Sumatra) or 'Buccaneer' (an attack on the Andaman islands). Either of these, given the resources, could be combined with the main campaign in Burma which, with Chinese co-operation, was to be a three-part affair. Myitkina in North Burma was to be the first objective, followed at a later, second stage by Mandalay and Rangoon. In the far north it was planned that two Chinese divisions which had been training in India, should advance under Stilwell's direct command into Upper Burma, while another Chinese force, also American-trained, should advance from the neighbouring Chinese province of Yunnan to join hands with Stilwell. These advances would be supported by British offensives in Central and Lower Burma. No doubt Mountbatten intimated to Roosevelt, Churchill, and the CCS that one unpalatable necessity of these plans might be that some transport planes might have to be diverted from flying supplies to China over the 'Hump'. This would not be popular with the Chinese, but they would have to choose which they wanted most—maintenance of 'Hump' supplies or the reopening of a land route from Burma.

It is probable, too, that at this informal gathering it was agreed that the plenary meeting of Roosevelt, Churchill, Chiang-Kai-Shek, and the military staffs should be held at 11 o'clock the next morning, rather than late in the afternoon as had previously been intended. It would then follow immediately on the separate meetings of the US and British staffs, and would clear the ground for a Combined Chiefs meeting in the afternoon, for part of which the Chinese military representatives would be present.

At the end of the first day of the conference then, the pattern for its course was set. It was already clear the South-east Asian and Chinese problems would take up much of the next day's proceedings and possibly the day after. In this sense the pattern imposed by Roosevelt was taking shape. Brooke had only the minor consolation that, as a result of the agreement to rearrange the agenda, the question of 'Overlord' versus the Mediterranean would at least be considered as a clear and separate issue, instead of being embedded in a mass of other and to some extent extraneous issues. Churchill, according to Brooke, was reasonably pleased with his first talks with F.D.R. Brooke himself was more dubious about prospects.[7]

23 November. Burma, the Andamans and Sumatra: Churchill, Marshall, and the Mediterranean: Roosevelt's plans for China: US bases in the Pacific: Chinese fear of Soviet aims: Korea and Indo-China

On the following morning the British and US Chiefs met early. The British staffs returned first to Churchill's *aide-mémoire*. This had contained a proposal for the establishment of a possible bridgehead on the Dalmatian coast, but Brooke expressed doubts about the wisdom of including this in the paper, in view of American phobias about a 'Balkan campaign'. Dill agreed, and added that the important thing was to get American agreement to a unified command in the Mediterranean. It would be up to the new commander, he remarked shrewdly—who would presumably be British—to deal with such problems. In this remark one can see some confirmation of Roosevelt's opinion in the *Iowa* discussions that a unified British command in the Mediterranean might lead to diversions of which the US did not approve. The Americans and the British, however, were not privy to each other's discussions, which was perhaps as well. At all events, it was agreed that it would be wiser to omit the reference and also the questionable statement that the Germans had withdrawn substantial forces from Italy and the Balkans, which Brooke had drawn attention to the day before. With one or two other amendments, the *aide-mémoire* was approved.

The C.o.S. then turned, as agreed with the Americans, to operations in South-east Asia. They had before them the JCS paper recommending the Andamans amphibious assault ('Buccaneer'). The US paper also stated the general claim that the Combined Chiefs should have some say in South-east Asian operations, to which Brooke had objected the previous day. Dill again pointed out the practical advantages of involving the US Chiefs in the approval of SEAC operations, and it was clear that Brooke was prepared in practice to concede the point. The CIGS soon made it clear, however, that he had no great love for the proposed Andamans operation. The amphibious

resources required for it would, he thought, be better used for operations in the Mediterranean—for example for an attack on Rhodes—
than for 'Buccaneer' which he suggested was 'not a particularly
attractive operation'. Echoing Churchill's thought, he pointed out
that to open the Dardanelles and the Aegean for supplies to Russia
would enable the Allies to close down the longer and more expensive
supply route across Iran. Admiral Cunningham introduced a fresh
demurring note in regard to 'Buccaneer'. The capital ships at present
in the Indian Ocean might, he suggested, be required for projected
operations in the Pacific, where US naval resources might be very
stretched. Optimistically, and quite inaccurately, the first Sea Lord
gave it as his opinion that King might welcome such assistance. In fact
King would probably not have welcomed a fleet dispatched by the
Archangel Gabriel in his Pacific sphere, let alone the Royal Navy, as
he was soon to make clear. However the C.o.S. took their cue from
Cunningham's point that naval requirements in the Indian Ocean
and the Pacific were interdependent. The whole pattern of grand
strategy against Japan was involved. It was pointed out that the
planners attached to the Combined Chiefs had not yet produced a
promised report on the general strategy for the war against Japan, on
which Pacific and other Far East naval allocations must be based. The
British Chiefs therefore agreed that they should propose to their
American colleagues that they should defer consideration of the US
Chiefs' paper (and with it a decision on 'Buccaneer') until the
planners' report was available: and the latter should be asked to
produce the report as soon as possible.

Having, as they hoped, side-tracked 'Buccaneer', the C.o.S. then
turned to a report from Mountbatten on his proposed operations in
Burma, a US proposal for long-range strategic air-bases in India and
China, and finally to Stilwell's paper on the future role of China in the
war. Mountbatten in fact was keen to carry out amphibious operations in the Indian Ocean; like Churchill he regarded an extensive
campaign in Burma as about the worst method of attacking the
Japanese position. Nevertheless, in accordance with his Quebec
remit, he had prepared a plan, as has already been noted, for at any
rate the first stage of a Burma campaign. Brooke made his reservations clear: the proposed operations in Upper Burma would be
'considerable in scope' and would probably of their own momentum
lead to further operations in South Burma. Nevertheless Brooke felt
that they were too committed to the Upper Burma operations to withdraw: and no doubt he also recognized the importance that Marshall
attached to Stilwell's plans for his American-trained Chinese troops,

which were to have their first real test in these operations. It was agreed therefore that the British Chiefs should recommend to the Americans that the Upper Burma operations should be carried out, subject to Mountbatten's proviso that he should have the use of thirty-four US transport aircraft (which as he had foreseen would probably have to be taken off the air supply route to China). On the question of amphibious operations, however, Brooke reminded his colleagues that they were committed by their previous conclusion to recommend postponement of a decision in this matter. On the question of long-range strategic bomber airfields, about which there was a separate US paper, and which were also referred to in Stilwell's memorandum, the British Chiefs could simply minute that the Prime Minister had already approved the proposal in so far as it affected India; the appropriate instructions had been sent for the construction of four such bases in the Calcutta area. Two of Stilwell's other proposals—for the Upper Burma campaign, which the British Chiefs had already approved, and the continuation of the US programme for training Chinese troops—passed without much comment. When it came to more ambitious proposals for Chinese operations however, the Chiefs of Staff parted company with the Stilwell programme. Stilwell's paper suggested that as more Chinese troops were trained, they could be used in 1944–5 for operations against Canton and Hong Kong, even, in conjunction with long-range bombing operations, against the Philippines and Formosa. The Chinese troops trained in India were to be moved as quickly as possible into China—Stilwell was anxious that his precious troops should not get further involved in SEAC operations designed to recover Britain's lost colonial territories. None the less, India was to remain their supply base. Lacking Stilwell's faith in the potential of the Chinese forces, the British Chiefs saw no reason why India should serve as a supply base for these ambitious proposals. Moreover General Riddell-Webster, who as Quartermaster General and therefore head of army supply attended many of the Cairo meetings, discounted the proposals as 'logistically impossible'. India could not feasibly serve as a base for such far-off operations, a polite way of saying that the US general could expect a pretty severe grilling at the afternoon CCS meeting.

The whole discussion illustrated the point that in the European war it was possible for Britain and the United States to work together in reasonable harmony for the defeat of Germany, neither State having territorial claims to make or lost territory to regain: whereas in the Far East they could only be, as Professor Thorne has described them, 'Allies of a Kind', since each was fighting a different war for different

ends. The Anglo-American situation in this theatre therefore re-
sembled the pattern of relations between the USSR and the Western
Allies in Europe; and discussion of Far Eastern operations tended to
bring out the worst on both sides. So far as the practical effect of the
discussion was concerned, it already looked as though Mountbatten
might be asked to fight the battle he least favoured (Upper Burma)
while being denied the amphibious operations he would have preferred. There were fierce arguments to come, however, before this
point was finally settled. It was also clear that this controversy about
SEAC operations and the role of China was about to break out in full
force. Simultaneously with the British meeting Marshall was informing the American Chiefs, during their discussion of Stilwell's paper,
that Chiang now seemed more in earnest about committing China's
vast manpower fully to the war. Given Stilwell's favourable opinion of
the potential value of the Chinese, if properly trained and led,
Marshall felt that there would be considerable scope for their use, once
the war with Germany was over and supplies to China could be
improved. Here were the seeds of much heated argument over the
next two days. The official US historians describe these differences of
view over SE Asia and China as being between Britain and China, in
which the United States had to act as moderator. It would be more
accurate to say that it was a difference of view between Britain and the
other two, in which, as in the early arguments over the 1942 Cross-
Channel Attack, Britain had an effective veto—and used it. [8]

It was now time for the plenary meeting at Roosevelt's villa between
the three heads of government and their respective staffs. The
President had spent the first half of the morning talking to Vyshinsky,
who was on his way through Cairo to take post as Soviet representative on the Italian Advisory Council. It provided an opportunity for
Roosevelt to hear at first hand the unfavourable Soviet views on such
dubious Allies as Badoglio and Mihailovich, which they had expressed
to Hull and Eden at Moscow. Roosevelt for his part spoke of his difficulties with de Gaulle, and touched on his trusteeship proposals.
There had also been brief courtesy calls by Churchill, accompanied by
Mountbatten, and Chiang-Kai-Shek with his military advisers. At the
plenary meeting Roosevelt took the chair, but appears to have
confined himself to formally welcoming Chiang and the Chinese delegation, and to have played little part in the discussion. Since South-
east Asia was the subject to be discussed, Mountbatten was called on
to outline his plans, and presented his plan of campaign for land
operations in Burma as set forth in his previous report to the British
Chiefs. He made it plain that the first phase of the British operations

in Central and Southern Burma would be on a fairly modest scale, and also that the land operations might interfere to some extent with the transit of airborne supplies to China.

Churchill then made use of the occasion to 'set out his stall' as it were on the general South-east Asia programme. He remarked of the Burma campaign, for which he had little enthusiasm, only that 'it would be examined by the Combined Chiefs that day', implying that no final decision had been made. He then passed on to paint a glowing picture of naval prospects in the Indian Ocean. A formidable British naval force of capital ships, aircraft carriers, and supporting warships would be assembled in 1944 in that area. Landing-craft and other vessels would be added, to make amphibious operations possible. Churchill however gave no assurance on the date of such operations, or indeed on precisely what operations would be undertaken. He still favoured the Sumatran attack, but if there was to be a contest for the use of amphibious resources, Churchill, like Brooke, wanted them to be used in the Mediterranean first. If, however, they were to be employed in SE Asia, he much preferred 'Culverin'—the attack on Sumatra—to the US-sponsored 'Buccaneer'. If the US Chiefs were not prepared to co-operate in the former operation, as seemed likely, he for his part was not prepared to give a very high priority to the latter.

Chiang-Kai-Shek's response was cautious. Burma, he asserted, exhibiting the characteristic myopia of the leader whose war is strictly limited, was 'the key to the whole campaign in Asia'. But a successful Burma campaign depended in his view on simultaneous amphibious operations, to block off the flow of Japanese supplies and reinforcements from the south via Rangoon. Churchill immediately expressed flat opposition to this view, and refused to guarantee such co-ordination. The fleet would certainly not be ready before late spring or early summer, *after* the scheduled date for the beginning of Burma operations; it would be based on Colombo in Ceylon, and its first object would be to block the Malacca Straits. The Prime Minister was again making it clear that his eyes were focussed on Singapore and Sumatra, rather than Burma. Seeing that an impasse existed, which was not likely to be resolved in a full plenary meeting, Roosevelt proposed that the Combined Chiefs should take the matter up with the Chinese at their meeting that afternoon. The plenary meeting then ended, leaving Churchill no doubt with a less favourable view of Chiang-Kai-Shek, and Brooke with a distinctly unfavourable one. Recording his impressions in his diary, he described the Chinese leader unflatteringly as 'shrewd and foxy', and judged that he had 'no grasp of the larger aspects of war, but was determined to get the best of all bargains'. One might fairly comment that this is usually the aim of most negotiators and is not a peculiarly Chinese characteristic. 'Foxy' or not, it was clear Chiang liked neither Mountbatten's limited proposals for British/Indian operations, nor the possible reduction in airborne supplies, nor Churchill's unaccommodating attitude on amphibious operations.[9]

Churchill and Roosevelt lunched with Hopkins and their personal staffs at the President's villa. It may have been on this occasion that Roosevelt put forward his suggestion that the British should make a gesture to the Chinese by handing back Hong Kong, which China might then lease back to Britain. Thirty years afterwards it does not seem a particularly outrageous suggestion, but like most similar approaches on imperial problems it received a dusty answer from Churchill. However the subject seems to have been concluded amicably, since the two leaders then departed on a sightseeing trip to the Pyramids, leaving the Combined Chiefs to wrestle with the Chinese problem. As was to be expected, the afternoon meeting proved a contentious one. Brooke indeed describes it as both 'heated' and 'stormy'.

It began however fairly quietly and amicably, in spite of the presence of General Stilwell, whose plans for large-scale operations in China, Brooke argued, were far too ambitious. Brooke received unexpected support from King and Leahy. The former remarked, echoing Brooke's view, that all these plans had to be seen in relation to the overall plans for the defeat of Japan, when those finally materialized. King's eyes were fixed as always on his Pacific campaign, and he was aware that the US strategic planners were now very much inclined to the view that the Central Pacific approach to the Japanese mainland should be the main one, and might well make large-scale land operations on the mainland of Asia unnecessary. Marshall alone of the US Chiefs had real faith in Stilwell's proposals. Loyal to his subordinate, he took it upon himself to make the case to the British. Reiterating the point he had made to his American colleagues that morning, he argued that Chiang was now for the first time really showing signs of a willingness to build up large properly trained forces, and to commit them against the Japanese. Stilwell's proposals therefore should be considered sympathetically. Stilwell himself, in fact, was not at all sure that Chiang really was prepared to play a full part even in the Burma campaign, but he did not say so. Instead he played down the Chinese leader's insistence on amphibious operations. 'Naval security' in the Bay of Bengal was all Chiang was really requesting—a highly dubious assertion. Mountbatten also rallied to Stilwell's defence, but specifically on the Burma campaign; as Deputy Commander of SEAC Stilwell was also his subordinate. Reverting to the plenary discussion, the SEAC commander pointed out that what-ever Churchill might now say, he, Mountbatten, had given Chiang to understand that there would be an amphibious operation in the spring, which would probably be synchronized with Burmese land operations. A large naval force at Colombo was of no great interest to Chiang, particularly if it was not intended to support the Burma campaign directly. What the Chinese wanted was the interdiction by sea and air of Japanese sea-lanes to Rangoon and Bangkok.

Marshall and Mountbatten were both faced with opposition, how-ever, since the British Chiefs were opposed to both 'Buccaneer' and land operations in China, and the other American Chiefs at best luke-warm on the latter topic. In the end a compromise formula was agreed, which gave Brooke most of what he wanted. Stilwell's more ambitious plans (that is, other than Burma) required, it was agreed, 'further study' by the planners, who should also look further into Chennault's and Stilwell's plans for strategic bombing of Japan from China. As for 'Buccaneer', the American proposal that it should take place 'as soon as possible' was accepted, but with the clear under-standing that it should be considered in relation to 'other operations' and that no date should yet be fixed.

The Combined Chiefs then turned briefly to the tentative US proposals (as they admittedly were) for Soviet and Chinese represen-tation on the Combined Chiefs of Staff. The American Chiefs con-ceded that they had only briefly discussed the idea themselves, mainly with a view to having some proposal with which to meet the expected Soviet pressure at Teheran. Brooke had no difficulty in securing acceptance for his view that they all needed further time to consider the matter; and a decision was accordingly deferred. A brief general discussion then followed of the expected shortfall of air supplies to China as a result of the demands of the Burma campaign, in which there seemed to be acceptance of this as a necessary consequence. The Combined Chiefs had now ventilated all the main aspects of South-east Asian operations, and were ready to have the Chinese military representatives in. There followed what Brooke regarded as an infuriating, farcical, and pitiful display, and even Stilwell thought a 'terrible performance'. Brooke asked for comments on the proposed operations in Burma and elicited only the reply that the Chinese staffs had not yet had enough time to study the plans and therefore wished only 'to listen to your deliberations'. As the Combined Chiefs had already finished their 'deliberations', this was an embarrassing request. Mountbatten and Stilwell between them managed to retrieve the situation and provide some basis for the meeting to proceed. Mountbatten asked for a report on the readiness of the Chinese Yunnan forces, which were to play an important part in the Burma campaign; and Stilwell then jumped in to give a reasonably optimistic account of the state of these troops, and an outline of their proposed movements. Very soon, however, Brooke impatiently brought the meeting to an end, with the suggestion that the Chinese generals should further examine the plans and come again on the morrow. It had all been, he complained to Marshall, a complete waste of time.

It should be remarked in fairness that Leahy, a slightly more impartial observer of the Chinese than Brooke, judged them to be 'fairly well informed'. Their silence Leahy surmised, correctly it seems, was probably under orders from Chiang-Kai-Shek. The latter had in fact decided that he would not commit himself on Burma until he had met Roosevelt and Marshall again privately, and seen what he could get out of them. It proved to be quite a lot, though ultimately the bonus for Chiang took mainly the form of political rather than military rewards.

Brooke, for his part, in spite of his annoyance and his growing conviction that Chinese affairs were dominating the conference just as he had feared, was probably not too displeased with the meeting as a whole. He had staved off a definite decision on 'Buccaneer' and also put a damper on what he regarded as unrealistic as well as unnecessary plans for operations in China. He and his colleagues were able to relax and enjoy a dinner party with their US colleagues, at which business matters were set aside in favour of a social evening. Churchill and Roosevelt, who had had their relaxation that afternoon, spent the evening on more serious business.[10]

Churchill devoted the evening to the man whom he recognized as his main opponent in the 'Overlord'/Mediterranean controversy— General Marshall. According to Marshall's account to his biographer, the Prime Minister kept him up till two o'clock in the morning, discoursing indefatigably on the advantages of maintaining pressure in the Mediterranean during the coming winter and spring. The familiar topics were covered—Rhodes, supplies to the Balkan resistance, the retention of landing-craft in the Mediterranean for Italian and Dodecanese operations, British objections to placing US strategic air forces in Italy under a central London command instead of the local commander-in-chief (General Eisenhower). Marshall, like Eisenhower, had considerable affection and respect for Churchill, but had developed by this stage a certain immunity to his persuasions. He was not much influenced, so far as the general strategic argument was concerned: but probably came away from the meeting feeling that pragmatically it might be necessary to make some concessions to Churchill's very strong feelings on the 'Overlord' date and Mediterranean operations, in order to retain full British co-operation in other areas such as South-east Asia.

Roosevelt for his part was entertaining Chiang-Kai-Shek and Madame, together with Hopkins and the Secretary of China's Defence Council, Wang Chung-Lui. As usual there is no US record of this meeting, but it is pretty clear that post-war problems rather than current military questions were the main subject of conversation. According to the Chinese records, it was at this meeting that Roosevelt made those large post-war promises to Chiang which were designed to keep the Nationalist leader in the saddle, stiffen Chinese determination to continue the fight, and ensure post-war Chinese friendship towards the United States. This is not to say, however, that Roosevelt did not believe in the intrinsic merits of his proposals. China, he assured Chiang, was to be a permanent member of the 'Big Four' in the projected international organization. Her lost territories—the North Chinese provinces, Manchuria, Formosa, the Pescadores islands—would be restored to her. China and the United States would work closely together to guarantee post-war security in the Pacific within the framework of a mutual defensive alliance, making use of each other's naval and air-bases when necessary. US military aid to China would be continued. The Ryukyu islands, lying just to the south of the Japanese mainland, would be placed under joint US–Chinese trusteeship. It seems probable, though the Chinese record does not mention it, that Roosevelt also touched on the question of Japanese-owned islands in the Pacific at this meeting and that the two men agreed that these should be placed under some form of United Nations supervision and administration: but that military bases in these islands should fall to 'those powers capable of exercising control', as Roosevelt subsequently put it. In this context the phrase was clearly a euphemism for the United States.

It seems that two of the problems that were likely to cause difficulties with the other two Allies were also discussed. Chiang made it clear that he maintained the Chinese claim to Hong Kong and Outer Mongolia. On the former question it seems that the Chinese leader asked Roosevelt to use his good offices with Churchill: on the latter, however, the Chinese record states that Chiang considered this a matter for direct Sino-Soviet negotiations. It may be that the record was 'doctored' at this point in order not to give the impression that Chiang gave Roosevelt *carte blanche* to negotiate with Stalin on his behalf; and was therefore to some extent approving in advance the kind of concessions which Roosevelt subsequently made to Stalin, at China's expense, at Teheran and Yalta. It seems unlikely, however, that so experienced a politician as Roosevelt would not have given some indication that Soviet claims and objectives in China might come up at Teheran, in the context of the US desire for Russia to enter the war. Possible concessions to Russia in terms of joint Sino-Russian rights in Manchuria and Mongolia and Soviet use of Chinese ports had already been mentioned in the *Iowa* discussions, and were clearly in Roosevelt's mind. One possible concession to the Soviet wish for a 'warm-water port'—the internationalization of Dairen—was certainly discussed with Chiang, either at this meeting or at a later one.

Roosevelt and Chiang also discussed other territorial problems in areas adjacent to China. On board the *Iowa* Roosevelt had told the Chiefs of Staff that Chiang wanted Korea to be under joint Soviet-Chinese-American trusteeship: but it appears the Chinese leader had now changed his mind and advocated straightforward independence for that country, to which Roosevelt agreed. Possibly Chiang now thought it would be safer not to concede a Soviet foothold in Korea. Siamese independence, it was agreed, should also be restored. On Indo-China Roosevelt, with his usual blithe disregard of French susceptibilities, suggested some form of UN trusteeship, presumably under Chinese or Sino-American auspices, as a prelude to independence. Chiang agreed, and emphasized that China had no desire to incorporate Indo-China in its own territory.

The two men also discussed China's economic future. Roosevelt promised to give serious consideration to the question of US economic aid to China after the war, and also intimated that China would receive reparations from Japan, probably—as Chiang wished—in the form of goods and raw materials rather than currency. Roosevelt's accompanying offer to give China a place in the occupation of Japan was, however, rejected, Chiang arguing sensibly that it would be too great a burden for China to bear.

On one other point Chiang received a temporizing answer, and was in the upshot to get little satisfaction. The Chinese leader proposed that China should become a full member of the Combined Chiefs of Staff or alternatively of a new Sino-American Chiefs of Staff Committee. In the light of his knowledge that the Combined Chiefs were considering the question, Roosevelt agreed to consult his Chiefs of Staff, but was ultimately obliged to return a negative answer.

However, Chiang must in general have been very pleased with the results of the conversation, which appeared to guarantee the recovery of virtually all China's lost territory with the possible exceptions of Mongolia, Tibet, and Hong Kong. Although very unwilling to allow US resources to be used in future in a way which might serve *British* interests, Roosevelt was apparently ready and willing to use them on China's behalf. The point is all the more noteworthy, since according to his son, Elliott, Roosevelt complained that the Chinese were doing very little fighting and keeping many of their troops in position to watch the Communists rather than employing them against the Japanese. Moreover Chiang had been obstructive until quite recently in relation to Stilwell's training of Chinese troops. Nevertheless, it was vital to keep China in the war. The reliability of Elliott Roosevelt's reporting must be a matter of conjecture, since it is based on his recollection of conversations with his father. But it does suggest that there is much that is not mentioned in the Chinese record, and this seems not unlikely.

According to Roosevelt, jnr. the President gave full vent to his anti-colonialism in his discussions with Chiang and indicated that US influence would be used to make not only France, but Britain also 'toe the line' in this area (that is, conform to the trusteeship ideas indicated in Hull's Moscow paper). If the account is accurate—and in the light of Roosevelt's known views it seems plausible enough—it probably seemed more tactful to the Chinese not to include it in the record. It seems unlikely in fact that this wide-ranging conversation about the post-war world did not include any reference by Chiang to his suspicions and fears of both Britain and the USSR. It seems likely, for example, that he sought American support against any British attempt to reassert former extraterritorial rights in China, or to make use of Chinese naval bases. As for the USSR, Roosevelt may or may not have seen at this time a memo drawn up by Hopkins on Chinese fears of Soviet intentions. That memorandum indeed, which is dated the 23rd, may have resulted from the evening's conversation. At all events Roosevelt was well aware, from previous exchanges, that Chiang feared Russian territorial claims on China and also Russian support for the Chinese Communists. No doubt he assured Chiang that his fears on both counts were groundless. Russia had recently withdrawn from the Chinese province of Sinkiang; and there was every indication (as Hopkins believed) that the Russians regarded Chiang as the best person to create a stable regime in China, though they would like to see the Communists brought into a 'unity' government. Naturally the Chinese record makes no mention of all this, nor of the undertaking that Roosevelt, according to his son, extracted from Chiang that he would soon create a democratic and unified government along these lines. According to Elliott Roosevelt, this understanding was contingent on US support for China against Soviet territorial claims, particularly in Manchuria, which the President said was, therefore, 'on the agenda for Teheran'. But it seems unlikely that Chiang had any intention of carrying out his undertakings.

The Chinese record implies that there was very little difference of views between the two leaders, and Roosevelt himself afterwards claimed as much. To a considerable extent it seems to be true, though, as in the above case this may have been due partly to a certain lack of frankness on the Chinese leader's part. [11]

24 November. The landing-craft stranglehold and the 'Overlord' straitjacket: Rome, Rhodes, and 'Buccaneer': Turkey and the Eastern Mediterranean: Chiang's three demands

As the third day of the conference began, Brooke must have reflected gloomily that things had turned out just as he had feared. Chinese affairs and particularly the Burma campaign had dominated the conference so far and would probably continue to take up some of their time on the third day. They had still not come to the main issue— Overlord and the Mediterranean. Yet, if the principle of 'Europe first' meant anything at all, the decisions on South-east Asian operations should not be taken until they had decided what to do in Europe. Moreover even in the context of Far Eastern operations what was planned in the China/India theatre should really depend on the over-all strategic plan against Japan, which was still awaited, and which would determine how much emphasis should be put on Central Pacific and South-west Pacific, as opposed to Burmese and South-eastern Asian operations. In two ways therefore they were putting the cart before the horse. Brooke blamed the Americans for this, but he may, and perhaps should, have blamed himself, too, for falling in with the logic of Roosevelt's arrangements. It was also becoming more and more apparent that the British Chiefs had to grapple not only with the 'straitjacket' imposed by the 'Overlord' timetable, but also with the stranglehold imposed on European operations by the shortage of landing-craft everywhere but in the Pacific. This question was more and more to dominate discussion at the conference. Had Brooke known it, another conference delegate was expressing his doubts about Far-Eastern plans at this very moment. General Chennault, the US air force commander in China, had confided to Averell Harriman at breakfast his view that the Chinese armies would not fight and therefore the Upper Burma campaign would be a disaster. Chennault, of course, like Brooke, was not exactly impartial. His faith was pinned to the air arm and strategic bombing, and he had no desire to see US supplies and aircraft diverted to support a Burma land campaign. Whatever Brooke and Chennault might think, however, the conference had already reached a point where the Allies were more or less committed to operations in Burma, which would ultimately develop into the largest single land campaign fought against the Japanese in the Second World War. [12]

Having heard Chennault's views on South-east Asian operations, Harriman now had to turn his attention to Europe. Aware that they would soon have to turn to the 'Overlord/Mediterranean controversy, the US Chiefs were anxious to get an up-to-date picture of Soviet attitudes on the matter from the US Ambassador in Moscow. Particularly they wished to know whether they could still expect Soviet support for the principle of 'Overlord' priority, or whether, as they were beginning to fear, the Russians had changed their minds on this. Harriman was partially reassuring. Soviet demands for continued allied action in the Mediterranean were, he said, due to their wish for continued relief from the constant German pressure. They still counted on 'Overlord' in the spring, but could not understand why two such powerful nations as Britain and the US could apparently do little in the mean time. General Deane, in all good faith but, as he later admitted, mistakenly, was still inclined to think that the Russians were now less concerned about the Cross-Channel Attack than they had been. General Arnold again raised the American bogy of a large-scale Eastern Mediterranean campaign. 'Is that what the Russians want?' he asked (as Churchill had on occasion implied, probably most recently at his dinner with Marshall). Harriman replied cautiously that he did not rule out the possibility that the USSR might accept 'a substitute' for 'Overlord': but it would have to be on the same scale and therefore equally effective in attracting German resources from the Eastern Front. The US Chiefs were left still in some doubt as to the attitude the Russians might adopt. [13]

The British Chiefs normally had their daily meetings at Cairo early in the morning at about the same time as the Americans—9.30 or 9.45. On this occasion after disposing of some less important items quickly they naturally turned to the major issue due to be discussed that day—'Overlord' and the Mediterranean. The C.o.S. had no need to discuss the matter at any great length since their views had been thoroughly formulated. They had to consider, however, whether Mountbatten's proposed operations in South-east Asia could be fitted in to the operational programme they wished to see in the Mediterranean. The landing-craft 'stranglehold' immediately came up. The British Chiefs had before them an optimistic paper from Churchill, backed up by a Joint Planners' report, which suggested that a not too serious delay of 'Overlord' might make it possible to keep the precious landing-craft long enough to launch an amphibious operation to capture Rome in January and Rhodes at the end of the same month. The latter operation of course would require Turkish co-operation, since use of their air-bases would be necessary to ensure allied air superiority. But Churchill clearly thought that the promise of a major assault on the Dodecanese would be sufficient to persuade the Turks where their best interests lay. Churchill's paper did not provide for 'Buccaneer', which he implied could be sacrificed or postponed for some time. That operation, he argued, was trivial compared with Rhodes. Admiral Cunningham thought this a slightly optimistic view so far as the dates of the operations was concerned. He doubted if the Rhodes attack would be possible before February, which would mean postponing 'Overlord' at least two months: and even that would require a degree of improvisation of assault craft for Rhodes. However, Cunningham in some respects was more optimistic than Churchill. He thought 'Buccaneer' could also be fitted into the programme, perhaps in March. Even if 'Overlord' were *not* postponed, the first Sea Lord still believed that Rome *and* Rhodes might still be possible, presumably by the kind of improvisation of landing-craft he had referred to. This was in fact to prove very over-optimistic, since in the event only the Rome amphibious operation (operation 'Shingle') was to prove possible, even with a month's postponement of 'Overlord'. However for the moment the British Chiefs were agreed. The order of priority should be first Rome, second Rhodes, and third—probably a long way third—the Andamans ('Buccaneer').

The British Chiefs then turned briefly to the US Chiefs' formal proposal on Soviet/Chinese participation in the Combined Chiefs' meetings, which they now had had time to consider. It had been evident during the previous day's discussions that of the US Chiefs only Marshall really thought any immediate action on those lines was necessary or desirable. Admiral King indeed had already put the practical difficulties involved, which Dill now reiterated. The proposal was indeed an impracticable one, in the light of these difficulties—the need to have separate meetings with the Russians and the Chinese and the language difficulties. Even with only two nations involved, and with the advantages of a common language, it was still necessary to supplement the regular Washington CCS meetings with fairly frequent full-scale conferences of the British Chiefs and their US counterparts (Cairo was the fourth such conference in 1943 alone). How then could a four-nation CCS play an effective part in the decision-making process, particularly as the Soviet and Chinese representatives were unlikely to be allowed much discretionary power by their governments? Fortified by their experience of meeting the Chinese the previous day, the British Chiefs had no difficulty in deciding that such arrangements would be farcical and they should confine themselves to inviting the Russians and Chinese to attend appropriate sessions of the CCS at Cairo, Teheran, and future full-scale conferences. The Secretariat were instructed to prepare a minute on these lines for the US Chiefs.

There was just time for the C.o.S. to give formal approval to the US paper on the 'enemy situation' in Europe (that is, the state of German troops and resources). This paper concluded (after much detailed examination of the German position) that the Germans had now been thrown on the general defensive in Europe, though still with the capability of some offensive operations in selected theatres. (These might, it was suggested, include an invasion of Sweden or Turkey—an implied confirmation of Turkish fears.) Brooke said that in general British intelligence sources agreed with the US appreciation, but added sarcastically that the US Chiefs' other papers certainly implied the necessity of maintaining Allied pressure on all fronts, which was rather inconsistent with a total sacrifice of Mediterranean operations during the next six months simply to strengthen 'Overlord'. [14]

The British and American Chiefs now adjourned to Roosevelt's villa for a further plenary meeting with their political masters, scheduled for eleven o'clock. As previously with South-east Asia, so with the European front, consideration of the problems by the military staffs was preceded by a general laying-down of guidelines by the two heads of government. Roosevelt began the meeting by pointing out that their final decisions on European operations must depend on the outcome of their conference with the Russians, and particularly on the current Soviet feeling on the importance of 'Overlord'. Reflecting his Chiefs of Staffs' doubts, Roosevelt said there seemed now to be some question whether Stalin regarded 'Overlord' as all-important or whether he attached as much or more importance to the continuance of unremitting pressure in the Mediterranean. It was questionable whether allied resources would permit the latter—to the extent the Russians might desire—and still allow a full-scale 'Overlord'. Roosevelt gave his opinion, no doubt reflecting impressions given to him by Harriman and Deane, that Stalin would probably expect both 'Overlord' *and* continued pressure in the Mediterranean.

Churchill now plunged into an eloquent exposition of the case for an ambitious programme of Mediterranean operations, taking as his general theme the 'blight' which preparations for 'Overlord' had cast on Mediterranean prospects, and the setbacks in Italy, the Balkans, and the Eastern Mediterranean which had followed the withdrawal of troops from that theatre. The 'flagging' of the Mediterranean offensive was due partly to this weakening of Mediterranean resources and partly to the 'artificial division' of command and resources between the two Mediterranean commands. The latter had contributed to the set-back in the Dodecanese which had cost the British five thousand men and eleven warships. If Turkey were brought into the war (and Stalin, Churchill reminded the Americans, had pressed for this at the Moscow conference) it would change the whole picture and, with control of the Dodecanese, would permit the supply route through the Eastern Mediterranean and the Dardanelles to be reopened. They should meet the Turks for a further discussion on their return from Teheran. Having made it clear where his priorities lay, the Prime Minister turned briefly to South-east Asia, and made it equally clear that he regarded these operations as of less immediate importance. If the United States was serious about the use of amphibious resources in that theatre, they must be prepared, he implied, to make a contribution to something worthwhile—namely the assault on Sumatra and the Malacca Straits. Britain would play its full part. If not, the landing-craft allocated to Mountbatten could be more usefully employed in the Mediterranean. Churchill was serving notice that he was not prepared to promise British support for the Andamans operation. Having thrown this bombshell Churchill then attempted a little belatedly to reassure the Americans. He was not advocating an all-out offensive in Italy. The immediate target was Rome and then a line corresponding roughly to Pisa on the west and Rimini on the east. The Prime Minister slightly spoiled the effect of this reassurance by saying that from that point allied forces in Italy could move 'left' (towards the South of France) or 'right' (through the so-called 'Ljubljana Gap' into central Eastern Europe). The latter phrase was calculated to rouse all the ever-present fears of the US Chiefs about a 'Balkan campaign'. Churchill continued his efforts at reassurance, however. The British, he said, were still zealous for 'Overlord', which remained 'top of the bill', but should not be such a tyrant as to rule out every other activity in the Mediterranean. In particular there should be some flexibility in landing-craft, and Alexander should be allowed to retain what he needed long enough to permit amphibious operations for Rome in January and for the Dodecanese in February. A limited postponement of 'Overlord', Churchill implied, would be justified for this purpose.

Churchill had done his best. But as is clear from Hopkins's reaction, as well as that of other Americans, the mention of Rhodes, Turkey, and the possibility of a 'rightward' turn from Italy merely confirmed the Americans in their fears that the Prime Minister was once again advocating 'strategic diversions in South-east Europe' at the expense of 'Overlord'. It may be remarked that if beauty is often in the eye of the beholder, eloquence is equally in the ear of the listener, and often depends as much on the intrinsic appeal of the arguments as on the ability of the advocate. Brooke and his colleagues might well judge Churchill to have given a 'masterly' performance, but to Leahy and Marshall the statement seemed 'lengthy and unconvincing'. They had succumbed to Churchill's eloquence too often, and were not disposed to do so again. Their minds were made up: they were not prepared to support adventures in the Eastern Mediterranean or the Balkans.

According to Marshall's biographer, the temperature of the meeting at this point, not surprisingly, rose somewhat. Even the usually calm and imperturbable Marshall was sufficiently roused to say that if he had his way, 'not one US soldier should die for Rhodes'. This in fact was slightly unfair, since Churchill had made it clear that it would be mainly a British operation. But it is indicative of the strength of the feelings aroused, a feature of the discussion which the US minutes tactfully conceal. Roosevelt himself now wielded the big stick. He read out the estimates of the disposition of US and British land and air forces at home and overseas, reminding Churchill that that the US would shortly be providing more of the global manpower resources than Britain and was therefore in the driver's seat. When Churchill asserted that Britain would play a full part with naval and air resources in the defeat of Japan, Roosevelt replied that in his opinion the defeat of Germany might lead to a fairly rapid end to the Japanese war, implying that not much in the way of a British contribution would probably be needed.

Roosevelt had made his point and contented himself with a brief statement of support for the US proposal of a unified strategic air command, eliciting, as was to be expected, an immediate rebuttal from Churchill. All the participants were by now probably both tired and heated, and Roosevelt wisely brought the meeting to an end, the two heads of government agreeing that the issue of European operations should be further considered by the Staffs with a view to obtaining agreement before the meeting with the Russians. In the light of the discussion they had just had this seemed somewhat optimistic.

It is difficult not to feel that this meeting illustrates all too well the point that at this stage of the war Churchill was not always the best advocate to convince the Americans. Brooke himself, though impressed by Churchill's forceful presentation, recognized that the Premier's obsession with Turkey and Dodecanese only served to increase US suspicions that the British still put Italy and the Aegean ahead of 'Overlord'. Brooke himself attached more importance to keeping up the impetus of the Italian campaign than to restoring reputations in the Eastern Mediterranean. But he was loyally prepared to sustain the Prime Minister's case, and during the next two days proceeded to do so.

During the same period, however, Chiang-Kai-Shek proceeded to raise the stakes. Pulled different ways between their two allies, with Churchill demanding a Dodecanese operation, while refusing to support 'Buccaneer' and Chiang laying down stringent conditions for his participation in the Burma campaign, the Americans savoured the joys of alliance diplomacy to the full. [15]

Marshall tackled the Generalissimo first over lunch, with Stilwell in attendance. Roosevelt's generous political offers the previous night had not elicited equal generosity from Chiang. Chiang had three related conditions for Chinese support of the Burma campaign (Brooke called them 'impossible demands'). The amphibious operations had to be simultaneous with the land operation in Burma: airborne supplies to China meanwhile must *not* be interfered with: even more fundamentally, Chiang showed that he was still almost as nervous about committing his best troops against the Japanese as he always had been. He wanted the British/Indian offensive to play a larger part in the proceedings. The British should advance on Mandalay in the first stage of the operation: the Chinese Yunnan force should only move as far west as Lashio, on the old 'Burma Road' to China, and fairly close to the Chinese frontier. Marshall, who had already spoken pretty bluntly to Churchill that day, was now equally frank with Chiang. Stilwell's plans for the Yunnan force he pointed out were conservative and not likely to be very costly. As for the amphibious operations, Chiang should talk to Mountbatten about British naval plans. Marshall clearly felt 'let down' by Chiang after his assurances to the CCS about Chinese readiness to fight: and he resented the demanding tone which both Churchill and Chiang sometimes adopted in regard to US lives and resources. Chiang, however, would not immediately give way. Stilwell was instructed to put his views to the CCS that afternoon.

While the Combined Chiefs were in session Roosevelt spent the afternoon obtaining more information about Balkan and Middle East affairs from brief chats with various visitors. These included the Egyptian Prime Minister, the Turkish Foreign Minister, the King of Yugoslavia and his Premier, the British army commander in the Middle East, the British ambassador to Egypt, and the British and US ambassadors in Turkey. Turkish participation in the war, the conflicts within the Yugoslav and Greek resistance, the possibility of landings on the Yugoslav Adriatic coast all appear to have been discussed. The President still had his son with him and during the day both Roosevelt and Hopkins stressed to Elliott that the US was now deploying more troops as well as outproducing the British and so were the 'senior partner'.[16]

Meanwhile the arguments continued to rage in the Combined Chiefs' meeting. Brooke's temper was further frayed by the need to set on one side the issue he regarded as crucial, in order to hold further 'futile' discussions with the Chinese and dispose of such irrelevancies (as he saw it) as the US proposal for Soviet/Chinese participation in the Combined Chiefs' discussions. However the meeting began, as they usually did, in an amicable spirit. Brooke sweetened the atmosphere a little with his announcement that the British Chiefs had arranged a special Thanksgiving Day service for the morrow as a courtesy to their allies. The previous day's conclusions were adopted, and the US 'United Chiefs of Staff' proposal was disposed of easily enough. As before, Marshall received relatively lukewarm support from his own colleagues and after Portal, Dill, and Brooke had expounded their previously agreed proposals these were accepted. The Combined Chiefs agreed they should not initiate the topic with the Russians, and if the latter raised it, they should merely propose that the Russian representatives should 'sit in' on relevant parts of the CCS meetings at Teheran and other such conferences. Having got his way, Brooke then took the meeting on to the related question of the agenda for a CCS/Soviet meeting at Teheran. It was agreed that Teheran would be primarily a political meeting, and the CCS discussions would take their cue from any decisions arrived at by Stalin, Churchill, and Roosevelt. Therefore they could not prepare a formal agenda, but it was clear that likely subjects to arise would include the Western desire for co-ordination of Soviet offensives with the 'Overlord' attack, the participation of Turkey in the war, and supplies to Russia (presumably in relation to the possible opening of the Dardanelles–East Mediterranean as a supply route).

The CCS now called the SEAC commanders Mountbatten, Wedemeyer, and Wheeler into the room and turned to the contentious

subject of South-east Asian operations. Marshall reported on his difficulties with Chiang and suggested Mountbatten should give the
Chinese leader details of the proposed British naval build-up in the
Indian Ocean. Marshall tactfully suggested that Chiang needed 'reassurance', a point which Brooke, who thought Chiang was simply
asking for as much as he could get, was inclined to brush aside. On the
question of an advance to Mandalay, Mountbatten pointed out that it
was his intention to resume the advance in that direction in October
after the monsoon, and Brooke underscored the point by reasserting
his conviction that the Upper Burma operations committed them to
an ultimate campaign to conquer the whole of Burma. He also mentioned Churchill's wish for the Sumatran operation rather than
'Buccaneer', but in the light of the US refusal to support it, virtually
conceded that it was 'out'. Mountbatten asked the Chiefs of Staff to
consider what further resources could be allocated to him, to enable
him to give Chiang concrete assurances that the campaign would
develop after the monsoon in the way the discussion had indicated.
The Combined Chiefs also raised the question of the future boundaries between Chiang's and Mountbatten's commands as South-east
Asian operations developed. Chiang had objected to the inclusion of
Thailand and Indo-China in Mountbatten's command area and
suggested that the question of future boundaries should be settled *ad
hoc*, according to the lines of advance reached by the various forces.
Mountbatten was prepared to agree to this, but would have nothing to
do with a further Chinese proposal that a 'political committee' should
be set up in Chungking to decide such matters. Such issues, he said
(and it was obvious the Chiefs of Staff agreed with him), should continue to be resolved by the heads of government directly. After
Marshall had repeated that Chiang clearly needed to be reassured that
the British effort in Burma would be a genuine one, and that his
columns advancing from Yunnan would not be left unsupported, the
Chinese generals were invited in to give their comments on
Mountbatten's plans. The Chinese proceeded to further annoy
Brooke by asking what he considered 'futile' questions about the
details of British strength in the Burma offensive, and then by reiterating Chiang's 'three demands'—a synchronized amphibious
operation in the Bay of Bengal, maintenance of airborne supplies at
10,000 tons a month, and a British advance to Mandalay in the first
stage of the campaign. The Yunnan forces, they stipulated, should not
go beyond Lashio. Stilwell was characteristically pleased to see the
tables turned to some extent, and the British effort called into question. The Chinese, he thought, had got 'under Brooke's skin'.

Mountbatten, however, was equally annoyed by what he saw as Chinese reflections on his Command's efforts, combined with their lack of willingness to co-operate with his plans. The question on an amphibious operation could not be answered yet, he said sharply: as for airborne supplies, the Chinese would have to choose between the reopening of the Burma road, for which they had pressed so long, and the 10,000 tons a month target. Brooke supported his SEAC commander on this point. The Chinese could not have both. Marshall with his usual fairness added his support for this view. The Chinese would have to settle for a small reduction in the air supply target for a limited period. An advance to Mandalay, Mountbatten added, in the first stage would be 'logistically impossible'. Stilwell, acting on Chiang's instructions, supported his Chinese rather than his British and American superiors. When General Shang, the leader of the Chinese, said that he was not authorized to make concessions, but must report back to his chief, the Combined Chiefs drew the discussion to a close. On Marshall's suggestion, Mountbatten was authorized to ask for a meeting with Chiang so that he could discuss the various issues directly. It was evident the Chinese generals would probably water down what had been said.

Prejudiced though Brooke was against the Chinese, it is difficult not to agree with his judgement that such meetings between those who were authorized to try to reach common policies to recommend to their political masters and those who clearly were not so authorized were bound to be 'a fiasco'. He found the whole business a waste of time. Marshall, for his part, was also beginning to find the Chinese something of a trial of his patience, and he cannot have been encouraged to persevere with his tentative suggestion that opportunities for Chinese participation in CCS meetings should be increased. It was the third day of the conference and they seemed no nearer a decision on their first item on the agenda—the Burma campaign. Brooke made the same point in his diary that night, 'after several days we have made no progress whatever'. Roosevelt however was more optimistic, as usual. He cabled Hull that same day that the conference was 'going well'. He expected to finish in two or three days, since he had now heard from Stalin that the latter would be at Teheran by the 28th or 29th. In the light of Churchill's wish to have talks with the Turks— and it was presumed that the Russians would also raise this at Teheran—Roosevelt also cabled Steinhardt in Ankara that he would soon be able to tell him whether President Inönü should be invited to come to Cairo or not. At the same time, however, he apparently made it plain to his son that he fully supported his Chiefs of Staff in their refusal to provide additional supplies for Turkey merely to gratify Churchill's wishes. It seemed unlikely therefore that further talks with Inönü would have results; and it is equally unlikely that the Americans wished them to have results.[17]

While Roosevelt had a restful evening at his villa, Churchill tried his hand with the Generalissimo over dinner. Chiang, however, hoped that he might still get what he wanted if he was stubborn enough. Before he would accept any diminution of his supplies even by the 1,000 tons a month Mountbatten proposed, or less ambitious plans for Burma, he insisted that the Combined Chiefs should again consider the provision of extra aircraft (it amounted in fact to 535 planes) to make the larger plan possible. And he still demanded the simultaneous amphibious operation. Churchill gave Chiang further details of the British Fleet which was to be built up in the Indian Ocean, and used all his eloquent resources to convince the Chinese leader that the amphibious operation was not essential to the land battle. But Chiang would not budge. This too would have to go back to the Chiefs of Staff. Chiang had also that day had a memorandum prepared incorporating his understanding of Roosevelt's assurances on China's status, and also including his further demands: China was to be a member of the 'Big Four' council in the post-war international organization: should be consulted on any peace negotiations with Germany: should immediately become a member of the Combined Chiefs, or a separate Sino-American military committee, as well as a Four-Power Council on Far Eastern operations: should take control of any Chinese territory liberated from the Japanese, whatever forces had liberated it: should regain all her lost territories from Japan: and be fully consulted both about the peace settlement with Japan and the disposition of Japanese territory in the Pacific. This memorandum was handed by Wang to Hopkins before the Chinese left Cairo. It could certainly be said of Chiang that he was not afraid to ask. Like Churchill, however, he was in danger of overplaying his hand so far as the Americans were concerned.[18]

25 November. The need to defer 'Overlord': US resistance to Eastern Mediterranean operations: F.D.R. intervenes on SEAC operations—the 'Buccaneer' promise: the Chinese Communists: Manchuria and Dairen

Roosevelt again had a quiet morning to begin the day. Sir Alexander Cadogan, who had now arrived with Eden, paid his obligatory courtesy call. Roosevelt then handed him over to Hopkins to discuss the communiqué which should be issued at the end of the conference, while the President got down to his paper work. That day the Staffs were to return to the Cross-Channel/Mediterranean problem, but Roosevelt had made it clear to his son the day before that he had little sympathy with British attempts to rehash the 'Overlord' issue, and would support whatever line his Chiefs of Staff adopted. Cadogan for his part was annoyed to find that Hopkins had already given a draft version of the communiqué to the Chinese before the British had been consulted. He was forced to spend the afternoon going over the communiqué with Wang and suggesting alterations (see Appendix B).

That morning the US Chiefs met only briefly. The CBI was again discussed, and Marshall made it plain to his colleagues that there could be no increase of aircraft for the China 'lift' and that he was opposed to sending US ground forces to China. The British Chiefs were less fortunate than their American colleagues. The Americans had little need to discuss their position on 'Overlord', which was established. The British, however, who wished to change things, had to discuss the tactics they were to adopt at the afternoon CCS meeting, to follow up Churchill's statement the previous day. Meeting at 10 o'clock, they disposed of a number of minor issues and then turned to the principal topic. They had their own *aide-mémoire* before them which included the principal heads of the British case—the changes in the war situation since Quebec, the need to keep up pressure in the Mediterranean and therefore, while observing the general commitment to 'Overlord', to be flexible about its timing. It was agreed that they should speak from this at the CCS meeting and circulate it afterwards to the US Chiefs. Coming to specific operations, it was agreed they should support Churchill in pressing for a fresh Dodecanese campaign, beginning with the assault on Rhodes and aiming to open the Dardanelles and knock Bulgaria out of the war. They should point out that the agreement to retain some landing-craft in the Mediterranean had already probably delayed 'Overlord' a little, and moreover that the US programme for moving troops to the UK (Operation 'Bolero') was already 35,000 men behind schedule—a further reason for delaying the date of 'Overlord'. (For this latter, King's demands on shipping for his Pacific offensive was partly responsible). The C.o.S. also agreed that they must now press for the command arrangements in the Mediterranean that would facilitate this strategy—the unified Mediterranean Command. Churchill had stressed the importance of this the previous day, ignoring the US idea of an overall European commander, which the British Chiefs also assumed at this point had been ruled out of court. The question of Turkish entry into the war was also vital to these plans, and it was agreed they should ask the Middle East Commanders to attend next day's CCS meeting to report on this and other aspects of East Mediterranean strategy.

After noting that the Combined Chiefs planners' report on the over-all plan for Japanese defeat would not be available till next week—which the C.o.S. had already concluded meant that no hard decisions should really be taken on South-east Asian operations (particularly 'Buccaneer') till then—the C.o.S. moved briefly to a consideration of a more distant subject: civil administration of Europe after 'Over-lord'. An Anglo-American Combined Civil Affairs Committee was at work in Washington under the direct supervision of the Combined Chiefs—which meant in effect that the US Chiefs and the US War Department had the most direct influence on it. It seemed to the British that the logical outcome of the setting up of the European Advisory Commission in London, together with the creation of the 'Overlord' Allied Headquarters there, was that civil administration planning should also shift to London. This, however, did not appeal to the US Chiefs. Dill, as usual, interpreted for the Americans. It was not simply a question of the Americans wanting to retain control in Washington, he implied. Marshall was worried that, if the centre of gravity in these matters shifted to London, the American public would lose interest in them. The possibility of a recrudescence of American isolationism was always at the back of Marshall's mind, as it was also at the back of Roosevelt's. The C.o.S. recognized there was some-thing in this, and that major issues of civil administration and occu-pation policy would in any event have to be cleared in Washington. They suggested the Prime Minister should talk to Roosevelt about the matter but first should have a word with McCloy, of the US War Department, who was present at the conference. (In the event it was Eden who did so.)[19]

While the C.o.S. were meeting, Churchill and Mountbatten, with Eden in attendance, had been making a further attempt to get some-where with Chiang-Kai-Shek at the latter's villa. Eden, whose mind was mainly focussed on the future problems of European adminis-tration referred to above, rather than military operations in South-east Asia, thought the talks had gone reasonably well, and Churchill and Mountbatten also seem to have thought they had made some pro-gress. It seems that Chiang now indicated a willingness to 'back down' on his three demands. Brooke was more doubtful. In his diary he re-corded 'The Chinese negotiations are not going well and Chiang is busy bargaining to obtain the maximum possible.'

After a photographic session of the Allied leaders, Roosevelt lunched that day at his villa and discussed supply problems with

McCloy, Winant, and the British Minister of War Transport, Lord Leathers: but his mind was already mainly on the forthcoming Teheran conference. He had received confirmation from Stalin that the latter would be at Teheran by the evening of the 28th. He himself had decided to fly direct from Cairo to Teheran on Saturday the 27th. Churchill meanwhile lunched with Eden. He was glad to see the Foreign Secretary, whose advice he valued, but like Brooke was in rather a gloomy mood about the progress of the conference. He had found Roosevelt's unsystematic methods and the waste of time on 'minor Chinese issues' very frustrating.[20]

The British, however, were to be somewhat cheered by that afternoon's CCS meeting at 2.30. The American reaction to the British *démarche* on the 'Overlord' timetable and the Mediterranean proved to be less violent than he had expected, and they made, Brooke considered, some progress. As usual they had first to deal with the long-running Chinese saga. Mountbatten, who was present for this item, reported on his and Churchill's attempts to modify Chiang's attitude on the 'three demands'. Arnold, speaking for the US Air Command, said that the 500 or so additional aircraft for a more extensive Burma campaign could *not* be provided. This was decisive. Brooke added, equally decisively, that there could be no decision on amphibious operations until the following week. As for the third demand, the maintenance of the 10,000-tons-a-month target, they had already agreed that Chiang would have to accept some reduction. As Mountbatten had pointed out to Chiang, it had never been more than a target-figure which had not in fact been reached. Without difficulty they agreed that Chiang would have to be told that his more ambitious proposals for the Burma campaign were 'out'. Mountbatten was asked to prepare a paper urgently for them to approve along these lines, which he should then ask Chiang to agree to.

The CCS then approved the conclusions of the previous day's meeting and, in the light of Brooke's point about the decision on amphibious operations, they instructed the joint planners to have their report on the overall plan for the defeat of the Japanese ready by 1 December. It was then agreed that they should have an 'off-the-record' informal discussion on the 'Overlord'/Mediterranean question. Brooke, as we have seen, found the US response fairly encouraging, but it seems that he got a false impression. Admiral Leahy in fact records that the US Chiefs found the proposals for Eastern Mediterranean operations (which he attributed to the British desire to maintain their hold on the Middle East) 'alarming'. According to his account, the US Chiefs resisted further 'diversions of forces' (that is, from 'Overlord') and 'no decision was reached'. This is confirmed by Roosevelt's remarks to his son about his determination to support the US Chiefs on this point. Hopkins too had complained to Churchill's doctor, Moran, about the Premier's obsession with Rhodes and Italy; and had confirmed how much the Americans resented the reopening, as they saw it, of the whole question of 'Overlord' priority, which they thought had been settled at Quebec. He assured Moran, no doubt deliberately concealing US doubts, that the Americans would line up with the Russians on this issue at Teheran. Moran adds that Churchill for his part was furious that the Americans obstinately resisted his plans for the Mediterranean while being willing to divert amphibious resources from 'Overlord' to an 'unnecessary operation in the Indian Ocean' ('Buccaneer'). It was quite clear that a battle royal was about to develop on this issue; and it was not long in coming. For the moment however the Combined Chiefs ended their session in a fairly amicable mood. [21]

Later that afternoon General Stilwell accompanied Marshall to a meeting with Roosevelt for a further discussion of the Chinese problem. It is evident that at this point conflicting signals were coming from the Chinese camp, reflecting perhaps a genuine indecisiveness on Chiang's part. Roosevelt was of the opinion that the Chinese leader would now accept the less ambitious Burma plan. Later that evening, however, Hopkins told Stilwell that this was not so.

Whatever may have been in the Chinese leader's mind, Roosevelt evidently decided that it was time he took a personal initiative to resolve the US–British–Chinese dispute on South-east Asia. In so doing he set aside the whole machinery of professional military advice represented by the Combined Chiefs, and in effect overrode the known British objection to any premature decision on 'Buccaneer' (which in Churchill's case amounted to a flat objection to *any* favourable decision). Roosevelt apparently concluded that the only way to pin Chiang-Kai-Shek down to active participation in Mountbatten's plans was to give the assurance the Generalissimo was seeking on simultaneous amphibious operations in the Bay of Bengal. This he proceeded to do at a meeting with Chiang at five o'clock. Chiang subsequently wrote to Roosevelt in terms suggesting that this had been agreed between them—though the Chinese later conceded that there had been no *written* agreement on this, or on another promise Roosevelt apparently gave to continue the US training and equipment programme until ninety Chinese divisions had been equipped.

One cannot admire Roosevelt's tactics as a negotiator. He had already made generous and gratuitous political promises to Chiang, which had produced no kind of quid pro quo on the military issues from the Chinese. (On the contrary it had encouraged Chiang to produce even more inflated demands in his written memorandum.) The President now proceeded to give Chiang a military assurance which his military advisers had so far refused to give, and which he must have known Churchill would fiercely resist. In all the circumstances Roosevelt was undoubtedly wise to conduct such conferences without a written record or written agreement.

As usual, however, with Roosevelt's talks at Cairo, the discussion with Chiang was not confined to one issue. It seems that the two leaders went back over other issues they had already discussed. Roosevelt again brought pressure to bear on Chiang to make his regime more democratic and representative, and in particular to heal the breach with the Chinese Communists and form a coalition government. Also as usual, Chiang wanted something in return: if he was to engage in *pourparlers* with the Chinese Communists, Roosevelt must obtain from Stalin an assurance that Russia would not interfere in matters, and particularly that Stalin would respect China's sovereignty over Manchuria. It is clear also that Chiang expressed his doubts about concessions which Roosevelt favoured to Russia on the use of North Chinese ports, and particularly Dairen. The two men again agreed that Indo-China should not return to French control, and that the other colonial powers, including Britain, must be made to see that their colonies must soon gain independence. It was a cosy scene. In contrast with the pressure he was clearly exerting on Chiang to make concessions to the USSR, the President was promising Chiang that he would support him against 'the imperialists' (primarily Britain). Whatever he was envisaging for Europe, Roosevelt was planning for the Far East a Sino-American-Soviet *entente* from which Britain would be excluded.

Having thus in effect gone behind Churchill's back and that of the Combined Chiefs, the President assumed the role of a genial host at a Thanksgiving Dinner for Churchill and Eden, at which he found no difficulty in addressing his guests, as Churchill put it, in terms of 'warm and intimate friendship'. During the course of this dinner Eden brought up his preoccupation with the Polish government, about which Hull had also sent a message to Roosevelt. Eden suggested that Roosevelt should take the matter up with Stalin at Teheran, but Roosevelt had no intention of fouling the air at Teheran by supporting the London Poles. The evening was a sociable one, and after a brief chat with Stilwell later that evening Roosevelt went to bed, no doubt with the feeling of having done a good day's work. The

American Chiefs at the same time were entertaining their British colleagues to dinner. The US Chiefs too, as we have seen, had their *arrière pensées*, but these were not allowed to surface at this friendly occasion.

All told it had been a bad day for the British, though at the time they did not fully realize it. There was to be a rude awakening on the morrow. [22]

*26 November. US Chiefs committed to 'Buccaneer':
doubts about Soviet wishes on strategy: need for co-ordination of
Soviet offensives with 'Overlord': the 'Overall' European Command,
Unified command in the Mediterranean, and strategic bombing:
Rhodes and Italy: Burma decision*

It is clear that Chiang had not finally capitulated the previous evening, in spite of Roosevelt's assurances. The next morning Roosevelt held further meetings with Mountbatten and Chiang with the object of reaching final agreement. Even so he found it necessary to arrange a meeting between Chiang and Arnold, the US Army Air Chief of Staff, later in the morning, so that the latter could explain to Chiang how impossible it was to find all the extra aircraft his demands would require. Afterwards Mountbatten relieved his feelings by telling Stilwell that he was thoroughly fed up with Chiang, on which the US general commented sardonically in his diary, 'as who is not?' Stilwell himself joined Arnold at 11.30 and attempted to 'talk Chiang down'. [23]

Meanwhile the news of Roosevelt's undertaking had obviously reached the US Chiefs of Staff. At their morning meeting Marshall made it clear that they would now have to take a harder line on 'Buccaneer'. If the British refused to support the operation, they must be told that any US landing-craft thus released would not be available for Eastern Mediterranean adventures. Instead they would go to support Admiral King's operations in the Pacific. As Marshall's biographer admits, this contrasted with the much milder reactions they had displayed earlier in the conference to British reservations on 'Buccaneer', and was the direct result of Roosevelt's assurances to Chiang. The US Chiefs' hands had been tied by their political master.

Unaware as yet of this development the British Chiefs at their morning meeting were making their way through a lengthy agenda. After disposing of a number of less important items they turned to a new memorandum from the US Chiefs on the forthcoming conference with the Russians. The Americans expressed the pious hope that they would be able to agree on European strategy before Teheran (which was now only two days off). They then revealed their fears that the Russians might after all join with the British in advocating Balkan/Mediterranean operations, by stipulating that the British and US Chiefs should consult privately on their response at Teheran, if such a proposal were put forward by the Russians. Mindful of the fact that the Russians might also continue their advocacy of getting Turkey into the war, the Americans put forward their customary ambivalent line on this—that there should be a common Anglo-American policy to this end, but no diversion of resources from 'Overlord'! The Combined Chiefs should also try to make the Russians understand that the Western Allies were waging a war in the Pacific as well as Europe, and had to provide resources for the former as well as the latter; and they should ask the Russians to co-ordinate their offensives with 'Overlord' when the time came.

Brooke and his colleagues approved these propositions without too much difficulty, but were a little sniffy about the rather detailed agenda the Americans had produced for a possible Combined Chiefs' meeting with the Russians. This included some of the more detailed suggestions for Soviet co-operation which the Americans had produced at Moscow, and which Brooke dismissed as subjects for the military missions, not the Chiefs of Staff. They agreed, however, that they might discuss with the Russians possible strategic bombing by the Soviet air force, the co-ordination of Soviet operations with 'Overlord', the Italian campaign, and Soviet entry into the war against Japan. (Under the latter heading the US Chiefs wished to find out what practical help the USSR might be prepared to offer the Americans by way of American use of their ports and airbases, and whether the latest Soviet intelligence appreciation of the Japanese position agreed with their own.)

The British Chiefs then turned to a more contentious matter: the formal US proposal for an 'Overall' commander against Germany, together with the proposal for a unified command of all strategic bombing. Ismay had produced a magisterial note on this matter, the burden of which was that the proposed overall commander and his staff would simply interpose an unnecessary link in the chain of command between the CCS and theatre commanders—unless the former were to hand over all their responsibilities in Europe to the new commander. The existing machinery had not failed, so where was the need for this? Drily, the note added 'there must be some limits to the responsibilities the Allied governments were prepared to delegate to a single commander'. The British Chiefs were of course in full agreement with this, as was Churchill, and the paper was approved as the

British response to the US proposal (it also served as the basis for a memo Churchill addressed directly to Roosevelt on the subject). The C.o.S. noted, however, with pleasure that the US note accepted the British proposal for a unified command in the Mediterranean. The effect of the latter was somewhat weakened, however, by a further US proposal, to place US strategic bombing forces in both the US and Italy under one commander responsible to the CCS in Washington. This also and predictably met with British objections, which Portal had formulated in a paper. This proposal, he pointed out, would remove strategic bombing forces in Italy from the control of the theatre commander, contrary to normal practice; and in the UK it would remove the co-ordinating powers over US and British strategic bombing forces which he himself, as Chief of Air Staff, had previously exercised. This proposal, of course, was a further exercise in the assertion of American power at the expense of the British, but must also be seen in the light of the 'Overlord'/Mediterranean controversy. The proposal ensured that all US strategic bombing resources could be directed to support 'Overlord' at the expense of the Mediterranean theatre commander's needs. The C.o.S. approved Portal's paper, but in the event the Americans went ahead with the proposal in a modified form.

Next the C.o.S. turned to the memorandum Mountbatten had formulated for Chiang in response to the CCS instructions on the previous day. The SEAC Commander's paper listed as the points on which the Combined Chiefs and Chiang must agree as being: (1) amphibious operations in the Bay of Bengal; (2) the assembly of the promised British fleet at Colombo; (3) the allocation to the SEAC command of control over air transport during the Burma battle, even at the expense of some diminution of airborne supplies to China; (4) command arrangements in the first stage of the campaign: the Chinese forces advancing into Upper Burma would be under the British General Slim's operational command to begin with and then pass under Stilwell; and (5) an undertaking that operations would be resumed in Burma in October at the end of the monsoon. The C.o.S. agreed with this identification of the points involved, but proposed that Chiang should be informed that the reduction in his supplies would probably be no more than 1,000 tons a month. They also thought it would be more prudent not to give an unqualified assurance on the resumption of operations after the monsoon. Subject to these changes the paper was approved. At this stage, of course, the British Chiefs were still ignorant of Roosevelt's promise to Chiang on amphibious operations.

Finally the C.o.S. turned again to 'Overlord' and the Mediterranean, with particular reference to the role of Turkey, on which the Secretariat had prepared a paper. The burden of the British memorandum was that the Turks must be restrained from an outright declaration of war against Germany in the planning stages of the Dodecanese operations, but should covertly make preparations for co-operation by preparing facilities on their airfields and in their ports. When the whistle was blown Germany would probably declare war on Turkey, and it would be up to the Allies then to provide air protection for Turkish cities and establish air supremacy in the Aegean. The Turks must be held back from attacking Bulgaria, which it was thought they might want to do. Instead they might attack some of the smaller Dodecanese islands while the British concentrated on the main target—Rhodes. The C.o.S. approved the paper subject to the tactful deletion of a reference to the possible occupation of Greece, which the British Chiefs knew would arouse all the lurking American suspicions of a Balkan campaign.

In point of fact, of course, all these elaborate plans were to come to nothing, since the Americans were unwilling to support the operations and the Turks were unwilling to take risks without a full allied commitment to the East Mediterranean theatre. When the British Chiefs again met their US colleagues that afternoon they were to find that the American price for any flexibility on the 'Overlord' date was now definite agreement to 'Buccaneer' at a date which might rule out any thought of using the same amphibious resources in the Eastern Mediterranean. The result was the most acrimonious session the Combined Chiefs had yet had at Cairo. [24]

The meeting began amicably enough with the Combined Chiefs' approval of Mountbatten's revised memorandum for Chiang-Kai-Shek. Essentially this repeated the argument that resources were not available for Chiang's more ambitious Burma plans (the attack on Mandalay) and indeed that even the less ambitious plan would require a small diminution of airborne supplies to China for a while: it expressed the 'hope' that the Burma offensive could be resumed after the monsoon without committing the Allies absolutely, and on Chiang's third demand—the amphibious operation—the memorandum again did not commit the SEAC command, but did not rule the operation out entirely. This was a form of words which was acceptable to both those who favoured 'Buccaneer' and those who did not, so the main argument did not break out at this point.

The CCS then moved on to Mediterranean operations and the consideration of British views, as expressed by Churchill earlier and encapsulated by the British Chiefs themselves in a memorandum which perhaps somewhat overdramatized the differences between the two sides. Before discussing this, however, the Combined Chiefs called in the Mediterranean and Middle East commanders to hear their views, beginning with Eisenhower. The burden of the latter's song was that the choice in Italy and the Mediterranean generally was between an 'all-out effort' which would permit an advance to the Po valley in 1944 and *then perhaps* an Aegean operation: or a 'limited effort' which would limit the Italian advance to the Pisa–Rimini line and thereafter make the Italian campaign a 'holding operation'. The 'all-out effort' would require the retention of landing-craft for amphibious operations at least till mid February and would require that there should be no further diversion of resources from the theatre to 'Overlord'. In effect what Eisenhower was saying was that only the 'limited effort' was consistent with the Quebec decision to give absolute priority to 'Overlord'. This was what the Americans wanted to hear and the British did not. It was also clear that in Eisenhower's opinion whichever choice was adopted, Aegean operations must await the attainment of minimum objectives in Italy, though in this regard Eisenhower spoke of course with the natural bias of one who commanded in Italy but not in the Eastern Mediterranean. It was difficult, as Marshall had remarked on the *Iowa*, for a theatre commander to take a global view.

The British Middle East commanders, Wilson (Army), Sir John Cunningham (Navy) and Douglas (Air) were then called in and presented (again perhaps naturally) a somewhat more optimistic view on Aegean operations. Provided Turkey entered the war and offered the use of their air-bases, the attack on Rhodes and subsequent occupation of the Dodecanese could be carried out with no more assistance from the Western Mediterranean (that is, from the Americans) than the provision of the vital landing-craft for a limited period. It was implied that British Middle East and Turkish forces could do the rest.

The Combined Chiefs then passed on to the British memorandum and the real argument began—but not at first. The US Chiefs were still prepared to be conciliatory on a limited postponement of 'Overlord', if that was all that was required. Leahy, speaking for his colleagues, said that they were prepared to accept the British paper and its recommendations at least *as a basis* for discussion with the Russians. These recommendations included the maintenance of the offensive in Italy to the Pisa–Rimini line: stepping up supplies to the resistance movements in the Balkans: and Eastern Mediterranean operations designed to open the Dardanelles and bring Turkey into the war. It helped, of course, that the British proposals envisaged only a limited objective in Italy (consistent with Eisenhower's 'limited effort') and made no mention of a 'Balkan campaign'—in both respects confirming Winant's original exposition of British views to the US Chiefs. The paper also recommended unification of the Mediterranean Command: but this the Americans had already agreed to. The real argument began when the discussion began to centre around the respective merits of the attack on Rhodes and 'Buccaneer', and the priority to be attached to each of them. It was clear that neither side were completely convinced that both were possible, and, if obliged to choose, the British preference was for Rhodes and the US preference was for the Andamans operation. Marshall made his (or rather Roosevelt's) position clear. 'Buccaneer' was necessary to gain whole-hearted Chinese participation in the Burma campaign. A heated argument developed—Brooke called it 'the father and mother of a row'— and the Combined Chiefs again decided to go into closed session off the record. Brooke felt that in the end the British 'had secured most of the points we were after'. Certainly the final decisions include a general acceptance of the British paper as a 'basis for discussion with the Soviets': also unification of the Mediterranean Command: and specific acceptance of a delay in the date for 'Overlord' and the retention of landing-craft in the Mediterranean for a longer period. On the other hand, it specifically minuted the US Chiefs' refusal to abandon 'Buccaneer' unless Roosevelt and Churchill agreed to do so: and if 'Buccaneer' went forward, it was still questionable if the attack on Rhodes would be practicable. However Brooke no doubt was confident that Churchill would refuse to co-operate in putting 'Buccaneer' into operation. What he did not know was that US and Turkish reservations would in the end make the Rhodes operation impossible also.

Having at length reached these conclusions, the Combined Chiefs approved the suggested agenda for the meeting with the Russians, with the amendments suggested by the British C.o.S. The items for discussion should be (1) the co-ordination of Soviet operations with Anglo-American operations; (2) the Italian campaign; (3) Turkish entry into the war; (4) supplies to Russia; (5) possible Soviet strategic bombing of German targets; and (6) Soviet entry into and collaboration in the war against Japan. The CCS then adjourned for the last time at Cairo.[25]

While all this was going on two other meetings were taking place, both also involving some Anglo-American argument. Eden and a senior Foreign Office official, Gladwyn Jebb, met Winant and

McCloy to discuss the general location of planning for post-war problems, including occupation policy and civil administration in Europe. The discussion began in the afternoon and went on over dinner. Eden at Moscow had secured—or thought he had—US agreement to the transfer of much of this planning to the newly-created EAC in London. The Foreign Office had followed this up by suggesting that the Anglo-American Combined Civil Affairs Committee should be transferred from Washington to London. It now appeared that Hull and the US State Department and War Department had considerable reservations about transferring so much authority to a London-based body. Hull of course had had his reservations about the EAC all along, and had not been completely frank about it: but Marshall was also concerned. Winant made the sensible point that the European Advisory Commission should not be overloaded with too many functions; and complained that the British attitude was making the Combined Civil Affairs Committee unworkable. He then pointed out that the Americans were sensitive about any shift of the centre of gravity from Washington. Eden, in what was probably a calculated show of temper, was pardonably annoyed. The Americans, he said, should not go back on their agreements: if they would agree to treat the EAC seriously, he would see to it that the Combined Committee was allowed to function. Eventually, however, he conceded that the EAC's recommendations should be cleared with the Combined Chiefs in Wasington, before being submitted to their respective governments: and the CCAC should remain where it was. It was another demonstration of the US determination at this stage of the war to assert its dominant position.[26]

At about three o'clock Roosevelt, Churchill, and Chiang met for the last time at Cairo. They were joined by Eden, Harriman, and Cadogan and the purpose of the meeting was mainly political—to approve the terms of the final communiqué in which were to be made public the generous promises about the return of Chinese territory. Military matters were also discussed, however, and it was at this meeting that Chiang finally capitulated and withdrew his more inflated military demands. Having received Mountbatten's paper, approved by the CCS, he agreed to co-operate in Mountbatten's less ambitious Burma plan and to accept a temporary reduction of 1,000 tons a month in airborne supplies. But Chiang's agreement must be seen in the light of Roosevelt's promises that an amphibious operation would definitely be carried out in conjunction with the Burma land operations—a promise which went much further than the carefully qualified assurances in Mountbatten's paper. It does not seem that Roosevelt made it clear to Churchill that he had now committed himself unequivocally to Chiang on this matter. At all events it was not until three days later that Churchill addressed to the British Chiefs a memorandum recording his unequivocal rejection of this assurance, a document which strongly suggests the mood of one who has only just discovered what has been going on. The 'Buccaneer' controversy would require further Anglo-American arguments before it was finally settled—in the negative. [27]

Churchill raised no objection to the promises to restore Chinese territory, always provided there were no references in the communiqué to Hong Kong. Nevertheless, the terms of the communiqué had been another source of Anglo-American friction. As we have seen, Cadogan and Eden had arrived on the 25th to find that Hopkins had already given a draft of the communiqué to the Chinese without showing it first to the British. Cadogan soon discovered 'flaws and omissions' from the British point of view, and had been obliged to spend that afternoon and the morning of the 26th arguing with Wang and Harriman on the subject. Churchill eventually had had to produce a revised version which was accepted by the three leaders.

The bases of the British objections were, firstly, that the communiqué talked about restoring territory conquered by the Japanese to China, specifically mentioning Manchuria, which Cadogan thought might cause difficulties with the Russians. It was also made clear that Japan would lose its Pacific island possessions. The communiqué did not specify who would be the beneficiary, but Cadogan had a pretty shrewd idea that it would be the United States. Nothing, however, was said on the subject of Japanese conquests in South-east Asia and the restoration of this territory to the British, French, and Dutch. Roosevelt of course was most unwilling to give any such assurance, particularly where the French were concerned. The most Cadogan and Churchill were able to obtain was the addition to the US draft of a statement that Japan would be expelled from all the territories she had taken, and a further statement that the Three Powers had 'no thought of territorial expansion' and 'coveted no gain for themselves', which might be of future use in dealing with Chinese claims on Hong Kong and Tibet and any Chinese ambitions in South-east Asia. It was no doubt these arguments with the British which prompted Hopkins to have a long conversation with Chiang that evening at which it appears he discussed both of these points— Chinese and British rivalries in the south and the difficulty of reconciling Soviet and Chinese aims in the north. During this discussion

Chiang apparently said that China would not give up its traditional claim to Tibet: that he wished Outer Mongolia to become an effective 'buffer' between China and the USSR rather than a Soviet puppet State: and that he did not wish Roosevelt to discuss with Stalin possible Chinese accommodations of Soviet interests in the north, such as the internationalization of Dairen. This was to be a vain hope.

The final communiqué approved, Roosevelt wisely dined quietly at his villa with Leahy and his personal staff, and then went early to bed in view of the long journey ahead. Churchill less wisely, but characteristically, kept Eden and Cadogan up till 2 o'clock in the morning discussing the conference, with the consequent loss of his voice the next morning.[28]

Departure for Teheran

On 27 November the British and American delegates left Cairo for Teheran. Neither side retained very pleasant memories of the conference. In many respects it was one of the most disagreeable Anglo-American meetings of the war. Churchill and the British were resentful of the attention devoted to the Chinese and their problems, the domineering attitude which the Americans seemed to them to adopt on various issues, and the general decline of the close and on the whole friendly relations they had previously enjoyed. Churchill's pressure for an Anglo-American conference before meeting the Russians had in fact had the worst possible results from the British point of view. Eden thought the conference one of the most difficult he had experienced; like Cadogan he resented the offhand behaviour of the Americans over the communiqué and could foresee many future difficulties over South-east Asia. Churchill felt that the main purpose of the conference from his point of view—to work out a common strategic policy to present to the Russians—had not been achieved. Brooke of course shared this view and deeply resented the amount of time 'wasted in academic discussion of South-east Asia and China'. However he found some consolation in the achievement of the unified command in the Mediterranean and the quashing of American proposals for an overall European commander (the proposal had not been referred to again after Churchill and the British Chiefs had firmly rejected it). Brooke also felt that the Americans had been less inflexible on the 'Overlord'/Mediterranean question than he had feared; and Eastern Mediterranean operations were still, so to speak, 'on the table'. Nevertheless British plans depended very much on the attitude the Russians adopted at Teheran. If they joined hands with the

Americans to impose an agreed strategy contrary to British wishes, there was not much the British could do about it.

The Americans for their part were hardly less disgruntled. They had been infuriated by what they saw as a British attempt to bring the whole Quebec agreement into question: and irritated by the British obsession with Mediterranean operations. Leahy felt that very little had been achieved militarily, an opinion shared, according to his biographer, by Marshall. In a sense this was true: the 'Buccaneer' operation, and therefore the whole conduct of the campaign in South-east Asia was still in question: nor had they really settled the question of what was to be done in the Mediterranean or just how much priority 'Overlord' should continue to have. All these decisions still waited on the conclave with the Russians and further discussions with the British and the Turks. Paradoxically the one decision which seemed to have been confirmed was that there should be a campaign in Upper Burma, which the British disliked and only Marshall of the US Chiefs really thought militarily worthwhile.

Whatever the case with the military decisions, however, the political discussions at Cairo had profound implications for the future. China had been promised the repossession of all her lost territories in the north, without, as it turned out, the necessity to do much fighting for them. This promise, however depended to a large extent for its fulfilment on Soviet acceptance, as Roosevelt and Cadogan had foreseen: and therefore made it inevitable, whatever Chiang might wish, that the question of Soviet claims in that part of the world should be discussed at Teheran. The boosting of China's position in the postwar world, also promised by Roosevelt, had equally important implications for the future. It is therefore surprising that Hopkins apparently passed on to the editor of his papers the impression that the conference had had 'a negligible influence' not only on the military conduct of the war, but also on the future history of the world. This seems an underestimate of promises and decisions which foreshadowed much that transpired at Teheran and indeed Yalta. Roosevelt certainly did not entirely share this view. He felt, according to Hull, that he had established a satisfactory personal relationship with Chiang-Kai-Shek—in his view one of the most important objectives of the conference. In a cable to Hull he said enthusiastically that he 'had had a very satisfactory conference with Chiang-Kai-Shek, and liked him'. As for Chiang, he departed from the conference 'with high hopes'. Politically he had been promised the earth, or a good part of it, and militarily, to quote Averell Harriman, 'he believed his main demands had been met'. This latter illusion was not to last for long.[29]

CHAPTER VIII

TEHERAN SUMMIT: STALIN DECIDES ALLIED STRATEGY

1. Stalin the Arbiter

As the British and Americans departed for Teheran on 27 November they both knew that in the military sphere many of the important issues—certainly the most contentious of all—would in effect be settled by the Russians. Politically, too, there was much they wanted to find out from their Soviet Ally. But their main concerns here were different. Roosevelt wished above all to confirm the Soviet promise to enter the Japanese war and if possible to obtain Stalin's approval for the broad outlines of the Far Eastern settlement which he had made with Chiang-Kai-Shek. To obtain these, and whole-hearted Soviet co-operation in the post-war international organization, he sensed there would have to be some gratification of Soviet wishes in the Far East, not only in relation to Outer Mongolia and the Kurile islands but also in terms of Soviet access to the Pacific via Chinese warm-water ports. Chiang, he clearly felt, must be prepared to make some concessions to Russia of this kind, in return for Stalin's approval of all that was promised to China. In Eastern Europe too, including Poland, territorial and other concessions might have to be made. Churchill and Eden on the other hand were thinking particularly of Poland, but in a much more anxious frame of mind than Roosevelt, and secondly of Germany. The need to obtain some solution of the Polish government and Polish frontier problem was becoming more and more urgent as Soviet forces approached the 1939 frontiers of Poland. But they seemed to be making no more impression on Roosevelt than they had been able to on Hull. The President, however, was well aware of the issues, and had been reminded of them, not only by Eden but by Harriman. He was aware that for there to be any hope of obtaining concessions from the USSR on the resumption of relations with the Polish government, there would have to be concessions to Russia on the frontier question. For his part he was prepared, as Churchill was, to accept the Curzon Line. But how to explain the surrender of large tracts of Polish territory to the large and highly nationalistic Polish population in the United States? Roosevelt felt he would have to tread carefully on this point. But unless he was prepared to commit himself publicly on the issue, Stalin would probably remain intransigent on the question of the Polish government. On Germany Roosevelt, Churchill, and Stalin each wished to sound out each other's views on the future settlement. Roosevelt and Stalin in fact were pretty alike in their thinking. Both thought the German people bad and dangerous and wanted to see Germany smashed for good. Only Churchill was concerned about preserving some kind of balance of power in Europe, for which Germany, or some form of German State, would be essential. Roosevelt and Stalin were also, as it turned out, pretty closely agreed on military matters. Both regarded 'Overlord' as all-important. Stalin also wanted the Anglo-Americans to maintain continuous pressure on Germany during the interim period, but did not wish to see any Mediterranean operations which might seriously interfere with the Cross-Channel Attack. As for Poland, he knew he would soon have all the cards in his hand and for that matter in the rest of Eastern Europe, if the military discussions went his way. He was prepared to listen to what the British and Americans had to say about Poland, but probably saw no reason why he should make any concessions to their point of view. What did Poland really matter to them? But it was life and death to Russia. On Far Eastern questions, he had, as Roosevelt surmised, his own list of objectives: basically these amounted very much to regaining for Russia the predominant influence in Manchuria and North China which Tsarist Russia had lost to the Japanese at the beginning of the century. The Chinese Communists, for whom he had no great love, might stand in the way. Chiang, however, in his weakness, might be more accommodating. Roosevelt's error was to suppose that Stalin was a Russian nationalist rather than a Communist. He was both.[1]

2. The Conference Day by Day

27 November. Roosevelt moves in with the Russians

Shortly after the Allied leaders arrived at Teheran there was much to-ing and froing on the subject of Roosevelt's residence. The British and Soviet Legations in Teheran stood side by side, separated only by a narrow lane. The US Legation was some distance away. For Roosevelt to visit the other two, or for them to visit him, required a journey through the narrow, crowded streets of the capital, with the risk of the assassin's bullet. Stalin and Churchill therefore had both invited Roosevelt to stay with them: Roosevelt, as we have seen, wished to offend neither. On the afternoon of the 27th Dreyfus, the US Minister, visited the Soviet chargé, Maximov, at the Soviet Embassy. Later Maximov paid a courtesy call on Roosevelt and no doubt renewed the Soviet invitation, since that evening at 6 o'clock Averell Harriman thought it necessary to go to see Molotov personally to explain further. Harriman conveyed Roosevelt's regrets and explained that the British might be rather upset if the President accepted the Soviet invitation but refused theirs. Molotov appeared to accept this for the moment, and after leaving the room briefly, apparently to consult Stalin, approved the arrangements which Harriman proposed, on Roosevelt's behalf, for the first day of the conference. For the President's convenience, in view of his disability, all their meetings should be at Roosevelt's quarters (at that time still in the US Legation). Stalin would call on Roosevelt at 3 o'clock for a brief introductory meeting, before a full plenary session with Churchill and the military staffs at 4 o'clock. Finally the three statesmen would meet again at 7.30 for dinner. [2]

Molotov signified his agreement, and then enquired if the Ambassador had an agenda for the conference. It was not an unreasonable request. It was the Americans, after all, who had repeatedly pressed for such a meeting; presumably they had some idea what they wanted to talk about. Harriman, however, explained that the President did not envisage a formal meeting with a prepared agenda and definite decisions but rather an informal 'get-together', which would give the two men an opportunity to establish their relationship on a personal footing and explore each other's minds. Roosevelt, he said, wished to consult with the Soviet leader on Allied strategy for the defeat of Germany, and then go on to discuss whatever political issues were in their respective minds, in an informal way. Such a procedure did not appeal at all to Molotov's precise and orderly mind, but he did not at first demur. Perhaps he was too taken aback to say much, but more probably he felt he should see what Stalin had to say about it.

When the British Ambassador, Clark Kerr, followed his American colleague a little later, Molotov brought the subject up again, and clearly found the British envoy more receptive. As a professional diplomat, Clark Kerr was accustomed to expect properly organized meetings, and furthermore knew that Eden and Cadogan felt the same way. This of course was also the view of the Chiefs of Staff. The US Chiefs, it will be remembered, had prepared a tentative list of subjects for Roosevelt to discuss with Stalin; and in agreement with their

British colleagues a similar list for their own discussions with the Soviet military representatives (see above, p. 212). Kerr promised to see what he could do, and repaired to the British Legation to discuss it with Eden and Cadogan.

When Harriman himself called at the British Legation, after dining with Roosevelt, he found Clark Kerr and Eden, as he put it, 'scuttling round to find an agenda'. Eden showed him a list of topics, including some of the problems connected with the operations of the Italian Advisory Council; one can guess that Poland was also on the list. Harriman himself had in fact already warned Roosevelt, following up similar representations from Eden and Hull, that unless the President dealt with Poland at Teheran, 'its fate would probably go by default'. However, in dealing with his British Allies his first responsibility was to carry out Roosevelt's wishes. He read the British a lecture. The President of the United States had not travelled all the way to Teheran to 'get into that kind of detail' (that is, the Italian Advisory Council), but to establish personal relations with Stalin and discuss the broad issues of war and peace. Eden and Cadogan, who thought they knew more about the conduct of international conferences than Harriman and who probably also thought his attitude high-handed, were some-what nettled, and the discussion became acrimonious. Eventually Eden gave way, and Harriman, realizing that they had all been up since 3.30 that morning and were very tired, took himself off.

The American Ambassador was not to get to bed yet, nor was Clark Kerr. Both were summoned a little later to see Molotov, though it was now past midnight. Molotov told them that there were German agents in Teheran who were planning 'a demonstration'; there might even be an assassination attempt. He again urged Roosevelt to join them at the Soviet Embassy, where the main building would be made available to him; or else to move in with the British. Wearily, Harriman agreed to discuss it further with his party, and returned to the Legation. Most of the American security men were agreeable. Apart from the security aspect, Harriman himself recognized the con-venience for the three leaders of being close together. They agreed to recommend the move to Roosevelt in the morning. The President readily agreed and the move was made the following afternoon. Churchill, as it happened, was not put out. His own ideas of proper accommodation were on a lavish scale, and he had come to the con-clusion that the British Legation would be a little cramped for both of them. So the issue was resolved amicably, and the Americans con-ferred with Churchill and Stalin under the ever-vigilant eyes of the Soviet secret police; and no doubt in their own quarters uttered their most casual remarks into the listening microphones.

It was already evident that the conference was to be a 'Roosevelt' conference—informal, not over-organized, and somewhat chaotic. 'The meeting', Cadogan confided to his diary, 'looks like being all over the place.' Identifying himself with a long line of diplomats and Foreign Ministers in his view of summit conferences, he added philosophically 'that is ever the way with the Great Men'.[3]

28 November. The crucial military decision: preliminary discussions of France, Poland, and Germany

Though the British and Americans did not know it, the first full day of the conference was to be decisive on the military issues. The British and US Chiefs began the day with their usual early meetings. Brooke conducted the C.o.S. meeting in a gloomy mood. Like Churchill, who had spent part of the journey to Teheran bemoaning the Mediterranean picture, the Chief of Staff felt that the lack of Anglo-American agreement at Cairo would prove disastrous. He thought, his diary says, that they were 'headed for chaos'. 'Buccaneer', the Chiefs of Staff agreed, was the most difficult of the many problems facing them. They had now gathered from the US Chiefs that Roosevelt had given an undertaking on this point to Chiang-Kai-Shek, and the Americans therefore had no latitude to discuss it. That meant the Prime Minister would have to be involved in the argument. It was agreed Ismay should ask Churchill if he was prepared to approve 'Buccaneer' after all, or if he would prefer to take it up with the President. Turning to the question of Turkey, the C.o.S. accepted Portal's view that the Turks should be advised to speed up the preparation of air defence precautions against possible future German raids. The C.o.S. also reaffirmed their previous view that the actual declaration of war by Turkey should be delayed until Allied forces were ready to mount the Rhodes operation, and that Turkish forces should not participate in the main assault. Ismay was instructed to draft a memorandum on these points for Churchill.

As for 'Overlord' and the Mediterranean, it was something that the Americans had agreed to the unification of command in the latter theatre and accepted the possibility of some delay to 'Overlord'. But the basic problem—the extent of future Mediterranean operations, and in particular the 'Rhodes versus Andamans' question—was still unsolved and awaited the result of their discussions at Teheran. When Brooke and Ismay reported to Churchill after the meeting, they found the Prime Minister still below par. He was suffering from a cold as well as a sore throat. Brooke sought to capitalize on the one important

point where the Americans had shown some readiness to be flexible—
the date of 'Overlord'. He tried hard to get Churchill to accept at least
the possibility that Italy, Rhodes, and the Andamans operation could
all somehow be fitted into the same timetable. There might be the
basis of some sort of compromise with the Americans here. Churchill,
however, was adamant; he would have nothing to do with 'Buccaneer'. It was unlikely, he felt, that enough resources, particularly
shipping resources, could be found for both Rhodes and 'Buccaneer'.

In the American delegation Averell Harriman was up betimes, in
spite of his late night. A brief chat with Hopkins and Ismay at the US
Legation convinced the former that Roosevelt should move. With the
President's agreement, arrangements were made to do so. Churchill,
as we have seen, was philosophical over this Soviet/American 'get-
together' but less so over another rebuff from Roosevelt. The Prime
Minister had asked to meet Roosevelt for lunch. As always, and ever
the optimist, Churchill still hoped to have some prior Anglo-American
agreement on the precise issues to be discussed and the line to be taken
with the Russians. But those days were over. Roosevelt was determined to see Stalin first and make it clear to the Soviet leader that he
had done so. He was equally determined not to be drawn into a discussion on Eastern Mediterranean operations with Churchill. He sent
back a polite refusal. Harriman's next task accordingly was to soothe
Churchill's ruffled feelings. It was less difficult than he had expected.
Churchill soon subsided into a mood of good-humoured grumbling.
He would follow, he said, the President's lead. He stipulated only that
he should be allowed to give a dinner party for the other two delegations on 30 November, his sixty-ninth birthday. Churchill, like
Eden at Moscow, was too much of a realist not to recognize the
weakness of the British position. Perhaps, too, the fact that he was
physically below par—and indeed was to be seriously ill not long
afterwards—persuaded him to conserve his energies for the struggles
ahead.

Before moving to his new quarters Roosevelt held a meeting with
the US Chiefs at the American Legation: as usual at these presidential
conferences Hopkins was also present. The theme of the meeting
revolved essentially around one point. If the Russians demanded
large-scale operations in the Mediterranean during the six months
before 'Overlord', as was still feared, what could be proposed with the
least damage to the Cross-Channel Attack? The conclusion was
equally simple: the safest course was to put more steam behind
Eisenhower's Italian campaign. Leahy, putting the issue more bluntly
even than he had put it to the British so far, argued that one had to

choose essentially between 'Overlord' and the Mediterranean. The implication was that they needed to avoid committing very much more even to Italy, let alone the Eastern Mediterranean. Marshall, achieving as usual, a greater degree of detachment and fair-mindedness than his colleagues, conceded that it might just be possible to launch the amphibious operation for the capture of Rome ('Shingle') *and* the Rhodes attack with a delay to 'Overlord' of at most two months. But the feasibility of this programme was not really the issue. It was the 'suction effect' of Eastern Mediterranean operations which was to be feared. Once start on that path and there was no telling where it might lead. Roosevelt raised the question of Turkish entry into the war, obviously with the thought that Stalin, as well as Churchill, might continue to press for this. Marshall was decisive on this point. The British might well have forces available in the Middle East, and the natural wish to use them: but the Americans could not spare anything for such operations from 'Overlord' and Italy, except just possibly the use of the necessary landing-craft for a limited spell. In these circumstances, Roosevelt said he did not see how they could press the Turks to change their cautious and reluctant attitude. As for the argument that the use of the Dardanelles route for supplies to Russia would be a great advantage, Marshall said that he had been advised that it would be six months before an effective switch could be made from the Iran/Arctic routes. Taking account of all the reorganiz-ation of supply routes which would be required, this could not there-fore be a major consideration.

The discussion continued to revolve around Italy. If the am-phibious operation were successful and Eisenhower could quickly take Rome and advance to the Pisa–Rimini line, what then? If Eisenhower were then instructed to adopt a defensive posture in Italy, it would be possible to use some of his forces for one of two purposes. Either they could be launched in amphibious operations against the south of France, to support 'Overlord', or they could be diverted east-wards to link up with and support Soviet forces advancing into the Balkans. The choice, it seemed, must largely depend on whether the Russians exerted any pressure for the latter course, in preference to a Southern France operation in support of 'Overlord'. Scenting danger, Marshall was quick to say that 'limited operations' on the Adriatic coast would be the safest commitment to make in that event, rather than any attempt to break northeastwards through the 'Ljubljana gap'. Marshall clearly was concerned lest the President's penchant for an adventurous and imaginative strategy should lead to unwise commitments at the expense of the main objective. Eisenhower, he pointed out, had alternative plans for the development of the Italian campaign either northeastwards *or* towards the south of France. The Army Chief of Staff left no doubts in anyone's mind which possibility he preferred.

Roosevelt seldom ignored Marshall's view, and he did not do so now. The 'Adriatic strategy', however, he said, would at least be better than Churchill's Eastern Mediterranean/Turkish adventures. If the latter succeeded, it would only lead to British demands for an invasion of Greece.

With landing-craft in everybody's mind, inevitably the subject of the Andamans operation came up. King stated his customary (and predictable) position. If resources had to be found for the Eastern Mediterranean they would have to come from 'Overlord', not from 'Buccaneer' (nor of course *a fortiori* from the Pacific). He rammed home his argument with a valid point, which often seemed to be over-looked by the Combined Chiefs in their discussions of the possible jug-gling of landing-craft between different operations and different theatres. Not all the landing-craft allocated to an operation could then be reallocated blithely in advance to another operation. Some would be sunk or damaged.

Restating what the US Chiefs already knew, Roosevelt reminded them that, with or without Churchill's by-your-leave, he had assumed a definite obligation to the Chinese, which it would be awkward to go back on. Marshall had already reminded the meeting of the equally obvious fact that Churchill would fight tooth and nail against 'Buccaneer'. The British, he added, thought the operation militarily unsound and 'politically motivated' (that is, prompted by the desire to give the Chinese something solid to take back from Cairo). Roosevelt's remarks of course virtually conceded that very point. Helping the President out, however, Marshall added that whatever the British view, the US Chiefs thought 'Buccaneer' a useful oper-ation militarily: for their part, too, they considered Churchill's sponsorship of the Rhodes operation equally 'politically motivated' (that is, influenced by the desire to strengthen British post-war influence in that area).

In closing the meeting, Roosevelt in turn sought to reassure the Chiefs of Staff. He would avoid being drawn into any discussion with Churchill of the respective merits of Rhodes and the Andamans oper-ations. He came back in conclusion to the point which had been in all their minds throughout. How hard would Stalin press for immediate relief for the Russian front pending 'Overlord', and where? That question was about to be answered conclusively by the Soviet leader, and in the most satisfactory manner from the US point of view.[4]

Roosevelt had apparently not made it clear to all the US Chiefs that he had it in mind not only to have a brief chat with Stalin that afternoon but also to call a plenary session. It maybe that this meeting was not definitely confirmed until after the Chiefs of Staff meeting, possibly not until Roosevelt and Stalin met for the first time. At all events, when the time came, Marshall and Arnold were not to be found, and King and Leahy had to represent the Americans at the plenary session. As would soon be apparent, on this occasion the US Chiefs were not required. Stalin did their job for them.

First, however, and as soon as Roosevelt had moved to his new quarters, Roosevelt and Stalin met alone, with only the interpreters present, for the first time. It is for this reason probably that the US record of the meeting appears to be so fragmentary (the published Soviet records do not refer to it at all). It seems to have been an odd disjointed conversation, and one wonders what Stalin made of it. After exchanging the usual courtesies, the two men apparently talked of the military situation first. Stalin gave the President the latest news from the Russian front, which was not quite as good as it had been all summer and autumn. The Russians had sustained a set-back as a result of German counter-attacks, and had lost two towns. The Germans were aiming to retake Kiev. The Soviet leader made it clear that this development had made it necessary to regroup and concentrate on the Ukrainian front; only on that front could they develop offensive operations for the moment, but it was still hoped that Soviet troops might cross the old Polish frontier very soon. Roosevelt did not pursue this theme, but, after an apparently irrelevant mention of the possible transfer of surplus merchant ships to the USSR after the war, plunged into a discussion of South-east Asian operations. This seems to have been partly prompted by a deliberate tactic, already agreed with the US Chiefs of Staff, that the Teheran meeting should be used to bring home to the Russians the scale of the Far Eastern war which the Anglo-Americans were fighting but Russia was not; partly also no doubt it was designed to elicit Stalin's opinion of the Chinese Nationalists and pave the way for the discussion of Soviet–Chinese relations and Soviet Far Eastern objectives which Roosevelt felt must occur some time during the conference; and partly to remind Stalin of the importance the Americans attached to future Soviet participation in the Far Eastern war.

Stalin's response cannot have been particularly encouraging. He was, it seems, contemptuous of the Chinese military effort and equally of Chinese leadership. Roosevelt switched to another topic, where

Soviet intentions were also slightly uncertain and a little worrying. He mentioned the trouble they had had with de Gaulle, particularly over the Lebanon. Stalin's response this time was very much to Roosevelt's taste. De Gaulle's posturing, they agreed, was 'unreal'. The 'real' France was the France of Pétain which had collaborated with the Nazis, and would have to suffer for it. Churchill's notion that France could soon become a great power again was wishful thinking. Via Indo-China, which Stalin, like Roosevelt, thought should not be restored to France, the conversation moved to European colonialism in general. Stalin made the valid point that they would need to fight Japan politically as well as militarily. The Japanese had given some of their conquered territories at least a semblance of autonomy and self-government. Were the Allies going to offer them nothing more than a return to colonial rule? Roosevelt reminded him of Hull's Moscow reference to the 'trusteeship' principle as a path to relatively swift independence. That principle, under the United Nations, should provide the pattern for future developments in this area. The United States itself had set an example in its treatment of the Philippines. Although the cynic might recall that there were other Pacific islands which the United States might be less willing to forgo, it is difficult not to feel that Roosevelt's position on colonialism was in essence ethically sound, and, in the long run, politically sensible. It is perhaps a pity he did not adhere to it as rigidly in relation to Soviet claims in the Far East. At the same time, as Averell Harriman noted, the President was almost totally ignorant of the vast and complex problems involved in preparing so many races at such different stages of development for self-government; more so than Stalin, who had hardly ever been outside his own country. Nor did Roosevelt really seem to grasp the immense consequences for the world balance of power and world stability of such a transformation of the political map in much of Asia and most of Africa.

It was, for a first meeting of the two most powerful men in the Allied camp, a curious affair. Roosevelt, as he later told his son, had not intended to transact any very serious business. He thought of it as a first opportunity for each of them to size each other up and begin to get to know each other. Most men who met Stalin, however much they might be repelled by his personality (which does not appear to have been the case with Roosevelt) formed a favourable impression of the Soviet leader's shrewdness and general capability. Brooke, for example, thought Stalin had 'ability, force, shrewdness, and a military brain of the highest calibre', in this last respect superior to both Churchill and Roosevelt. Roosevelt certainly found the man impressive. Moreover they had seemed to think alike on a lot of things. He told Elliott Roosevelt that he was sure that they would 'hit it off' and that the mistrusts of the past would be cleared up. It was Churchill who was really the problem. His viewpoint was so far from Stalin's that it would be difficult to reconcile them. But Roosevelt was prepared to try.

What Stalin's first impressions were we can no more be absolutely sure now than then. If Djilas' testimony is to be believed, he trusted Roosevelt very little more than he trusted Churchill. But whatever his impressions, it seems certain that Stalin must have been much encouraged by Roosevelt's frank expression of how far apart his and Churchill's ideas were. Unless the President were playing a very deep game, he was apparently prepared to see France permanently weakened and British influence as a world power much reduced, at least in Asia. If Roosevelt was prepared to take an equally drastic and simplistic view of the 'proper solution' to the German problem—and Stalin was soon to find out that he was—there would be little to stand in the way of Soviet objectives in Europe; while in the Far East the removal of European colonial power and the defeat of Japan would relieve the USSR of most of her fears and open up a wider scope for her ambitions. Did it cross Stalin's mind that Roosevelt was, wittingly or unwittingly, pointing towards a world of Soviet/American dictatorship—that system which the Chinese were much later to stigmatize as 'hegemonism'? Probably it did. All Stalin's suspicions and prejudices, however, must surely (and almost certainly did) have prevented him from thinking of this as much more than a temporary *modus vivendi* based on *realpolitik*. It is difficult to believe that the Soviet leader ever thought possible the kind of partnership and genuine cooperation between capitalist America and communist Russia which Roosevelt desired. *Mutatis mutandis* these considerations probably still define the limits of *détente* today.[5]

The discussion between the two men had lasted for about three-quarters of an hour. There was only a brief break before Stalin returned with Molotov and Voroshilov, and Churchill appeared with Eden and the British Chiefs, for the first plenary meeting at four o'clock. Because of the misunderstanding already noted, Roosevelt had only Hopkins, Leahy, King, and Deane with him.

This was to be the decisive meeting, so far as allied strategy was concerned. Churchill and Stalin had already agreed that Roosevelt should preside. The latter opened by stressing again, for Stalin's benefit, the fact that for the Anglo-Americans and particularly the United States, it was a 'two-front war'. In relation to the Pacific he underlined the vast distances and great efforts required, touched on the 'island-hopping' strategy and the naval war of attrition against Japan and, turning to China, emphasized that the essential purpose of the Burma operations was to keep China in the war. The forces involved were seeking to reopen a land route for supplies to China and they were also hoping to increase the air bombardment of Japan via this theatre. Cautiously, in view of Churchill's presence, Roosevelt added that amphibious operations in this area were also 'under discussion'.

Roosevelt then turned to Europe and the main issue. 'Overlord' was planned for May 1944, but in the meantime the British and Americans wished to aid their Soviet Ally as much as possible through Mediterranean operations. The problem was landing-craft, since most of the options available required amphibious operations. Because of this, a very big effort in the Mediterranean would involve giving up 'Overlord' altogether. 'Lesser operations' might involve delays of one, two, or three months. The possible options were stepping up the Italian offensive, operating against the Adriatic coast, or, in conjunction with Turkish entry into the war, operations in the Aegean. It was on these points that they particularly wanted to hear Marshal Stalin's views. Which course would help Russia most? Roosevelt concluded, according to the US record, by making it clear that he personally regarded 'Overlord' as the most effective way of helping Russia, and therefore wished for as little delay to it as possible: which meant in effect, the minimum for Mediterranean operations which the Russians would accept.

The US Chiefs must have felt that Roosevelt could not have expressed their views more forcibly. Conversely Churchill no doubt thought the President had presented Mediterranean operations in just about as unfavourable a light as it was possible to do, invited the answer he wished, and at the same time grossly overstated the case. The British had always argued, sincerely, though perhaps optimistically, that they could do everything they wished to do in the Mediterranean at the cost of at most two months' delay to 'Overlord'. But this of course was on the assumption that the Andamans operation, with its demands on landing-craft, could be dropped or at any rate postponed, an assumption Roosevelt was not prepared to make—not as yet. However, Churchill elected to postpone his remarks till Stalin had spoken. (This was a tactical mistake. But he was not without hope still that the Russians might support his case.)

If this plenary meeting was the decisive encounter of the conference from the viewpoint of future allied strategy, the moment that was now upon them was the decisive moment of that meeting. Both the British and the Americans waited for Stalin to speak with mingled hope and anxiety. By laying stress on the drain to American resources constituted by the war against Japan, the President had tacitly invited Stalin to reaffirm—or not—his Moscow promise that the USSR would eventually enter that conflict. By posing the Mediterranean/'Overlord' alternative so starkly, he had then invited Stalin to settle that issue also one way or the other.

Stalin proceeded to answer the first question immediately. So long as the German war continued, Soviet forces in Siberia could only be maintained at a level adequate for defensive operations. To take the offensive against Japan these forces would need to be trebled. But with Germany defeated it would be possible to reinforce the Far Eastern Army. It seems clear (though the Soviet record, for reasons best known to its editors, omits this passage) that Stalin then repeated his promise to enter the war against Japan after Germany was defeated.

Having gratified his American listeners by this assurance, Stalin was about to do so even more. However, he kept his listeners in suspense a little longer by first describing operations on the Russian front, evidently in much the same way as he had to Roosevelt. Then he turned to the main business and administered the *coup de grâce* to Churchill's hopes. The Russians, he said, had never denied that the Italian campaign had some value, but that value was mainly in opening the Mediterranean and freeing much Allied shipping. As a route to the heart of Germany, however, Italy itself was clearly not very suitable, since the Alps stood in the way. Similarly it would be helpful to the Allied cause if Turkey opened the way to the Balkans, but the Balkans, too, were a long way from the heart of Germany. France was closest of all to the German heartland and the best route to it. The Cross-Channel Attack, therefore, was the best of all the options mentioned, supported perhaps by a landing in the south of France. The clear implication was there. Whatever may have been the case at the time of the Moscow conference, or since, Russia was not now pressing for extensive Mediterranean operations.

Stalin had said exactly what the Americans had wanted him to say, and dreaded not to hear. Conversely, Churchill must have known from this moment that he was fighting a losing battle, with all the odds against him. But such considerations had never deterred him from entering the fray, and they did not do so now. His first purpose was to challenge the idea which Roosevelt had established of an antithesis between the Cross-Channel Attack and Mediterranean operations. They were not inconsistent: they were complementary. It had always been the British argument that only by weakening Germany through persistent pressure in the Mediterranean could the success of 'Overlord' be assured. They were all, Churchill said, agreed on 'Overlord' in the spring or early summer of 1944. That was not in question. Thirty-five Anglo-American divisions would be used in the first assault, rising within a few months to a total of fifty or sixty divisions. Britain would play its full part initially, though subsequent reinforcement must come from the United States. Churchill pointed out that Anglo-American divisions, with all their complex supporting arms, were numerically much larger than German divisions—about twice the figure of 12,000 (which Stalin himself had given) for a German division. To put the matter simply, this meant that an Anglo-American army group would be landed in the first assault, and a second army group within a month or two: and these army groups would be numerically equivalent to a German or Soviet army group, though containing a smaller number of divisions.

But in the mean time, Churchill continued, there would be an interval of at least six months, even if the earliest possible date (1 May 1944) was adhered to. He had always regarded Mediterranean operations as a 'stepping stone' to 'Overlord', not 'the main theatre' (a remark which somewhat oversimplified a series of complex and sometimes inconsistent attitudes). But the British and Americans could not remain idle in the Mediterranean during this long period. In Italy the target was Rome, which it was still hoped would be taken quite soon, and then the Pisa–Rimini line. The British had no plans prepared for an invasion of Austria from Italy, and certainly did not propose to send a large army into the Balkans, though it was obviously good policy to assist Tito's resistance in Yugoslavia. As the President had said, if a defensive posture were adopted on the Pisa–Rimini line, some of the forces in Italy could then be used amphibiously for a 'right-hand' movement on the Adriatic. Alternatively there was the possibility of an operation in southern France. Then there was the Eastern Mediterranean. Great things might be achieved if they could neutralize the German outpost in the Dodecanese, open the Aegean and the Dardanelles to Allied shipping, and bring Turkey into the war. The effect on Germany's satellites, Romania and Bulgaria, and on the conquered Greeks and Yugoslavs would be profound. They might start a 'landslide' in favour of the Allies in the Balkans. All this, Churchill implied, could be achieved without taking resources from 'Overlord'. Only two or three British divisions with air support would be required, which were already in Egypt and the Middle East. They could not be brought back to participate in 'Overlord' because there was not shipping available. Why not use them? Putting the same question as Roosevelt to Stalin, but hoping for a rather different answer, Churchill then asked the direct question. Were these operations of sufficient interest to the USSR to warrant a delay of two or even three months to 'Overlord'? How should they approach Turkey, and how hard should they try to get Turkey into the war?

At this point Roosevelt again weighed in, somewhat to the consternation of the US delegation, by reiterating that 'he had thought of a possible operation at the head of the Adriatic, to make a junction with the Partisans under Tito and then operate north-east into Romania in conjunction with the Soviet advance from Odessa'. Hopkins passed a note to King. 'Who's promoting the Adriatic business the President keeps returning to?' Equally bewildered, King replied, 'As far as I know it's his own idea.' Even Churchill was surprised, after Roosevelt's strong presentation in favour of absolute priority for 'Overlord', though no doubt pleased. It was probably this episode which prompted Churchill to say in his memoirs, 'the President drifted to and fro in the argument'.

Stalin then questioned Churchill closely, in what the latter regarded as the crucial point of the discussion, about the effect of these various operations on 'Overlord', particularly in terms of the allocation of troops. Would a development of operations from Italy affect the troops for 'Overlord'? 'No', replied Churchill; seven divisions had already been withdrawn from Italy for 'Overlord'; further reinforcements for 'Overlord' would come direct from the United States. Shrewdly Stalin asked if the capture of Rome, landings in the south of France and in the Adriatic were *all* envisaged. Churchill replied that no definite plans had been worked out for the Southern France operation. They were, he implied, discussing possibilities and alternatives. In answer to a further question from Stalin, the Prime Minister repeated that if Turkey came into the war, this would only draw on the two or three divisions needed to capture the Dodecanese—which were already in the Middle East. It was precisely on this point—whether the effects of Aegean operations could be thus limited—that the US Chiefs had most doubts. Perhaps Stalin did too.

At all events Stalin now made the decisive thrust. It was not wise strategy, he said, reproducing almost exactly the American view, to disperse forces all over the Mediterranean in these varied operations. 'Overlord' was the best way of assaulting Germany and everything else should be subordinated to it. It would be best to use any surplus troops in Italy for a landing in the south of France, perhaps even before 'Overlord'. It was sound strategy to attack the weakest spot

(France) from two directions in a pincer movement. Even the capture of Rome was less important. As for Turkey, he very much doubted if she would enter the war though it would be helpful if she did. But neutrals, he said, knew when they were well off and preferred to stay that way, to which Roosevelt subsequently added that if he were President Inönü of Turkey, he would demand a very high price for entering the war. Churchill continued the argument vigorously. He was not necessarily opposed to a landing in the south of France; he accepted that Turkey might remain obdurate, and so limit possibilities in the East Mediterranean. But the British public would never understand, if Rome were not captured after all the hard fighting in the Mediterranean. In any case the Allies needed the airfields north of Rome to support any invasion of France: and he personally would not tolerate large British forces in the entire Mediterranean being left virtually idle during a critical period of the war.

It was quite evident, however, that the British Prime Minister was making little impression on Stalin. Seeing this Roosevelt proposed that the military staffs should meet the following day and work out plans for a landing in the south of France, possibly even to precede 'Overlord'. Not quite willing to concede defeat, Churchill insisted the staffs should also consider Turkey—what they should ask the Turks to do, what inducements they could offer, what consequences followed if Turkey agreed to enter the war. Making it clear that he now had very little interest in or expectations from Turkey, Stalin said all that would be up to the Anglo-Americans to decide. Turkey was their responsibility. He then agreed, though rather reluctantly, that the staffs should meet the next day, adding rather unkindly that he had not brought his military men with him, but the unfortunate Voroshilov would 'do his best'. Roosevelt then proposed that the staffs should meet at 10.30, Marshall and Leahy for the Americans, Brooke and Portal for the British, and Voroshilov for Russia, before a further plenary meeting at four o'clock in the afternoon.[6]

With that the first meeting of the three leaders ended, with the strategic argument largely resolved in favour of the Americans. Churchill had been outvoted two to one—and those two both more powerful than he. Naturally the Americans were delighted, even surprised by Stalin's enthusiasm not only for 'Overlord' but also for the South of France operation. Predictably they formed a high opinion of Stalin's intelligence and strategic abilities. So did Brooke, but for different reasons. He had never personally had as much enthusiasm for Turkey or East Mediterranean operations as Churchill. But he was horrified by the suggestion that the Italian campaign, even perhaps the capture of Rome, should be completely sacrificed; and even more by the idea of a premature landing in southern France. To give the Germans a chance to mop up an inadequate force in the south before the main 'Overlord' landings took place was military nonsense and he thought Stalin must know that. The latter, he thought, was simply concerned that the Anglo-Americans should divert some German forces, and did not care what the consequences were.

Certainly the Soviet view as presented by Stalin at Teheran differed widely from what it had been a few months earlier and even more recently. After the Moscow conference Molotov and the Soviet military representatives had continued to needle Harriman and Deane on Turkey, and the need to keep things going in the Mediterranean. Now the Russians were once again all for 'Overlord' and nothing but 'Overlord'. Brooke's view was that things had gone so well for the Soviet forces recently that they now felt they could afford to wait for a crushing 'Overlord'. By the same token they were no longer prepared to take the risk of obstacles to their political objectives in Eastern Europe which Anglo-American activity in the Aegean and perhaps in the Balkans might engender. This was probably a pretty sound diagnosis. Whatever the cause, there was gloom in the British camp. Brooke felt that the day's proceedings had gone 'from bad to worse' and 'confused things more than ever'. Churchill put it more succinctly. According to his doctor, he said 'A bloody lot has gone wrong', attributing this largely to 'the prejudice of Roosevelt's military advisers'.[7]

In this somewhat chastened mood Churchill, Eden, and Clark Kerr joined Stalin and Molotov with Roosevelt, Harriman, and Hopkins for dinner. The President was not feeling well, which may indeed have accounted for what Hopkins as well as the British thought a rather inept performance at the plenary meeting. At all events Roosevelt soon pleaded indisposition and retired for the evening. Before he left, there had been some discussion between the three men about France, Germany, and Poland. Stalin and Roosevelt again vented their spleen against France and agreed that the French did not deserve to retain their empire. In any event various important strategic points such as Dakar should be put in safer hands. Churchill did not for the moment choose to take up the thesis. He contented himself with the remark that it would be wise for 'certain strategic points' to be under UN control. Stalin also took the opportunity to develop the argument which Molotov had foreshadowed during the Moscow discussions— namely that the harshest possible treatment should be administered to Germany, including the dismemberment of the German State. Most of the measures of control so far mentioned by the Americans—disarmament and so forth—were inadequate to prevent a revival of German power and aggressive militarism. Roosevelt took the point about dismemberment up and suggested the establishment of an international zone of some kind in north Germany to control the Kiel Canal and safeguard the approaches to the Baltic. In addition the Polish–German frontier, Stalin remarked, should be moved westwards to the Oder, slicing off a considerable portion of pre-war Germany. Roosevelt then left the party, but Churchill, though also not feeling at his best, was not disposed to miss his first real chance of a talk with Stalin. He wanted to discuss Germany and Poland further——particularly Poland. Stalin discoursed further about his view of Germany. Unless they dealt with the Germans with the utmost severity, Germany would soon rise again. The Soviet leader clearly had no sympathy with the gentlemanly view that one should not kick a man when he was down. Having got the Germans down, one should kick them and go on kicking them, or they might get up again. Churchill suggested there was a distinction to be made between the Nazi regime and the ordinary German working people, but Stalin waved away this unexceptionably proletarian statement. The Germans were all much of a muchness, he implied. They were dangerous because they would always do what they were told. Churchill in turn took up the point about dismemberment and floated his idea of a 'Danubian federation'. He had always felt that Prussia, which he implied was the heart of German militarism, should be detached from the rest of Germany and treated 'more severely'. Then perhaps south Germany could form a 'peaceful confederation' with Austria and Hungary. Stalin was non-committal, but on this occasion apparently did not reject the idea out of hand. That would come later.

Churchill then took the conversation on to the sticky Polish ground. It seemed best to begin with the frontier question, on which British and American views might not be too far away from the Russians, since they were both willing to concede that the Soviet frontier should extend to the 'Curzon Line', with compensation for Poland in the west. If they could work out something satisfactory to the Russians on the frontier question, perhaps that might make it easier to discuss the thorny question of the London Polish government: at all events they could establish definitely what Stalin wanted in the way of frontiers. Stalin's response was chilly to begin with, but as it became apparent that Churchill and Eden for the moment only wished to discuss frontiers, not the London Poles, he thawed somewhat. Churchill emphasized that though Britain had gone to war for Poland, they had not guaranteed any particular frontiers, only that an independent Polish State should be preserved. Stalin cautiously agreed that Polish culture and language should be respected, but evaded the question of Polish political independence. However, the two men agreed without too much difficulty that Poland should move westwards on the map and gain in the west (at the expense of Germany) what she lost in the east to Russia. Eden was encouraged by this conversation. He felt they had made the 'opening moves' on Poland, and they had not gone too badly. The problem would be to get Roosevelt to commit himself publicly on the frontier issue: Hopkins had told him that with the presidential election due next year, the Polish question was 'political dynamite'. Eden in turn had pointed out to him that if they did not get a settlement *now* with Stalin it would be much more difficult to get a satisfactory one later, when Soviet troops had occupied Poland.[8]

29 November. The military decision confirmed: the world organization: China and Germany

The first day's discussion had really decided the crucial military issue, as Churchill and Brooke both realized. Churchill, who saw his cherished Eastern Mediterranean strategy receding into the distance, was the more downcast. He was appalled by the final realization that he could no longer count on Roosevelt's support, and that consequently he now had little power to influence Anglo-American strategy. For Brooke, who had always been less enthusiastic for the Eastern Mediterranean strategy, all this was less catastrophic. The important thing was to ensure that the Italian campaign was not wantonly jeopardized and that no plan was approved for a premature landing in the south of France which would invite disaster.

In this mood Brooke went to the meeting of the military representatives at 10.30 on the morning of the twenty-ninth. As he must have expected, he had to spend most of the meeting arguing with Voroshilov. The latter had obviously been well briefed, and repeated stolidly Stalin's arguments of the previous day and his 'two demands': (1) that 'Overlord' should take place on the agreed date, or at any rate with as little delay as possible; and (2) that it should be supported by a landing in the south of France. Brooke for his part drew Voroshilov's fire by pointing out that both 'Overlord' and the Southern France operation could easily fail if the conditions were not right.

Brooke began by restating the familiar British argument that it was vital to keep as many German divisions as possible engaged prior to 'Overlord', which at the earliest could not take place before the first of May. This objective could only be achieved through Mediterranean operations. There were about twenty German divisions in Italy and another twenty or so in the Balkans, plus some Bulgarian units. The Germans must not be able to transfer any of them to France. He reminded the meeting of the possibilities mentioned by Churchill—Italy, increased aid to the Yugoslav resistance, or operations in the Aegean—and loyally stressed the advantages to be gained from the latter. Without calling on any troops not already in the Mediterranean they could, if Turkey co-operated, open a shorter supply route to Russia and acquire air-bases for attacks on targets in Romania. But both Italy and the Aegean would require amphibious operations and therefore the retention of landing-craft in the Mediterranean, with some delay to 'Overlord'. According to the British record, Voroshilov at this point asked whether Brooke's arguments applied particularly to Italian operations. Still loyal to his brief Brooke replied that they applied equally to Italy and the Eastern Mediterranean: however he revealed his own priorities by going on to stress particularly the advantages for strategic bombing of south Germany of taking the airfields north of Rome. He added the valid point, in the light of the fact that the Russian air force did not engage in strategic bombing, that the Anglo-American strategic air effort kept a million Germans occupied who might otherwise be employed elsewhere. Brooke then turned his attention to the suggested operation in southern France, soon to be code-named 'Anvil'. Even a defensive strategy on the Italian front would still require a considerable force, leaving a relatively small one —perhaps six to eight divisions—for a southern France operation. A force of that size, landed several weeks before 'Overlord', would almost certainly be defeated. A simultaneous landing would, however, he conceded, stand a better chance. Taking up another Soviet argument, which Brooke obviously regarded as simplistic, the CIGS added that one could not compare the problems of a pincer movement in a land campaign with those involved in two widely separated amphibious operations, such as 'Overlord' and 'Anvil', where forces depended on seaborne supply and reinforcement. The crucial period for example for 'Overlord' would be the immediate follow-up of the initial assault—the build-up from four or five to thirty-five divisions. During this period it was essential that the enemy should not be able to bring large reinforcements to bear.

Marshall then restated the US case firmly, but with his usual moderation. He conceded Brooke's argument as to the danger of a premature landing in the south of France and the relative slowness of a build-up over open beaches (since one must assume that the enemy would put any nearby ports out of action). On the main issue, he reaffirmed American belief in the Cross-Channel strategy; he had always considered it much the most advantageous. The problems now before them, however, was what Mediterranean operations should be undertaken during the period before 'Overlord'. The limiting factor was not trained troops, of which they now had plenty in the United States, but air-cover, and more especially assault shipping and landing-craft. The latter had now become so crucial as almost to determine strategy. The Pacific war was largely a matter of amphibious landings, and the Americans had four such operations currently in hand, with four more to follow. Summing up, Marshall said the question was where and when to use the limited number of landing-craft in the Mediterranean; and this in turn depended on whether any delay to 'Overlord' was acceptable. Where should they strike the balance between the two extremes of 'very reduced' operations in the Mediterranean and a large-scale plan involving perhaps several operations? Undoubtedly the former would involve the least interference with 'Overlord'.

Although Marshall had put the case fairly, he had by his summing-up invited Voroshilov to give the required answer. The latter probably needed no encouragement. Also no doubt he saw an obvious opportunity to drive a wedge between the British and Americans, and to discomfort Brooke who, together with Churchill, was clearly the main antagonist. This he did by misrepresenting Brooke's argument. It was clear to the Russians, he said, that the United States thought 'Overlord' of first importance. But did General Brooke think the same, or did he believe that Mediterranean operations could take its place? In any case was it really necessary to use the same landing-craft for both? At Moscow they had been told the building of landing-craft was being speeded up and given priority. Marshall had already implied the true answer to this second question, which was that Admiral King had commandeered the lion's share of the increased production for his Pacific operations. However he contented himself with saying that in spite of every effort, there were still not enough landing-craft to go round. The main question, however, had been aimed directly at Brooke, and he now answered it in his customary unyielding fashion. Yes, he did believe 'Overlord' to be not only important, but essential—but only if the right conditions obtained: and these conditions depended among other things on keeping the maximum number of German divisions employed in the Mediterranean. That would not happen if the 1 May date were adhered to, because that would mean withdrawing landing-craft from the Mediterranean *now* and thereby making it impossible to maintain the most effective pressure on the Germans through amphibious operations. Mediterranean operations were indeed 'auxiliary' to 'Overlord'—but a necessary auxiliary.

Voroshilov then restated the Soviet position, which of course differed not a whit from that enunciated by Stalin the previous day. The Soviet marshal did not attempt to answer Brooke's arguments. He ignored them. 'Overlord' was what really mattered, therefore no operations should be undertaken elsewhere which would interfere with (that is, delay) it. The meaning was clear. There should be no amphibious operations in Italy or the Eastern Mediterranean. The Anglo-Americans should 'dig in' in Italy and if possible attempt a landing in the south of France. However the important thing from the Soviet point of view was that 'Overlord' should take place at the beginning of May. They would like the Southern France landings also, but, Voroshilov added, 'they did not insist on it'. He was sure the Allies would overcome the technical problems of these two operations, if only (no doubt looking at Brooke) the will to launch them was there. The Red Army had faced similar problems in making crossings of large and bitterly defended rivers. Although almost every word Voroshilov said was supporting his own general views, Marshall found this last over-simplification too much to swallow. There was a difference between the failure of a river crossing and the failure of an amphibious operation, he said. The former would be a set-back: the latter was a catastrophe. For himself, the need to grapple with the problems of amphibious operations had required a complete personal military re-education; Soviet generals, and even Soviet marshals, he implied, had not had to cope with that part of the curriculum.

As could be foreseen, the meeting had simply provided an opportunity to restate the main positions already adopted, and had served little useful purpose, except perhaps to confirm the absurdity of expecting the CCS to function and produce agreed recommendations if representatives were added to it who had no latitude to vary their government's position. There was clearly no agreement, there could be no agreed recommendations, and there was little point in continuing. Voroshilov, however, attempted to get a decision, which of course in the situation could not have been a unanimous decision but a 'majority' decision. When Brooke intimated that he would have a good deal more to say before he agreed to anything, it was provisionally agreed that they should meet again the next morning, the unspoken condition being, 'if our political masters think there is any point in our so doing'. Both the Americans and the British were agreed on one point. They had got nowhere.⁹

It would not be quite true, however, to say that the meeting had had no effect. It clearly confirmed the view which Brooke had probably already formed, that if the Americans were determined to let Russia decide their strategy, it would be necessary to make some concession to the Soviet point of view. It probably seemed a rather one-sided arrangement to Brooke, since no one was suggesting that the Anglo-Americans should directly influence Soviet strategy in Europe, save for a request that the Red Army should try to launch an offensive to coincide with 'Overlord'. But it could not be helped. Nor was Stalin to blame. The Anglo-Americans had chosen to submit the question to him and he had given the answer which suited him best. What was the consequence? The Eastern Mediterranean strategy would probably have to go and they would have to consider at any rate the practical possibilities of a landing in the south of France. But that would at least have the advantage that so long as the operation were seriously under consideration, there would be a strong case for retaining landing-craft in the Mediterranean. The important thing was to make sure that 'Anvil' was not launched prematurely, which meant for Brooke not *before* 'Overlord'. Marshall had shown some sympathy with the British point of view on this at the meeting. If that point were gained, the landing-craft could be used for an operation against Rome before they were required for the south of France.

Immediately after lunch therefore the British Chiefs met to consider the question. Marshall had given them a preliminary note on the requirements of 'Anvil', and discussion centred around this. Considerable anxiety was expressed as to whether adequate air-cover could be provided. The nearest Allied-controlled airfield would be 190 miles away, on Corsica. The other possibilities—Sardinia and mainland Italy—were even more distant. Portal summed up on the matter. Land-based fighter support would be very meagre, which meant that aircraft-carriers would be required. These would have to be held back, Cunningham pointed out, from the Indian Ocean, delaying the naval build-up there, and prejudicing the chances for 'Buccaneer'. So far as the land forces were concerned, the American note seemed to envisage transferring the bulk of the Italian troops to the Southern France operation, leaving what the British Chiefs agreed would be a totally inadequate force even to hold a defensive line in Italy.[10]

The Americans had in fact been taken by surprise by the Soviet enthusiasm for the South of France operation. They had not brought a copy of Eisenhower's latest plan of 27 October with them and had to work from an out-of-date 'outline' plan. Marshall, however, set his planners to work that afternoon and by the following morning they had produced a more realistic plan. Meanwhile, they conferred with the President, indicated their general support for the Southern France operation, and presented him with memoranda to discuss with Stalin on possible measures to be taken in anticipation of Russian entry into the war against Japan.

Roosevelt had refused to meet Churchill privately so far. None the less, the President had another private talk with Stalin at 2.45 that afternoon. Roosevelt stressed the importance of forward planning in advance of Soviet entry into the Far Eastern war and handed Stalin the US memoranda dealing with possible US use of Soviet air-bases and naval facilities in that eventuality. He also brought up again the possibility of American strategic 'shuttle-bombing' of Germany in co-operation with the USSR. General Deane had made this proposal at the Moscow conference, but had since been able to make little progress with the Russians. Stalin said he would give these matters his personal attention.

Roosevelt then unfolded to Stalin his ideas on the kind of structure he envisaged for the new international organization, which had been foreshadowed by the Four-Power Declaration at Moscow. He sketched out a plan whereby there would be a large consultative, world-wide body on which all the United Nations would be represented and a smaller Executive Committee of ten members in which the 'Big Four' would be joined by two European States, and one each from South America, the Near East, the Far East, and the self-governing members of the British Commonwealth. This body, Roosevelt suggested, should take decisions on non-military matters —agriculture, food, health, and the other economic areas which Hull had suggested at Moscow required international co-operation. When Stalin asked him if this body could make decisions which would be binding on its members, Roosevelt was somewhat evasive, but indicated that the 'Big Four' would probably have a veto if they chose to exercise it. Finally there would be a Four-Power Council which would deal with immediate threats to peace. Stalin saw an objection to this. The European States would not like to be ordered about by China, which in any case in his view would not be very powerful immediately after the war. This of course had been the consistent Soviet view, and was probably a sincere expression of opinion; though it is also probable that Stalin had no particular desire to see a powerful China emerge, whether Communist or non-Communist. According to Roosevelt's son, the President took the opportunity to mention some of the steps which would be necessary to raise China to the status required and some of the anxieties which Chiang felt. In the first place the European States would have to give up all their extra-territorial rights including the British colony of Hong Kong. Roosevelt also mentioned Chinese anxieties about Soviet intentions in Manchuria, to which Stalin replied that 'respect for the sovereignty of other countries was a cardinal principle with him'. No comment seems necessary on this interesting observation, if indeed it was made. Roosevelt may also have mentioned the promise he had extracted from Chiang that the Chinese Communists would be taken into his government and that free national elections would be held in China as soon as possible after the war. Stalin pressed his point about China, however, no doubt with the thought that it would not be desirable from the Soviet point of view to give China the right to meddle in European affairs. Would it not be better, he queried, to have two councils, one for Europe consisting of Britain, Russia, the US, and perhaps one other European State, and the other including China for the Far East? Roosevelt replied that Churchill thought there should be three councils—for Europe, the Far East, and the Western Hemisphere: but he himself doubted if Congress would agree to US membership of a purely European body which could commit US troops to the settlement of intra-European disputes. He added that it might not have been possible to involve the United States in the present war if the Japanese had not forced the issue in the Far East by attacking Pearl Harbour. Stalin replied logically that after all the proposed 'Big Four Council' would presumably be able to commit US troops in Europe, but Roosevelt indicated, as he had to his Chiefs of Staff in the *Iowa* talks, that the US would hope to confine its part to the use of American naval and air power: it would be up to Russia and Britain to use armies. This intimation that Roosevelt hoped to see all American ground forces withdrawn from Europe soon after the war —the first though not the last such intimation of the kind that Roosevelt was to give to Stalin—must have been welcome news to the Russian. It looked like a recipe for Soviet dominance in Europe. Roosevelt went on to say that economic sanctions might well be a sufficient weapon to use against small States which threatened peace and stability, but they would need to use military force for 'more serious threats'. As the editor of the Hopkins papers comments, it does not seem that the possibility of one of the Big Four being an aggressor was mentioned. Roosevelt, however, was aware of this contingency, and had concluded pragmatically that the new body would not be able to coerce the Big Four. He told his son that he had discussed the 'veto power' with Stalin, and they had both agreed that it was necessary, since the Council could not operate effectively unless the 'Big Four' were united. If these remarks were made—and it does not seem unlikely—it was presumably on this occasion. It may have been during this meeting also that Stalin gave Roosevelt an assurance that the Manchurian railway system should remain Chinese property, rather than passing wholly or partly under Soviet control: and also put in a Soviet claim to South Sakhalin and the Kurile Islands. But more probably this came later, probably over dinner, after the three leaders had discussed the possibility of Soviet access to warm-water ports in north China.

At the end of the conversation Stalin raised the question which was clearly on his mind—the necessity for a harsh settlement of the German problem. Unless the most stringent measures were taken, Germany could easily become a threat to peace again in fifteen or twenty years. He reiterated that the measures proposed in the US paper at the Moscow conference (see above, pp. 85–6) were good as far as they went, but not enough. Stalin mentioned his conversation with Churchill on the subject the previous night. The Prime Minister, he said, was far too optimistic on this score. The Big Four would need to retain control of German naval and air-bases for a considerable time—and similar strong points elsewhere, including islands near Japan. Roosevelt of course agreed whole-heartedly with this view which exactly coincided with his own. The conversation came back to China, and Stalin again expressed his doubts. Roosevelt replied by saying, as he had to others, that he was thinking far into the future. China was a nation of over four hundred million people, which represented an enormous potential power. It would be better to have them on the side of the new international order than against it. [11]

The conversation seems to have ended at this point and the two men moved to another room where Churchill, in an impressive ceremony, presented the specially made Stalingrad Sword to Stalin. Then, after a photographic session, the three heads of government met at four o'clock with the US and British Chiefs of Staff plus Eden, Molotov, Hopkins, Generals Somervell and Deane, and Voroshilov for the second plenary session.

The plenary session, like the Staff meeting, followed predictable lines. Stalin restated the Soviet position—'Overlord' on 1 May and a landing in the south of France at the expense of all other operations— and did his best to rush the Anglo-Americans into an immediate decision. Churchill in turn argued that this meant nothing would be done in the Mediterranean to weaken or hold down the German military effort for a period of at least four months. Was this really what they wanted? Surely it was worth a month or so's delay to 'Overlord' to achieve the objectives he had indicated? Roosevelt as usual seeking for a compromise, but leaning effectively to the Soviet side, said the issue was the timing, not the fact of 'Overlord'. It would still be possible, he said, to launch the main operation on or near the agreed date provided one of the three operations—the south of France, Rome, or Rhodes—were given up. The President left no doubt in anyone's mind that it was the Aegean operation which should be sacrificed.

Before the discussion reached that point, however, Stalin introduced a new point, and in so doing made it quite clear that he at any rate was by no means convinced by the President's assurance that the Anglo-Americans would launch 'Overlord' in 1944. Stalin had asked who the commander for 'Overlord' would be, and on being told by Roosevelt that the appointment had not yet been made, said bluntly that in this case 'nothing would come of the operation'. He himself, it was implied, would not be convinced that the Anglo-Americans were serious about 'Overlord' until they had appointed someone, the sooner the better. It was a valid point. Roosevelt must have appreciated this but felt he could not go into the personal problems involved with Marshall in the room. He pointed out, however, that planning for the operation had been in progress for months under the British General Morgan. Churchill added that he and Roosevelt had already agreed that the ultimate commander should be an American. Sensing Roosevelt's concern for Marshall's feelings, Churchill suggested the three leaders should discuss the matter privately rather than in a large meeting. Stalin was not to be deflected from his point. The information that a British general was in charge of planning probably was not particularly reassuring to him. He made a further valid point. It was not just a question of planning for the operation, he said, but its execution. The commander when appointed might well want to alter the existing plan, and that would cause further delay. All the Russians asked, Stalin continued, was to know the name: they were not seeking to influence the choice. When Churchill assured him that the appointment would probably be made within two weeks, Stalin was satisfied for the moment. But the interchange had revealed how far the Russians were from being convinced that 'Overlord' would take place; and in all the circumstances that was not altogether surprising.

Churchill, indeed, then added to these suspicions by going over the familiar British view with considerable force and eloquence. He could never agree to the proposition that substantial forces in the Mediterranean should remain virtually idle for six months. But there was no need for that if 'Overlord' were postponed for about six weeks.

That much delay would make it possible to retain enough landing-craft in the Mediterranean for a two-division 'lift'. That in turn, he believed, would enable them to undertake the operations for the capture of Rome and Rhodes, and still make a landing in the south of France in May or June. Churchill emphasized the point made by Brooke at the Staff meeting. The size of the force which could be spared from Italy for the latter operation would in any case have to be studied very carefully: too small a force would be annihilated. They should also give what help they could to the Yugoslavs, who were holding down about thirty enemy divisions in the Balkans: but, he repeated, there was no British proposal to send large Anglo-American forces into the Balkans. As for the Turks, the British government was prepared to bring the strongest possible pressure to bear on them and he hoped the US government would do the same. Equally he hoped that if Bulgaria attacked Turkey, the USSR would declare war on Bulgaria. If Turkey would not bear her share of the sacrifices, Churchill continued, she could not look to Britain for help in defend-ing her rights in the Bosphorus and the Dardanelles. The object of all Mediterranean operations, he insisted, was firstly to relieve the pres-sure on the Russian front and secondly to help the success of 'Over-lord'. With that thought in mind, the military staffs should be told to meet again and do better: and since the Aegean and Balkan operations raised political as well as military questions, it might be helpful if the British and Soviet foreign ministers also met, with a representative of the President, to discuss these matters.

Stalin at this point showed signs of impatience, feeling no doubt that they had gone round and round the same arguments long enough. Yes, he said, if Bulgaria attacked Turkey the USSR would declare war on Bulgaria; and they all agreed on giving help to the Yugoslavs. But these things were all of minor importance compared to 'Overlord'. If the British and Americans were concerned to help the USSR, the way to do it was to launch 'Overlord' as early as possible, and ensure its success by supporting it with an operation in the south of France, if possible before 'Overlord' or simultaneously with it. But even a landing there after 'Overlord' would be better than these other diversions. 'Overlord' in May was what counted and the commander should be appointed now. These were the directions which should be given to the military staffs if they really needed to meet again.

It was at this point that Roosevelt suggested his compromise. If one of the three amphibious operations were abandoned, 'Overlord' could still go ahead near enough to the prescribed time. If all three were to be undertaken, it would mean, as the Prime Minister had said, at least six weeks' delay to 'Overlord'. The President then made it crystal clear which operation he thought should go and why. The trouble with operations in the Eastern Mediterranean, he said, was that they might, if Turkey entered the war, lead to 'bigger commitments' (that is, in the Balkans) which would perhaps delay 'Overlord' by even more than six weeks.

It seems that Roosevelt, like the US Chiefs, had convinced himself that Churchill was determined there should be, one way or another, a 'Balkan invasion'; and that the motive, as he afterwards asserted to his son, was not primarily because Churchill thought this the better strategy, but because he wished to forestall the Russians in Central Europe. Stalin, Roosevelt thought, was equally aware of the political implications of the opposing strategies. In giving this subsequent account of the meeting to Elliott Roosevelt, if indeed he did, the President conveniently forgot that he himself had mentioned the possibility of a 'right-hand swing' from Italy through the 'Ljubljana gap' into the Balkans, while Churchill for his part had repeatedly disclaimed any intention of sponsoring large-scale operations in that region (as opposed to the Eastern Mediterranean). However, Roosevelt was determined to adopt the strategy which would bring the war to the speediest end, and had been convinced by his Chiefs of Staff that the Cross-Channel/Southern France strategy was the best choice from that point of view. (One may assume that Marshall had had a word with him on the subject of Adriatic adventures.) Churchill was thinking too much about post-war Europe, Roosevelt said, and afraid that Russia would be 'too strong'. He for his part 'would not put American lives in jeopardy to protect real or fancied British interests on the European continent'.

Stalin had hastened to support the President's suggestion. In his view, 'Overlord' should not be launched later than 20 May. Churchill replied equally bluntly that as far as Britain was concerned, he could give no such undertaking. Then, seeking to be more conciliatory, he added that there was after all no fundamental divergence, since they all wished 'Overlord' to go in as early as possible. But it would be wrong to let the armies in Italy stand idle for nearly six months and sacrifice great possibilities in the Mediterranean, merely in order to launch 'Overlord' on 1 May instead of early June. He reminded Stalin of the conditions or prerequisites for a successful 'Overlord' stated at Moscow. These included the stipulation that there should be no more than a limited number of German divisions in France at the time and no more than a limited number which could be sent from other theatres to reinforce them. Therefore it was necessary to hold as many German divisions as possible on other fronts. Taking up the President's point that Eastern Mediterranean operations might lead to an unlimited commitment, Churchill emphasized again that only small forces, and those already on the spot, were required for the operations he had proposed. Equally they would require only a small number of landing-craft, and these would have to be retained in the Mediterranean till May anyway, or how were they to undertake landings in the south of France?

Stalin now showed his impatience openly. He clearly felt there had been enough talk. The President had asked him to meet him for three or four days, and he himself could certainly not stay in Teheran beyond 2 December. He could see no point in referring things to military or political subcommittees. They themselves were the heads of government, and it was up to them to make the important decisions, namely the date of 'Overlord', the choice of its commander, and 'the need for an auxiliary operation in southern France'. He wanted as early as possible a date for 'Overlord' but whatever date was fixed he must know it, if the Red Army was to plan an offensive to coincide with the main operation. This was a fair point. Roosevelt then read out a directive to the military staffs, which he hoped would satisfy both Stalin and Churchill. It was to the effect that they should assume 'Overlord' to be 'the dominating operation' and consider what subsidiary operations should be included in the Mediterranean, 'taking into careful account any delay in operation "Overlord"'. Churchill, who was determined that they should not be rushed into a decision, said that he was certainly in favour of the military staffs committee meeting again, and also thought a meeting of Molotov, Eden, and a US representative would be useful on the political issues. This was too much for the Soviet leader. Turning to Churchill he directed at him the same thrust as Voroshilov had directed at Brooke that morning. 'Did the British believe in 'Overlord' or were they just saying so to pacify the Russians?' Churchill gave him the same answer as Brooke had given to Voroshilov. 'Yes, if the right conditions [that is, those stated at Moscow] prevail.'

Roosevelt obviously realized that the tension was rising. Soothingly he suggested that there was a good dinner awaiting them and no doubt they were all hungry. The Staffs should meet tomorrow and reach an agreed decision. Churchill added, no doubt with considerable feeling, that it was the British and US Chiefs alone who should meet to coordinate their views, so that they could at least present an agreed programme to the Russians. Stalin, according to the Soviet record, replied drily that that would certainly 'accelerate their work'. Grudgingly he added that the foreign secretaries and the representative of the President could also meet, if the British and Americans thought it important. Finally it seems to have been agreed that the Anglo-American Staffs should meet in the morning, the heads of state should lunch together at 1.30, while the foreign ministers lunched separately, and there should be a further plenary session at four o'clock. Talking to his son afterwards, Roosevelt apparently said 'Winston knows that he is beaten'. Probably indeed he did. [12]

Beaten or not, Churchill still had plenty of spirit left, as was to be obvious later that evening, when the three leaders met for dinner at 7.45, with Stalin as host. Molotov, Eden, Hopkins, Harriman, and Clark Kerr were also present, and so apparently, and some might think inappropriately, was Elliott Roosevelt, which proved to be rather an unfortunate circumstance. The various records by the participants have to be accepted with some caution, since the wine and vodka, as usual at Soviet banquets, seem to have flowed freely. However all the accounts agree that Stalin expressed his resentment at Churchill's opposition to his plans by 'needling him unmercifully', as Harriman puts it. Roosevelt's obvious hope that the tensions generated by the afternoon's arguments would be assuaged by food and drink can hardly be said to have been fulfilled. Stalin repeatedly implied that Churchill had a secret liking for the Germans and therefore wanted to let them off with a soft peace. 'We Russians are not blind', he remarked at one point, implying presumably that Churchill's real motive was to maintain Germany in some form as a bulwark against Russia. In his view, he repeated, 'really effective measures were necessary, or Germany would rise again in fifteen to twenty years'. These should certainly include the liquidation of the entire German general staff. Making his meaning absolutely clear, Stalin said this would require the execution of 50,000 or perhaps 100,000 officers.

At this point the inevitable explosion occurred, as no doubt Stalin expected. Churchill replied heatedly that he personally would never agree to cold-blooded murder or 'barbarous acts'. Only proven war criminals should be punished after a proper trial. Roosevelt tried to lower the temperature with a bad joke to the effect that perhaps 49,000 would do. It seems that the unfortunate Elliott Roosevelt was drawn into the argument by Stalin; and this reference to a young officer, who probably in his opinion should not have been there at all, provoked Churchill even more. According to his own account he left the party and went into an adjoining room, from which Stalin and Molotov had to persuade him to return.

When the discussion was resumed, and turned again to the necessity for the 'Big Three' to retain control of bases and strong points all over the globe, Churchill relieved his ruffled feelings further by saying categorically that Britain desired no extension of territory, but would not give up what she had, and that included Hong Kong and Singapore. If they advanced any portion of the Empire towards self-government it would be in accordance with their own principles of what was right, not, he implied, in accordance with any blueprint imposed upon her. Britain might, however, occupy certain bases if that was the wish of their Allies. In his now conciliatory mood Stalin assured him that the British had fought well in the war, implying that they deserved some reward. He personally thought the British Empire should increase its territory round Gibraltar at the expense of Spain. Franco had shown that he was their enemy, and they should install 'more suitable governments' in both Spain and Portugal. Scenting that Stalin might well think it would be difficult for the British to oppose Soviet territorial demands if they themselves were being equally greedy, Churchill immediately asked what Russia would demand as extra territory, but Stalin refused to be drawn. The time for Russia to make its demands would come later, he replied, doubtless reflecting that almost every day's operations on the Eastern front served to strengthen the Soviet bargaining position.

After the dinner Hopkins, very probably on Roosevelt's instructions, visited Churchill, and apparently advised him to give in on the military question gracefully. He pointed to the strength of US feelings on the 'Overlord' issue and the fact that the United States and Russia were agreed. Britain could not expect to impose its wishes on its two more powerful Allies. Churchill as well as Brooke was probably coming to this conclusion by now, however reluctantly. But Hopkins's visit must have served to confirm it.

It had been another bad day for the British, particularly Churchill. Brooke for his part felt that a lunatic asylum would not seem strange after the arguments of the last two days, in which the Americans, in his view, as at Cairo, were forcing them to put 'the cart before the horse'. It must have seemed strange to him that the British should be accused of framing strategy for political reasons when Roosevelt had first tried to force an operation on them ('Buccaneer') of uncertain value in order to please Chiang-Kai-Shek and was now sponsoring another dubious operation in the south of France in order to win Stalin's favour. But he saw that they would have to agree to consider the latter seriously, in order to save the Italian campaign: in return the

Americans would have to accept a limited postponement of 'Overlord' in order to get what they wanted.

Stalin for his part must have been pretty well pleased by the day's events, which in general had confirmed his advantage. Churchill certainly was still being obstinate, but he could hardly hold out indefinitely against the two of them. The Americans had made it plain that they would go as far as they could to satisfy Soviet military demands, and had no enthusiasm whatever for strategic ventures which might place substantial Anglo-American forces in the Red Army's bailiwick. Moreover if Roosevelt meant what he said, not only would there be no Anglo-American military presence in Eastern Europe, but very soon after the war there would be no American military presence in Europe at all. The Red Army would be the only substantial military power on the Continent. It would still be necessary of course to deal adequately with Germany, but Roosevelt had not shown any opposition to the idea. Therefore any opposition which Churchill might put up on that subject would probably be as ineffective as his resistance to Soviet military wishes seemed likely to be. The same applied even more to Eastern Europe. Not only was Roosevelt ostentatiously refraining from offering Churchill support either political or military, but he had not protested at Stalin's rough handling of the Prime Minister that evening. Roosevelt hoped that his accommodating attitude would lead Stalin to be equally accommodating. It probably had the reverse effect. The Soviet leader could now see a situation emerging where he would not be obliged to make any concessions to the Western point of view on any issue which the USSR deemed important. [13]

30 November. The military decision ratified:
Turkey and the Dardanelles: warm-water ports

As was usually the case at Teheran Brooke faced the coming day with no great enthusiasm. As his diary records, he expected an unpleasant day with more prolonged and wearing argument. First of all the British Chiefs themselves would have to agree on the tactics to be adopted with the Americans. Then they had to try to persuade the American Chiefs to accept whatever compromise the British had agreed to put before them. In both meetings the main burden of argument, as Brooke well knew, would fall on him.

However, the line of approach was now fairly clear. Both he and Churchill could see that it was a question of salvaging what they could. In return for the final acceptance by the British of a date for 'Overlord' acceptable to the Americans and the Russians, the US Chiefs must be willing to agree to maintain sufficient pressure in Italy to provide the minimum conditions for a successful 'Overlord'. This in turn meant their agreement to the retention of landing-craft in the Mediterranean long enough to permit the amphibious assault for the capture of Rome: and secondly a sufficient head of steam to carry the armies forward to the Pisa–Rimini line. The parameters for the 'Overlord' date were then set. On the one hand it would not be possible, in Brooke's view, to get sufficient landing-craft together for 'Overlord' till June at the earliest. On the other hand it was improbable the US Chiefs and Stalin would agree to anything later than June. A final argument was that on previous experience it seemed unlikely that the Russians would be ready or willing to launch their major summer offensive before June. Everything therefore seemed to point to a June date for 'Overlord'.

Other operations would then have to be fitted in to this main pattern in the light of what was then possible. The date of an assault on the south of France, for example, would depend on when sufficient troops could be spared from Italy, after their main task was accomplished; and whether enough landing-craft could be found when 'Overlord' needs had been met. Brooke felt it was not unlikely, when they got down to detailed planning for the operation, that they would find that the Southern France operation could not physically take place before 'Overlord'—very likely indeed not till afterwards. Equally the need to find landing-craft for the operation might well persuade the Americans that 'Buccaneer' should be given up, or at any rate postponed. Stalin himself had now provided the British with a fresh argument they could use on this thorny topic. If Russian participation in the war against Japan was assured, the need to launch expensive and ambitious operations in the Bay of Bengal was surely much diminished. After all, if the Balkans were 'a long way from the heart of Germany', as Stalin had argued, it was equally true that the Indian Ocean was a long way from the heart of Japan. The thought may also have occurred to Brooke that, if Stalin believed in 'pincer movements', the most effective one against Japan would be by Russian power from the north and west and American power from the south and east. British forces in the Bay of Bengal were rather a long way off to constitute part of an effective pincer movement.

As for Aegean operations, the practicability of these depended in any case on Turkish entry into the war. Brooke had never been fully convinced that large-scale operations in that area could safely be reconciled with the demands of the Italian campaign. He probably now felt that it was pretty unlikely that the Turks could be cajoled or bullied into action. That being the case there was no point in wasting too much energy on arguing with the Americans about it.

The C.o.S. convened early, at 8.45, in the British Legation. It was not difficult for them to reach agreement, in the light of the situation as revealed in the military staff talks and the two plenary meetings. Brooke pointed out that Eisenhower's original plan for a landing in the south of France had been accompanied by a caveat to the effect that sustained pressure on the German forces in Italy might well be a more valuable help to 'Overlord' than a diversion in the south of France. If true, this diminished somewhat the effective case for 'Anvil'. None the less the Chiefs agreed that, since Stalin had asked for this operation and the US Chiefs had supported him, it would have to form part of a compromise, provided that its precise timing and scope were related to an agreed priority for the Italian campaign. If possible, therefore, they must avoid being drawn into another absolutely rigid timetable agreement for 'Anvil'. In return for British agreement to this operation, which the Russians and Americans wanted, the Americans for their part must agree to an advance to the Pisa–Rimini line in Italy. The Americans must also accept that this latter decision would require the retention of the precious landing-craft in the Mediterranean at least until mid January: and allowing for the time taken for the craft to return to the UK, with additional time for repair, replacement, and retraining, this in turn meant, in Brooke's view, that 'Overlord' could not take place till the 1 June at the earliest. These were the important decisions the C.o.S. wished to see submitted by the CCS to Churchill, Roosevelt, and Stalin.

As minor elements in the package the C.o.S. suggested firstly a programme of increased assistance to the Yugoslav guerillas, but no military action on a larger scale than commando raids. This was not controversial, since all three leaders had expressed their approval of such a policy. Finally, on the more controversial question of Aegean operations, the British proposed simply that the decision should be postponed pending further talks with Turkey, on whose co-operation the feasibility of such operations depended. It was agreed that they should also ask the American Chiefs whether Stalin's definite commitment to enter the Far Eastern war at some future date had in any way altered their views as to the necessity of 'Buccaneer'. After all, landing-craft had still to be found for the South of France operation as well as perhaps for the Dodecanese. Brooke hoped, as did Churchill, that the Americans now might be willing to reallocate the landing-craft for 'Buccaneer' either to the Mediterranean or 'Overlord', whichever might need them most.

It was not in fact too difficult to reach agreement with the US Chiefs along these lines. Throughout the discussions with the British the Americans had been moving in the direction of accepting a limited postponement for 'Overlord'. Their insistence on 1 May had been from the beginning prompted mainly by the fear that any weakness on this point might open up a gap in agreed strategy through which Churchill might drive a coach and horses. The particular coach they most feared, of course, was that marked 'Rhodes'. Not only would that operation in Marshall's opinion make demands for landing-craft which would probably impose an unacceptable delay to 'Overlord'; there was also the risk that it would lead to further and 'open-ended' commitments. But a strictly limited delay to 'Overlord', to make possible operations in Italy and the south of France which could be shown to help 'Overlord' directly, was not in itself unacceptable. Marshall in any case was too good a soldier not to know that absolute rigidity in the timetabling of operations was militarily impossible. Probably Stalin did too. With Cross-Channel operations in particular, conditions of moon and weather and many other factors might always cause a change of a week or more on either side of the target date.

On the Southern France operation, too, there was ground for agreement, provided always the British accepted the basic concept of the operation. Marshall had already concluded that it should not take place more than three weeks or so before 'Overlord' and that probably the best thing in fact would be to aim at two more or less simultaneous operations. The British proposals therefore offered the possibility of a compromise on everything except the Rhodes-versus-Bay-of-Bengal controversy, where the US Chiefs felt only Roosevelt, who had given the promise, could make a concession.[14]

So it proved, when the Combined Chiefs met at 9.30 at the British Legation: but not without a good deal of argument, in which each side contended that the operations they most favoured could be achieved without affecting the main objective. Brooke began the meeting by indicating the main lines of a possible compromise, namely: (1) British acceptance of a Southern France operation; (2) US acceptance of a continued offensive in Italy to the Pisa–Rimini line; (3) some delay—but not too much—for 'Overlord'. They had to find, he said, an agreed basis for presentation to the Russians at the afternoon's plenary meeting. He then indicated the basis for such an agreement, stressing the point that the capture of Rome and the Pisa–Rimini objective would require an amphibious operation. It had always been generally agreed among them that the natural advantages of defence in the mountainous country of central Italy made some kind of out-flanking operation mandatory. The retention of landing-craft for this purpose till mid January would of itself mean, in the British view, that 'Overlord' could not take place till June. Finally Brooke added that obviously there was no agreement between them on Aegean oper-ations but if Turkey did not enter the war, this question would not arise. A decision on this matter could be left, he implied, till they had talked to the Turkish leaders again, with the further implication that it very likely would not arise at all.

For once it was King rather than Marshall who replied and his re-sponse was for the most part conciliatory. The US Chiefs entirely agreed that the Italian operations, of which Brooke had spoken, should be carried out: but for their part they did not believe that the required retention of landing-craft in the Mediterranean till 15 January would impose any measurable delay to 'Overlord'—and that was their only real concern. The sting in this otherwise concili-atory remark was the implication that Aegean operations *would* cause an unacceptable delay.

Brooke was not disposed to let King get away with this neat anti-thesis between Rome and other operations. Using the same argument which King himself had brought up in a previous Joint Chiefs' meet-ing, Brooke said that the need for repair, replacement, and retraining of landing-craft and crews after the Rome operation probably would mean that 1 May would be an unattainable date. Marshall now inter-vened in support of King. Their planners, he said, did not think either the Italian operations or the Southern France operation would inter-fere with 'Overlord'. Their view was that the necessary landing-craft for the Italian amphibious operation could be retained in the Mediterranean till as late as 1 March and still be available for 'Over-lord'. That would still leave enough landing-craft in the Mediter-ranean to lift nearly 27,000 men for the initial assault on the south of France. Admiral Cunningham questioned the first assertion. Speak-ing with the authority of a naval commander with more experience of Mediterranean operations than anyone else present, he said that in his view 15 February was the latest possible date the 'Overlord' craft could be retained without affecting its date. This was still a small con-cession to the American argument, since it admitted a little more flexibility than Brooke, while at the same time still allowing ample time for the Rome operation to be carried out. Seeking to remove all possible risk to 'Overlord', King used Cunningham's point to argue that to be on the safe side perhaps they should say 'no later than Feb. 1st', not perhaps quite noticing that on this particular point he was contradicting Marshall and the US army planners. The discussion at this stage showed signs of reaching that point where it is not clear who is arguing with whom and about what. Marshall brought them back to the main US contention, which was that the Rome and the Southern France operations were compatible with an 'Overlord' very close to 1 May. If, however, the Rhodes operation had to be fitted in to the programme, using the same landing-craft, then almost certainly that would mean at the very least that the Southern France operation would be delayed until long after any date the Americans (or the Russians) would agree to for 'Overlord'. In other words 'Anvil' could not then be simultaneous with 'Overlord'—or very close to it. Half the point of 'Anvil', he implied, would then be lost. Even worse, when they really got down to it, they might well conclude that the Rome–Rhodes–South of France programme might require the retention of the heavy tank-landing ships required for 'Overlord' much longer than allowed for, with a consequent unacceptable delay for 'Overlord'. Brooke seized the opportunity to make the point he and Churchill both felt to be valid. Since their problem was landing-craft, and arose from the fact that they were trying to fit a quart into a pint pot, why not increase the size of the pot? The only way he could see to do that was to reallocate the 33 landing-craft needed for 'Buccaneer' to either 'Overlord' or the Mediterranean.

Marshall, however, refused to be drawn on this point, having already made it clear at Cairo that only the President could tamper with 'Buccaneer'. The discussion continued to revolve round and round the same points, but gradually more concessions were made. Marshall made it quite clear that he personally did not really favour Stalin's view that 'Anvil' should be launched before 'Overlord': he would be quite prepared to settle for a simultaneous or near-simultaneous operation. This removed one potential difficulty. Marshall also sought to reassure the British that it was not intended to denude Italy of troops completely: enough would have to be left to maintain a secure defence even after the Pisa–Rimini line was reached. Arnold for his part admitted to Portal that adequate air-cover for the Southern France operation was a worrying factor and they would have to look at it carefully. They were getting close to the point where Brooke's main contention would be accepted: namely that planning for 'Anvil' should be dependent on and subject to the needs of both Italy and 'Overlord' being fully met; and its date therefore based on real military possibilities, not Russians demands and US hopes. King and Leahy were still unwilling to admit that this programme necessarily meant delay for 'Overlord', even if Rhodes were ruled out, but Marshall was clearly looking for a compromise.

Brooke finally brought them to the point of decision. They had to decide what to say to the Russians on the date of 'Overlord' and they had to decide now, or they might as well end the conference. The date of 1 May for 'Overlord' imposed, in his view, too tight a schedule to make it certain that they could successfully undertake the Mediterranean operations (Italy and the south of France) on which they now seemed to be all agreed: 1 June, however, was just feasible—and would give them another month's production of landing-craft. If they threw in the 'Buccaneer' landing-craft it would be even better. They could then strengthen the initial assault for 'Overlord', which probably ought to be done anyway, without affecting the Mediterranean. Portal supported him, arguing that they should concentrate on the defeat of Germany first, as had always been their intention. Portal added the argument about Stalin's promise to enter the Far Eastern war and the consequent lessening (in his view) of the urgency of operations in the Bay of Bengal against Japan. Cunningham added his support to his colleagues on this point. With the 'Buccaneer' landing-craft they could strengthen either 'Overlord' or the Southern France assault—perhaps both.

It was not likely that the British would get any change out of the US Chiefs on 'Buccaneer', nor did they, but on the other issues the latter were clearly weakening. Leahy and King continued to argue for the 1 May date for a while, but with lessening conviction. Eventually Leahy, with almost too pat a reproduction of Voroshilov's and Stalin's questions, levelled at Brooke the charge that had clearly been in his mind all along. Did Brooke really believe 'Overlord' was possible in any conditions other than complete German collapse? In other words did he really believe in the operation? He got the same unbending response. Yes, said Brooke, if the enemy were engaged continuously on other fronts. At last Leahy gave way. He conceded that the Russians would accept 1 June as the date for 'Overlord': but it would have to be 'rock-hard'. Brooke's patience very nearly evaporated at this suggestion that their main concern should be what the Russians would 'accept'. The date of 1 May, he replied brusquely, had been fixed at Quebec solely as a compromise between the preferred American date of 1 April and the British preference for 1 June. It was not based on any strategic consideration. Brooke certainly did not feel that what Stalin wanted was the main 'strategic consideration'. They should tell the Russians the date was 1 June, and ask them to time their offensive to coincide with it.

It was not particularly tactful for Brooke to remind the Americans that the date the British had wanted in the first place was in fact the date they would now have to settle for. However, since the Combined

Chiefs had now been arguing for nearly three hours, he can perhaps be forgiven. At any rate his bluntness seems to have worked. The Combined Chiefs agreed at last to recommend: (1) that the momentum of the Italian campaign should be sustained until the Pisa–Rimini line was reached and the 68 LSTs retained till mid January for the Rome operation: (2) that there should be an operation in the south of France on as large a scale as available landing-craft would permit; that there should be no rigid fixed date for the latter, but for planning purposes it would be assumed that the date would be the same as for 'Overlord': and (3) that 'Overlord' would be carried out 'by 1 June'. The President and Prime Minister should inform Stalin accordingly. Finally the Combined Chiefs recorded their inability to reach an agreed conclusion on Aegean operations without further instructions from their political chiefs. The latter were requested to give their respective Staffs their assent or refusal to these recommendations before the plenary session that afternoon.

So ended, in effect, the long argument about the respective merits of Mediterranean operations and the Cross-Channel strategy, which had occupied the British and Americans for the best part of two years. For most of that time British conceptions had prevailed, leading in turn to the North African campaign, the Sicilian operation and the Italian campaign. Now the strategy which the United States had always favoured and the Russians had always desired had at last prevailed. Naturally enough American and British accounts of what happened put a slightly different gloss on these decisions. The official US historians temperately talk about the British Chiefs 'gradually giving ground'. Admiral Leahy characteristically records that 'the British finally fell into line'. Sir Arthur Bryant on the other hand stresses the achievement of Brooke and Churchill in snatching so much from the jaws of defeat. There is some truth in both these viewpoints. For Brooke in particular, obtaining a firm US commitment to maintain pressure in Italy, at least to Rome and beyond, and the avoidance of premature and unrealistic plans for the 'Anvil' operation was a considerable gain. As has been shown, he had in general been less enthusiastic about an 'Eastern Mediterranean strategy' than Churchill. As against that, he had felt obliged to agree to a date for 'Overlord' probably rather earlier than he would have wished; and to the elevation of the Southern France operation from the position of one of many alternatives (possibly not the best or most likely) to that of the second Mediterranean priority. Brooke doubted whether this dispersion of effort from Italy was wise.

Churchill, of course, had suffered a rather worse defeat. Almost certainly he genuinely believed in the military advantages of the Eastern Mediterranean strategy. But over and above that, he could see the political consequences of leaving the whole of Eastern Europe as the exclusive military preserve of the USSR. His mind indeed was probably already turning to the possibility of still achieving a breakthrough in Italy and through the 'Ljubljana gap' early enough to bring some Western military power to bear at least in Central Europe, or alternatively at some stage in Greece. But he now felt it would be a very uphill fight to salvage anything in Eastern Europe.[15]

The Combined Chiefs went straight from their meeting to report to Churchill and Roosevelt. Roosevelt made a characteristic change intended to mollify Stalin. The commitment to launch 'Overlord' should be 'during the month of May', not 'by 1 June'. Semantically it could be argued that 'by 1 June' meant '31 May at the latest' and therefore amounted to the same thing as 'during May'. But in fact the nuances of the two expressions were different and 'during May' was misleading. It is better to be frank, especially with an ally as suspicious as the USSR, and one feels Roosevelt should not have suggested the change, nor Churchill agreed to it. Be that as it may, both men felt no doubt that Stalin would be pleased with the decision

It is worth noting, perhaps, that while 'Overlord' was eventually launched on 6 June (as compared with Combined Chiefs' 'by 1 June'), the main Soviet summer offensive was begun on 23 June; which may be compared with Stalin's undertaking to begin an offensive to coincide with 'Overlord'. This slight discrepancy is not necessarily an indication of Soviet bad faith. But it is perhaps a commentary on the difficulty of fulfilling exactly commitments of this kind.

Having finally achieved the military decisions that he wanted, Roosevelt could now turn his attention to political matters. Immediately after the Chiefs of Staff had left he had a short meeting with the young Shah of Iran. As usual there is no formal record of this discussion. Elliott Roosevelt implies that the conversation was largely concerned with Iranian economic problems and 'the economic grip Britain had on Iran's oil wells and mineral deposits'. There is no doubt that Roosevelt, reinforced by Patrick Hurley in this case, would have tended naturally to suspicion of British 'imperialistic policies' in this part of the world and been sympathetic to any attempt to undermine them. No doubt this came up in the conversation. The whole background to the meeting, however, makes it clear that the Iranians' principal immediate concern at this time was to get the occupying British *and* Soviet forces out of the country as soon as may be. The

Shah and his ministers certainly put this point forcibly to Roosevelt, though also anxious to obtain US economic aid for post-war development and reconstruction. The upshot of the meeting indeed illustrates this point very well. Moreover Roosevelt, jnr. does not mention the fact that, as Cordell Hull puts it, 'one facet of [US] diplomacy consisted in supporting the efforts of American companies to obtain petroleum concessions there', a policy which smacks more of sharing in the exploitation of Iran than the 'unselfish American policy' Roosevelt later referred to. However, the text of the tripartite declaration which Hurley prepared on Roosevelt's instructions after this meeting confined itself to pledging economic assistance to Iran and the maintenance of Iranian 'sovereign independence and territorial integrity'. The declaration was issued at the direct request of the Iranian government, made even before the meeting with Roosevelt, and reflected both aspects of Iranian concern. There is no doubt that the Shah and his ministers were equally concerned about both Russian and British designs; and on the evidence of past history they had good reason to be.[16]

While Roosevelt was pursuing his slightly tortuous path on Near Eastern matters, Churchill received the British Staffs' report, and then turned to correcting what he regarded as Soviet misconceptions, in his first private talk with Stalin. By this stage of the conference the Prime Minister was of course deeply concerned about the way the British had been relegated to a position of splendid isolation, while the President and Stalin enjoyed their cosy chats together. He felt that the Americans had deliberately set out to make the British seem the 'odd man out' and the main obstacle to Soviet wishes; and that Roosevelt, moreover, had misrepresented the British position to the Russians, particularly in the first plenary session. Stalin's hostile attitude the previous evening must have confirmed these views. He had, therefore, suggested that he and Stalin should meet privately for a change.

Churchill's main concern was to put the strategic controversy in what he regarded as a juster perspective. The impression had been given, he told Stalin, that the issue was simply one of 'Overlord' versus Mediterranean operations: but it was not as simple as that. There were other factors in the equation. The basic problem was landing-craft, and the shortage derived as much from the demands of Pacific and Indian Ocean operations as from those in Europe—more so indeed, in view of the scale and nature of the Pacific campaign. If the Americans were willing to cancel or postpone the 'Buccaneer' operation, that would release enough landing-craft to make possible *both* Mediterranean operations *and* a punctual 'Overlord'. Equally, he had suggested to the Americans that some landing-craft might be spared from the vast numbers allocated to the Pacific either for 'Buccaneer' or to help European operations. But the Americans (that is, Admiral King) were 'very touchy' about the Pacific. The British were not in the least 'lukewarm' about 'Overlord' and wanted to launch it as close as possible to the planned date. But they also wanted to keep the Mediterranean campaign alive on a sufficient scale to ensure the success of 'Overlord' when it came. Moreover it was impossible for him to keep large British armies idle in the Mediterranean, where they had twice as many troops as the Americans. British public opinion would not understand or accept the virtual cutting out of these forces from operations at a decisive stage of the war. The armies in Italy should maintain unremitting pressure on the Germans until they reached the Pisa–Rimini line, which should be before the date of 'Overlord': after that he personally was not opposed to the diversion of forces to the Southern France operation proposed by Stalin, at the same time as 'Overlord' or 'at whatever time was judged correct'. Stalin had also indicated that he would not believe in the seriousness of Allied intentions in regard to 'Overlord' until a specific commander was designated for it. Well, it was not the British who were holding up the announcement. They had agreed that it should be an American appointment back in August, which made it Roosevelt's responsibility. The President had found it difficult to make up his mind for 'domestic reasons' which were important to him. He, Churchill, had repeatedly urged Roosevelt before the conference to make up his mind, and had now suggested to the President that the appointment should definitely be made before they left Teheran.

One may doubt if all this made very much impression on Stalin. Whether it was Churchill or Brooke who was really the arch-villain he may not have been sure. But he was quite convinced that it was the British who were mainly responsible for the delay in acceding to Soviet wishes, as he was to make clear again that evening; and in simple terms he was of course quite right. He now answered Churchill, and it is difficult not to sympathize with his argument. The 'Overlord' operation was crucially important to Russia not simply in strategic terms but in terms of the need to bolster Soviet morale. After over two years of bitter fighting the Red Army was war-weary. If 'Overlord' were not launched in May, then, after so many previous disappointments, it would be difficult to convince his soldiers and his people that it would take place in 1944 at all. The effect would be deeply discouraging and it would be difficult to combat feelings of 'isolationism' in the Red Army. This was the only occasion during the conference when Stalin hinted that if they did not receive more direct assistance from the West, he might feel obliged to consider a separate peace with Germany. It was blackmail, but, in all the circumstances, it may be thought legitimate blackmail.

Churchill replied that 'Overlord' would certainly take place, provided that the Germans were not in a position to reinforce the Northwest theatre during the crucial build-up period. This was the point of Mediterranean operations. They could not afford to take the risk that 'Overlord' might fail. Stalin again made the valid point that even if it did, the attempt would indicate to the Red Army that the Western Allies were serious in their desire to help Russia and that would itself have a good effect. In any case he wished to prepare a Soviet offensive in May or June to coincide with it, and therefore needed a reasonably firm date. When would that be? Churchill told him that the date had now been definitely agreed by the Anglo-American staffs that morning. Roosevelt wished to tell Stalin the news himself at lunch, but he, Churchill, could give the assurance now that the date would be satisfactory from the Soviet point of view.

With that the two leaders repaired to their luncheon appointment with the President. Roosevelt immediately conveyed the Staffs' recommendations and his own and Churchill's approval to Stalin, and the latter indicated, and we may be sure quite sincerely, that he was very satisfied with the outcome. Roosevelt also promised that he would name the commander in 'three or four days' and that separate commanders would be appointed for the Mediterranean and the Southern France operation. Churchill interpolated the comment that the last-named would come under the 'Overlord' commander (presumably after lodgement had been achieved), no doubt with the thought in mind that the supply and reinforcement of the force would then cease to be a Mediterranean Command responsibility.

Over lunch the conversation turned to the Far East and possible Soviet claims in that area. The British and US records differ over who first raised the subject but it is agreed that the matter of Soviet access to ice-free warm-water ports came up in the context of the proposed Cairo communiqué. In effect the two leaders, particularly Roosevelt, were asking Stalin to approve the generous treatment of China which the communiqué promised, but indicating that this imposed on them an .obligation to treat legitimate Soviet claims sympathetically. Churchill put the thought into very practical terms. It was important that if the three of them were to be responsible for keeping peace after the war they should emerge as satisfied powers with no further claims or grievances. Poachers, he implied, (if the thought is not too cynical) should only turn gamekeepers when they had no need to go a-poaching any more.

Stalin replied cautiously that he approved in general of the Cairo communiqué, including, it may be noted, the promise to restore Manchuria to China, and Korean independence: but so long as the USSR was neutral in the Pacific conflict he could make no public commitments. As for Soviet claims, perhaps the USSR should wait until she had done some fighting before making any. The Chinese, he added, should do a bit more fighting, too, if they wanted generous treatment. Perhaps the thought was also in Stalin's mind that when Russia had entered the war and Soviet troops were on the march, then the USSR would be in a better position to enforce any claims she might make. Stalin, the supreme realist, made it fairly clear on a number of occasions during the conference that he regarded the moral validity of any national claim as directly proportionate to the amount of fighting a nation had done and the power of that nation to enforce its claims. Russia, however, he said, had virtually only Vladivostok in the Far East and that was not ice-free all the year round, and moreover was closed off at each end by Japanese-held straits. (At some stage during the conference, as has been noted, Stalin put in a claim to Soviet annexation of South Sakhalin and the Kuriles on this ground.)

Roosevelt then made the suggestion that he had discussed with Chiang-Kai-Shek at Cairo, namely that the Chinese port of Dairen should become a 'free port' under an international regime. Shrewdly Stalin observed that the Chinese might object to this. Roosevelt indeed had every reason to know, from his Cairo discussions, that Chiang-Kai-Shek did not view the suggestion with great enthusiasm. None the less he replied easily that the Chinese probably could be persuaded, thinking presumably that if the Chinese did not like it, they would have to lump it. The contrast between Roosevelt's attitude to British extra-territorial rights in Shanghai and putative Soviet rights in Dairen is noteworthy. Roosevelt would presumably have argued that the regime he envisaged for Dairen was different, and Soviet interests more 'legitimate' than British. At all events, Stalin indicated that the idea would be acceptable to the USSR.

The subject of Soviet access to the Baltic and the Mediterranean also came up. On the former, Roosevelt again mentioned his idea of an international regime for the Kiel Canal, with Hamburg, Lübeck, and Bremen as 'free ports' under international control on either side of it, and Stalin indicated that this too would be a good idea. Then there was the question of the Dardanelles, lying within Turkish

sovereignty, but entirely controlling Soviet access to the Mediterranean. Russia found the existing system of control under the
Montreux Convention unduly restrictive, and would like to see it
revised. Churchill cautiously replied that the present moment, when
they were trying to induce Turkey to enter the war, was not perhaps
the time to raise the matter, but the British for their part would
welcome Soviet ships anywhere. To this anodyne comment, Stalin
replied a little acidly that in Lord Curzon's day the British had 'other
ideas', but perhaps they would be more helpful now. According to the
British record, Roosevelt remarked, and Churchill assented, that the
Dardanelles should be free to the commerce of the whole world
(whether designedly or not, the President did not mention warships).
With that the discussion apparently ended, and the three men agreed
that they would hold one more plenary session with the Staffs that
afternoon at 4.30, to 'wrap things up' in the military sphere, but they
would meet again the following afternoon at 4.00 with their foreign
ministers to discuss other 'political matters'. Poland, Finland, and
Sweden were apparently mentioned as subjects for discussion, presumably by Churchill and Roosevelt rather than Stalin.[17]

While the three heads of government were thus engaged, the two
foreign ministers and Hopkins were meeting separately at the British
Legation to begin political discussions, as Churchill had requested.
Nominally the purpose of this meeting was to discuss the Eastern
Mediterranean, particularly the political implications of Turkish participation in the war and of Yugoslav operations, but these were not
subjects to which either Hopkins or Molotov wished to devote much
attention. The two men therefore immediately plunged into a quite
different topic which did interest them both, namely the question of
'strong points' or bases which the Big Three should control after the
war. Bizerte and Dakar were specifically mentioned together with
various points in the Far East. Molotov linked the former with the
Soviet view that France should be punished for her collaboration with
the Nazis. Eden expressed his disagreement with the view that the
entire French nation could be stigmatized as collaborators and
generously added that the fall of France was due partly to the lack of
adequate British help at that time. He made it quite clear that in his
view France should be treated as a liberated and friendly country, not
as an ex-enemy, and was quite candid in expressing the British view
that France was a long-standing ally of Britain, and the British wished
to see her become strong again. However, though French sovereignty
over these places must be recognized, the French might be willing to
make some strategic points available to the United Nations under

international control. Britain for instance had leased bases to the United States in the West Indies and been glad to do so. Hopkins turned to the question of bases in the Far East, and said that the United States would expect to have such bases by agreement in both the Philippines and Formosa, even after the former became independent and the latter reverted to China. Eden remarked that Britain certainly sought no additional territory, but would be prepared to share in the international control of strategic points in former enemy territory. Hopkins agreed that the difficulty would be more with bases in 'friendly territory' and Molotov, in response to Eden's firm championship of France, conceded that some form of voluntary French participation might be appropriate. Hopkins brought this part of the discussion to a close by stressing that the United States wished all these arrangements to have some kind of international sanction and emphasizing that they were of course directed primarily at Germany and Japan.

Eden now turned the discussion to the problem of bringing Turkey into the war, which was the ostensible purpose of the meeting. He repeated what Churchill had said earlier—that if Turkey continued to show reluctance, it should be made clear to her that she could not expect much consideration from the victorious powers after the war. If Inönü would not come to Cairo, they should send a special envoy to Turkey for the purpose. He knew that the Russians no longer thought the Turks could be persuaded, but it was worth trying. Molotov agreed that Soviet views had changed since the Moscow conference, but that was because the first round of talks with the Turkish leaders had been so disappointing. Putting his finger on the point that most interested the Americans, Hopkins asked if that meant the Russians were now less anxious to get Turkey into the war, or simply less optimistic? The Americans assumed from the vigour with which the Russians had pressed the point at Moscow that they *did* want it. Eden added rather plaintively that he had certainly thought he was speaking for all of them to the Turks. Molotov agreed that under the Protocol they had signed Eden had every right to, and in answer to Hopkins pointed out that the USSR had given a commitment to declare war on Bulgaria if it were necessary to help the Turks, which indicated that they were quite serious about it. But the Turks should not keep them waiting too long. For his part, he had been interested in Churchill's and Eden's advocacy of a tough line with Turkey. What sanctions precisely did they propose to apply? Did it mean Turkey would have to give up her rights in the Bosphorus—that is, agree to renegotiate the Montreux Convention?

Eden, who was obviously already regretting that Churchill had been quite so specific on this matter, replied according to the US record that he really did not know, but he assumed Churchill simply meant that the Turks could no longer count on British support on this matter. He would ask Churchill exactly what he had meant. (The latter in fact had perhaps already regretted that he had been so definite, and at that very moment was also being much less precise in his commitments in response to Stalin's questions.) Molotov, however, agreed that Roosevelt and Churchill should try their hand on Inönü at Cairo and said he would ask Stalin if Russia should send a representative to the talks.

Hopkins then revealed what was really on the Americans' mind and, in so doing, their essential lukewarmness on the whole issue. They were concerned, he said, that 'large military commitments' might follow from Aegean operations consequent on Turkish entry into the war, with perhaps further delay to 'Overlord'. However he admitted there might be advantages which would make that worthwhile. One is tempted to comment that Hopkins as usual was efficiently reflecting Roosevelt's views, even in this case the latter's 'wavering to and fro in the argument'. Molotov at once indicated that Russia would strongly object to anything that might delay 'Overlord'. Hopkins amplified the point. Clearly the Turks would demand that the Allies mopped up the Dodecanese and the Greek islands, which indeed Churchill wanted. But he wondered if Churchill had not underestimated the size of the force required, and that might also be the opinion of the Turks, and their reason for refusing. The British and Americans would need to examine this aspect carefully before seeing the Turks. Obviously intent on reassuring Molotov about the American priorities, Hopkins went on immediately to say that he was very hopeful that Stalin's principal demands—'Overlord' in May, the immediate appointment of a commander for the operation and the question of a Southern France operation—would be satisfactorily answered that day. Molotov commented that if the three heads of government, including Stalin, agreed to the Combined Chiefs' proposals, he was quite sure that these proposals meant no delay to 'Overlord'; and that anything to do with Turkey would be fitted in to that order of priorities. Hopkins indeed had made it pretty clear that the Americans would not allow Churchill's Eastern Mediterranean ideas to interfere with the main operation.

After a short discussion of supplies to Yugoslavia and the establishment of a possible Soviet supply base for this purpose in Egypt, Eden then seized the opportunity for a brief reference to the Polish problem.

Again he started with what seemed the easiest part of the problem from the point of view of tripartite agreement. If the Poles were to agree to the kind of adjustment of frontiers which Churchill and Stalin had discussed, they should perhaps look at the precise nature of these adjustments more closely. He recognized that perhaps the Americans felt unable to make precise commitments in the matter at the moment. Hopkins gave Eden no encouragement. He at once made it clear that he did not feel authorized to discuss Poland, and that it was up to the President to deal with it if he chose. Eden emphasized that his only purpose was to prevent the matter becoming a source of friction between them, but obviously realized he could get no further with it at the moment. With no more ado he proposed they should meet again for luncheon the following day, Molotov indicating that it was his turn to be host.[18]

At four o'clock the conference gathered in plenary session for the last time—the heads of government, the Chiefs of Staff, the two Foreign Ministers, plus Hopkins, Harriman, Deane, and Voroshilov. The meeting was brief—hardly more than half an hour. Roosevelt as usual opened the proceedings. He said that he and the Prime Minister were pleased the Combined Staffs had reached an agreement which had satisfied Marshal Stalin. After Brooke had gone over the various points—'Overlord' during May and a Southern France operation on whatever scale available landing-craft permitted, Churchill in a valedictory speech stressed the importance of maintaining close collaboration between all their Staffs, but took a last and slightly forlorn opportunity to stress the importance of the Italian campaign and the potentialities further east in Yugoslavia and the Aegean (a reference which the Soviet record pointedly omits). Stalin said that he fully understood that 'Overlord' was a dangerous undertaking, particularly during the build-up period, and repeated his undertaking to prevent the transfer of German reserves from the Eastern Front by launching a big offensive 'by May'. Roosevelt reverted to Stalin's 'third demand'. He would announce the appointment of the Supreme Commander for 'Overlord' within three or four days, as soon as he had conferred with his Staffs again. In the mean time he suggested the latter should return to Cairo at once to get on with the detailed planning required by the decisions they had taken. Both Churchill and Stalin agreed that there was no need to detain the military staffs at Teheran any longer, and Churchill added that since they had finished with the military discussions he presumed the three heads of government could devote the following two days to political discussions. He hoped they could reach agreement on these matters, having reached a successful conclusion on the military topics. Roosevelt and Stalin signified that they were willing to stay for the next two days if necessary. Roosevelt then suggested that before they left, the military staffs should work out a draft communiqué for them to approve. Churchill in conclusion stressed the necessity of confusing and misleading the enemy about 'Overlord' by deception and 'cover plans', on which Stalin commented that the USSR used such methods to conceal the location and timing of their offensives, and therefore were thoroughly familiar, he implied, with the necessity for them. The meeting then ended with an agreed decision that the heads of government should meet with their foreign ministers on the following day.[19]

That evening a large party assembled at the British Legation for the dinner to celebrate Churchill's sixty-ninth birthday. As this was essentially a festive occasion and was not intended to provide an opportunity for any business discussions, not only the official delegates, but also members of Roosevelt's and Churchill's entourage were invited. These included Roosevelt's son and son-in-law, Hopkins' son and Churchill's son and daughter, as well as various aides and secretaries. It was on the whole a jovial affair with many toasts, but there was one revealing moment of tension during the evening. After Roosevelt had proposed Brooke's toast in a pleasant speech, Stalin remained on his feet. He joined in drinking Brooke's health, he said, but he regretted that he was 'unfriendly' to the USSR and seemed 'grim and distrustful' in his relations with them. As he came to know the Russians better, he hoped Brooke would find that they were 'not so bad after all'. Hopkins tactfully lowered the tension with an amusing toast to Churchill in which he remarked that the Prime Minister had an advantage over the Americans in that the British Constitution was unwritten and the powers of the British War Cabinet were undefined. This meant, he said, that they could both be interpreted any way Churchill wanted.

Brooke, however, was the last man in the world to take an attack lying down, and in any case he thought as a matter of policy it was necessary to stand up to Stalin. After meditating his reply he rose to say he was surprised that Stalin considered him unfriendly. He referred to the discussion of deception and 'cover plans' earlier in the day. Friends and allies too could sometimes be misled by appearances. Perhaps he had been misled by Soviet actions earlier in the war and possibly Stalin had also been misled and had misjudged his real wishes, which were for closer collaboration with the Russians. According to Churchill Stalin was impressed by this speech, and this is not unlikely. At all events the two men shook hands at the end of the dinner in a cordial fashion and the evening ended with Roosevelt expressing the optimistic hope that the varying political complexities represented by the three States would combine to form a rainbow, which was the 'symbol of hope'.[20]

1 December. Turkey, Finland, Poland, and Germany

The military issues had now been decided. The staffs departed for Cairo, to put these decisions into effect. The politicians remained in Teheran. They had further business to discuss. Stalin had agreed to remain for two more days, if necessary, to discuss political issues, but in the event the forecast of bad flying conditions very soon determined Roosevelt to leave the following day. Thus the best part of three days had been devoted to military issues but as it turned out only one day entirely to the political questions. This suited Roosevelt better than it suited Churchill and Eden. The President had already secured Stalin's general approval to his concept of a Four-Power Directorate as the foundation of future international peace-keeping. Stalin had also given his blessing to the broad outlines of the settlement for the Far East agreed between Roosevelt and Chiang-Kai-Shek at Cairo, and given Roosevelt some idea of Russian objectives in that area, which seemed to be moderate. So far so good. Roosevelt did not wish to have long discussions with his colleagues over Poland and East Europe: in fact he was determined to avoid them, together with any embarrassing commitments in that regard. It remained only to obtain, if possible, some agreed principles on which to base the future treatment of Germany; and to secure some hope of leniency for Finland, the one country in Eastern Europe for which Roosevelt showed a lively concern. There was one other thing. It had to be reaffirmed for Stalin's benefit that if the Soviet attitude towards Turkish participation in the war was now lukewarm, the American attitude was equally so: and it must be made clear to the British that the United States could not guarantee that landing-craft could be found for the Dodecanese operations, and therefore no commitments of that kind must be made to Inönü in the forthcoming talks.

With all this in mind, at noon Roosevelt entertained the two leaders to lunch, with Hopkins, Harriman, Eden, Clark Kerr, and Molotov. The first purpose of their meeting was to hear from the foreign ministers a report on their discussions of the previous day. As the ostensible purpose of that meeting had been to consider what inducements could be offered to Turkey in the talks with Inönü, they began on that subject. It had been agreed in a pre-lunch talk, probably over Roosevelt's favourite Martinis, that the three leaders should send telegrams to their ambassadors in Ankara, definitely inviting Inönü to meet Churchill and Roosevelt. From the discussion which followed, two things emerged. Firstly, Roosevelt and Hopkins made it clear that they did not expect the Turks to commit themselves without positive assurances that the Aegean would be cleared of the Germans; and the Americans for their part had no intention of promising landing-craft on the scale they thought would be necessary—or other resources for that matter. Secondly it soon became apparent that Churchill was about to abandon his long fight for Aegean operations. He emphasized much more the value of limited Turkish participation in the Allied war effort. Stalin said comparatively little, though what he said was not unhelpful to Churchill. But he was probably not much interested.

Hopkins went to the point straight away. They had to decide before seeing Inönü what military assistance they were prepared to offer the Turks. Catching the ball, Roosevelt remarked that Inönü would certainly want to know what he could expect. Churchill reiterated the limited nature of the British commitment so far. He and Eden had promised the Turks only that they would receive adequate protection against German air attacks, in the form of three anti-aircraft regiments and twenty fighter squadrons. These forces, except three of the latter, were already in Egypt. The British had not promised any ground forces to the Turks, who had a substantial army of their own. Stalin commented, not unhelpfully to Churchill's case, that Turkish participation, even without Aegean operations, would make air-bases available. (The US record, deliberately or not, omits this remark.) Churchill agreed. One advantage would be that targets in Romania could then be attacked more easily. He again emphasized that there would be no demands on US resources, other than landing-craft, though it would of course help if the Americans could spare a few bombers. The landing-craft would be required only in March, if the Rhodes operation were undertaken. It could be 'sandwiched' between the Rome attack in January and 'Overlord' in midsummer. Roosevelt immediately expressed the US Staff's objection: losses of landing-craft and casualties in two such operations might be heavy, and they would need all the craft they had for 'Overlord'. These would in any case need to be back in the Western Mediterranean in full strength no later than 1 April. He felt the Staffs would have to examine this question very carefully. Until they had done so, there should be no undertakings to the Turks.

Churchill thought the difficulties were not as great as Roosevelt implied. So far, at least, the British had promised nothing to the Turks which was not theirs to give, he remarked pointedly, and had made no further promises. As for the Cairo talks with Inönü, he said, betraying perhaps for the first time slight weariness with the subject, it was possible that Inönü might not come at all. Sardonically Stalin remarked that the Turkish President might find it convenient to develop a diplomatic illness. The Soviet leader, of course, was fully conversant with the usefulness of this particular ploy. Churchill replied firmly that if Inönü did not come to Cairo, he himself would go to Turkey and convey to Inönü how little Turkey could expect from the Allies if she did not co-operate.

Hopkins then demonstrated his two outstanding characteristics— absolute fidelity to Roosevelt's wishes and an eye for the root of the matter. The British might have considered the possible commitments involved, he said, but the Americans had not yet done so in any detail. Some of the US planners, however, thought bomber groups *would* be necessary. The whole of the Mediterranean was now one Command and had to be considered in terms of the needs of each part of it. Was it wise to talk to Inönü before the Combined Chiefs had thoroughly thrashed this out and agreed what could be offered? Churchill countered with his previous argument. Let them repeat their offer of adequate air protection (accompanied, he implied, by heavy diplomatic pressure), and they might at least get the use of Turkish airbases. They need not wait until the landing-craft question was sorted out, and a decision made on the Rhodes operation.

Stalin picked up the implications of Hopkins's intervention with his usual quickness. Did Hopkins mean then that they should *not* invite Inönü to Cairo after all? And was it really necessary for the Anglo-American Staffs to have another long discussion? As on previous occasions, Stalin obviously thought the Staffs were there to carry out their leaders' orders, not to tell them what they could do. Churchill unwisely trod on Roosevelt's toes, by suggesting that landing-craft might be found from the Indian Ocean or the Pacific, eliciting from the President the sharp retort that transfers of landing-craft from the Pacific were out of the question. The distance was too great for them to be transferred to the Mediterranean; anyway they were all required for current Pacific operations. Churchill (or according to the Soviet record, Eden) repeated that they had made no commitment about amphibious operations to the Turks: to which Roosevelt replied that he was sure the latter would demand Aegean operations as the price of entry. Hopkins tried to make the US position absolutely clear to Stalin. The question of landing-craft was a technical matter, which only the Staffs could resolve. At the moment they felt far from sure that landing-craft could be found for any Aegean operation. The Staffs must work out exactly how many would be required, and if they could be provided.

Churchill tried a slightly different tack. The assumption was being made that there was no point in talking to the Turks, since they would not enter the war without a guarantee of large-scale operations in the Aegean. But even without a declaration of war on the Axis, the Turks might still be induced to grant the use of their air-bases, which in turn would enable the Allies to gain air superiority. With air and naval power the Allies could then blockade the islands and perhaps starve the Germans out without a direct assault. Stalin conceded that might work, and Roosevelt agreed that there was no objection to the use of purely British air and naval power for the purpose, providing the precious landing-craft were not involved. But he was obviously not hopeful that the Turks would agree.

Eden shared Roosevelt's doubts. In their conversations with him the Turks had asserted that the grant of air facilities would in any case provoke a German air attack on them. They would rather wait until they were ready and then take the initiative, than be dragged into the war at a time not of their own choosing. Churchill remarked in exasperation that if you asked the Turks to go part of the way, they said either that the Germans would still attack them, or that they would rather go *all* the way: and if you asked them to go all the way, they said they were not ready. The time had come to substitute harsh words and if necessary threats for mild requests. Eden said they had better agree on what they wanted. Did they want to ask for a full declaration of war (at this point Stalin assented), relying on the incentive that the USSR would 'look after' Bulgaria and the threat that not to do so would cost the Turks much at the peace conference? Or did they want something less? Churchill, with one eye on Roosevelt, replied that he would settle for 'strained neutrality' (that is, the grant of air-bases). It was clear that Churchill had by this point almost given up hope of the Rhodes operation, in view of the American attitude, but was still prepared to try to persuade the Turks to take some risk which fell short of actually declaring war.

Molotov now asked the same awkward question which he had put to Eden the day before. Mr. Churchill had spoken of threats in connection with Turkish rights in the Straits. Could he be more precise? The USSR was interested. Churchill, with whom Eden no doubt had had a quiet word on the subject, now showed belated caution. He thought the regime of the Straits probably 'needed to be reviewed'.

Falling back on his last refuge, he added lamely that he would of course have to consult the War Cabinet, a remark which probably made Hopkins smile a little. Molotov was a sufficiently experienced hand to recognize a diplomatic block when he saw one. He did not press the point. Churchill added, however, that he and Roosevelt would discuss these matters with the Turks 'in a friendly spirit', but if they would not co-operate, they would be told that they could expect no support from the West against any future Soviet demands. With this the Russians had to be satisfied for the moment. Stalin indicated again that he was content to leave the negotiations to Churchill and Roosevelt, but since they wished it, he would send Vyshinsky and his ambassador in Ankara to represent Russia at the talks.[21]

Feeling that they had devoted enough time to Churchill's pet idea, Roosevelt now turned to his own. He asked Stalin if he would discuss Finland, and the Russian assented. Roosevelt then asked if the US could do anything to get the Finns out of the war. Should they encourage the Finns to send a peace delegation? Stalin said preliminary exchanges with Finland through Swedish channels had shown that the Finns were not yet in the mood to pursue serious peace talks. Powerful elements in that country were still hoping for a German victory, and were not prepared to sever Finnish links with Germany. He for his part had let them know that the USSR did not, as they feared, wish to annexe Finland. However he thought a peace delegation would be of little use in their present mood. Churchill tried to explore the possible basis of a peace settlement. Russia must of course have security for the approaches to Leningrad, and an assured naval position in the Baltic —implying some cession of Finnish territory and naval bases to Russia. He was glad to hear that Russia did not contemplate the annexation of Finland, and hoped she would not demand heavy indemnities, which a poor country like Finland could not pay.

Stalin expressed disagreement with this view, but in moderate terms. Russia did not want monetary transfers from Finland: but the Finns needed a lesson, and ought to make some reparation for the damage they had done. They could help to do so by supplying such things as wood and paper for five to eight years. Churchill reminded him of the Bolshevik slogan of the First World War—'no annexations and no indemnities'. Stalin acknowledged the thrust and returned it. His attitude in these matters was, he said, becoming less Bolshevik, and 'more like that of a Conservative'. The Finns, he pointed out, had recently reinforced their front, which did not fit very well with their assertion that they wanted peace. Molotov reminded the company that the Finns had bombed and bombarded Leningrad, in alliance with the Germans, for over two years. The Russians, he implied, could hardly be expected to forget this.

Roosevelt now tried to get down to details. The Finns, he thought, might be willing to cede the Karelian Isthmus but would hope to retain Viborg and Hangö. The latter perhaps could be demilitarized, so that it could not be used against Russia. Churchill indicated that for his part he sympathized with the Soviet viewpoint. They had suffered much at the hands of the Finns and had a right to say what the peace terms should be. When he knew what these terms were, he would decide whether to plead for leniency or not. The twin foundations of any peace should be Soviet security and Finnish independence. Stalin also decided the time had come to be specific. The basis of any treaty would have to be a restoration of 'the 1940 frontier', which meant Viborg, Hangö, and the Karelian Isthmus would be Russian. However he would accept Petsamo, which would give Russia a common frontier with Norway, instead of Hangö. He would respect Finnish independence, but they must pay up. He regretted Roosevelt had not been able to persuade the Finns that this was what they had to accept. According to the British records, Roosevelt indicated that he thought Stalin's proposal to take Petsamo instead of Hangö was reasonable. He added that he was prepared to tell the Finns to send a peace mission to Moscow, with no stipulations in advance about what they would or would not be prepared to concede. Stalin thought it a mistake not to have any prior conditions or understandings. It would only be a propaganda victory for the Germans if the negotiations failed. However, let them come; he was prepared to negotiate with anyone, pro-German or not, provided it produced results. Churchill brought up a point which Eden had made at the Moscow talks. If Russia treated Finland with reason and moderation, it would reassure the Swedes, and perhaps encourage them to enter the war. Stalin did not show irritation, as Molotov had done, but instead outlined the limits of Soviet reason and moderation. Apart from the territorial concessions already mentioned, the Finns must make compensation for up to fifty per cent of the damage they had done, 'in kind' (that is, goods and services rather than by monetary payment.) They must also break with Germany, expel German forces, and demobilize their own armed forces. Churchill again expressed his doubts about the wisdom and indeed practicability of extorting large reparations in any form from a small, poor country like Finland. Germany—large, populous, and with great resources—was a different matter. Stalin was quick to take the point. So the Prime Minister was not against indemnities in all circumstances? Churchill agreed some reparation for damage was reasonable, if it could be obtained. Stalin made it clear that he would see to it that it was obtained. Russia would occupy part of Finland, until the Finns had paid. Anyway, would his allies accept the other points he had indicated as reasonable? Roosevelt and Churchill promised their support on these points in the negotiations, though in slightly ambiguous terms, and with that the discussion ended on a note of amity. [22]

According to Churchill's recollection, based on the British records, it was at this point, and before they left the luncheon table, that Molotov raised the subject of the transfer of Italian shipping to the USSR. As they had just discussed Finnish reparations, the topic would have followed quite naturally. However the US and Soviet records both agree that it was not until after the resumption of the talks later that afternoon that this matter was discussed. Whenever it took place, the discussion was brief. In answer to Molotov's query, Roosevelt said that the Western Allies were quite willing to hand over some of the Italian ships for Soviet use in the common war effort. He suggested only that the question of permanent possession should await the end of the war. Molotov said this was agreeable to the USSR, which could certainly use the ships. They would like them sent to northern ports, unless Turkey entered the war, in which case they could go to the Black Sea via the Dardanelles. Churchill remarked that the Soviet request was moderate in view of Russian sacrifices in the war. He would ask only for a month or two to make the arrangements carefully and avoid the threat of mutiny or scuttling by the Italian crews. Thereupon this subject too was concluded amicably and a loose end left from the Moscow talks was finally tied. Other loose ends, however, were to require a good deal more attention than was possible at Teheran. [23]

During the adjournment Roosevelt had a short conversation with Stalin and Molotov, with only Harriman and the interpreters Bohlen and Pavlov present. Knowing that Churchill was going to bring up the subject of Poland, he wanted to tell Stalin privately what his difficulties were. The President began by telling Stalin that if the war was still going on in the autumn of 1944, he would probably feel it his duty to stand for election again, though he did not personally want to do so. There were six or seven million American voters of Polish extraction and he did not wish to alienate them. He could say now, informally and privately, that he personally accepted the idea of moving the Polish–Soviet frontier to the west and the Polish–German frontier also westwards to the Oder. But for the reason he had given, he could not 'participate in any decision' on these matters, or 'take part publicly' in any arrangement until after the election. Stalin was probably a little mystified by all this, but signified that he understood. As far as he was concerned it was quite all right if Roosevelt did nothing at all about Poland for the next year or so.

The two other Americans present were less happy with the President's remarks than Stalin. Harriman felt 'profound misgivings'. Once the Red Army had occupied Poland 'it would be too late for a negotiated settlement'—Russia would impose what it wanted, without regard for American or British wishes. Bohlen, who also knew the Russians pretty well, records in his memoir that he was 'dismayed'. Churchill and Eden would have been even more so if they had known: according to Eden they did not find out what Roosevelt had said to Stalin until long afterwards. As Eden comments in his own account, this assurance of American inaction 'was hardly calculated to restrain the Russians'. Bohlen felt that Stalin must have been relieved that there was to be no American pressure over Poland at the crucial time and that the President apparently felt the issue to be of such minor importance that he was prepared to let it hang fire for another year. Moreover Roosevelt had not even mentioned the question of relations with the London government.

Continuing the conversation, Roosevelt turned to the other Soviet claim which raised some difficulty—that for the reincorporation of the Baltic States in the USSR. Unfortunately there were also a fair number of American voters of Baltic descent, which made it difficult again for him to say publicly that he was prepared to accept this. He could assure Stalin that the United States would not make an issue of the matter when the time came, but he hoped that the USSR would make some sort of gesture in favour of the principle of self-determination. Perhaps the Russians might hold a plebiscite. He was sure the Baltic peoples would vote for incorporation in the USSR.

Stalin, who was equally sure they would, given the right circumstances, made it quite clear what those circumstances would be. The peoples of the Baltic states would have their opportunities to vote— under the Soviet Constitution. But there could be no question of an internationally supervised plebiscite or any nonsense of that kind. One is reminded of Molotov's surprise when Churchill was ousted in the elections of 1945. After all, the Conservatives had supervised the elections, hadn't they? Roosevelt however seems to have been quite happy to leave it like that. He remarked that there were only two subjects for them still to discuss with Churchill—Poland and

Germany—and it seems to have been agreed between the two men that these could be disposed of when the talks were resumed that afternoon, which would enable them to leave the following day, while flying conditions were still good. Roosevelt referred to the proposed world organization again. He and Stalin had discussed it already, and he did not want to take it up with Churchill just at that moment. One may surmise that the reason for this reluctance was that on this issue, unlike most of those discussed at the conference, Churchill and Stalin seemed to think alike. Both leant towards the idea of separate regional councils, rather than one world-wide council. Stalin seems to have sensed the reason for Roosevelt's concern. He had been thinking it over, he said, and he had come to the conclusion that Roosevelt was right. There should be one world-wide council. Roosevelt was pleased, though he was not quite sure how firm Stalin's actual attitude was. They ageed that further study should be given to the mechanics and structure of the organization, as had been suggested at Moscow, and the conversation ended. [24]

The two men then repaired to the conference room for the resumption of the plenary talks with Churchill. At last the Polish question came under discussion. Roosevelt began by expressing belatedly the hope that relations could be resumed between the USSR and the London Poles. It would facilitate the settlement of the question if they were. This was a tactical mistake. If Roosevelt had wanted to do any good on this matter, he should have mentioned it in his private talk with Stalin beforehand. One feels the remark may have been made simply for Churchill's benefit. Stalin was obviously annoyed to have this subject sprung on him without warning, and showed it. He replied in his most uncompromising manner, accusing the London Poles of collaborating with the Germans, and adding that the London-inspired resistance were killing left-wing partisans. The Americans and the British, he told Roosevelt bluntly, had no idea what was going on in Poland. Eden thought the accusation of collaboration 'outrageous', though he conceded Stalin seemed to believe it. Churchill tried to pour oil on troubled waters. He said he understood that for historical reasons Russia had a very different viewpoint on Poland from the Western Allies, but he hoped Stalin would also understand that Britain had gone to war as a result of a specific guarantee to Poland. She had obligations, therefore, in that quarter. Seeking to turn the discussion into safer channels for the moment, he brought up the subject of frontiers again. They all wanted to achieve security for the USSR in the West *vis-à-vis* Germany. The Marshal, he reminded them, had mentioned the possibility of moving the Polish western frontier to the Oder, in compensation for the westward movement of the Soviet frontier to the Curzon Line.

Stalin was not completely mollified. It now seemed to be implied that the Allies would only put a frontier settlement to the Poles if the USSR resumed diplomatic relations with them. That had not been his understanding when they had discussed the matter earlier. The Soviet leader obviously thought that it should be the other way round—if the London Poles were prepared to be reasonable about frontiers, he might consider resuming relations with them. But he doubted if the leopard could change its spots, and an anti-Soviet government become a pro-Soviet government; and he questioned if the London government really represented the Polish people. However, if the London Poles were to give some indication of a change of heart—for example by collaborating with the pro-Soviet partisans instead of attacking them—he might change his mind. He reminded the conference that Poland was more vital to Russia, because it affected her security, than it could be to Britain, whatever promises the latter had made.

Churchill responded that they wanted to devise a solution of the frontier question which was acceptable to Russia. If they could do that, he was quite prepared to take it back to the London Poles and tell them this was the best they could expect. If the London Poles turned it down, then Britain would still support the solution at the peace table. Reverting to a familiar, but misleading formula, the Prime Minister said Britain wished to see 'a Poland which was strong and independent, but friendly to Russia'.

Stalin replied drily that this was no doubt desirable, but it must be made clear to the Poles that they had to accept the 1939 frontier (that imposed by Russia after Poland's defeat). The whole of the Ukraine and Belorussia must return to the USSR. That was ethnologically just and right. Eden interpolated that Stalin was talking about the so-called 'Molotov-Ribbentrop' Line, which had been agreed between Russia and Nazi Germany in 1939. The introduction of the Nazi Foreign Minister's name into the discussion was perhaps rather below Eden's usual standard of tact, and Molotov hastened to say that the '1939 frontier' corresponded in fact to the 'Curzon Line'. Stalin was less put out. 'Call it what you like', he said, 'the USSR thought it was just'. Eden pointed out that the Curzon Line was in fact slightly more favourable to the Poles, though the differences were admittedly small. After some discussion around the maps and the establishment of the precise position of the Curzon Line, Stalin seems to have conceded that in one or two places the Curzon Line did pass a little to the east of the 1939 partition line and said that he did not want to take any territory which had a Polish population. The city of Lwów, however, though admittedly largely Polish, was surrounded by territory inhabited by Ukrainians, so it would have to remain part of Russia.

According to the US record, Roosevelt at this point intervened to ask if the area of the land between the existing frontier of Poland and the Oder was roughly comparable to that which the Poles were being asked to give up. Stalin replied, as though the matter was not really important, that he did not know and it had not been measured. Churchill effectively answered the substance of Roosevelt's query. The German territories in question, being both agricultural and industrial, were a good deal more valuable than the Pripet marshes in the east. He felt he could tell the Poles that they were getting a good bargain and should accept it. He personally was not prepared to break his heart over the destiny of Lwów. Roosevelt added finally that some transfer of population would probably be necessary, and he assumed could be arranged 'on a voluntary basis', to which Stalin assented. [25]

Churchill would have liked to continue the discussion of Poland and get all the loose ends tied, but Roosevelt obviously felt they had spent long enough on this sensitive subject, which had already led to some friction. He suggested they should turn to the more important subject of Germany, and remarked that if they decided to split up Germany, there were different ways it could be done. The various records have interesting divergences at this point, and show signs of having been edited. The British and US records, for example, agree that Stalin expressed himself 'in favour of dismemberment', which the Soviet record omits. Stalin then went on to say that the Prime Minister would object to discussing this, since he wanted Germany to remain united (and therefore presumably strong). Churchill replied that he was not 'against' dismemberment exactly. In fact he was particularly interested in detaching Prussia from the rest of Germany, since Prussia and the Prussian military class was 'the root of the evil'. Roosevelt then suggested a possible plan which he and his advisers had thought up. It involved the division of Germany into five parts: (1) a smaller and weaker Prussia; (2) Hanover and north-west Germany, excluding the Ruhr; (3) Saxony and Leipzig; (4) Hesse-Darmstadt, Hesse-Cassel, and the Rhineland; and (5) Bavaria, Baden, and Württemburg. In addition there would be two regions placed under international control for the benefit of all Europe: (1) the Ruhr and the Saar (the main regions of heavy industry); and (2) the Kiel Canal.

Churchill was clearly taken aback by the sweeping nature of Roosevelt's plan, which he said was quite new to him. He thought that any plan should have constructive as well as destructive elements. Prussia, he again said, should be destroyed, but they should offer some hope to the inhabitants of the rest of Germany, who were more peaceably inclined. He would like to offer them the constructive alternative of inclusion in a larger unit—a 'Danubian Confederation'. There was an obvious weakness in Churchill's argument on which Stalin immediately fastened. Whatever might have been the case in the Kaiser's Germany, to which Churchill's mind was obviously returning, the Nazis had certainly had as much support in South Germany as anywhere else. When Churchill had suggested his Danubian Confederation earlier, Stalin had held his fire. He now made his opposition quite clear, and made some reasonable points. If Germany was going to be dismembered, they had better do a proper job, and he therefore preferred Roosevelt's plan to Churchill's. To include a large number of Germans in a large confederation would merely give them the opportunity to revive a powerful German State, which they would dominate. The Russians had not been able to discover any difference between the German soldiers from different areas. They all fought equally hard and willingly, except the Austrians. In any case, a Danubian confederation including different races such as the Hungarians would be quite artificial. In his opinion not only Hungary but Austria as well should be independent States. He agreed that the Prussian military caste was particularly dangerous, but he had already said that the Prussian officers and staffs should be 'eliminated'.

Churchill repeated that he was not against dismemberment, but he felt that a division into tiny pieces would merely mean that those pieces would seek to come together again. Give them something worthwhile to attach themselves to, he implied, and it might last. In his memoirs Churchill subsequently added that to some extent he was indeed consciously seeking to re-establish the Austro-Hungarian Empire, which 'if it did not exist would have to be invented'. Stalin, however, replied that of course whatever they did the Germans would seek to reunite, but it would be their business to see that they did not. Churchill for his part revealed more fully what was in his mind—the need to create a Central Europe which was reasonably stable and viable, politically, economically, and, if it came to that, militarily. To Stalin he put the direct question 'Do you want a Europe of little States, which would be completely disjointed?' Stalin replied that he was only talking about Germany. Presumably France, Italy, and Poland would be 'strong countries'. The Soviet record omits this last remark, and indeed one cannot help feeling that it was somewhat inconsistent with Soviet intentions towards all three countries, and the contemptuous attitude Stalin had adopted towards France in particular. Roosevelt interpolated that Germany had been a good deal less dangerous when it had been divided into a hundred or so principalities, but Churchill repeated that he would hope for larger units to be preserved. However, he added, their present discussion could only be a 'preliminary survey' of a vast problem, to which Stalin assented.

At this point, the discussion on Germany having apparently reached an impasse, Churchill reverted to the topic which was clearly still on his mind—Poland. He asked Stalin if he would agree to the formula that the new Polish State should lie between the Curzon Line and the Oder, with East Prussia and the German district of Oppeln included in Poland. Roosevelt was probably somewhat nettled by this revival of a topic he had thought safely disposed of. He would have liked to get a bit further with the much more important matter of Germany. However, he merely remarked that it would be a good idea to ask some body—either the European Advisory Commission or a body specially constituted for the purpose—to consider the question of Germany's future treatment. Stalin supported the idea, and Churchill did not dissent. According to the US record, it was agreed that the EAC should undertake the task—though in fact it never did so. Stalin also answered Churchill's query. He took up Churchill's point about East Prussia which had not previously been mentioned, and which was not covered by the Curzon Line. Then, for the first time, Stalin made a Soviet claim on German territory. Russia, he said would like that part of East Prussia which included the port Königsberg. He indicated a frontier line along the River Niemen on the map. Königsberg (now called Kaliningrad) would give Russia another large ice-free port on the Baltic. If this were conceded, he said, he would accept Churchill's formula. As the American record puts it—'although nothing was stated, it was apparent that the British were going to take this suggestion back to the London Poles'.[26]

At this point the discussion was ended and the three men adjourned to prepare for their final dinner together. The latter part of the discussion had been revealing, but its importance lay mostly in what was *not* decided. On Germany Churchill had effectively prevented Roosevelt's sweeping partition plan from becoming the basis of all future discussions. On Poland, Stalin had graciously accepted the frontier settlement that he had all along intended to have, but equally effectively avoided any commitment to resume relations with the

London Poles. Both men had therefore scored a negative victory. Roosevelt had shown again that he was not prepared to press Stalin on the Polish question at this time. It could be argued that Churchill and Eden are to be censured also for not pressing the cause of the London Poles much harder. But in view of Stalin's unyielding posture and Roosevelt's lack of support (save for the one introductory remark), they no doubt felt that there was not much point. The best they could do was to take the frontier formula back and try to sell it to the London Poles. If the London government proved accommodating on this issue, it might then be possible to persuade Stalin to relax his attitude, particularly if at a later stage Roosevelt were willing to play a more active and supportive role. But the two British leaders were not very optimistic, particularly as they knew how intransigent the London Poles were. Eden felt that the frontier proposals would probably not be acceptable to the Poles. He had hoped for some Soviet concessions, particularly as regards Lwów, and some progress on the resumption of relations. As he records in his memoirs: 'I began to fear greatly for the Poles'. We need not doubt it.

Shortly after the tripartite meeting broke up, at 7.40, Cadogan hurried over to Roosevelt's quarters to work on the draft communiqué to be issued. He had already prepared a draft in correct Foreign Office language, but found that the Americans had got out a draft of their own, which he described humorously as 'better, that is more journalistic' (see Appendix B below). It was prepared by the American delegation, and subsequently worked over by Roosevelt and Hopkins. It is very general and vague in its terminology and has no particular historical importance except for the American optimism it reveals. At dinner that evening it was approved by all three leaders, together with the Declaration on Iran worked out by Hurley. No business was transacted at this dinner, which was purely a social and farewell gathering. At about 10.30 that evening the three men exchanged farewells, and early the following morning flew out for Moscow and Cairo respectively. The Teheran conference was over.[27]

CHAPTER IX

RETURN TO CAIRO AND CONCLUSION

1. Epilogue in Cairo

There is little need to describe the second half of the Cairo conference in great detail. The outcome of the five days' discussion amounted to little more than three negative decisions in the military sphere, and a political/military 'non-event'. The negative decisions were that neither the Andamans nor the Aegean operation should be undertaken in the immediate future; and that General Marshall should not be appointed to the 'Overlord' command. The non-event was the entry of Turkey into the war—at least in time to exert any influence on the course of European operations.

In one sense it could be argued that the above overstresses the negative side of the second Cairo conference. It could be said that the essential positive decision of that conference was to give *absolute* priority in 1944 not only to 'Overlord' but also to 'Anvil'; and that when the implications of that decision were examined, it was found that they involved the postponement, if not the abandonment of both the Andamans and the Rhodes operation; and further that the un-likelihood of any major Aegean operations or large-scale American involvement in that area made it doubly certain that Turkey would not be prepared to commit herself in the foreseeable future. But all of this was really inherent in the Teheran concept of European operations for 1944. That concept amounted, in sum, to the following five decisions: (1) that there should be no more than one month's delay to the planned date of 1 May for 'Overlord'; (2) that, of the various alternative Mediterranean operations for 1944, 'Anvil', as the one most calculated to help 'Overlord', should be the 'preferred' operation subject only to the attainment of limited objectives in Italy; (3) that 'Anvil' should, if possible, be simultaneous or near-simultaneous with 'Overlord'—that is, as soon after 1 June as possible; (4) that before 'Anvil' the Allies should take Rome and advance to the Pisa–Rimini line, with the consequent necessity of an amphibious operation in Italy in January or February; and (5) that it was still desirable that Turkey should enter the war, but the Allies could not promise large-scale Aegean operations in the near future.

Once they had focussed their minds on the decision for 'Overlord' and 'Anvil' in midsummer, the British Chiefs had no real difficulty in concluding, at their first meeting, on the morning of 3 December, that 'Anvil' (and probably 'Overlord' too) needed to be strengthened to be certain of success. Since the most dangerous period for both would be the initial assault and 'build-up' phase, this meant a more powerful assault than the tentative plans envisaged, and therefore more landing-craft. In turn this meant that unless 'Overlord' were to be weakened to strengthen 'Anvil', more landing-craft would have to be found from some other source—and this could only be 'Buccaneer' or the Pacific. The British Chiefs therefore recommended (1) that 'Anvil' should be launched with at least a two-division assault, and consequently allocated more landing-craft and escort assault vessels; and (2) that 'Buccaneer' should be postponed or cancelled to permit this, unless the Americans were prepared to make up the deficiency from the Pacific.

There remained the question of the Rhodes operation. The British Chiefs had by now probably concluded that it was unlikely Turkey would agree to enter the war, since the Americans would not permit them to be offered the one inducement that might have worked. However, since they had not received definite instructions from Churchill to abandon the quest, the C.o.S. piously added the hope, but probably without much conviction, that the Rhodes operation could still be undertaken about 1 March, if Turkey entered the war.

There were numerous ironies in the position which the British and US Chiefs had now reached. By the wish of the Americans rather than the British, the crucial decisions on Allied strategy had been submitted to the arbitrament of Stalin. The Soviet leader had pronounced in favour of an early 'Overlord' and a simultaneous Southern France operation. Having jumped on the 'Anvil' bandwagon, as a means of finally pinning the British down to the North-west European strategy, the Americans now found they had risked jeopardizing not only Aegean operations, which they disliked, but also the Andamans operation, to which their political chief had assumed a binding commitment. Moreover the long-sought promise that the USSR would enter the Japanese war had given the British a further argument against 'Buccaneer'—namely that the logical strategy to pursue for the defeat of Japan would be to combine attacks across the central Pacific with the threat from the Soviet Union. The latter could provide bases much closer to Japan than any the Chinese Nationalists could offer. This made China itself less important to the Allied war effort, and consequently reduced the importance of keeping China in the war—though that in any case could probably be achieved by maintaining supplies to China 'over the Hump'. As for 'Buccaneer', and indeed the whole Burma campaign, these now fell back into a position of comparative unimportance. All this suggested the British had been right to feel that the Chinese should have come after Teheran, rather than before: and gave further cause for regret that Churchill's tactics beforehand had so prejudiced American minds against this.

A further irony arose. As the official British historian points out, the American Chiefs now found themselves arguing for the Andamans operation, which they had originally regarded with relative indifference, at the possible expense of 'Overlord' and 'Anvil', which they regarded as all-important: while the British Chiefs were in the position of arguing against the operation in South-east Asia which their own theatre commander most favoured, on behalf of an operation ('Anvil') which they had originally regarded with disfavour. The final irony was this: at the first Cairo conference the British and Americans had spent long hours arguing about the possibility of fitting both the Rhodes and the Andamans operations into the same timetable, but with the unspoken assumption on both sides that it might be necessary to choose between them. In that case, the Americans wished to rule Rhodes out, and the British 'Buccaneer'. Now it seemed that both would have to go.

So far as Marshall, at least, was concerned, the British arguments did not fall on wholly unreceptive ears. 'Anvil' would undoubtedly serve to support 'Overlord', the operation he had always regarded as the most important of the European war. Logically therefore he could see that there were strong arguments for strengthening it to ensure its success. As for South-east Asia, it was the Burma campaign which Marshall thought important, not 'Buccaneer'. They were only committed to the latter because of Roosevelt's promise, which in turn depended on the assumption that without it Chiang would not tell his troops to march, and the whole Burma campaign might fall to the ground. Worse still, China might effectively withdraw from the war. If Marshall could be satisfied that these consequences did not necessarily follow, perhaps 'Buccaneer' was not so important.

It required, in fact, some days' argument before the logic of all this prevailed. Neither Roosevelt nor Churchill were inclined to give up their preferred operations easily. At their first meeting with the American Chiefs later on the morning of the 3rd, the British found their US colleagues prepared to accept the thesis that 'Anvil' should be strengthened to a two-division assault at least, and that the planners should be told that they must investigate the problem of providing landing-craft for this, with no other operation except 'Overlord' to be considered sacrosanct. This was a step in the direction of abandoning 'Buccaneer', but King and Leahy in particular still denied that this consequence necessarily followed. Nevertheless, progress had been made; and the Americans also agreed to an agenda for the remainder of the conference which included the consideration of the overall plan for the defeat of Japan, which now at last was ready. This included the statement 'the main effort against Japan should be made in the Pacific', while operations elsewhere should be 'subsidiary'. It also contained recommendations for action if Russia should enter the war, which envisaged the use of Soviet bases in the north, and operations from that quarter. This reinforced the British Chiefs' arguments against the necessity of extensive operations in South-east Asia. The agreed agenda also included the possibility of Turkish entry into the war, thus just keeping the Rhodes operation on the table. Events were moving towards a final decision, but there was still a little way to go before agreement was reached.

Churchill and Roosevelt dined together that evening and spent some time discussing the respective merits of the two contentious operations. But Roosevelt, as Leahy puts it, still 'would not budge', citing his promise to Chiang. Churchill was extremely perturbed. While he was aware, with the more realistic part of his mind, as was Brooke, that the prospects for the Rhodes operation were now far from good, his inveterate optimism still persuaded him not to give up; particularly as the 'Anvil' commitment ensured that a larger number of landing-craft would now have to be kept in the Mediterranean. But 'Buccaneer', he was convinced, would rule out Rhodes: they would never find enough landing-craft for 'Anvil', 'Buccaneer', *and* Rhodes.[1]

A further day's argument therefore followed. Throughout 4 December Churchill and the British Chiefs continued to pound away at 'Buccaneer', at a plenary meeting with Roosevelt and the US Chiefs, and at a Combined Chiefs' meeting which followed it. Further arguments were brought into play. Cunningham argued authoritatively that enough escort and assault vessels simply could not be provided for 'Buccaneer' in March and a Southern France operation in June or July. Portal pointed out that one of the supposed purposes of 'Buccaneer' was to increase the allied capacity for an interdiction of Japanese sea and land supply routes: in fact, in his view, the Andamans would not make a major contribution, since its airstrips were small and those that might be constructed would be similar. The 'overall plan' for the defeat of Japan also came formally before the Combined Chiefs for the first time, enabling Brooke to argue that the heavy commitment which would develop from 'Buccaneer' and the Burma land campaign (Operation 'Tarzan') was incompatible with the overall plan's main premiss, namely that 'the main effort should be made in the Pacific'. Finally Mountbatten added fuel to the flames, so far as Churchill was concerned, by demanding an assault force of 37,000 men for 'Buccaneer', against a Japanese garrison of not much over 10,000. Even the US Chiefs boggled a little at this. Roosevelt, however, was not yet willing to concede defeat, and Brooke thought they had made no progress. But in fact the President was weakening. Summing up at the end of the plenary meeting, he had said that they were all agreed that 'Overlord' and 'Anvil' must have top priority, which meant other operations could only be fitted in if they found they could 'scrape together' the resources for them. This applied both to Aegean operations (which the British Chiefs were still optimistically discussing) and South-east Asia. It certainly looked, Roosevelt added, as though Mountbatten would have to do the best he could with the resources he already had. It was no good his asking for more.

However, the Combined Chiefs could get no further that day than to agree to exchange memoranda on the subject, in the hope of clarifying their minds further on the question of precisely what resources could be found for the various operations. The final decision on both the Rhodes and the Andamans must rest with the politicians, since both operations depended on political factors. Would Roosevelt be prepared to risk offending Chiang, with the consequent possible loss of the entire Burma plan? Would the Turkish representatives, who had arrived that day, commit themselves sufficiently for Operation 'Hercules' (the assault on Rhodes) to remain at least a faint possibility?[2]

The next day's discussions in fact decided one issue and virtually decided the other. On 5 December, after the usual preliminary meetings of the American and British Chiefs, the Combined Chiefs met again. Brooke, with what had become at this stage habitual pessimism, recorded that 'negotiations remained at a deadlock'. But this was not quite true. Just as Roosevelt had begun to give ground the day before, so Marshall now conceded an important point. At their own meeting the British Chiefs had agreed to put a crucial question to Marshall. Shorn of its political aspects (the promise to Chiang), did the US Chief himself really think 'Buccaneer' was militarily vital to the success of the Burma campaign? Marshall's innate honesty triumphed over his loyalty to his political chief. No, he conceded, he did not. The problem was the possible effect of abandonment on Chiang and the Chinese. If he thought the Burma campaign would still go ahead as planned, he would not worry too much about the fate of 'Buccaneer'. A gap had been made in the wall: but King and Leahy still held firm to Roosevelt's presumed wishes. Consequently the Combined Chiefs could only report back that they were now fully agreed on absolute priority for 'Overlord' and 'Anvil'—which probably meant the allocation of additional resources to both—and therefore that Aegean operations could only take place if there were eventually some landing-craft left over from the main operations. But they had still not agreed on 'Buccaneer'.

At the plenary session the same morning Roosevelt commented, probably somewhat wearily, that he would have preferred an agreed recommendation. He was however faced with the consequences of his own actions. He had committed himself to an operation which he knew Churchill opposed, and which the British Chiefs therefore were unlikely to accept: while the US Chiefs for their part would feel that they had to insist on it. Consequently an agreed recommendation on this matter from the Combined Chiefs had become a virtual impossibility. It was a deadlock similar to that over the 'Second Front' in 1942, which only Roosevelt or Churchill could break. One or the other of them had to give way, and Churchill for his part probably felt that he had made enough concessions on other issues. Let them go ahead with the Burma campaign and defer 'Buccaneer', he argued. Chiang might be annoyed, but he would not drop out of the war, provided supplies continued to flow over the 'Hump'.

Roosevelt began to give ground. He agreed that Mountbatten should be told to explore with his subordinate commanders the possibility of smaller alternative operations in South-east Asia, on the assumption that the landing-craft allocated to 'Buccaneer' might be withdrawn. As Brooke commented, they were now looking for ways to save Roosevelt's face with Chiang. At their afternoon meeting the Combined Chiefs agreed to telegraph Mountbatten accordingly, and also that 'Overlord' should be strengthened in its assault phase, while 'Anvil' it was definitely agreed should have at least a two-division assault. Eisenhower was directed to prepare a definite plan for the latter on these assumptions. All this meant that 'Buccaneer' and 'Hercules' were now fast receding into the distance.

Roosevelt in fact had made up his mind after the plenary meeting. At five o'clock he summoned the US Chiefs. It was clear, he told them, that no further resources could be found for 'Buccaneer', such as Mountbatten was demanding. It was time to stop the argument. They could not let the conference end in a deadlock. With great reluctance he had concluded they should abandon 'Buccaneer' and offer Chiang-Kai-Shek some lesser alternative. If the latter wished to postpone the whole Burma campaign till the autumn as a consequence, it could not be helped. Immediately after the meeting, Roosevelt and Hopkins drafted a telegram to Chiang along these lines, while Churchill received the laconic message, '"Buccaneer" is off'. To Stilwell Roosevelt said the same day that he had been 'as stubborn as a mule for four days. But the British just won't do it'. In this manner one of the bitterest strategic arguments of the war between Britain and the United States finally ended.[3]

The Reluctant Ally

While 'Buccaneer' was being finally disposed of, Operation 'Hercules' (Rhodes) was also receiving its quietus from the Turks. President Inönü arrived in Cairo with his Foreign Minister, Numan Menemencoglu, and other members of the delegation on the morning of 4 December. Three days of talks followed, but produced little result. five tripartite meetings were held: Roosevelt had one meeting with Inönü separately; Eden and Churchill met with the Turkish Foreign Minister; and Eden and Hopkins also had talks with Numan on a subsequent occasion. Finally on the 7th Churchill had one last meeting with Inönü, after Roosevelt's departure. But all these hours of talks produced in the end, as Eden remarked, very little of a positive nature. Inönü and his colleagues were cautious men, and their caution was understandable, for the Turkish army was inadequately trained and equipped with out-of-date weapons. The British plan was for the preparation of Turkish air-bases to be speeded up throughout December and January, with the necessary British advisers and technicians being admitted to Turkey in civilian clothes. Some time during February it was hoped the bases would be ready for Allied (that is, British) use. At that point British planes would fly in and begin air operations against the German positions in the Dodecanese, with naval support. Once air mastery over the Eastern Aegean had been obtained, there would be a 'best case' and a 'worst case'. The best case would be that landing-craft would be available and the Rhodes assault could take place, preferably in late February or early March. It could be argued, for the benefit of the Americans, that the landing-craft could still return to the Western Mediterranean in plenty of time for 'Anvil'. The worst case was that no landing-craft would be provided, and 'Hercules' would therefore be ruled out. In that case the British would try to starve the Germans out of the Aegean islands by air and naval blockade. But it was only the latter possibility that Churchill could discuss with the Turks. The Americans had stipulated at Teheran that he should not even tentatively promise amphibious operations. Either of the two alternatives, however, would require the use of Turkish air-bases.

In view of the relatively small inducements they could offer, Churchill and Eden did not ask for an immediate Turkish declaration of war against Germany, or for direct Turkish participation in operations. Their requests were limited, for the moment, to the use of Turkish bases; in return for which they promised adequate air and anti-aircraft protection against possible German raids. They hoped Inönü would agree to the first stage and give at any rate conditional assent to a British 'fly-in' some time in February. Even this was too much for the Turks, however. Inönü argued that the mere preparation of air-bases and certainly their use by the British Air Force would bring a German declaration of war, for which the Turkish army was not ready. Then there were also the Bulgarian divisions on their northern frontier, very much better equipped (by the Germans) than the Turkish army. In effect Inönü demanded that the Allies should equip the Turkish army with generous supplies of up-to-date weapons, before they could take that risk. This would take much longer than six or eight weeks; several months would be needed.

By this stage of the conference Churchill was exhausted, after two weeks of arduous negotiations. A day or two later he was to succumb to an attack of pneumonia. None the less he rallied his powers for a last effort, and, supported by Eden, used every argument to persuade the Turks. The war situation, he pointed out, was very much better for the Allies than it had been a year earlier; Germany was now on the defensive and the risks of action for Turkey were correspondingly less, since the Germans would probably not attack her unless they were obliged to. As for the Bulgarians, the Soviet Union had undertaken to look after them. By entering the war now, Turkey would secure for herself a privileged position as an Ally at the peace table, and in particular 'would put Turco-Russian relations on the best footing'. By not doing so the Turks would lose these advantages, and, it was implied, perhaps lose British support against possible Soviet pressures.

Eden was more blunt than Churchill. The Allies, he said, could not afford to wait for endless negotiations. The time when Turkish help would be valuable to them was during the next few months; after that, allied offers would be withdrawn. The Allies could not afford to dispose of valuable resources without a firm guarantee that they would soon be used against the Germans. Roosevelt's attitude during the talks was not directly unhelpful, but rather aloof. He was well aware of his Chiefs of Staff's fears that the Eastern Mediterranean could become a bottomless pit, draining away valuable resources from more important operations. He had said all along that he thought the Turks would put a higher price on their services than the United States at any rate was willing to pay. He displayed sympathy for the Turkish point of view on more than one occasion. One feels too that Steinhardt had probably made the American attitude pretty clear to the Turks beforehand.

However that may be, the Turkish government could not be moved from its cautious attitude. Inönü would only agree that military talks should begin between British and Turkish officers, and in the meantime the preparation of air-bases should continue. He would give no guarantee that in mid February these bases would be activated. Nor were they. In the months that followed the question of active Turkish participation in the war slipped off the urgent agenda, and with it the Rhodes operation. Whatever Churchill may have felt about this, the Turkish people have every reason to be grateful to Inönü. He had ensured that Turkey, which had suffered much in the First World War, should not suffer equally in the Second. Nor were the dire consequences which had been hinted at in fact forthcoming, since it remained a Western interest to support Turkey against undue Soviet pressure.[4]

Problems of Command

During the last days of the Cairo conference most of the Command problems which had exercised the Combined Chiefs and their political masters were also resolved. It had already been agreed in principle that the whole of the Mediterranean area which was the scene or the possible scene of active operations should be placed under one commander. This had been strongly urged by the British and, thanks to Marshall, conceded by the Americans. The Final Report of the Combined Chiefs to Churchill and Roosevelt on 6 December formally ratified this recommendation. The previous day the British and Americans had approved a directive to Eisenhower adding Turkey and the Balkans to the existing Western Mediterranean Command. In the immediate future this meant only that the new command would be responsible for unifying and co-ordinating all allied assistance to resistance movements in the Balkans, and any allied operations connected with them. Had the talks with Inönü had a different outcome, the Rhodes and Dodecanese operations would also have come under the new Command. It had been agreed between Churchill and Roosevelt at Quebec that this new Mediterranean Command should be a British appointment, since the 'Overlord' Command was to go to an American. The obvious man for the post was the successful commander of the allied armies in Italy, and previously in North Africa, General Alexander. Brooke, however, felt that Alexander could not be spared from the Italian campaign, and persuaded Churchill to appoint the Middle East commander, General Maitland Wilson, instead. Immediately after the conference Eisenhower set about initiating the new Command, and handed it over to Maitland Wilson on 10 January.

There had also been much discussion at Cairo on the American proposal to combine the US Strategic Air Force in the Mediterranean (the heavy bombers of the 15th US Air Force) with similar American forces in the UK, under one Command. The new commander would be responsible directly to the Combined Chiefs. The American purpose was to ensure that all of these strategic bomber forces would be used at need against targets which would directly help 'Overlord'. Portal, for the British Chiefs, had objected to this proposal on the ground that it would simultaneously diminish his existing authority to co-ordinate all strategic bomber operations from the United Kingdom and at the same time diminish the power of the new British commander in the Mediterranean to support his own operations. On this issue a compromise was reached during the second stage of the Cairo conference. The British accepted the new arrangement (though under protest) and agreed to support it and make it work. The Americans made two important concessions. The new Strategic Air Force commander would continue to come under the general direction of Portal, acting for the Combined Chiefs, for the time being. The Mediterranean Command would continue to have first call on a proportion of the US Strategic Air Forces in Italy until Rome and the airfields to the north of it were captured; and even after that could still use the whole of the 15th Air Force in a 'strategical or tactical emergency'. On this basis an amicable agreement was reached, and the American Air Force General Spaatz was appointed to the new Command. In addition Arnold agreed to have further discussions with allied commanders in the Mediterranean before bringing the new arrangements fully into operation.

Two other tentative American proposals had already fallen to the . ground. British opposition, plus the experience with the Chinese and Russians during these meetings, had put an end to the idea of a

'United Chiefs of Staff' with Russian and/or Chinese representation. This was formally laid to rest in the Combined Chiefs' final Report. Similarly the proposal for an 'Overall Commander' of all European operations had been quietly abandoned in the face of vehement British objections. This proposal was not put forward again after the British and Americans left Cairo for Teheran. Its abandonment, however, had important consequences for the most important Command decision of all—the command of 'Overlord'.

Roosevelt had hesitated for so long over the 'Overlord' appointment largely because of his unwillingness to lose Marshall, the obvious choice, from the supreme strategic direction of the war. In addition there had been suggestions in Washington, inspired largely by the desire of Hopkins's enemies to find a stick to beat him with, that the President on Hopkins's advice was proposing to 'downgrade' Marshall. To that charge Marshall's appointment not just to the command of the 'Overlord' operation but to the supreme direction of the war in Europe, would have been an effective answer. Since that possibility was now ruled out, Roosevelt's natural predisposition not to lose Marshall's services in Washington reasserted itself. On 5 December he summoned Marshall to his villa. The President asked him directly which appointment he would prefer—to remain Chief of Staff or to command 'Overlord'. But Marshall, in accordance with his code, would not express a preference. He was a soldier and would do as he was told. Roosevelt then told him that no one could really replace him in Washington. The 'Overlord' appointment would go instead to Eisenhower. Immediately Marshall drafted for the President a message to Stalin conveying the decision. In this way, after months of hesitation on Roosevelt's part, the most important Command appointment of the war was made.[5]

'The Captains and the Kings depart'

Generally speaking, therefore, on Command arrangements the British had got their way, and the Americans had had to abandon their more ambitious plans. But this was comparatively unimportant compared with the operational decisions. The British left Cairo committed to overriding priority for 'Overlord' and 'Anvil', and with the possibility of extensive operations further east, whether in the Aegean or the Adriatic, virtually ruled out. They had been able to save a little for the Italian campaign, but that was all. It mattered little whether the Mediterranean commander were British or American, if most resources were to be directed elsewhere, and he would eventually have to part with even some of those he now had.

The American Chiefs then were on the whole pleased with the results of the conferences. So was Roosevelt, in spite of his annoyance over 'Buccaneer'. He had successfully defended the American strategic concept. He had made, he felt, progress in establishing relations with Stalin, and winning his confidence. He had secured Stalin's general approval for his concept of a future international organization and the broad outlines of a Far Eastern Settlement; and he had obtained a reaffirmation of the Soviet promise to enter the Far Eastern war, once Germany had been defeated. Churchill for his part was depressed. But he was never downcast for long. His mind seems to have turned to the possibility of doing something to retrieve the situation, even though some of the more promising options had been foreclosed. As usual, there was a 'best case' and a 'worst case'. The best case was that the Italian amphibious operation in January might be completely successful, and the fall of Rome follow almost immediately. With Alexander's military skill, it might still be possible to break into the Po valley by midsummer, before formations committed to 'Anvil' had to be withdrawn. Building on success, it might then be feasible to persuade the Americans that it was worth retaining enough resources in Italy to permit an attempt to debouch through the 'Ljubljana gap' into Central and Eastern Europe before the winter closed in.

The worst case was that none of the above would come about; that Anzio would fail, or subsequent operations prove disappointing. This in fact is what occurred. In that eventuality, the only recourse would be to see what could be salvaged in Eastern Europe by diplomacy. It would probably not be much, since Stalin would have all the cards in his hand. But the attempt would probably have to be made. Perhaps Stalin's appetite would be reasonably moderate. It was this line of thought which led to the East European 'percentages' agreement of October 1944, by which Churchill sought to limit and define the boundaries of Soviet influence. True, Churchill argued that this arrangement was intended only for the 'short-run'. But 'short-runs' have a way of becoming 'long-runs' when one is dealing with the Soviet Union, as experience in Germany was to show.

It is clear, looking at the record of the Cairo and Teheran conferences as a whole, that neither Churchill nor Roosevelt was at his best. Both men arrived at Teheran already tired by the long hours of wrangling at Cairo. Since the first Cairo conference was largely fruitless in producing agreed decisions, one has to admit that it would have been better if it had not taken place at all. If things had been otherwise—if the American attitude had been different, if the Chinese had been held back until after Teheran, as they should have been, Cairo

1 might have produced worthwhile results. As it was the British and Americans arrived at Teheran not only without an agreed plan, but further apart than ever, and in a state of mutual irritation. It was not the best situation in which to confront Stalin. For all of this Churchill must take his share of the responsibility, both because he had insisted on the conference, and because he had handled Roosevelt and Marshall with none of his previous skill. When they returned to Cairo, as we have seen, the crucial decisions had been made and it was largely a matter of absorbing the consequences. By this time both Roosevelt and Churchill were exhausted, and far from well. Only this can explain and excuse one or two petulant actions by Roosevelt in this last stage of the conference, particularly an ill-advised and unwarranted intervention in the murky waters of Greek politics. Churchill for his part was, by his own account, 'at the end of his tether'.

On 7 December Roosevelt left from Cairo West airport for Tunis and then for Washington. The Chiefs of Staff and Churchill remained for one more day, to tie up the loose ends in a last series of separate and joint meetings, and to gather for a final dinner together at Churchill's villa. The next day the US Chiefs departed, and on the 10th Brooke and Churchill flew to Tunis, where the latter was to go down with pneumonia. The long series of tripartite conferences which had begun on 18 October in Moscow had finally come to an end. [6]

2. The Consequences of Moscow, Cairo, and Teheran

President Roosevelt returned to Washington well satisfied with what he had achieved. He had set out to establish a good relationship and understanding with Stalin and the Soviet leaders, as a basis for further progress towards continuing and closer military co-operation in the war and post-war co-operation in international peace-keeping. To achieve this he had consciously distanced himself from Churchill and the British, with the aim of convincing Stalin that the United States and Britain were not allied in a common bloc against the USSR. He felt he had made considerable progress along these lines and garnered some of the hoped-for-harvest, in the shape of Stalin's specific agreement to a Four-Power, world-wide structure for the future international order. On the Far East also he felt he had made progress towards the kind of settlement he had in mind, based on Sino-Soviet-American 'tripartism', with Britain and other European States as far as possible excluded from any effective say in the China/Pacific area. Stalin had seemed willing to accept that China should be restored to unity and strength, to recognize Chinese sovereignty over Manchuria, and to acknowledge Chiang as the leader of China. As a quid pro quo it appeared Stalin would only require a rather more effective outlet to the Pacific and a more predominant 'influence' for Russia in Manchuria than other powers. In return he was apparently willing to recognize an equally predominant position in the Pacific Ocean generally for the United States; and had indicated that he would give his support to the United States in helping Chiang to rid his country of the last vestiges of European imperialism.

It seemed to Roosevelt also that there had been no diminution of the general agreement on Western and Central Europe which had apparently emerged from the Moscow conference. Stalin evidently shared Roosevelt's low opinion of France—something which had not been clear before—and a belief that the French neither could nor should play a major role in Europe or the world after the war; both men were disposed to deal harshly and firmly with Germany, in a way which would prevent any possibility of that country exercising the predominant influence in European affairs in the future. They had agreed on the principles which should be applied in Italy and France, along democratic lines which were perfectly acceptable to the United States. Presumably the Russians would not object to the same principles being applied in Germany when the time came, and if in Germany, why not in Eastern Europe also? The discussions on Finland had been not unpromising. Stalin had been severe, but not extreme in his attitude, and had disclaimed any intention of annexing Finland. If the Russians were prepared to treat a small enemy State which had done them considerable harm with some degree of restraint, there was no reason to suppose that other States in Eastern Europe which had not been enemies but allies—such as Poland and Czechoslovakia—would fare too badly. *Mutatis mutandis*, the same might apply to the ex-enemy States—Hungary, Romania, Bulgaria. What Stalin had had to say on Poland probably did not sound too unreasonable either. Roosevelt, like Hull, was not too familiar with the complex problems of Polish and East European frontiers, but there seemed to be a basis for a settlement acceptable to Russia, which would also help to weaken Germany, and which the British apparently regarded as not too bad for Poland. Of course it would help matters along if the London Poles could patch up their differences with the USSR, but again, Stalin's attitude to this group of rather obstreperous and highly nationalistic exiles cannot have seemed to Roosevelt so very unreasonable. It was, after all, very much the same as his own attitude towards de Gaulle and the Free French, and included the same concern that these people might hamper and obstruct military operations. Anyway it was up to Churchill to make the London Poles see reason. Roosevelt was not willing to risk what he had achieved by involving himself.

All of this would of course mean, especially if US troops were quickly withdrawn from Europe after the war, that the USSR would then be the most powerful military and political force on the Continent. This was the theme of Bohlen's celebrated memorandum after the conference. Especially would this be the case in Eastern Europe. Roosevelt made it clear by his actions at Teheran, and, if his son is to be believed, by his specific utterances, that this was in his view a consequence that had to be taken on board, and an acceptable risk. 'Maybe the Russians will get strong in Europe. Whether that's bad depends on a whole lot of factors', he is reported to have said. Whether he actually said these precise words is not of great importance. Roosevelt's actions only make sense if he thought along these lines. The gamble was twofold: that Soviet/American world-wide co-operation would become a reality, and that Soviet demands in Eastern Europe would not be so immoderate as to make nonsense of the principles on which most Americans, no less than the British, believed the post-war settlement must be based. Historians of course are still arguing about which half of the package came unstrung first. Was it, as cold-war orthodoxy had it, that Soviet ruthlessness and tyranny in Eastern Europe made genuine post-war co-operation impossible? Or was it rather, as revisionist historians would have us believe, that the American failure to pursue the path of genuine co-operation made for Soviet intransigence and obstinacy in Eastern Europe—and elsewhere? It is not the purpose of this book to enter the well-worn paths of this controversy, but to show the sequence of events and patterns of thought which led to these questions being posed.[7]

On the military side Roosevelt and his Chiefs of Staff were on the whole equally satisfied. At Quebec they had finally pinned Churchill and the British down to a definite date for 'Overlord'. At Moscow they had given definite assurances to the Russians along these lines. Then there had been alarms and excursions. Churchill had once again shown signs of backsliding. The Russians had displayed a tendency to be far too interested in Mediterranean operations and in setting off dangerous diversions in the Aegean. But at Teheran all had come right. Stalin had thrown his weight unequivocally on the side of 'Overlord' and against unnecessary diversions. Faced with this Soviet/American axis, Churchill and Brooke had been forced to give way. An agreement to keep Western Mediterranean operations going for the time being had been for the Americans a reasonable price to pay for this agreement, particularly as the weight of those operations would soon shift westwards, in a way which would assist the main strategic effort. As Marshall's biographer puts it: 'General Marshall could feel gratified that he had pinned down the British to a May date for the invasion of northern France and to an assault on southern France.' Moreover, it had been agreed that these operations should have priority over all others, once the limited objectives agreed in Italy had been reached. The Americans had not succeeded in obtaining the Command arrangements that ideally they would have wished for, but the operational decisions were really what counted. The important thing was that the Aegean/Turkish threat to 'Overlord' had been firmly pushed aside. It was slightly unfortunate, as Pogue puts it, that 'if "Overlord" and the landings in southern France were to be mounted on a proper scale, something would have to give—and it would be "Buccaneer"'. But the importance of 'Buccaneer' had always been political rather than military. The logic of the US planner's recommendation that the Central Pacific thrust against Japan should be the main Far Eastern priority, no less than Stalin's promise to enter the Pacific war, reduced the military significance of South-east Asian operations, as the British had argued. Even if Nationalist China did effectively opt out of the war, or refuse to take part in the Burma campaign, this would now have less military significance. Roosevelt could reasonably and with satisfaction say to Stimson 'I have brought "Overlord" back to you safe and sound, and on the ways for accomplishment'. To Stalin he cabled 'I consider the conference a great success' and to the American people he reported 'I believe we are going to get along well with [Marshal Stalin] and the Russian people'. Not all Americans, however, were quite so starry-eyed, especially those in close touch with the Russians. Averell Harriman, it is true, was cautiously optimistic but worried about the future of Poland: he was concerned particularly about the probable conflict between the main Polish resistance and the Red Army, if a settlement was not reached between Moscow and the London Poles. Bohlen, however, thought even Harriman was too optimistic about the extent of the understanding between Russia and the Western Allies, which he, Bohlen, felt was purely military, not political. Looked at coldly, the political reality was that in Europe the Russians were hoping to dismember Germany and seemed to want a weak France, a subservient Poland, and the continued division of the Balkans into small, weak States. In the Far East it seemed that they wished to restore the position which had existed before the Russo-

Japanese War at the turn of the century—an effective Russian 'sphere of influence' in Manchuria and part of North China. It was difficult to see how this latter could be reconciled with a strong and independent China, possessing 'full sovereignty' over Manchuria; while the complete fragmentation of Central and South-eastern Europe could only be a recipe for Soviet dominance in Europe as a whole. [8]

The picture from the British angle at the time bore of course a very different aspect from that presented and probably believed in by Roosevelt. It was much closer to that of Bohlen. While Churchill lay sick in Carthage and Marrakesh, Eden and Brooke both reported to the War Cabinet. It is interesting to compare what they said then with what is said in Eden's (and Churchill's) memoirs and to view both in the light of all the information now available about their mood at the time.

In his report to the War Cabinet Eden displayed his customary tendency to put the best face on things. True, so far as the military issues were concerned, he complained, as did Brooke, that Chiang's presence at Cairo had distorted the proper order of business and made it impossible to reach decisions with the Americans on combined plans for European operations. Thus they had been forced to argue their differences in front of the Russians. None the less he said 'a reasonable solution [on the military issue] had been reached' and Stalin had been 'co-operative and friendly; there had been no retrogression from the position reached at Moscow'. The accounts given above of the Cairo and Teheran conferences will enable the reader to judge how far these remarks softened the harsh outline of the picture.

Eden however admitted that they had been forced to accept a disappointing conclusion to the Turkish discussions: but he did not 'spell out' to his colleagues the extent to which Churchill's strategic plans had been thwarted. Brooke explained the consequences of the Soviet-American agreement on strategy more specifically. They had been forced to accept the Southern France operation; this admittedly had the advantage of facilitating the Anzio operation and so assisting the Italian campaign. But now that the full consequences of 'Anvil' had been digested, it was clear that it also ruled out the Rhodes assault, and Aegean operations generally. Stalin, Brooke reported, 'was showing little interest in possible Anglo-American operations in the Balkans or the opening of the Straits', adding that this lack of interest probably sprang from other motives than purely strategic ones. Brooke, like Roosevelt and Churchill, judged that Stalin saw as clearly as they did that these decisions would make Russia the arbiter of the future for all the Balkan States.

It was not in Eden's nature to concede that the combined effect of
Moscow and Teheran amounted to a series of defeats for British policy
in the Balkans and Eastern Europe. He confined himself to saying that
the Russians were now showing some disposition to seeking a
common policy *vis-à-vis* Tito and the Yugoslav government-in-exile;
and on Poland that they had worked out a frontier agreement which
might form the basis of a *rapprochement* between Moscow and the
London Poles. There was no mention of Stalin's extreme bitterness
against the London Poles; or Roosevelt's aloofness; nor was the fact
stressed that none of the reciprocal assurances had been given by
Stalin which had been hoped for, in exchange for a British undertaking to persuade the Poles of the virtues of an acceptable frontier
agreement. In particular very little progress had been made towards
the resumption of diplomatic relations. None of his colleagues was
apparently tactless enough to remind Eden of this. It must have been
apparent to them, however, that there was no alternative to the policy
of trying to secure the agreement of the London Poles to this settlement, in the hope that Stalin's heart might then be softened.
Circumstances had changed a good deal since the War Cabinet had
last discussed the basis of a reasonable bargain with Russia over
Poland. Soviet inflexibility and Polish intransigence had both played
their part in this, but it had been the lack of American support at
Teheran, following a similar lack of interest at Moscow, which had
been decisive in tilting the balance.

The more perceptive of Eden's colleagues must also have been perturbed by what he told them of Roosevelt's and Stalin's apparent
agreement in denigrating and wishing to weaken France: and the
contrast in the Cairo communiqué between the open and generous
promises on the restoration of Chinese territory and the lack of
reference to South-east Asia. Altogether it cannot have been a particularly reassuring report. In his memoirs, of course, Eden is a little more
forthcoming. In contrast to his assurances to the War Cabinet, he says
that 'his feelings at the close of the Teheran conference were less easy
than they had been at Moscow', and attributes this to a number of
factors: the evidence of a much less forthcoming attitude on the part
of the Russians; the continued unwillingness of the Americans to
concert common Anglo-American policies; and Roosevelt's positive
'unhelpfulness' over Poland. All of these, he says, gave him deep concern. He knew how difficult it would be to persuade the London Poles:
and even if he did, there was no guarantee that Stalin would be more
amenable. Once the Red Army crossed the Polish frontier, the possibilities of further conflict with the Resistance and increasing

Soviet–Polish bitterness might make a reconciliation impossible. Not surprisingly he adds: 'I felt that my power to help the London Poles might be limited'. This was all too accurate an assessment.

Churchill for his part softens the outlines of the picture in his memoirs more than can be justified, either by the facts or his own feelings at the time. On the outcome of the military argument he even goes so far as to say 'I personally was well content'. The picture of Churchill exhausted, sick, and defeated, which Brooke and Moran give, is hardly consistent with this frame of mind. Churchill indeed in the same paragraph admits that he would much have preferred the 'rightward movement' from Italy (through Istria-Trieste and the 'Ljubljana gap' towards Vienna) to the 'Anvil' operation which had been foisted on them. He makes it clear that he hoped that the decision could later be changed. But this possibility depended on a breakthrough in Italy during the next few months, with at least the possibility that exploitation to the Po valley and Istria would be feasible during the summer months. The first requirement for this was the launching of the Anzio operation in sufficient strength to bring those results. To that Churchill turned his attention, even while still recovering from his illness in North Africa, sacrificing the last remote possibility of Aegean operations to do so. Moran, who was with him at the time, believed he had concluded that only by getting troops into central Eastern Europe before the Red Army arrived could he now help any of those countries, in the face of Soviet attitudes and American indifference. Exploitation in Italy was the only remaining chance of doing so. But if these were Churchill's hopes, they were not to bear fruit. It was to prove impossible to reverse the effects of the Teheran strategic decisions.

Churchill's judgement in his memoirs that the political consequences of Teheran depended on 'the results of great battles to be fought' must be seen in the light of this appraisal. His comment on the Western approach to Russia at Teheran 'it would not have been right to let suspicion rule our attitudes' is surely more of a defence of Roosevelt's memory—and perhaps of his own deference to the latter's wishes—than a reflection of his own attitude at the time. Churchill was certainly unhappy at the prospect of Soviet dominance in Eastern Europe, though it is not necessary to make the further deduction that he was largely motivated by his long-standing anti-Bolshevism. Churchill and Eden were opposed to Soviet dominance for the same reasons that they had opposed German dominance. The ideological coloration of the oppressor was a secondary consideration.

Churchill and Eden both realized of course that they could not just hope for a problematic success in Italy to reverse the political/military results of Teheran and Moscow. Both also turned their attention in 1944 to exploring the possibilities of salvaging something from the wreck in Eastern Europe through a diplomatic bargain; and the evidence suggests that Stalin may not have been entirely averse to such a deal along the lines indicated in the 'percentages agreement' of October 1944. Similarly, and with even more urgency, the two men applied themselves to the task of getting the agreement of the London Poles to the frontier settlement, and so facilitating a last attempt to save their position before Russian troops entered Poland. But the lack of concerted Anglo-American effort and a real agreement on policy continued to hamstring these efforts. As for Germany, Roosevelt's mood at Teheran made it best to shelve the whole issue of the post-war settlement for the time being, and indeed to give the Germans no inkling of their probable future. As Churchill puts it, at Teheran 'retribution' was the dominant German theme, at any rate so far as America and Russia were concerned. Better to wait and hope that wiser counsels would eventually prevail in Washington.[9]

Stalin's real thoughts, and those of his associates, about Teheran are, as always, more difficult to assess. In the short term they had every reason to be satisfied. With American assistance they had finally pinned the British down to 'Overlord' in the summer and a Western Mediterranean strategy which effectively ruled out Aegean or Balkan operations in the near future. In the Balkans, as in Poland and the rest of Eastern Europe, it was now almost certain that the Red Army would have virtually a free hand. It might be good policy to make a few 'compromises' (the phrase is Djilas') over Yugoslavia and Greece, to avoid friction with the British. But essentially the game was in their hands—always assuming the Anglo-Americans could be trusted to carry out their strategic promises, of which Stalin was by no means sure. In view of Churchill's *arrière-pensée*, one cannot argue that Stalin's doubts about British intentions were entirely unjustified, but it is probable that he was almost equally suspicious of Roosevelt. This last judgement is not dependent on a few *obiter dicta* of Milovan Djilas. Stalin's whole life and character—and beliefs—would have predisposed him to suspicion of someone who purported to be as frank and unreserved as Roosevelt. However, if the military promises given at Teheran were really meaningful, they represented everything that the USSR could have hoped for.

Politically, too, Stalin and Molotov must have felt that the omens of the discussions at Teheran, informal and inconclusive though they had been, were promising. At Moscow they had received Anglo-

American assurances on the specific principles for the political settlement in Italy, France, and Germany which committed the West to the
extirpation of Fascism and its allies—which previously they had much
doubted. In return they had been obliged to give no specific assurances on the political principles to be applied in Eastern Europe other
than the vague and qualified acceptance they had already given to the
Atlantic Charter and the UN Declaration of January 1942. They had
staved off every attempt at Moscow to limit in any way Soviet freedom
of action in Eastern Europe. At Teheran Stalin had not felt it necessary to give any assurances on the matter, and except in the specific
case of Finland had been put under no pressure by the Americans to
do so. He had felt no need, therefore, to be other than uncompromising on the question of relations with the London Poles, when
pressed by the British. As one historian has put it, 'he had thrown
down the gauntlet both to the London government and to the [Polish]
underground movement'. The proposed Soviet–Polish frontier was
perfectly satisfactory as far as it went, and both Churchill and
Roosevelt had committed themselves to it. What eventually happened
on the other side of that frontier would be entirely at the discretion of
the Soviet Union. There remained the crucial question of Germany.
No doubt it was a disappointment to Stalin that he had not been able
to secure a definite commitment to the dismemberment of the German
State. But here too the American mood—if Roosevelt really meant
what he said—looked distinctly promising, as indeed was the latter's
attitude to de Gaulle and his pretensions.

Finally, on the Far East, Stalin had staked his claims. Long before
there was any question of honouring the Soviet promise to enter the
Far Eastern war, it should be possible to enlarge the scope of the
generalities exchanged on the subject and make specific the extent of
Soviet gains in the Far East. Stalin would probably have agreed with
Bohlen's judgement (again if he could believe in Roosevelt's sincerity)
that he was being offered assured Soviet dominance in Europe: and in
addition to that, a large sphere of influence in the Far East and the
position of one of the two major partners in a Four-Power world
directorate. It would be hardly surprising if he had his doubts about
these large promises. Certainly he felt that the Soviet Union could not
afford to lower its guard in its relations with the West.[10]

This was probably the mood of the principal participants immediately
after Teheran. Hindsight of course is different. Writing a dozen
years or so after the conference, a distinguished American historian
rightly judged that it was Roosevelt's optimism rather than Bohlen's

pessimism which reflected the general mood of the US administration at the time. The same historian believed Stalin may have been misled by Roosevelt's frankness and responsiveness into thinking that the American attitude to breaches of the Atlantic Charter would be more compliant than it turned out to be. In this, too, Herbert Feis may well have been right. He appears, however, to have been misled by Churchill's comments into thinking the British mood more optimistic than it was. Feis himself, after quoting Bohlen, rightly concludes that 'Soviet territorial aims in Europe had been advanced, and Stalin had managed to get all proposals which might have resulted in opposed strength discarded or deferred'; while in relation to the Pacific war commitment, there would be 'time and opportunity to decide what advantage might be secured in that connection'. Churchill's view in 1943 would not, one feels, have differed very much from this summary.

To ask the question 'what were the consequences of Moscow, Cairo, and Teheran?' is to ask two different questions, one of them factual, the other speculative. The answer to the factual question is concerned with what actually happened as a result of decisions which were taken; and the historian by and large knows the answer to this question. But how he or she interprets and judges the actual consequences often depends on the answer given to the much more speculative question 'what would have happened if the decisions had been different?' It is when it is possible to argue and believe that the results of alternative decisions would have been much better than those that occurred, that strong feelings are aroused. But it is important to remember that such statements are never susceptible of absolute proof. No one can be absolutely sure what would have happened if different decisions had been taken on any occasion from those which were taken. Some contemporary historians, particularly those who deal with the Cold War, have tended to forget this simple truism. The war-time conferences, which served as a prologue to the Cold War, invite the same kind of oversimplification. It is necessary, therefore, to distinguish between these two questions—and their answers.

Politically the result of these conferences was mainly important for Eastern Europe, even more than for the Far East. Stalin was a realist: he needed American goodwill because he needed Lease-Lend and he needed a powerful ally. He was far less concerned about British goodwill, since British supplies and the British war-effort were less important. It mattered of course that Britain should remain an active ally, but he probably calculated that the British would not withdraw from the conflict, after sacrificing so much, when victory was in sight. It was not necessary therefore to conciliate the British particularly. The United States was a different matter. Its goodwill was important. American policy and American attitudes could therefore influence Stalin, on Eastern Europe, as on other matters. At Moscow and Teheran Roosevelt and Hull made it clear that the fate of Eastern Europe was not their primary concern: post-war co-operation, the post-war security organization, and a satisfactory arrangement in the Pacific and Far East were their main priorities. Roosevelt and Hull believed in fact that if they could secure genuine long-term co-operation with the USSR, all these territorial and other issues in Eastern Europe could be settled on a reasonable basis. If Soviet/American co-operation were not secured, the outlook was bleak for Eastern Europe in any case. General Deane, a participant in these conferences, judged that Stalin and Churchill knew exactly what they wanted, whereas Roosevelt did not. But this does Roosevelt an injustice. Roosevelt knew what he wanted. The question is firstly, was what he wanted practicable? And secondly, did he go the right way to obtain it?

It is at this point that the factual question merges into the speculative. The practical result of the American posture at Moscow and Teheran was that no effective political obstacles were placed in the way of Soviet objectives in Eastern Europe. Moreover Stalin and Molotov may well have been given the impression that the United States did not really regard the fate of the Eastern European countries as of great importance. The conclusion would have been natural enough, and was probably reinforced by Roosevelt's apparently rather cavalier attitude towards the rights of the Baltic peoples and the Poles. If the issue *was* important to the Americans, why did they not make a stand on it when their Allies, the British, wished them to and the opportunity was there? This or something like it may have been Stalin's reasoning.

When one asks the question whether a different American stance could have achieved better results for Eastern Europe, one is entirely in the realm of speculation and caution is necessary. There is some evidence for the view that it might have done. Finland was the one Eastern European country for which Roosevelt demonstrated real concern at Teheran, and Finland certainly emerged with a greater degree of independence than the other East European countries (save for Yugoslavia which had to fight a bitter battle with Moscow for the privilege). It cannot be proved that Roosevelt's stand over Finland made any real difference to Soviet policy in that respect, but it seems not unlikely. In this one case the Americans had hoisted a warning signal; and Stalin was accustomed to take notice of warning signals. Cordell Hull could have acted similarly at Moscow on a succession of proposals which Eden put forward, without any real risk of breaking up the conference. The Russians had no wish for the Moscow conference to fail. However bitter the arguments which might have developed, they would still probably have sought a face-saving compromise. Hull however, did not merely refrain from supporting Eden. He indicated at best American indifference and at worst outright American hostility to the proposals, without suggesting alternatives of his own. If the Russians misinterpreted the signals as indicating permanent US indifference to the fate of Eastern Europe and an American willingness to waive the principles of the Atlantic Charter in that area, they can hardly be blamed. If the main cause of the ultimate Soviet/American conflict, as some historians believe, was their 'misperceptions' of each other's aims and beliefs, some of those misperceptions may have begun at Moscow and Teheran. The same can be said of the even more crucial question of Germany. Certainly Roosevelt gave the impression at Teheran that he believed wholeheartedly in the total destruction or 'dismemberment' of the German State. If Cordell Hull is to be believed, he was not by any means as sure that this was the correct policy as his remarks on the subject at Teheran suggested. The conclusion cannot be avoided that Roosevelt, as so often, was 'thinking aloud' and trying out the effect of ideas to which he had given insufficient thought. This practice may have worked reasonably well in domestic matters, though it contributed to Roosevelt's reputation with some people for a certain 'trickiness' and unreliability. But it was a far more dangerous practice in international diplomacy. In this case it must surely have given Stalin a false impression of what consistent US policy was likely to be. Again, a different, a more cautious approach, such as Hull himself adopted at Moscow on this issue, would have been beneficial. It could of course be argued that Churchill also favoured German dismemberment (of a kind) at Teheran. But Stalin was well aware that Churchill was aiming at something quite different from the power vacuum in the heart of Europe indicated by Roosevelt's approach. Stalin was not misled about Churchill's intentions and said so, explicitly.

If such speculations are tentative in regard to Europe they must be no less so in regard to the political implications of these conferences for the Far East. It was for long customary to identify the Yalta conference as the occasion when these latter issues were really decided: but for the Far East, as for Eastern Europe, much that happened later was foreshadowed by the discussions at an earlier period. The concessions made to Stalin, largely at the expense of China, at Yalta were the logical outcome of the basis for a Far Eastern settlement sketched by Roosevelt at Teheran. The difficulty of dividing fact and speculation is here exacerbated by the question of where one draws the line and says 'here the consequences of this particular set of decisions end'. The long-term outcome of the wartime strategy and diplomacy was in fact a united Communist China; and this outcome was not in all probability foreseen or intended by Stalin and certainly not by Roosevelt. Roosevelt wished for a united but non-Communist China, and the fact that he singularly failed to achieve it has somewhat obscured the probable fact that Stalin might well have preferred a weak and disunited China. It is improbable that either a blank American refusal to countenance Soviet objectives, or a larger and more positive military and political commitment to Nationalist China would have fundamentally altered the outcome. Soviet ability to achieve its objectives in Manchuria depended largely on the military situation at the end of the war. But one cannot entirely discount the possibility that firm American opposition to Soviet claims might again have served as a warning signal, and that Stalin might have been influenced by it. In the end it mattered little, so far as these specific issues were concerned, since Stalin felt morally obliged to surrender these gains, when it became a question of dealing with a brother Communist State.

The larger question of course is whether a different military and political policy on the Far East from that pursued at Teheran and Yalta (to which Churchill, it must be stressed, was a willing partner) could have 'saved' the Nationalist regime in China. Leaving aside the question whether this was a proper objective of American (or British) policy, only one conclusion can be advanced with any certainty. So great was the weakness, the political and military debility of that regime that a major American military commitment would have been required. Other things being equal, the Far Eastern war would then presumably have ended at a time when the United States had become deeply involved in the Chinese civil imbroglio. How long Congress and American public opinion would have supported such a commitment; whether it would have been possible for American policy to have created a regime in China acceptable to Western public opinion generally and to absorb the Chinese Communists successfully in such a regime; what would have been the effect on Soviet objectives in Manchuria of all this, are questions involving too many imponderables to admit of any certain answer. On the whole it seems unlikely that satisfactory results would have been attained. Roosevelt's Far Eastern policy, with the concessions to the USSR which it involved, was a complex package in which the adoption of the central Pacific strategy, Soviet participation in the Pacific war, and the political objective of obtaining post-war Soviet/American co-operation all played a part. Hindsight tells us that the atomic weapon made Soviet assistance unnecessary for the West; and indeed that it may have been unnecessary anyway, if Roosevelt and his military advisers had been prepared to contemplate a much larger American casualty rate in the later stages of the Pacific war. Hindsight, however, cannot tell us that any combination of US policies would necessarily have preserved the Nationalist regime or any non-Communist regime. Such a proposition is not demonstrable.

In relation to Eastern Europe political policy and military strategy were equally interwoven. As will be evident, the effects of the political stance adopted on these issues by the United States at Moscow and Teheran were reinforced by the strategic policies adopted, policies recommended by the US Chiefs mainly, though not entirely, on military grounds. Roosevelt was not unaware of the political implications of this strategy. It is certainly hard to fathom all the nuances of Roosevelt's complex attitudes towards British objectives in this area. One has the feeling that he regarded 'imperialist Britain' as a convicted criminal, whose intentions must be viewed with suspicion, while the USSR had a clean sheet and could be given the benefit of the doubt. The risk that he might, in the process of thwarting 'illegitimate' British interests, be fostering the creation of a Soviet Empire in Eastern Europe does not seem to have worried him as much as it might have done.

Two British historians have put the connection and to some extent antithesis between military and political factors in relation to Eastern Europe in the following way: 'From a purely military viewpoint it was perhaps fortunate that the Turkish adventure was never embarked on, for it might have seriously hampered operations in Italy and France.' This is the purely military side of the argument, which weighed so strongly with Marshall, and to some extent with Brooke. It is very probably correct. Wheeler-Bennett and Nicholls go on to say, however, 'The decision to put the major weight of the Anglo-American effort into Western Europe meant that the liberation of the Balkans would have to be postponed.' The delay was probably fatal for the independence of those countries. These quotations encapsulate the whole US–British controversy over strategy and 'the political motive'. Foreshortening a very long and complex argument, the case is that the pursuit of an all-out Mediterranean strategy in 1944 might have postponed the Cross-Channel Attack and so (possibly) have prolonged the war: but this would have been worthwhile if the end-product had been a freer Europe. One of the 'included assumptions' in this thesis is that Western Europe would still have emerged free and democratic, if large Anglo-American forces had been employed in Central-Eastern Europe, and the Cross-Channel invasion had been later and on a smaller scale. This may not be an unreasonable assumption, since the Red Army would have had little excuse or incentive to go far beyond Berlin—and perhaps lacked the resources to do so. Western Europe could therefore to some extent have 'looked after itself'. But this thesis is a long step—or rather a series of long steps—from the simple and reasonably factual statement that the decision to put the main Anglo-American thrust into Western Europe removed any serious obstacle to Soviet policy in Eastern Europe. Every one of the various assumptions involved—both military and political—can be argued about: none can be proved or disproved. None the less it may be a tenable thesis.

When one describes a particular moment, a particular series of decisions, as a 'turning point', one is implying at very least that a decisive shift of some kind took place at that point: one may be implying also that the decisions taken, the choices made were absolute in a particular way—that they foreclosed options which had previously been open. In the first and simpler sense the end-of-year conferences of 1943 marked such a turning-point in a number of ways. It was the moment when the balance of military power within the Anglo-American alliance shifted decisively in favour of the United States: simultaneously, and closely connected with this was a two-fold shift in American diplomatic policy and Anglo-American strategy. The United States turned its main attention within the alliance from Britain to the Soviet Union: Western strategic policy changed from a Mediterranean focus, largely inspired by British ideas, to a Western European focus reflecting largely American concepts. In all these ways this was a 'turning-point'—a decisive shift—for the wartime alliance. In the Far East also Allied strategy moved decisively towards a central Pacific emphasis and away from China and South-east Asia.

In the second sense also it can be argued plausibly that the meetings resulted in a 'turning point', that is in the sense of 'a point of no return', a foreclosing of options, for Eastern Europe: less certainly for the Far East. The option of resisting effectively the creation of a Soviet sphere of interest in Eastern Europe probably ceased to exist after this point. I have argued that it is less certain that any alternative political or military policy towards China and the Far East could have substantially altered the outcome. But for Eastern Europe 1943 was perhaps the turning-point.[11]

One other point is worth discussing briefly, namely to what extent did Moscow, Cairo, and Teheran foreshadow the Yalta decisions? So far as the Far Eastern settlement is concerned, the answer is 'to a very considerable extent'. The published records clearly do not give anything like a full account of what was discussed at the latter two conferences between Roosevelt and Chiang or Roosevelt and Stalin. But both Roosevelt and Stalin subsequently agreed that not only Soviet access to the port of Dairen, but also the Manchurian railways, Sakhalin, and the Kurile islands were discussed between them. Stalin also asserted that Soviet use of another Chinese port—Port Arthur— was mentioned, and this does not seem unlikely. Whether Roosevelt had actually secured Chiang's consent at Cairo to Soviet use of either of these ports, or to Soviet privileges in regard to the Manchurian railways seems uncertain. The evidence is not conclusive. It is probable that Roosevelt told Chiang that he would have to make some concessions to Russia in return for Soviet acceptance of the Cairo agreement. For his part Chiang may have gone no farther than to say that he might consider such concessions at some future date. If so, Roosevelt probably ignored Chiang's reservations at Teheran, and at Yalta made further concessions to Stalin, going beyond what had been agreed at Teheran. But in the broad sense the Yalta agreements in this area were certainly foreshadowed at Cairo and Teheran.

The Polish frontier settlement was also largely foreshadowed at Teheran, though more specifcially in detail on Soviet–Polish boundaries than on the Western frontier with Germany. More important, however, for the future of Poland and Eastern Europe than what was done was what was not done. The failure to bring any effective pressure to bear on Stalin, either politically or militarily, presaged future Western impotence in this area,

On the general question of the treatment of Germany also the Moscow and Teheran discussions presaged much that was formally decided later. The total destruction of Nazism, the occupation of Germany, German disarmament and demilitarization were all indicated as agreed lines of policy for the future. On two other crucial issues, however, future disagreements rather than agreements were foreshadowed. It was clear for example that the Soviet Union wished for much larger reparation payments to be extracted from Germany than either Britain or the United States thought practicable: and though there was apparent agreement between the Big Three that Germany should in some way be dismembered, it was also evident that Churchill did not favour as drastic a plan as Roosevelt and Stalin wished to see implemented. In the final result German partition came about more as a result of the supposedly temporary division into occupation zones than from anything which was agreed at Teheran or Yalta.

Finally in relation to the future world organization there were some indications at Teheran of what it would be like. But what was finally agreed at San Francisco made more concessions to the idea of the 'sovereign equality' of nations than the outline Roosevelt sketched to Stalin at Teheran. The Teheran proposals consigned the power of effective decision-making in a much more wholesale fashion to the 'Big Four' than was finally thought acceptable to the smaller powers. It must be said, however, that in the absence of Roosevelt's hoped-for Soviet/US co-operation, it made little difference what structure was finally adopted. [12]

SELECT MOSCOW CONFERENCE DOCUMENTS

Documents in Appendix A and B based on U. S. text (FRUS, 1943, Vol I and 'Cairo and Teheran Conferences').

1. Secret Protocol

AGENDA

1. Consideration of measures to shorten the duration of the war against Hitlerite Germany and her Allies in Europe.

(Proposed by U.S.S.R.)

2. (*a*) Four-Nations Declaration concerning general security.

(Proposed by U.S.A.)

(*b*) The establishment of a Commission of the three Powers.

(Proposed by U.S.S.R.)

3. The setting up of machinery for dealing with questions requiring current and close collaboration, with particular reference to the functions and scope of the Politico-Military Commission in Algiers.

(Proposed by U.K.)

4. Exchange of views on the situation in Italy and the Balkans.

(Proposed by U.K.)

(*a*) Information about the position in Italy and the Balkans.

(*b*) Proposal of the U.S.S.R. about policy in regard to Italy.

(*c*) Proposal of the Soviet Government as regards the transfer to the Soviet Union of part of the Italian Navy (one battleship, one cruiser, eight destroyers, four submarines) and of the Merchant Fleet (to a total of 40,000 tons) which was at the disposal of the Anglo-American forces as a result of the capitulation of Italy.

5. Methods of dealing with current political and economic issues and those which may arise as the war progresses.

(Proposed by U.S.A.)

6. Attitude towards the French Committee with special reference to its position in Metropolitan France and the establishment of eventual French government.

(Proposed by U.K.)

7. A. Treatment of Germany and other enemy countries in Europe.

(*a*) International military, political, and economic control over Germany during the armistice period.

(*b*) Steps toward ultimate settlement of future status of German Government, frontiers and other questions, length of armistice period.

(Proposed by U.S.A.)

B. Agreement in principle in regard to treatment of Germany and other enemy countries in Europe.

(*a*) During the armistice period, e.g. control commission, etc.

(*b*) At peace settlement, e.g. frontiers, military occupation, disarmament, reparations, decentralization of the German Government etc. (Austria)

(Proposed by U.K.)

8. Question of agreements between the major and minor Allies on post-war questions.

(Proposed by U.K.)

9. Common policy towards Turkey.

(Proposed by U.K.)

10. Common policy in Persia.

(Proposed by U.K.)

11. Relations between the U.S.S.R. and Poland and policy in relation to Poland generally.

(Proposed by U.K.)

12. Future of Poland and Danubian and Balkan countries, including the question of confederations.

(Proposed by U.K.)

13. Peace feelers from enemy states.

(Proposed by U.K.)

14. Policy regarding Allied territory liberated through the advance of the Allied forces.

(Proposed by U.K.)

15. A. Post-war economic cooperation with the U.S.S.R.

(Proposed by U.K.)

B. Economic matters for reconstruction.

(Proposed by U.S.A.)

(a) Cooperation in the rehabilitation of war damage in the U.S.S.R.

(b) Joint action for assistance to other countries.

(c) Collaboration on an international basis dealing with matters such as food and agriculture, transport and communications, finance and trade, and the International Labor Office.

(d) Questions of reparations.

16. Common policy towards resistance movements in Yugoslavia.

(Proposed by U.K.)

17. Question of joint responsibility for Europe as against separate areas of responsibility.

(Proposed by U.K.)

18. Declaration about the responsibility of the Hitlerites for atrocities.

(Proposed by U.K.)

19. Mutual exchange of military information.

(Proposed by U.K.)

20. Publication of Conference documents.

AGREED ACTION ON ABOVE POINTS

1. See the Most Secret Protocol of the Conference.

2. (a) The text of a declaration was agreed. The Declaration was signed on October 30th.

(b) It was recognised as desirable that representatives of the United States of America, the United Kingdom and the Soviet Union should conduct, in a preliminary fashion, an exchange of views on questions connected with the establishment of an international organisation for the maintenance of international peace and security, the intention being that this work should be carried out in the first instance in Washington, and also in London and Moscow.

3. (a) It was decided to set up a European Advisory Commission in London.

(b) It was decided to set up an Advisory Council for Italy.

4. (a) A written and oral exchange of information took place.

(b) The text of a declaration was adopted.

(c) Mr. Eden and Mr. Hull did not raise any objection to the proposal of the Soviet Government but reserved their final answer.

5. See the decision under point 3(*a*).

6. An exchange of views took place upon the document presented to the Conference by the Governments of the U.S.A. and the U.K.: "Basic scheme for Administration of liberated France".

In connection with questions put by the Soviet Delegation and observations made by them, the document in question was referred for examination to the European Advisory Commission.

7. An exchange of views took place, which showed identity of view on the main questions.

The question was referred for detailed study to the European Advisory Commission.

The text of a declaration about Austria was adopted.

8. An exchange of views took place. Note was taken of Mr. Eden's statement that he had no objection to the conclusion of the Soviet-Czechoslovak Treaty, the draft of which had been communicated to him.

9. The question was considered in the discussion on point 1.

10. The following proposal, which was worked out by a committee appointed by the Conference, was accepted: "(*a*) After an exchange of views, the Committee detects no fundamental difference in the policy towards Iran of any of the three Governments; (*b*) the Committee was unable to reach agreement on the expediency of making any immediate declaration or declarations with regard to Iran; and (*c*) the issue of such a declaration or declarations might be further considered by the representatives of the three Govern-

ments in Tehran, with a view to the three Governments coming to a decision about the expediency of issuing such a declaration or declarations after the signature of the proposed Irano-American Agreement and after appropriate consultation with the Government of Iran."

11. An exchange of views took place.

12. An exchange of views took place. Note was taken of the statement of the Soviet Delegation.

13. An exchange of views took place. The following resolution was adopted on the line to be taken in the event of peace-feelers being received from enemy countries:

"The Governments of the United Kingdom, the United States of America and the Soviet Union agree to inform each other immediately of any peace-feelers which they may receive from the Government of, or from any groups or individuals in, a country with which any one of the three countries is at war. The three Governments further agree to consult together with a view to concerting their action in regard to such approaches."

14. An exchange of views took place. The question was referred to the European Advisory Commission.

15.A. It was considered necessary to continue the examination of the questions raised.

B.(*a*) It was considered desirable to start conversations between the People's Commissariat for Foreign Affairs and the United States Embassy in Moscow.

(*b*) The statement of the United States Secretary of State on paragraph (*b*) "Joint action for assistance to other countries" is attached to this Protocol.

(c) The memorandum of the United States Secretary of State on paragraph (c) "Bases of our program for international economic collaboration" is attached to this Protocol.

(d) An exchange of views took place in the course of which there was some difference of opinion on some points in the memorandum which had been put forward.

16. This question was removed from the Agenda of the Conference at the suggestion of Mr. Eden.

17. This was dealt with under point 12 of the Agenda.

18. The text of a declaration was adopted.

19. The following resolution was adopted: "It is agreed that in order to ensure that all information regarding the common enemy is available to all the Allies engaged in his destruction, the Allies should keep each other mutually and constantly informed of all technical military information reaching them regarding the German Army, Navy and Air Force, the fighting value of enemy formations and the tactics used."

CORDELL HULL
V. MOLOTOV
ANTHONY EDEN

2. Most Secret Protocol (Military)

"THE CONSIDERATION OF MEASURES TO SHORTEN THE DURATION OF THE WAR AGAINST HITLERITE GERMANY AND HER ALLIES IN EUROPE"

(Proposed by the Soviet Delegation on the 19th October, 1943)

On the question put on the agenda of the Conference of representatives of the Governments of the United States of America, United Kingdom and the Union of Soviet Socialist Republics by the People's Commissar of Foreign Affairs, V. M. Molotov on the 19th October, 1943, made the following proposals which were handed in writing to Mr. Anthony Eden and Mr. Cordell Hull:

"For the purpose of shortening the duration of the war it is proposed:

(1) To put into effect such urgent measures on the part of the Governments of Great Britain and United States of America in 1943, which will ensure the invasion of Anglo-American armies into Northern France and which, together with the powerful blows of the Soviet forces against the main forces of the German army on the Soviet-German front, must radically undermine the military strategic situation of Germany and lead to a definite shortening of the duration of the war.

In this connection the Soviet Government considers it necessary to determine whether the statement made by Mr. Churchill and Mr. Roosevelt in the beginning of June, 1943, to the effect that Anglo-American forces will carry out the invasion of Northern France in the spring of 1944, remains in force.

(2) To propose to the Turkish Government on behalf of the three Powers that Turkey immediately enters the war.

(3) To propose to Sweden on behalf of the three Powers that she should provide the Allies with air bases for the struggle against Germany."

With regard to point (1) of the proposals of the Soviet Delegation of 19th October 1943, the Minister of Foreign Affairs of Great Britain, Mr. Eden, and the Secretary of State of the United States of America, Mr. Hull, on the 20th October 1943, endorsed the statement made by the British Lt-General Ismay and the American Major-General Deane (see appendices: statement of Lt.-General Ismay and statement of Major-General Deane) as being an accurate presentation of the most recent decisions of their Governments, taken at the Quebec Conference in August 1943.

With regard to the question put by the Soviet Delegation: whether the statement made by Mr. Churchill and Mr. Roosevelt in the beginning of June, 1943, to the effect that Anglo-American troops will carry out the invasion of Northern France in the spring of 1944, remains in force, Mr. Eden and Mr. Hull gave an affirmative reply declaring that the decision to undertake the invasion of Northern France in the spring of 1944 had been reaffirmed at the recent conference in Quebec, subject to the conditions quoted by General Ismay in his statement. Mr. Eden and Mr. Hull added that this decision has not been changed and that preparations to carry out the above mentioned operation are being pressed forward as rapidly as possible.

The United States delegates placed the following proposals before the conference.

(1) That, in order to effect shuttle bombing of industrial Germany, bases be made available in the U.S.S.R. on which U.S. aircraft could be refueled, emergency repaired, and rearmed.

(2) That more effective mutual interchange of weather information be implemented. In order to effect this, it is essential that means of communication between the U.S.A. and the U.S.S.R. be strengthened.

(3) That air communication between these two countries be improved.

The People's Commissar of Foreign Affairs, V. M. Molotov, stated that the Soviet Government take note of Mr. Eden's and Mr. Hull's statements, as well as of the statements of Lt-General Ismay and Major-General Deane, and express the hope that the plan of invasion by Anglo-American troops of Northern France in the spring of 1944, contained in these statements, will be carried out on time.

Mr. Hull, Mr. Eden, and V. M. Molotov recognise the desirability of the Governments of the United States of America, United Kingdom and Soviet Union continuing to study the question of Turkey and Sweden.

V. M. Molotov said that the U.S.S.R. agrees to the United States proposals in principle and that the appropriate Soviet authorities will be given instructions to meet with Generals Deane and Vandenberg for the consideration of concrete measures which would be necessary to carry out these proposals.

CORDELL HULL
V. MOLOTOV
ANTHONY EDEN

1 Nov 1943.

3. Four-Nations Declaration on General Security (Annex 1 to Secret Protocol)

N.B. Original US wording in [ ] omitted in final text or replaced by words printed in italics.

The Governments of the United States of America, the United Kingdom, the Soviet Union and China;

united in their determination, in accordance with the Declaration by the United Nations of January 1, 1942, and subsequent declarations, to continue hostilities against those Axis powers with which they respectively are at war until such powers have laid down their arms on the basis of unconditional surrender;

conscious of their responsibility to secure the liberation of themselves and the peoples allied with them from the menace of aggression;

recognizing the necessity of ensuring a rapid and orderly transition from war to peace and of establishing and maintaining international peace and security with the least diversion of the world's human and economic resources for armaments;

jointly declare:

1. That their united action, pledged for the prosecution of the war against their respective enemies, will be continued for the organization and maintenance of peace and security.

2. That those of them at war with a common enemy will act together in all matters relating to the surrender and disarmament of that enemy [and occupation of enemy territory and territory of other states].

3. That they will take all measures deemed by them to be necessary to provide against any violation of the terms imposed upon the enemy.

4. That they recognize the necessity of establishing at the earliest practicable date a general international organization, based on the principle of the sovereign equality of all peace-loving states, and open to membership by all such states, large and small, for the maintenance of international peace and security.

5. That for the purposes of maintaining international peace and security pending the reestablishment of law and order and the inauguration of a system of general security, *they will consult with one another and as occasion requires with other members of the United Nations with a view to joint action* [they will consult and act jointly] on behalf of the community of nations.

6. That after the termination of hostilities they will not employ their military forces within the territories of other states except for the purposes envisaged in this declaration and after joint consultation [and agreement].

7. That they will confer and cooperate with one another and with other members of the United Nations to bring about a practicable general agreement with respect to the regulation of armaments in the post-war period.

4. European Advisory Commission
(Annexe 2 to Secret Protocol)

N.B. Original British wording in [ ] replaced by text printed in italics.

1. The Governments of the United Kingdom, United States of America and the Soviet Union agree to establish a European Advisory Commission composed of representatives of the three Powers. The Commission will have its seat in London and will meet as soon as possible. The presidency will be held in rotation by the representatives of the three Powers. A joint secretariat will be established. The representatives may be assisted where necessary by technical advisers, civilian and military.

2. The Commission will study and make joint recommendations to the three Governments upon *European questions connected with the termination of hostilities* [any European questions other than military] which the three Governments may consider appropriate to refer to it. For this purpose the members of the Commission will be supplied by their Governments with all relevant information on political and military developments affecting their work.

3. As one of the Commission's first tasks the three Governments desire that it shall as soon as possible make detailed recommendations to them upon the terms of surrender to be imposed upon each of the European states with which any of the three Powers are at war, and upon the machinery required to ensure the fulfillment of those terms. The Commission will take into account, as part of the material for its study of these matters, the memorandum of July 1st, circulated by the United Kingdom Government to the Governments of the United States of America and the Soviet Union, regarding the principles which should govern the conclusion of hostilities with European enemy States. The Commission will also take account of the experience already gained in the imposition and enforcement of unconditional surrender upon Italy.

4. Representatives of the Governments of other United Nations will, at the discretion of the Commission, be invited to take part in meetings of the Commission when matters especially affecting their interests are under discussion.

5. The foregoing terms of reference will be subject to review by the three Governments if circumstances should arise which call for an extension of the membership and competence of the Commission.

6. The establishment of the Commission will not preclude other methods of consultation on current or other issues which the three Governments think it desirable to discuss. There may for example be questions calling for special consideration. These questions may be handled by tripartite discussions in one or other of the three capitals (Washington, London, or Moscow, as may be found most convenient) between the head of the Foreign Ministry and the permanent diplomatic representatives of the other two Governments.

7. There may also be questions calling for international or special tripartite conferences.

5. 'The Self-Denying Ordinance'

"His Majesty's Government in the United Kingdom, bearing in mind the obligation upon themselves and the Soviet Government under the Anglo-Soviet Treaty of May 26th, 1942, to collaborate with regard to post-war matters, and having regard to the importance of securing in the final post-war settlement a just balance between rival views and claims that may be put forward by other European Governments, consider it in principle advisable that, pending that settlement, the two Governments should avoid entering into any commitments or agreements with other European countries allied with them in the common struggle relating to the period after the cessation of hostilities in Europe.

"His Majesty's Government in the United Kingdom therefore propose that pending final post-war settlement, the two Governments should agree that neither of them will negotiate any commitments or agreements with any other European countries allied with them in the common struggle in respect of questions covering the peace settlement or post-war period. The two Governments will consult one another whenever necessary so that observance of this agreement may harmonize with their respective and joint interests."

Statement of the Soviet Delegation on Point 8 of the Agenda

On the question of agreement between the principal Allies and the Small Allies concerning post-war questions the British Government has presented a proposal, put forward in a draft note which has been presented in the form of a proposal of the British Government regarding this point of the Agenda. According to this proposal, the British Government and the Soviet Government would conclude an agreement not to conduct negotiations concerning any obligations or agreements whatsoever with the Governments of other European states which are their allies in the joint struggle, regarding questions relating to the post-war period.

The Soviet Government cannot give its assent to this proposal of the British Government.

The Soviet Government is prepared, in so far as that corresponds to the desires of the British Government, to conclude an agreement with the Government of the United Kingdom obligating both parties not to conclude, with governments of European states which are Allies in the common struggle against Hitlerite Germany, any agreements or treaties whatever concerning post-war questions without previous consultation or agreement.

The Soviet Government, at the same time, considers it the right of both Governments, both the Soviet Union and the United Kingdom, for the purpose of preserving peace and resisting aggression, to conclude agreements on post-war questions with bordering Allied states, without making that action dependent on consultation and agreement between them, in so far as agreements of such a character concern questions of the direct security of their boundaries and of the corresponding states bordering on them.

6. Draft Declaration on Joint Responsibility for Europe

The three Governments
Fully conscious of their common responsibility as members of the United Nations, aware that once the Nazi and Fascist powers are crushed the welfare of Europe depends on the widest possible cooperation among the nations concerned, disapproving of those separate combinations which have in the past spread jealousy and suspicion and led to economic and armed rivalries, declare: –

1. That they affirm the principle that each people is free to choose for itself its form of government and way of life, provided that it respects equally the rights of other peoples;

2. That all States are accordingly free to associate themselves with other states in order to increase their mutual welfare by the establishment of institutions on a wider scale than each can separately maintain, provided that such associations shall not be directed against the welfare or stability of any other States and are approved by any general international organization that may be set up in accordance with paragraph 4 of the Four Power Declaration adopted at . . . . on . . . .

3. That, subject to the considerations advanced in paragraph 2 above, they regard it as their duty and interest, so far as lies in their power, to assist other European States to form any associations designed to increase mutual welfare and the general prosperity of the Continent;

4. That for their own part they will not seek to create any separate areas of responsibility in Europe and will not recognize such for others, but rather affirm their common interest in the well-being of Europe as a whole.

[No action was taken on this document.]

7. Draft Declaration on Liberated Territory

The Governments of the United Kingdom, the United States, and the U.S.S.R. desire that self-government should be restored as soon as possible in all Allied territory in Europe liberated from enemy occupation. To that end it is their common policy to facilitate the resumption of authority over liberated territory by the Allied Governments concerned; or, where no such government exists, by an appropriate authority recognized as capable of exercising governmental powers pending the formation of a freely elected constitutional government.

The application of this policy must however, in the opinion of the three Governments, necessarily be conditioned by paramount military requirements, which will make it essential that there shall be a first phase in which the Commander-in-Chief of the Allied forces of liberation in each theatre of operations must exercise supreme authority in areas where he is conducting active military operations. During this first phase, the three Governments, having regard to the conditions of modern warfare and to the confusion that is likely to prevail in newly liberated territory, consider it indispensable that the supreme responsibility in civil as well as military affairs should *de facto* be concentrated in the hands of the Allied Commander-in-Chief. This will be without prejudice to the principles—first, that this responsibility shall be transferred to the appropriate Allied authorities as soon as the progress of operations permits; and second, that the reorganized administrative and judicial services in liberated territory shall be conducted so far as possible by citizens of the Allied country in question who have shown their loyalty to the Allied cause.

[This document was referred to the European Advisory Commission.]

8. Soviet Statement on East European Federations (Annexe 7 to the Secret Protocol)

The Soviet Government consider the liberation of small countries and the restoration of their independence and sovereignty as one of the most important tasks in the post-war arrangement of Europe and in the creation of lasting peace. For this purpose the defeat of aggressive force, as a result of the victory of the Allies and the removal of the threat of new aggression, at any rate in the first years after the war, will create favorable conditions. The Soviet Government consider that the small countries will require some time, which cannot yet be definitely calculated and which will not be the same for all of them, to enable them fully to orientate themselves in the new situation created as a result of the war and in the re-created relationships with neighboring and other States, without being subjected to any outside pressure to join this or that new grouping of states. The premature and possibly artificial attachment of these countries to theoretically planned groupings would be full of danger both for the small countries themselves, as well as for the future peaceful development of Europe. Such an important step as federation with other states and the possible renunciation of part of their sovereignty is admissible only as a result of a free, peaceful and well-considered expression of the will of the people. It is to be feared that neither the existing *émigré* governments nor even the governments which will be set up immediately after the conclusion of peace under conditions still not sufficiently normal, will be able fully to ensure the expression of the real will and permanent aspirations of their people. The creation of such federations by the decision of *émigré* governments, which, in virtue of their special situation, cannot be closely bound with their people, might be interpreted as imposing on the people decisions not in conformity with their wishes. It would be particularly unjust if countries which had become satellites of Hitlerite Germany should at once be placed, as equal members of any such federation, in conditions as favorable as those of other small states which had been the victims of attack and occupation at the hands, among others, of those same satellites, and thus freed from the consequences of their part in the Hitler-Mussolini crimes.

Moreover, some of the plans for federations remind the Soviet people of the policy of the ''cordon sanitaire'', directed as is known, against the Soviet Union and therefore viewed unfavorably by the Soviet people.

For these reasons the Soviet Government consider it premature from the point of view of the interests both of the small countries themselves, and of the general post-war settlement of Europe, now to plan and thus artificially to encourage combinations of any states in the form of federations and so forth. They will in due course be ready to re-examine this question in the light of the experience of post-war cooperation with other United Nations and of the circumstances which may arise after the war.

APPENDIX B

CAIRO AND TEHERAN DOCUMENTS

1. The Cairo Declaration

President Roosevelt, Generalissimo Chiang Kai-Shek and Prime Minister Churchill, together with their respective military and diplomatic advisers, have completed a conference in North Africa. The following general statement was issued:

"The several military missions have agreed upon future military operations against Japan. The three great Allies expressed their resolve to bring unrelenting pressure against their brutal enemies by sea, land and air. This pressure is already rising.

"The three great Allies are fighting this war to restrain and punish the aggression of Japan. They covet no gain for themselves and have no thought of territorial expansion. It is their purpose that Japan shall be stripped of all the islands in the Pacific which she has seized or occupied since the beginning of the first World War in 1914, and that all the territories Japan has stolen from the Chinese, such as Manchuria, Formosa, and the Pescadores, shall be restored to the Republic of China. Japan will also be expelled from all other territories which she has taken by violence and greed. The aforesaid three great powers, mindful of the enslavement of the people of Korea, are determined that in due course Korea shall become free and independent.

"With these objects in view the three Allies, in harmony with those of the United Nations at war with Japan, will continue to persevere in the serious and prolonged operations necessary to procure the unconditional surrender of Japan."

2. The Teheran Communiqué

WE—The President of the United States, The Prime Minister of Great Britain, and the Premier of the Soviet Union, have met these four days past in this, the capital of our ally, Iran, and have shaped and confirmed our common policy.

We express our determination that our nations shall work together in war and in the peace that will follow.

As to war—Our military staffs have joined in our round table discussions, and we have concerted our plans for the destruction of the German forces. We have reached complete agreement as to the scope and timing of the operations which will be undertaken from the East, West and South.

The common understanding which we have here reached guarantees that victory will be ours.

And as to peace—we are sure that our concord will make it an enduring peace. We recognize fully the supreme responsibility resting upon us and all the United Nations, to make a peace which will command the good will of the overwhelming mass of the peoples of the world, and banish the scourge and terror of war for many generations.

With our diplomatic advisers we have surveyed the problems of the future. We shall seek the cooperation and the active participation of all nations, large and small, whose peoples in heart and mind are dedicated, as are our own peoples, to the elimination of tyranny and slavery, oppression and intolerance. We will welcome them, as they may choose to come, into a world family of democratic nations.

No power on earth can prevent our destroying the German armies by land, their U-boats by sea, and their war plants from the air.

Our attack will be relentless and increasing.

Emerging from these friendly conferences we look with confidence to the day when all peoples of the world may live free lives, untouched by tyranny, and according to their varying desires and their own consciences.

We came here with hope and determination. We leave here, friends in fact, in spirit and in purpose.

Signed at Teheran, December 1, 1943.

ROOSEVELT
STALIN
CHURCHILL

APPENDIX C

J.C.S. MEETINGS

After this manuscript was completed, I was able to inspect the full records of the U.S. Joint Chiefs of Staff in Washington. This information has not required any major changes in the manuscript, but a full list of J.C.S. meetings at Cairo and Teheran, with the principal subjects discussed, is appended for completeness. (Reference: Box 195, National Archives, Modern Military Section, Washington, D.C.)

J.C.S.124. 'Iowa' 10.00 a.m., Nov 17th.
1) Command of Allied Forces, Europe (overall Supreme Command): J.C.S. recommends President should press for this, or failing that, at least for unified Strategic Air Command. (J.C.S.602).
2) 'Rankin': Division of Allied occupation zones in Germany. (J.C.S.577).
3) Further ops in S.E.A.C.: J.C.S. approved 'Buccaneer' as opposed to 'Culverin' (operation against Sumatra). (J.C.S.582).

J.C.S.125. 'Iowa' 10.00 a.m., Nov 18th.
'Rankin': J.C.S. agreed to put to President difficulty of U.S. in N.W. zone.

J.C.S.126. 'Iowa' 10.00 a.m., Nov. 19th.
1) Recommended line of action and agenda at Cairo: J.C.S. approved J.C.S. 533/1, App.A, as proposed agenda and J.C.S.533/7 (Unified Strategic Air Command).
2) Topics for Roosevelt-Chiang talks: J.C.S. suggested should include Soviet entry into war and question of Manchuria occupation.
3) Overall Supreme Command: Leahy reported Roosevelt supported proposal.
4) Collaboration with U.S.S.R.: Leahy reported Molotov would not come to Cairo but Soviet military representative might do so. J.C.S. directed their planners to make a study of possible Soviet participation in C.C.S. mtgs.
5) E.A.C.: J.C.S. discussed difficulties which would arise for the U.S. govt. and War Dept. if this body became too important as a rival to the C.C.A.C.

J.C.S.127. Cairo. 11.00 a.m., Nov 22nd.
1) E.A.C.: J.C.S. discussed further difficulties with McCloy.
2) British and Soviet attitudes to conferences: Reports of Winant and Harriman (see text).

J.C.S.128. Cairo. 0930 a.m., Nov 23rd.
1) Role of China: J.C.S. discussed need to maintain 'Hump' supplies,

possibilities of Burma campaign and expectations of Chiang, Mountbatten and Stilwell re. 'Buccaneer'. J.C.S. approved these ops (C.C.S.405) but reserved judgment on Stilwell's suggestions for further ops.

2) United Chiefs of Staff: With reservations J.C.S. approved planners' paper recommending creation of four-power body (J.C.S.607).

J.C.S.129. Cairo. 0930, Nov 24th.

1) Collaboration with U.S.S.R.: General discussion of possible methods of collaboration, including United Chiefs of Staff, Soviet entry in Jap. war and Soviet preferences as between 'Overlord' and Mediterranean ops. No immediate action resolved.

2) European ops: Marshall reports Churchill set on Dodecanese, expansion of Italian and Adriatic ops, with 'O/L' delay of 5–6 weeks. Marshall opposed to this. J.C.S. agreed must know Soviet view before deciding.

J.C.S.130. Cairo 0930, Nov 25th.

1) Overall Supreme Command: J.C.S. ordered Secretary to prepare memo advocating this.

2) Collaboration with U.S.S.R.: Leahy reported Presidential order not to discuss Soviet participation in Jap. war unless Soviets initiated it. J.C.S. approved J.C.S.606/2 (C.C.S.407).

3) Overlord and Mediterranean: J.C.S. decided to seek British assent to U.S. view, and if not obtainable, defer decision till they knew Soviet view.

4) S.E.A.C. ops: Marshall reported Chiang would demand 'worthwhile military help'. J.C.S. agreed on necessity of maintaining 'Hump' supplies, but that Chiang must accept Mountbatten's plan for Burma operations.

5) Eisenhower report on Med. ops: If Italian operations expanded, Eisenhower recommended advance to Po and possibly limited Adriatic ops, in preference to Dodecanese ops, as more helpful to Southern France invasion.

J.C.S.131. Cairo. 0930, Nov. 26th.

1) S.E.A.C. ops: J.C.S. approved Mountbatten memo. for Chiang on points requiring agreement, with minor changes (C.C.S.411).

2) Overlord and Mediterranean: J.C.S. considered Br. memo. recommending changes in 'Quadrant' decision, with possible O/L delay of 2 months (C.C.S.409), also J.C.S. Planners' comments (J.C.S.611). J.C.S. reaffirmed need to seek Soviet views, if Br. persisted, and to insist (on presidential instructions) on 'Buccaneer'. Subject to this, J.C.S. accepted C.C.S.409 as 'basis for discussion'.

J.C.S.132. Teheran. 10.00, Nov 28th.

Overlord and Mediterranean: Somervell and Cooke (for J.C.S. Planners) reported on relative lack of value of Rhodes op., both militarily and from supply point of view (opening of Dardanelles). J.C.S. all agreed, and concluded choice was between full-scale 'Overlord' or concentration on Med. ops plus very limited O/L ('Rankin'). Reaffirmed must await Soviet view.

J.C.S.133. Cairo. 0930, Dec 3rd.

1) Overall Supreme Command: J.C.S. took note of Br. unfavourable reply (C.C.S.408/1) to U.S. proposal (C.C.S.408).

2) Overall Plan for Japanese defeat: J.C.S. considered Combined Planners' report, recommending Central Pacific thrust (C.C.S.417) with J.C.S.614 (Joint Chiefs' Planners' suggested amendments.) King wished to adopt immediately, and after hearing MacArthur's Chief of Staff on advantages of S.W. Pacific ops, J.C.S. approved C.C.S.417 with minor amendments.

J.C.S.134. Cairo. 0930, Dec 4th.

1) Integrated Command of U.S. Strategic Air Forces: J.C.S. approved modifications of original U.S. proposal (C.C.S.400) in light of Br. reply (C.C.S.400/1) and Planners' suggestions (C.C.S.400/2).

2) Unified Med. Command: J.C.S. approved directive to new Med. Cdr (C.C.S.381/2).

3) German occupation zones ('Rankin'): McCloy advised this could only be decided at highest level (i.e. Roosevelt and Churchill).

4) Expansion of India as base for S.E.A.C. ops: in face of King's doubts, J.C.S. approved J.C.S.617 (C.C.S.421), recommending committee to make plans for this.

J.C.S.135. Cairo. 0900, Dec 5th.

1) European and S.E.A.C. ops: J.C.S. agreed differences between Br and U.S. now boiled down to 'Buccaneer', tho' Br. also dubious about Burma campaign, which Marshall argued necessary to bolster Chiang, ensure 'Hump' supplies and draw Jap troops from S.W. and Central Pacific. King argued 'Buccaneer' essential to Burma campaign. J.C.S. decided, if no agreement possible, must be referred to Roosevelt for solution. Otherwise Br and U.S. were agreed. (C.C.S.423, 423/1, 423/2).

2) Integrated Command of Strategic Air Forces: Arnold recommended his compromise, leaving Portal and Med. Cdr with existing functions for a period. J.C.S. agreed, but deferred action.

3) Unified Med. Cd: J.C.S. approved immediate setting-up of new cd. (C.C.S.387/2) and directive to support Yugoslav resistance (C.C.S.425).

4) Southern France op. ('Anvil'): J.C.S. approved plan and directive to Med. Cdr. (C.C.S.424).

5) S.E.A.C. ops: J.C.S. agreed Mountbatten could receive no additional resources (C.C.S.419, 423/2).

J.C.S.136. Cairo. 0900, Dec 6th.

1) S.E.A.C. ops (alternatives to 'Buccaneer'): J.C.S. discussed Combined Planners' report (C.C.S.427) and decided proposals not sufficient to safeguard Burma campaign and draw Jap. resources. Agreed Leahy proposal——'Buccaneer' postponed and landing-craft transferred to European ops: but left decision on continuing Burma campaign open, pending further consultation with Mountbatten and Chiang.

2) Plan for defeat of Japan: Discussion of Combined Planners' amendments to C.C.S.417 in light of 'Buccaneer' cancellation. J.C.S. approved.

3) Final Report to Roosevelt and Churchill: Somervell made point all 'Quadrant' decisions not requiring modification in the light of their discussions should be *reaffirmed* as 'Sextant' decisions.

J.C.S.139. Cairo. 0900, Dec 7th.

1) Unified control of U.S. Strategic Air Forces: J.C.S. approved revised draft presented by Arnold for forwarding to C.C.S. (C.C.S.400/3).

2) Alternative ops. to 'Buccaneer' in S.E.A.C.: J.C.S. discussed opinion of Mountbatten that suggested alternatives not adequate and might cause Chiang to withdraw participation in Burma campaign. J.C.S. took note of this; and opinions of Stilwell and Wedemeyer that Burma campaign still practicable without 'Buccaneer', if Chiang participated.

NOTES

(*Guide to Documentary Sources and Bibliography, pp. 359–63.*)

INTRODUCTION

1 *The North African Landings*, Davis–Poynter, 1976.

CHAPTER I

1 *Hull's decision to attend, and correspondence between Roosevelt, Stalin, and Churchill*:
Cordell Hull, *Memoirs* ii. 1253–6; *Foreign Relations of the United States, 1943* i.
518–20, 530–1, 538 (this volume contains the relevant published docu-
ments and minutes of the Moscow conference: referred to hereinafter as
US: other volumes as *FRUS* with the appropriate year and/or subtitle); F. L.
Loewenheim *et al.*, *Roosevelt and Churchill, Their Secret Wartime Correspondence*
362–3, 368; ed. R. S. Sherwood, *The White House Papers of Harry L. Hopkins*
ii. 752–3; W. S. Churchill, *The Second World War* v. 247–51; The Earl of
Avon, *The Eden Memoirs, The Reckoning* 401–3, 405–6; Ministry of Foreign
Affairs of the USSR, *Correspondence between the Chairman of the Council of
Ministers of the USSR and the Presidents of the USA and the Prime Ministers of
Britain during the Great Patriotic War of 1941–45* (hereinafter referred to as
Stalin Correspondence) ii. 90–2. Welles resigned on 25 September on Hull's
insistence. *Hull–Welles relationship*: Avon 377, 380, 402; Hull ii. 1227–31,
1256; PREM 3/172/1, p. 46, Eden to Churchill, CONCRETE 748,
5.9.43, CONCRETE 767, 6.9.43. Eden had doubts at first about the value
of such a meeting, in view of US unreadiness to commit themselves on
many issues important to the USSR (Avon 402–3). Flying was an ordeal for
Hull. Part of his journey, however—from Puerto Rico to Casablanca—was
by sea (see C. J. Marion, 'Ministers in Moscow' 44–7). *Roosevelt's attitude
to Hull*: Marion 49–51; and below, Ch. III n. 5. Eden judged Hull's
presence essential because of the latter's weight with Congress (PREM
3/172/1, p. 73).
2 *Roosevelt to Stalin (Dec. 41)*: *FRUS (1941)* iv. 752. *1942 overtures*: *FRUS 1942*
iii. 662–3, 665–6, 675, 678; *Stalin Correspondence* ii. 22, 44–5. *Roosevelt's view
of Churchill–Stalin relationship, and need for US mediation*: E. Roosevelt, *As He
Saw It* 176; cf. Churchill iv. 247; Loewenheim 292, 297; Hull ii. 1248.
3 *Stalin on difficulty in leaving Moscow*: *Stalin Correspondence* ii. 22, 44–5; *FRUS
(1943)*: *Conferences at Cairo and Teheran* (hereinafter referred to as *CT*), 6,
17–18. *Roosevelt's constitutional difficulties*: Roosevelt 24; cf. PREM 3/172/1,
pp. 16–17, 31, 114–15; Hull ii. 1248–52.
4 *Churchill and Roosevelt–Stalin* à deux *meeting*: *CT* 10–11; Loewenheim 340,
347–8; Averell Harriman, *Special Envoy to Churchill and Stalin* 216–17. Hull

attributes Stalin's 'cooling-off' in the summer of 1943 to Churchill's desire to be present, but there were other reasons for this (see n. 6 below); Hull ii. 1250. Cf. E. L. Woodward, *British Foreign Policy in the Second World War* ii. 557–64.

5 *Churchill's belief in Anglo-American co-operation after the war*: Churchill v. 110–11, 115; Harriman 222. Cf. PREM 3/172/1, p. 19, Churchill to War Cabinet, WELFARE 736, 14.9.43. Cf. FO 954/22/197. *Roosevelt on Russian and Chinese post-war role*: Hull ii. 1265–6, 1595–6; *FRUS (1943)* iii. 9–41, 541. *Churchill on China*: Churchill iv. 504, 837; Woodward iv. 521–4, citing FO 371/25.

6 *Stalin's favourable response to invitation, May 1943*: *CT* 6: *Washington conference military decisions*: M. Matloff, *Strategic Planning for Coalition Warfare, 1943–1944*, Ch. VI; principal relevant document is final Report, Combined Chiefs of Staff, CCS 242/6, 24.5.43 (filed Br. records CAB 88/5–22). *Stalin's reaction*: *CT* 7–8; Loewenheim 340–1; Woodward ii. 555–9, citing Churchill to Br. Embassy, Moscow, T 792/851/3. Cf. I. Maisky, *Memoirs of a Soviet Ambassador* 362–5; *Stalin Correspondence* ii. 67–71. *Churchill's reaction*: Woodward ii. 555, 561–3; Loewenheim 340; PREM 3/172/1, p. 126, Churchill to Clark Kerr, T 552, 11.6.43 and T 852/3, 19.6.43. Soviet breach with London Polish Exiled Government resulted from discovery of bodies of several thousand Polish officers in Katyn forest, territory occupied by German armed forces, but part of the USSR 1939–41. German propaganda claimed these officers had been shot by the Russians. British attempts to heal breach, half-heartedly supported by Washington, got nowhere. Cf. J. K. Zawodny, *Death in the Forest* (Notre Dame, 1972); S. Micalojczyk, *The Pattern of Soviet Domination* 30–49; Churchill iv. 678–81; Woodward ii. 625–44; Hull ii. 1267–73; Stalin Correspondence i. 61, 120; *FRUS (1943)* iii. 399, 403–5, 432–4, 445–6, 453, 461–7; FO 371/34571; FO 371/34573; PREM 3/345/8. Churchill and Eden considered that since the murdered men could not be restored to life accusations could only damage alliance, and prejudice Poland's future. *Arctic Convoys*: Woodward ii. 566–73; Churchill v. 228–9, 231–9; British War Cabinet Minutes, WM(43) 44/2 (filed under CAB 65/33). Convoys were suspended March–November 1943. Cf. Loewenheim 380–3. *Italian surrender*: PREM 3/172/1, Stalin to Roosevelt and Churchill, 22.8.43; *FRUS: Conferences at Washington and Quebec* 1086–7; Harriman 224–5; *Stalin Correspondence* ii. 84. This message contains first demand for a political/military tripartite commission in the Mediterranean. The War Cabinet felt that to refuse would encourage the USSR 'to deal independently with Germany and Eastern Europe'. Cf. references below, Ch. III n. 1.

7 *Roosevelt's overtures to Stalin and Stalin's reply*: *CT* 16–19; PREM 3/172/1, pp. 114–15, 133–4; *Stalin Correspondence* i. 387; Hull ii. 1252. *Clark Kerr's attitude*: PREM 3/172/1, p. 130; Woodward ii. 561–2, citing Clark Kerr to Churchill, T 992/3, 1.7.43. *Suggested Eden visit to Moscow*: PREM 3/172/1, pp. 131–3 (Eden to C. Kerr, T 827 and 977). Churchill supported

Roosevelt's approaches (PREM 3/172/1, pp. 96, 134; WM(43) 114/2.) Stalin suggested preliminary meeting should be 'practical and preparatory' (*US* 514, Churchill iv. 247–9; PREM 3/172/1, p. 89).

8 Eden advised Churchill to agree to a preliminary meeting at 'Foreign Office level' (WM(43) 114/2; PREM 3/172/1, p. 111, Eden to Churchill, CONCRETE 85). *Roosevelt's and Churchill's acceptance*: *US* 513–15. *Discussions about date and venue of Foreign Ministers' meeting*: Hull ii. 1252–5; *US* 518, 530–1; PREM 3/172/1, pp. 20–90; Churchill v. 249–50; Avon 401–6; *Stalin Correspondence* ii. 90–2; FO 371/37031, pp. 73–4, 77; WM(43) 123/2; Woodward ii. 578. Eden thought Roosevelt's objection to London ungenerous, 'in view of number of times we have been to Washington' (Avon 405; PREM 3/172/1, Eden to Churchill, CONCRETE 692 and 838, 2 and 10 Sept. 1943). Roosevelt and Churchill finally agreed to Moscow on 10 Sept. (*US* 520; PREM 3/172/1, Churchill to Stalin, WELFARE 681; Hull ii. 1254). Roosevelt tried to reopen the subject on Hull's account, but Stalin was obdurate (*US* 530–1). The date gradually narrowed down to mid October (PREM 3/172/1, p. 83, Eden to Churchill, CONCRETE 886, 13.9.43; *US* 520, 530–1).

CHAPTER II

1 *Soviet insistence on agenda and proposals*: PREM 3/172/1, p. 115; WM (43) 114/2; Churchill iv. 247, 249; *US* 513–14, 519–20. *Churchill's and Roosevelt's desire for 'exploratory' character of conference*: PREM 3/172/2, pp. 81–6, 96, 101; WM(43) 134/6; *US*, 514, 519; *CT* 21. *Roosevelt's informal list of subjects: FRUS (1943)*i. 520. Churchill thought there should be 'four or five large issues for discussion' (PREM 3/172/1, p. 70). Hull submitted a draft agenda to Roosevelt on 14 Sept. suggesting discussions be kept to 'the broad basis of security within which detailed questions would be more easily solved' (*US* 521). This set keynote for US approach to the conference. Standley, US Ambassador in Moscow, gives slightly different slant on Hull's views (W. Standley, *Admiral Ambassador to Russia* 497, cited Marion 56); cf. also Sir O. Harvey, *War Diaries* 295. Hull's proposals included draft of Four-Power Declaration (*US* 522–3) shown to Eden at Quebec (Br. ref. WM(43) 124/2, WP(43) 389). *British–US exchanges on agenda*: PREM 3/172/2, p. 187; *US* 525; Hull ii. 1254–6. *Soviet comments on US/UK agendas*: *US* 534.

2 *The economic dimension*: *US* 521–2; Hull ii. 1303–4, 1643. Cf. J. M. Burns, *Roosevelt, The Soldier of Freedom* 513–14.

3 *Soviet objections to Chinese participation*: *US* 534–5, 537–8, 541–2, 548. *Quebec discussions on Four-Power Declaration*: Hull ii. 1238–9.

4 *US desire for acceptance of China as one of 'Big Four'*: *US* 541–2; Hull ii. 1256–8; *FRUS (1942)*: *China* 185; *CT* 47. Hull remarks Britain was 'not so convinced' that China deserved this ranking.

5 *US policy for Germany*: *US* 521, 542; Hull ii. 1233–4, 1265–6; these illustrate Hull's and Roosevelt's varying attitudes on the partition of Germany; cf. Harriman 227. *Eden's general agreement with Hull on this*: Avon 370–1, 373, 378. *Churchill's view*: Churchill v. 252, 318; cf. also PREM 3/172–5, p. 279. *Roosevelt on reparations*: Hull ii. 1266. *US Moscow proposal on Germany*: *US* 720–3, 740.

6 *Roosevelt's intention to discuss territorial problems with Stalin*: Harriman 227; *US* 542; Hull ii. 1266.

7 *US preliminary planning for relief, reconstruction, and economic co-operation*: Hull ii, Chs. 116–18; *US* 665–6, 739, 763–8, 820, 1127. *Roosevelt's wish to link aid to Russia with Soviet postwar co-operation etc*: Harriman 227.

8 *US attitude to de Gaulle* Hull ii. 961–2, 1120–32, 1158–63, 1193, 1213, 1215; Harriman 227; Sherwood ii. 627, 646, 659–60. *St Pierre and Miquelon*: Hull ii. 1128–37. *Giraud, de Gaulle, and FNCL*: ibid. 1220–6, 1232–3, 1241–6; Sherwood ii. 719, 729. *De Gaulle's attitude*: C. de Gaulle, *War Memoirs, Unity* 77–8, 82–4, 101, 215, 216–18, 227 (relations with Giraud: 82–4, 86–9, 123–4; Ch. IV *passim*). Contrasting US and British attitudes to de Gaulle are illustrated by their views on French membership of the political/military commission (*US* 784–5, 788, 792, 798; Woodward ii. 582; WM(43) 120/4; PREM 3/172/1, pp. 49–50, 70). Churchill's support for de Gaulle varied more than Eden's (Churchill v. 155, 158–62). *Roosevelt's reluctant approval of French civil administration plan*: Hull ii. 1244. *British wish for recognition of FNCL*: Avon 396–403, 447–8. 'Recognition' was extended to the FNCL on slightly different terms by the US and UK. Both formulae fell short of acceptance of FNCL as a 'provisional government'. This was delayed by US obstinacy until Oct. 1944 (Avon 467, 477, 486).

9 *Italian invasion and armistice negotiations*: above, Ch. I n. 6; cf. H. Feis, *Churchill, Roosevelt and Stalin* 158–76; *Stalin Correspondence* ii. 78–86.

10 *US proposal on 'current issues'*: *US* 522. *London as better centre for 'more important body'*: Woodward ii. 578, citing Churchill to War Cabinet, WELFARE 582, 3.9.43.

11 *US priorities*: Hull ii. 1256, 1258, 1260–3 1265–6. *Hull's view of Four-Power Declaration as 'principal item on agenda'*: idem 1256. Roosevelt gave Hull general guidance in relation to Germany, Poland, the Baltic States, and the Far East, at White House meetings on 4 and 5 Oct.; but made it clear he reserved serious discussion on these points for the heads-of-government meeting (*US* 541–3; Hull ii. 1265–6). *US/British acceptance of political/military commission*: *US* 785–6; WM(43) 119/1; WM(43) 120/4; FO 371/37031, p. 77, Churchill to War Cabinet, WELFARE 449, 27.8.43, War Cabinet to Churchill, CONCRETE 665, 31.8.43.

12 *Eden's proposal on 'joint versus separate responsibility' and federations*: PREM 3/172/2, p. 185; FO 371/37028; FO 371/36955–6; Avon 405–6; Roosevelt papers, Roosevelt Library, Hyde Park, N.Y., Winant to Roosevelt, 1.9.43, cited Marion, p. 42; *US* 525, 544, 736–7. Roosevelt commented on Eden's other and closely related proposal on 'agreements between

major and minor powers' (the 'self-denying ordinance') that 'it smacked too much of spheres of influence policies, the very thing it was supposedly designed to prevent'. It would be difficult to carry suspicion of an ally much further than to suppose its Foreign Minister means the precise opposite of what he says (*US* 544). *Hull's views on Polish issue before the conference*: Hull ii. 1269–73; *US* 622–3. The Polish ambassador requested British/US guarantees of Polish 'independence and integrity' (i.e. Poland's pre-war frontiers) and that Anglo-American troops should enter Poland; the former was politically and the latter militarily unrealistic. *Declaration on Liberated Territories*: Woodward ii. 643 n. 1; PREM 3/172/2, p. 186; Hull ii. 1239–40; *US* 517. *Soviet negative reaction*: *US* 524, 529–30. The Soviet government suggested it should be referred to political/military commission for consideration. *Eden's Moscow conference proposal*: *FRUS (1943)*i. 552, 738. *Hull's caution over Poland*: Avon 416; *US* 572 seems to be less than frank, if Eden's account is correct. Hull had, however, made some attempts in July to bring about a resumption of Soviet–Polish relations—attempts which demonstrated his ignorance of the real issues at stake. His unwillingness to discuss frontiers vitiated these attempts (Hull ii. 1270–3). *Foreign Office policy on federations*: Avon 366, 371; E. Barker, *Churchill and Eden at War* 263–5.

13 *US/UK view of Conference as 'not primarily military'*: PREM 3/172/1, pp. 50–1, 68–70; WM(43) 122/2, 3.9.43. Churchill cabled War Cabinet (WELFARE 582) and Stalin (WELFARE 61314) on 5 Sept. along these lines. However he offered to send Ismay to Moscow to explain Washington/Quebec strategic decisions (PREM 3/172/2, p. 171; Churchill v. 250, 253; Lord Ismay, *Memoirs* 321). Roosevelt as usual was vaguer. He referred loosely to 'a political and military meeting on State Department level' in a message to Stalin on 4 Sept., but made it clear he did not think conference should be mainly concerned with military matters, though assault on France could be discussed (*US* 518–19, 540; Hull ii. 1264). The nature of the Soviet agenda with its one item made Soviet priorities crystal clear (*US* 534, Molotov to Hamilton, 29.9.43). Same message, however, indicated Soviet willingness to discuss other issues raised by Western Allies (cf. PREM 3/172/1, Eden to Churchill, CONCRETE 715, 3.9.43, account of Eden–Maisky conversation).

14 The British Government was first to submit agenda (on 3 Sept.). *First draft*: PREM 3/172/1, pp. 59–60, shown to Roosevelt by Churchill on 5 Sept. *British agenda*: ibid. 81–2, Eden to Churchill, CONCRETE 887, 14.9.43; Avon 410–11. Churchill's approach was altogether less precise than Eden's (PREM 3/172/1, p. 70; Churchill v. 251–2; *FRUS (1943)*i. 534, 525–8; WM(43) 137/4; WP(43) 447).

15 Eden, though less inclined to defer to the US than Churchill, was equally aware of need for US post-war aid and co-operation (PREM 3/172/1, pp. 70–3, Eden to Churchill, CONCRETE 692, 2.9.43). War Cabinet discussed the Four-Power Declaration at meeting of 6 Sept. (WM(43) 124/2). Doubts were expressed about the phrase 'sovereign equality of

nations', as implying all States would have equal weight, even the smallest; also about universal membership, as implying immediate admission of ex-enemy States. The USSR raised no objection to the items proposed by Britain and the US (*US* 534; PREM 3/172/2, p. 179.)

16 *Anglo-American agreement to take up Iranian questions*: Woodward iv. 432–7; FO 371/35075; FO 371/35102; *US* 545–7; Hull ii. 1503–4. *Moscow proposals*: *US* 730–6.

17 *Churchill's earlier approaches to Turkey*: Churchill iv. 623–35. On 5.9.43 he wrote to Smuts 'I think it better not to demand entry into the war at present [but] the question may be put to Turkey later this year' (Churchill v. 114). *Eden's scepticism of Turkey's military value*: Avon 196–7, 221, 411–12. C.o.S. however favoured Turkish entry by end 1943 (Sir A. Bryant, *Triumph in the West* 59; C.o.S. mtg. 149, 11.11.43. (filed under CAB 79); *Dodecanese operations*: Churchill v. Ch. XII; Bryant 45–9; J. Ehrman, *Grand Strategy*, v. 88–100. Roosevelt and the US Chiefs were not very sympathetic or helpful (Churchill v. 186–91). *US view of these operations*: Matloff 252–9, citing OPD memo of 9.9.43, and British Chiefs' memo CCS 365 of 3.10.43. *Eisenhower's view (as Allied C-in-C Western Mediterranean)*: D. D. Eisenhower, *Crusade in Europe* 210–11. Cf. US documents BIGOT-OVERLORD, Eisenhower to Marshall, 2 and 4 Oct. 1943, CM-IN 2303 and 1703; F. Pogue, *The Organizer of Victory* 295–6, citing OPD msg. File and OPD Exec 10, Item 64.

18 *Roosevelt on Baltic States and Poland*: Harriman 227; *US* 542. Eden put his 'declaration on liberated territory' on the agenda after the USSR had rejected the previous Anglo-American draft.

19 *Soviet-Czech treaty etc.*: Woodward ii. 595–9; FO 371/34338, 34532, 36957, 34407, 36956; WM(43) 93; WM(43) 135; WP(43) 423; *Eden's Moscow proposal*: *US* 544, 724–7. This item was added to agenda by Eden, and item on Finland enlarged to cover all 'peace-feelers' (PREM 3/172/2, p. 187).

20 *US attitude to Finland*: *FRUS (1943)* iii. 213 ff.; Hull ii. 1449–50; Sherwood ii. 575–6, 707.

21 *Br.–US discussions on agenda*: PREM 3/172/2, p. 187: *US* 532–3, 526; Hull ii. 1254–6: WM(43) 124/2, and WM(43) 131. Roosevelt had discussed his ideas for future international organization with Churchill and Eden. Maisky records that Bracken, British Minister of Information, discussed a scheme similar to Roosevelt's with him in April 1943 (Maisky 356–7).

22 *Revision of agenda*: PREM 3/172/2, p. 187; *US* 526. *Austria*: *US* 514–17. Eden was unwise enough to remind the Americans Stalin had previously raised objections (in talks with Eden, Dec. 1941) to inclusion of Austria in a federation. This did not recommend the idea to them (*US* 549–50).

23 *War Cabinet discussion of Germany*: WM(43) 135/4; WP(43) 421, and WP(43) 447; WP(43) 413 (Chiefs of Staff paper on Germany); PREM 3/172/2, pp. 146–60. There were diverse opinions on question of dividing Germany. Some ministers foresaw that even division into occupation zones might lead to permanent partition. Another thought it unwise to split up Germany too much in view of Russia's probably dominant position after the war.

24 *War Cabinet discussion of Poland*: WM(43) 137/4; FO memos WP(43) 439, 438, WP(43) 447. There was general agreement Soviet demands on Poland would have to be conceded, but that acceptance of these should form part of wider package, including resumption of Soviet–Polish relations and reconciliation of Soviet conceptions of security with Polish independence. The latter hope represented a circle that was never squared, and perhaps never could be. Much the same line was taken in relation to Soviet claims on the Baltic States, Finland, and Romania. Eden was authorized to express informal acceptance of these claims but not to sign written agreements. Churchill's general 'note of advice' on the conference reminded Cabinet that the USSR had acceded to the Atlantic Charter on the basis of 'the frontiers of 1941' (i.e. before the German attack on the USSR) (PREM 3/172/2, pp. 160, 194–5; Churchill v. 251).

25 *War Cabinet discussion of political/military commission*: WM(43) 137/4; FO memo WP(43) 444.

26 *War Cabinet discussions of Four-Power Declaration*: WM(43) 124/2; WM(43) 131. *Turkey*: WM(43) 135, WP(43) 420; Eden reminded Cabinet that UK would have to supply Turkey if she entered the war. *Eden's concern for Iran*: PREM 3/172/2, p. 161, Eden minute to Churchill, 6.10.43. *Hull's avoidance of prior meeting with Eden*: PREM 3/172/2, p. 164; *US* 538–9, 547; Hull ii. 1277, 1286.

27 *Soviet agenda and Cross-Channel Attack*: PREM 3/172/2, p. 178; *US* 534–8, 547; Hull ii. 1264.

28 *Soviet desire to discuss territorial claims at earlier stages of war*: Avon 289–301.

29 *Dissolution of Comintern*: Harriman 270; Hull ii. 1248–52.

CHAPTER III

1 *Preliminary discussion of 'political/military commission'*: Much of the relevant correspondence from the time of Stalin's first suggestion (22 Aug. 1943) is contained in a separate section of *FRUS (1943)* i. 520, 541, 552, 782–800; Woodward ii. 577–81 gives British side. *War Cabinet discussions*: WM(43) 119/1; WM(43) 120/4; WM(43) 137/4; WM(43) 119/1; WM(43) 137/4; WM(43) 142; FO Paper WP(43) 444. *Telegrams between Churchill, War Cabinet, and Stalin*: CONCRETE 570, 665, and 907, WELFARE 582, and 681 (PREM 3/172/1); cf. Hull ii. 1243–5, 1274. These documents show gradual evolution of ministerial and FO thinking on scope and location of commission, towards creation of two separate bodies. A Soviet suggestion that commission should deal with future surrender and armistice terms for Germany and other enemy States, as well as Italy, contributed to this.

Churchill and Eden thought London more suitable than Algiers for discussion of these 'wider issues'. In September Churchill nominated Macmillan, and Stalin Vyshinsky as representatives on commission: these appointments clearly reflected Br. view of the original commission as purely Mediterranean, and Soviet view of it as a 'wider body'. *British unwillingness to allow Soviet interference in Allied military government*: WM(43) 120/4, 137/4, 142/3; cf. *US* 553. *Question of French and other States' membership*: WM(43) 120/4; Woodward ii. 578, citing WELFARE 582, 3.9.43; WM(43) 122/3; Hull ii. 1274; *US* i. 552. *de Gaulle and Harriman*: Harriman 231–2. *Growing strength of French Committee*: Hull ii. 1242–5. *US Vichy policy*: W. L. Langer, *Our Vichy Gamble* (New York, 1947); G. Warner, *Pierre Laval* (London 1968); K. Sainsbury, *The North African Landings* (London, 1976) 45–54. *For typical Roosevelt comments on the future of France*: *CT* 195, 484–5, 509; cf. references at Ch. II n. 8.

2 *Arctic Convoys*: Woodward ii. 572–4; WM(43) 142/3; Lowenheim 381; Avon 409, 412; Churchill v. 237–42. FO 371/36989–90.

3 *Eden on order of agenda*: *US* 548. *Eden at Algiers*: Ismay 323; H. Macmillan, *The Blast of War* 413–14. *Allied position in Italy*: Churchill v. 216–22; S. Ambrose, *The Supreme Commander* 289–92; H. C. Butcher, *My Three Years with Eisenhower* 371. Alexander's discouraging report gave further emphasis to Churchill's frenzied activity on behalf of Mediterranean operations (Earl Alexander, *Memoirs* 117; Churchill v. 216–18). Eisenhower's covering note was somewhat less pessimistic (A. D. Chandler, *The Papers of Dwight David Eisenhower* E.P.1360/1370 of 25/31 Oct. 1943). Churchill's use of Alexander's rather than Eisenhower's appreciation annoyed the Americans (cf. Stimson Diary, Reel 8, 28/29 Oct. and 4 Nov. 1943, cited D. Carlton, *Anthony Eden* 227). Pogue (p. 294) thinks Stimson not quite fair to Churchill. *Dodecanese*: see above, II n. 17. *Eden in Cairo*: Avon 407–9; PREM 3/172/5, p. 274. *Yugoslavia*: Avon loc. cit.; Churchill v, Ch. XXVI; F. Maclean, *Eastern Approaches* (London, 1949) 227–79; Barker, *Eden* 271–5; F. W. Deakin, *The Embattled Mountain* (Oxford, 1971) 139, 204–6; E. Barker, *British Policy in South-East Europe in the Second World War* 157–64, 170–2; cf. *US* 551 for Moscow proposal. *Greece*: Avon, loc. cit.; Barker, *Eden* 182–6. *British policy towards Yugoslav and Greek resistance*: Auty and Cloggs (eds.), *British policy towards Wartime Resistance in Yugoslavia and Greece (passim)*. *Helphand approach*: FO 371/37031/N 6851, 15.9.43. Helphand's proposals bear a close resemblance to Soviet terms for a settlement with the West, as they emerged at Moscow, Teheran, and Yalta; which suggests Helphand was well informed on Soviet attitudes. *Stockholm peace-feelers*: *US* 502–3; there was also a Japanese attempt to bring about a Soviet-German armistice at this time (Hull ii. 1263–4). Cf. Sir A. Cadogan, *Diaries* (ed. Dilks) 516. Senior Foreign Office officials of the period have confirmed to me that the possibility of a separate Soviet peace was always at the back of their minds, but was not an especially pressing worry at this time (Lord Gladwyn, Sir Frank Roberts, and Lord Sherfield to the author).

4 *Hull in Algiers*: Hull ii. 1274; de Gaulle 195; Macmillan 415–16; Butcher 369–70; R. Murphy, *Diplomat Among Warriors* 258–9. *Hull in Cairo*: Marion 60, citing Kirk to Stettinius, 26/9/43, Decimal File 740.0011, Moscow 1169, National Archives. *Eden–Hull meeting at Teheran*: Hull ii. 1277; Avon 410; PREM 3/172/5, p. 274; Ismay 324.

5 *Hull's character, views on international diplomacy, and relations with Roosevelt*: Burns 23, 350, 359, 398, 427, 429, 452, 483; Sherwood ii. 658, 752–4; J. M. Blum, *From the Morgenthau Diaries: Years of War*, 1941–5, 441–2; C. Bohlen, *Witness to History* 128–9; Harriman 177–8. Dr. Marion (pp. 48–51) thinks Hull's personal influence with Roosevelt by the time of the Moscow conference 'about nil'. This contrasts with Burns' estimate (p. 452). The truth is somewhere between these two extremes. Hull's influence on foreign policy as opposed to administration seems to have been quite considerable on a limited range of issues: to some extent it was in inverse ratio to that of Hopkins, which was at its zenith in 1943. Sherwood's judgement (ii. 811) that Hopkins at Teheran served as 'acting Secretary of State' is valid. *British views of Hull*: Avon 380; The Earl of Halifax, *Fulness of Days* (London, 1957) 254–7; Macmillan 450–1.

6 *Eden's character and relations with Churchill*: Barker, *Eden* 15–28; Earl of Chandos, *Memoirs* (London, 1962) 221–9. For an interesting and not much discussed illustration of Eden's tendency to overvalue his own achievements, cf. F. de Guingand, *Operation Victory* (London, 1947) 54–9. Eden's estimate of the results of the Moscow conference provides another example.

7 *Eden's attitude to France and relations with de Gaulle*: Avon 249–50 (NB the veiled reference to Anglo-American relations), 347, 387, 396–406; Eden consistently believed that French greatness should be restored. De Gaulle's appreciation of this in his *Memoirs* is, to say the least, grudging. *Eden and future of Germany*. WP(42) 8; WP(43) 144; WP(43) 217; WP(43) 421; cf. Avon 284, 370–9; Woodward ii. 222–3, 247, 589; Hull ii. 1233–4; Sherwood ii. 710–14. Foreign policy in wartime depends much on changing events, public opinion, the attitudes of allies, and tends to expose its practitioner to charges of inconsistency and opportunism. Eden's most consistent view is probably reflected in his statement 'when regenerated, Germany should find a place again in the family of nations' Cf. K. Sainsbury, 'British Policy and German Unity', *English Historical Review*, no. 373 (Oct. 1979), 768–804. *Eden's 'tilting of the lance' with Roosevelt and Hull over France*: Avon 402–3; Hull ii. 1213–16, 1218, 1232; cf. Churchill v. 154–164. *Over Germany (Morgenthau Plan)*: Avon 475–6; Hull ii. 1615; cf. PREM 3/192/2, no. 45; Churchill vi. 138ff. *Eden's views on world organization*: Avon 366, 443. *Differences with the US over colonialism*: Avon 514; Hull ii. 1234–5, 1237–8; see Ch. IV below for trusteeship issue at Moscow. Much light is thrown on Eden by the Harvey and Cadogan Diaries.

8 *Molotov, Stalin, and Western Allies*: A. Werth, *Russia at War* (1965 edn.) 107–8, 355; M. Djilas, *Conversations with Stalin* (1963 edn.) 56–62. *British*

and US views of Molotov as negotiator: Avon 297, 299, 327–8, 411–18; Hull ii. 1174–5, 1282; Churchill iv. 296–301, 436–7, v. 261–2; Bohlen 130.

9 *Harriman's character* Bohlen 127; G. C. Kennan, *Memoirs, 1925–50* (London, 1968) 231–4; Avon 255. *Harriman and Churchill*: Churchill iv. 185, 425–7, 428–9, 434–44, v. 122, 255; Sherwood ii. 750–1. *Harriman on Eastern Europe*: Harriman 236, 243–5, 249–50.

10 *Roosevelt's attitude to State Department*: Bohlen 121–2; Burns 352. Dunn, like Hull himself, was regarded as right-wing and anti-Soviet by Washington newspaper critics (Burns 398). *Soviet territorial demands, declaration on liberated territory*: Hull ii. 1166–70, 1240.

11 *Ismay's personality and role*: Lord Moran, *Winston Churchill, the Struggle for Survival* (1968 edn.) 132–3; Sir J. Kennedy, *The Business of War* pp. xv. 50, 100, 239; Pogue 7, 70; W. D. Leahy, *I Was There* 195. Ismay and Hollis both published memoirs (Ismay, op. cit.; J. Leasor, *War at the Top*). *Hollis' opinion of Ismay*: Leasor, op. cit. 11. *Strang's diplomatic career*: Cadogan 838. Strang had served at Moscow Embassy at the time of the 'treason trials' and later participated in abortive Anglo-French mission to Moscow, 1939; cf. his own memoirs (Lord Strang, *At Home and Abroad*).

12 *Western opinions of Vyshinsky*: Bohlen 48–9, 130–1; Kennan (op. cit. n. 9 above) 525; Harriman 339–40; Cadogan 708 n.; Macmillan 468–75. *Of Litvinov*: Harriman 198–9; Bohlen 32–5, 64–5; Strang 165, 182, 192; Eden 53–4. *Of Voroshilov*: Ismay 338; Deane 14–16, 30–4, 45.

CHAPTER IV

Note: British minutes of the conference are in Foreign Office file FO 371/37031 in the Public Record Office (hereinafter referred to as BR: unless specified, reference is to FO 371/37031 throughout); US minutes are in *FRUS (1943)* i. (*US*); Soviet record, in Russian, is in *Moscow Conference of Ministers of Foreign Affairs of the USSR, USA, and Great Britain* (*SOV*). As texts of proposals are normally identical I have usually given only British and US references. A selection of conference documents is printed below in Appendix A.

1 *Agreed agenda*: BR, p. 216; *US* 703–4; *SOV* 273–4.

2 *Soviet proposals for shortening the war*: *US* 534, 581, 771–2; *SOV* 91–8, 365–6; BR, pp. 89–90, 234, 304–6. *Soviet proposals on Italy*: *US* 714–15; *SOV* 284; BR, pp. 248–9, 292–3. *Soviet proposal for Three-Power commission*: *US* 705; BR, p. 302.

3 *US proposal on current issues*: *US* 719–20; BR, p. 247. *US economic proposals*: *US* 739–41, 763; BR, p. 308–9. *US proposal on Germany*: *US* 720–3; BR, pp. 297–300.

4 *US proposals on military co-operation*: *US* 773; BR, 'Most Secret Protocol'. p. 6.

5 *Original Br. proposals for pol./mil. commission*: *US* 554–6, 705–6; BR, pp. 74–5. Cf. discussion 22 Oct. (*US* 604–5; BR, pp. 243–4). *Later Br. proposals for terms of reference, EAC and IAC*: *US* 710–12; BR, pp. 306–8, cf. p. 290. *Br. proposal for 'self-denying ordinance'*: *US* 724–6; BR, p. 295. *'Joint responsibility'*: *US* 736–7; BR, p. 297. *Liberated Territories*: *US* 738–9; BR, pp. 303–4. *Austria*: *US* 724; BR, p. 300. *Br. 14 July proposal on end of hostilities*: *US* 708–10; BR, p. 290. *Peace-feelers proposal*: *US* 737; BR, pp. 300–1. *Iran*: *US* 732–6; BR, pp. 316–17. *Exchange of military information*: *US* 755; BR, 'Most Secret Protocol', p. 6.

6 *Scheme for liberated France*: *US* 760; BR, p. 224. *War Crimes*: *US* 768–9; BR, p. 229.

7 *Eden–Hull*: Avon 414–15 *Eden to Churchill (cables of 21st and 24th)*: PREM 3/172/5, pp. 258, 262. *Hull–Stalin mtg.*: Hull ii. 1292–6; Harriman 241. *Hull–Molotov talks 25 and 27 Oct.*: *US* 634–5, 653–4. Eden's cables reflect characteristic tendency to put favourable gloss on events.

8 *Harvey's comments*: *Diaries* 313–14. *Eden's rebuffs on E. Europe and Churchill's 'Overlord' démarche*: see below, n. 32. *Churchill's earlier telex to Eden (20 Oct.)*: PREM 3/172/5, p. 263. Harvey thought the *démarche* 'might wreck conference' (op. cit. 314–15). Eden and Harvey were also annoyed by Churchill's approach to Roosevelt for fresh Anglo-American mtg. without Russians. *Eden on later stages of conference*: Avon 415, 418.

9 *19 October*: Hull's comment on 'taking decisions' perhaps implied more leeway than he possessed. *Roosevelt's comment on Three-Power participation*: *US* 540. *Stalin's reply*: *US* 548. *Hull–Eden conversations*: *US* 570–2. *Hull–Molotov conversation*: *US* 576–7.

10 *Harvey's comment on luncheon*: *Diaries* 310. The appropriate volumes of official British and US war histories cover earlier stages of Anglo-American strategic argument in detail: M. Howard: *Grand Strategy* iv; Matloff and Snell, *Strategic Planning for Coalition Warfare, 1942–3* (Washington, 1953). I have added a few points in my *North African Landings* (London, 1976). See also M. Stoler, *The Politics of the Second Front*. *Quebec Surrender*: Churchill v. 75–6; Matloff 227–30; Ehrman 7–10; CCS 319/5, 24.8.43, (CAB 88/5–22). *Harvey's comment*: *Diaries* 312. *Anglo-American strategic presentation*: Ismay 325; J. R. Deane, *The Strange Alliance* 18–19; Avon 411: *US* 583–9, 774–81; BR, pp. 99–114; *SOV* 99–114; Hull ii. 1280; Harriman 238–9; PREM·3/172/5, p. 259, Eden to Churchill, SPACE 48.

11 *Turkey and Sweden*: Deane 21 – 2; Avon 411–12; Churchill v. 256 – 8. Eden's first reaction was lukewarm, but he felt bound to report proposals to Churchill (PREM 3/172/5, p. 259), stressing however Soviet overall commitment to 'Overlord'. *Alexander's appreciation*: Churchill v. 216 – 20. Churchill's use of this and support for Turkish entry antagonized Americans, as Eden foresaw. Cf. Loewenheim 387. *Roosevelt's negative reply*: *US* 644.

12 *21 October*: *US* 590–9, 600–; BR, pp. 604–13; *SOV* 114–33. *Molotov–Harriman mtg.*: Harriman 238–40. *Four-Power Declaration*: Deane

23; Woodward ii. 587; Hull ii. 1280–2.

13 *Eden–Stalin mtg.*: Avon 412–14; Woodward ii. 574; BR, FO 371/36899; *SOV* 130–3; Churchill v. 243–4.

14 *22 October*: *US* 604–13; BR, pp. 244–9; *SOV* 133–48. Successive stages of British proposals may be compared in *US* 708–10 (14 July); 554, 705–8 (12 and 22 Oct.); 710–12 (24 Oct.). Also BR, pp. 74–6, 290, 304–7; Hull ii. 1283; Strang 202. Eden's explanation on the 22nd differed from both previous proposals. Not surprisingly Molotov was confused. *US proposal (Item 5)*: *US* 719–20. *US suspicion of London-based body*: *CT* 260, 352–3. *Br. proposals, Italy*: BR, p. 76; *US* 712. *US attitude to French membership*: *US* 75, 562–3. *Brazilian/Chinese membership*: *US* 792–3, 795–8. *Drafting Committee*: *US* 604–6; BR, p. 243.

15 *Soviet attitude on Italy*: *FRUS (1943)* ii. 377; Hull ii. 1283–4; *US* 714–15 (Soviet proposal, also BR, pp. 292–3). *Italian ships*: BR, pp. 248, 292–3; *US* 715.; *US/UK notes on Italian policy*: BR, pp. 291–4, 302; *US* 715–19.

16 *Soviet–Czech treaty (6th-session discussion)*: *US* 624–7; BR, pp. 254–8; *SOV* 164–7. *Cadogan's reaction*: Barker, *Eden* 266–7, citing Cadogan minute PREM 3/114/2, 25.10.43. *Earlier stages of argument*: above, Ch. II n. 19. See also FO 371/34338, FO 371/36955–6.

17 *23 October*: *US* 613–21; BR, pp. 249–54; *SOV* 148–64. *Eden to Churchill*: PREM 3/172/5, p. 258; Avon 414. *Yugoslavia*: see above, Ch. III n. 3; cf. Avon loc. cit. *Hull–Molotov conversation*: Hull ii. 1288. *Soviet attitude to Yugoslavia resistance*: Djilas 12–15.

18 *Br. terms of reference EAC and IAC*: BR, pp. 306–7; *US* 710–12; *SOV* 303–6. Preparation of these and other fresh briefs required many hours' work by British delegation (Strang 200–2).

19 *Final terms of reference, EAC, IAC*: *US* 756–9.

20 *Churchill on Turkey*: Churchill v. 256–7; *US* 621.

21 *24 October*: *US* 622–8; BR, pp. 254–8; *SOV* 164–76. *Eden–Hull conversation*: Hull ii. 1305; Avon 416; *US* 622. At this discussion link with Br. support for Chinese part in Four-Power Declaration seems implicit in Eden's approach. *Italian declaration*: *US* 624; cf. BR, pp. 292–4, 302.

22 *Stalin on US German proposal*: Hull ii. 1285. *Soviet–Czech treaty*: see above, n. 16. *Molotov's statement and subsequent talks*: *US* 726–30; BR, pp. 295–6; cf. FO 371/33882. G. Wilson and K. V. Novikov constituted Anglo-Soviet subcommittee. See also FO 371/34340; FO 371/34588–9.

23 *Iran subcommittee and proposals*: *US* 636–7, 654–9, 674–9, 736; BR, pp. 311–17.

24 *Br. draft, spheres of responsibility, federations*: *US* 736–7; BR, p. 297. For prior history: Woodward 591–3; Barker, *Eden* 263–4, citing FO 954/4(16), 954/19(438), 954/4(21); Avon 366–7. *US response*: *US* 637–9; Hull ii. 1298.

25 *Bohlen–Vyshinsky*: *US* 628.

26 *25 October*: *US* 629–35; BR, pp. 259–65; *SOV* 176–89. *US German proposal*: *US* 720–3; BR, pp. 297–8; Hull ii. 1284–5, 1287–90. Hull had opposed German dismemberment. His comment that Moscow discussions revealed 'identity of view' is misleading. Cf. Woodward ii. 593. *Austria*

proposal: *US* 724; BR, p. 300. Phrase envisaging possible association with other States, already modified by Eden, was further modified by Drafting Committee (*US* 761).

27 *'Peace-feelers' proposal*: *US* 737; BR, p. 300. *Approaches from Hungary, Bulgaria, Rumania*: *US* 484–512. Molotov suggested 'unconditional surrender' should be added to proposal, but withdrew this because of US concern for Finland (final version, *US* 753–4; cf. Hull ii. 1297).

28 *Hull's response to later Br. suggestions*: Hull ii. 1452, 1456, 1458. *Hull's subsequent comment (after April 1944)*: Hull ii. 1451.

29 *Hull–Stalin mtg.*: Hull ii. 1292–6; Harriman 241. Minutes of mtg. are not in US or Soviet published records. *Hull–Molotov conversation*: *US* 634–5.

30 *26 October*: *US* 636–42; BR, pp. 265–8, 311–12; *SOV* 189–203. *Spheres of influence and federations*: *US* 736–7; BR, p. 297; Hull ii. 1298–9. It was suggested that those parts of declaration acceptable to both Hull and Molotov (as they asserted)—self-determination and no spheres of influence—should be included in Four-Power Declaration. Eden withdrew proposal on professed (and possibly genuine) ground he did not wish to disturb harmony on Declaration. Br. record is somewhat brief, as though drawing veil over unpleasant episode. Eden's memoirs, perhaps for same reason omit all reference. Hull's memoirs show no second thoughts on his attitude. *Molotov on 'cordon sanitaire'*: *US* 762–3; BR, p. 225. Molotov insisted this be included in protocol of conference (see above, Appendix A).

31 *Hull to Roosevelt and Chinese on Four-Power Declaration*: Hull ii. 1301; *US* 644–5. Dr. Marion (p. 107) suggests a major purpose of Declaration was to restrain Soviet ambitions in Eastern Europe; however Hull specifically denies in *Memoirs* having 'any particular area in mind'. Moreover, he allowed language of Declaration to be modified in such a way as to preclude this effect. During previous 18 months Roosevelt and Hull had shown anxiety to restrain Soviet territorial demands, but this is not apparent here. US concern at this time seems more directed to Br. than Soviet ambitions. *British observations on Art. 6*: *US* 533. Hull thought proposed tripartite commission premature and persuaded Molotov accordingly (Hull 1300).

32 *Eden–Hull talk*: n. 7 above. *'Overlord'*: Harvey, p. 312; Churchill, v 258; Bryant, ii 51–2; CoS mtg, 907, 26.10.43; cf. Pogue, 293–4; WM(43) 147/1.

33 *27 October*: *US* 645–53; BR, pp. 268–71; *SOV* 203–12. *Hull/Eden memo, Italy*: *US* 718–19; BR, pp. 293–4, 302. *Roosevelt on Sov proposal*: *US* 643. *War Cab. reaction*: WM(43) 147/2. *Sov. memo, Bulgaria*: *US* 712–14; BR, p. 302; cf. PREM 3/172/3, 25.10.43. This memo was, as Barker remarks 'thin and unrevealing'. Sov. attitude to Br. contacts Romania and Bulgaria was consistently discouraging (Barker, *Eden* 276). *Declaration, Liberated Territories*: *US* 738–9; BR, p. 303. Woodward (ii. 590–1) rather surprisingly says declaration had 'an easy passage'—but that was merely to EAC which might or might not act on it. No declaration actually issued

from conference, but ultimately it emerged at Yalta—too late.

34 *Hull–Molotov talk*: *US* 653–4. *Anglo-American memo on France*: *US* 760; BR, p. 244. Hull's reference to this unpalatable subject is as brief as acct. of matter in US records (Hull ii. 1301; *US* 653). BR record reveals probing nature of Molotov's questions and Sov. record even more so (*SOV* 210–12). Molotov's questions to Eden also hinted at Br. difficulties with de Gaulle.

35 *Eden–Stalin talk*: BR, PREM 3/172/5, pp. 255–6; *SOV* 212–21; Churchill v. 259–61; Avon 415; Ismay 326; Woodward ii. 584–7. *US Embassy on Molotov's status*: *US* 786–7. *Eden to Churchill*: Churchill v. 261–2, SPACE 97. Dr. Marion (p. 85) thinks Stalin preferred to leave it to Molotov and Voroshilov to raise awkward questions next day.

36 *28 October*: *US* 656–62; BR, pp. 272–4; *SOV* 225–38. Br. record omits awkward questions raised by Molotov and Voroshilov which *US* and *SOV* include. Cf. Ismay 327. *Turkey*: Br. and US memos: *US* 655–6; BR, pp. 304–6; Avon 416–17. *Exchange of mil. information*: *US* 692; BR, MSP, p. 6; Deane 20–3. *Br. Embassy dinner*: Ismay 328; Harriman 242.

37 *29 October*: *US* 662–72; BR, pp. 274–81; *SOV* 239–55.

38 *US economic proposals*: *US* 739–41; BR, pp. 308–9; Hull ii. 1303–4. *Differences between records*: *SOV* agrees with *US* in making Soviet attitude to future econ. co-operation, 15(*b*) and 15(*c*), seem encouraging. However, *SOV* on reparations, 15(*d*), agrees with BR in bringing out strong dissent of USSR from US approach. Molotov remarked bluntly US memo did not 'get to grips' with problem, which was 'not clearly stated'. Cf. Hull ii. 1303–4.

39 *Dependent territories*: *US* 747–9; Hull ii. 1234–8, 1304–5; Sherwood ii. 716–17; Avon 514. Eden had made reasonable point in previous discussions with Hull that no one formula could cover all territories.

40 *Poland*: Avon 416; Hull 1305–6. Eden records episode 'left sour taste in the mouth'. Cf. BR, N 6789 (Warner memo). D. Carlton (*Eden* 226–7) is one who thinks Eden put up too little fight on Poland and Eastern Europe. But US attitude was most discouraging.

41 *Italian shipping*: Roosevelt cable, *US* 643–4; Churchill v. 262–3; Hull to Roosevelt, *US* 672; Roosevelt to Hull, *US* 683.

42 *Hull–Molotov talks*: *US* 670–2; Hull ii. 1306–7.

43 *30 October*: *US* 673–92; BR, pp. 282–314; *SOV* 256–69. *Eden–Hull talk*: *US* 673; Avon 417. Harvey (p. 315) presumably reflects Eden's attitude on Sov. participation in future US/UK military conferences. Cf. Churchill v. 279–80.

44 *Eden on Molotov's new attitude*: Avon 415. *Minute doctoring*: Two nice examples here. BR omits Litvinov's awkward query why spheres of influence should only be barred in Europe. *US* omits Eden's remark that some smaller European States believed UK and Russia wanted division of Europe into such spheres, and welcomed Eden's initiative; cf. Woodward ii. 592–3.

45 *Final meeting of Iran subcommittee*: *US* 674; BR, pp. 311–16. *Eden on Poland*: Avon 415–16.

46 *Signature, Four-Power Declaration*: *US* 755–6 (final text); *FRUS (1943) China* 819–35; Hull ii. 1280–3, 1299–1301, 1306–8; Deane 23. *Press communiqué*: *US* 741–4, BR, pp. 309–11. *Conference Protocols*: see Appendix A for this and other Moscow Conference documents.

CHAPTER V

1 *Farewell Banquet*: *US* 685–92; Hull 1308–10; *CT* 147; Harriman 246–7. Hull's and Eden's cables both showed optimism about future Soviet collaboration. PREM 3/172/5, Eden to Churchill, SPACE 131, 158. Ismay and Clark Kerr agreed with Eden conference was 'high tide, if not of good, at least of tolerable relations' with USSR; cf. Harvey 315–16; Churchill also reported optimistically to War Cabinet (WM/43/148/2: FO 371/37031/N 6635). Churchill pointed out however that there had been no progress on Poland.

2 *Eden–Hull mtg. 31 Oct.*: *US* 688–9; Avon 417; Hull ii. 1312. *Eden–Molotov talk*: Avon, loc. cit.; *US* 693; Hull, loc. cit. *Eden–Hull talk 1 Nov.*: ibid. *Eden–Molotov agreement*: Churchill v. 266; *US* 697; Hull, loc. cit.; WM(43) 148/2. *Hull–Roosevelt cables*: *US* 694, 698–9. US consent was attached to Most Secret Protocol, containing military discussions and assurances (*US* 697). This and Secret Protocol (*US* 749–69; BR, pp. 219–26) detailing political agreements was signed by Hull, Molotov, Eden 1 Nov.

3 *Eden–Menemencoglu talks*: Avon 418–19; Harvey 319. Turks sent temporizing reply 15 Nov., asking for further talks (Cadogan 572–3). Eden thought, rightly, further talks would produce little result (Avon 423; WM(43) 151/3). *Eden Mid.-East talks*: Avon 419–20; PREM 3/172/5, Eden to Churchill, T 1850/3; Barker, *Eden* 185–6, citing PREM 3/211/6, GRAND 102, WP(43) 522; Harvey 320.

4 *Poland*: Avon 421–2. Eden states London Poles were in an embarrassing position 'through no fault of their own'. His comment at the time was 'they seem to have learned nothing'. *Eden's talks with Poles*: Micolajczyk 49–51; Harvey 332; Woodward ii. 642–50. Among the relevant memoranda are WP(43) 438 and 528; FO 371/34562, 34563; WM(43) 137/4. After Moscow Poles agreed to consider compensation in West for surrendered territory in East; cf. WM(43) 156.

5 *Hull and Poland*: Hull ii. 1315–17. *Hull to Roosevelt*: *CT* 381. Hull told Polish ambassador (Hull ii. 1315) that he had 'emphasized and re-emphasized his interest in Poland'. This seems an overstatement. Roosevelt ignored Micolajczyk's request, as did Churchill a similar approach (FO 371/34562).

6 *US representation, EAC*: *CT* 616, 625, 784. Hull did have doubts about Winant's appointment. Roosevelt overruled them. Hull's comment is very revealing: 'We of course have no intention of playing up importance of this body.' Cf. Gaddis 106–9.

7 *Yugoslavia and Greece*: Cadogan 575–6; Barker, *Eden* 186, 274; WM(43) 155, 160.

8 *Lebanon*: Churchill v. 164–5; Cadogan 575–7; Woodward iv. 268–89; Macmillan 420–9 (also for Giraud episode); de Gaulle 198–202; Harvey 321–3; FO 371/35185–92; WM(43) 153–9. War Cabinet threatened withdrawal of recognition from FNCL. Churchill's attitude was pugnacious and was supported by Roosevelt. Eden suprisingly ignores episode in memoirs.

9 *Hull to Congress*: Hull ii. 1314–15; FO 371/37031/N 6879; *Roosevelt's reaction*: Hull ii. 1313; Harriman 242; Marion 280, citing Roosevelt papers (Roosevelt Library) 942, 22: 184–5. *US Press comment*: New York Times 2 Nov. 20, 43; Washington Post 4 Nov. 7, 43.

10 *Harriman report*: *CT* 152–5; Harriman 242–50. *Bohlen*: *Witness to History* 128. Marion (p. 281) quotes Moseley's view that Hull 'fuzzed the issues' of Soviet territorial claims, and herself states Hull 'dangerously exaggerated value of Four-Power Declaration', overemphasizing international organization as 'cure-all for all world problems'. This belief 'helped to foster US policy of postponement' (op. cit. 108–11). However Marion feels Hull 'could not have pressed Russians harder on E. Europe without destroying the conference' (p. 281). This seems an overstatement.

11 *Eden Commons' report and debate*: FO 371/37031/N 6776. *Cranborne*: ibid. N 6775; cf. PREM 3/172/5, p. 245.

12 *Churchill*: WM(43) 148/2, 149/2; FO 371/37031/N 6635, 36; Churchill v. 265–6.

13 Avon 411; Clark Kerr, FO 371/37031/N 6575; Ismay 328.

14 *FO Memo*: PREM 3/172/3, pp. 209–10, FO 371/37031/N 6789 (Warner, head of Northern Department, FO).

15 FO comments on Hull (FO 371/37031/N 6789) are by M. Butler, G. Wilson, and F. Roberts.

16 *Soviet press comment*: FO 371/37031/N 6685. Cf. Werth 678–9. *Litvinov*: *US* 700–3; FO 371/37031/N 6647, 6665, 6755.

17 *Later stages of discussion on heads of government mtg.*: *CT* 23–68; PREM 3/172/1, pp. 19–86; Loewenheim 369, 378, 381; Hull ii. 1292–6; *US* 688–91; Churchill v. 272–282.

18 *US reactions to reopening of Quebec decisions*: Matloff 259–64, 305–6, 334; Pogue 293–6.

19 *Roosevelt's attitude to China*: Burns 374–8. *Invitation to Chiang*: *CT* 13, 16. *Soviet military representation*: Loewenheim 391–2; Churchill v. 279–80: *US* 691–2; Harvey 315; *CT* 41.

20 *Churchill to Roosevelt*: *CT* 34, 38–9; Churchill v. 220–1, 276–8; Loewenheim 386–9. *Mediterranean situation*: Matloff, Ch. XI; Ehrman

67–75, 88–103; Churchill v, Chs. XII, XIV; Eisenhower 203–11; Ambrose, Ch. 20.

21 *Churchill–Roosevelt cables*: *CT* 34, 38; Loewenheim 384–9; Churchill v. 254–6.

22 *Roosevelt to Churchill, 25 Oct.*: *CT* 42. Roosevelt said Chiang and Molotov could join them 'towards the end of their talks'. *Marshall*: *CT* 41. *Churchill–Roosevelt cables, 26 Oct.*: *CT* 41–2; Churchill v. 279; Loewenheim 391–2. *Roosevelt–Chiang, 27 Oct.*: *CT* 47. '*Balkan campaign*': Churchill v. 187; Loewenheim 371. Churchill may well have believed (1) that no large-scale Balkan campaign was necessary and (2) objectives in E. Mediterranean could be achieved without detriment to some form of 'Overlord' in 1944. But cf. Kennedy (pp. 305, 307, 309) 'Had we had our way . . . invasion of France would probably not have been done in 1944'; cf. also D. Fraser, *Alanbrooke* 372. Undoubtedly Churchill hankered after some form of 'Balkan Strategy' from the early days of the war. The remarks quoted by Ehrman (op. cit., Appendix VI) seem to justify this statement, though after Cairo and Teheran Churchill realized this was 'not on'.

23 *Stimson and 'Overlord' Command*: Stimson and McBundy, *On Active Service in Peace and War* 430–9. '*Overall European Command*': Matloff, Ch. XII; Pogue 272–5.

24 *Hull's return*: *CT* 53, 66–7. *Roosevelt's stop in N. Africa*: *CT* 50. *Churchill and Soviet general at CCS*: Churchill v. 279–80; *CT* 47–50. Roosevelt suggested to Chiang they might meet 'about 26 Nov.'. Chiang accepted but insisted it must be 'before the mtg. with Stalin'; *FRUS (1943): China* 156. *Roosevelt–Churchill, 30 Oct., 3 Nov.*: *CT* 55, 64; Churchill, v. 281.

25 *Roosevelt–Churchill, 5 and 6 Nov.*: *CT* 67, 69.

26 *Stalin–Roosevelt, 5 Nov.*: *CT* 67–8. *Ismay*: Churchill v. 281; *CT* 69–70. *Harriman: Special Envoy* 241; *CT* 70. *Roosevelt to Stalin and Chiang, 8 Nov.*: *CT* 71–2, *FRUS (1943): China* 160. *Stalin–Roosevelt, 10 Nov.*: *CT* 78.

27 *Churchill's reaction*: Churchill v. 282; *CT* 78.

28 *Roosevelt–Churchill, 11, 12 Nov.*: *CT* 79–80; Churchill v. 283. *Stalin–Roosevelt, 12 Nov.*: *CT* 82; Churchill v. 284. *Churchill–Roosevelt, 14 Nov.*: *CT* 86.

29 *Hopkins' Quebec report*: Sherwood ii. 744–5.

CHAPTER VI

1 Every textbook and memoir of the wartime period refers extensively to Roosevelt and indeed to Churchill. A selection from the extensive literature is in the bibliography at the end of this book.

2 *Roosevelt's ideas, habits of mind, and work*: Burns 58, 62, 92, 143, 253, 299,

342, 347–55, 451–3, 549–50; Stimson and Bundy 333; Bohlen 136; Sherwood i 73–6, 159–60, 209–12; Avon 373–4. *China*: Avon 377; Sherwood i 713–15; J. M. Blum, *From the Morgenthau Diaries* iii. 658; FO 371/35739. Gaddis Smith, *American Diplomacy during the Second World War* 90–4; *FRUS (1943): China* 185; *CT* 47, 532; *Burma*: Matloff 232–40; Ehrman 148–54.

3 *Roosevelt and colonialism*: Gaddis Smith, Ch. V; Burns 217–22, 378–81. Roosevelt 36–8, 74–6, 111, 165. *India*: Sherwood ii. 516–17. *Future of France*: *CT* 195.

4 *Roosevelt on UN*: Sherwood ii. 715–16; *CT* 530–3; Burns 513–15.

5 *Roosevelt and Churchill*: G. Smith 10–11; Barker, *Eden* 125–38, 216; Sherwood i. 364–5; Loewenheim 7–13; Moran 824–5; Roosevelt 155–6, 165; Avon 424. *'Political motive'*: Leahy 237; *CT* 252–4, 256, 259. Cf. also Trumbull Higgins, *Winston Churchill and the Second Front*, and M. Stoler, *The Politics of the Second Front, passim. Imperial Preference*: Hull ii. 975–6, 1151–3, 1211, 1476–7; Sherwood ii. 809. *Churchill and growing US superiority*: Bryant ii. 63. *Eden on Roosevelt*: Avon 373.

6 *SE Asia crisis*: Churchill iv, Ch. IV. *Tobruk*: op. cit., Chs. XXIII, XXIV; Moran 59–60; Avon 331–2.

7 *Military/economic situation in China late 1943*: *FRUS (1943): China* 168–74 (Gauss to State Dept). *Chiang's 'Fascist' tendencies*: Thorne 68, 310, 436, 571, 575. *US estimate of Nationalist strength*: *CT* 242.

8 *Western impressions of Chiang*: Churchill v. 290–1; Avon 424; Bryant ii. 66–9; Moran 150–1; Sherwood ii. 703; Leahy 236–7; Pogue 304; Carton de Wiart, *Happy Odyssey* (1955 edn.) 197–8 (for more favourable impression than most); Thorne 22–3, 37, 67–8, 172–5, 181–5, 192–3, 306–7, and *passim*. Roosevelt's private view of Chiang's and Chinese war effort are probably pretty accurately reflected in Elliott Roosevelt 142–3, 153–4, 163–5. Clark Kerr, when Br. Ambassador, described Kung as a 'cancer' (Thorne 65). *Chiang's suspicion of UK and Russia*: *FRUS (1943): China* 164, 172. *Chiang's political position*: op. cit, pp. 260–2.

9 *Extra-territorial rights*: Thorne 68, citing FO 371/27721; Hull i. 565–6, ii. 1257–8, 1583; Avon 366; Woodward iv. 510–15. *Br. suspicion of Chinese aims*: FO 371/35776, 371/35739. *Estimate of Chinese war effort*: FO 371/35616, 371/35729. *Churchill on Burma*: Churchill iv. 702; PREM 3/147/3, 3/143/10. Cf. Ehrman 148–53. *Churchill on China*: PREM 4/100/7, 4/30/5.

10 *Roosevelt's Chinese hopes*: Burns 82. *Unfavourable US reports*: *FRUS (1943): China* 27, 116, 125, 127–9, 139, 150, 168–74; Thorne 181, 323. *Hornbeck*: FO 371/35779. *Hurley*: *FRUS (1943): China* 165; cf. Roosevelt 143, 154.

11 *Stalin's character*: I. Deutscher, *Stalin, passim*. M. Djilas, *Conversations with Stalin* (1963 edn.) 68. *Churchill, Eden, and Stalin*: Barker, *Eden* 221–4, 231–2, 242, citing WP(42) 48, WM(45) 26/5; FO 800/302 (Warner 25/1/44, Wilson 19/3/44); WM(43) 114, CONCRETE 85, 10.8.43. *Stalin on Churchill*: Djilas 61, 90.

12 *Stalin on Roosevelt*: Djilas, loc. cit. (if Djilas is reliable, Roosevelt failed to

win Stalin's trust). *Roosevelt's confidence*: PREM 3/486/3, Roosevelt to Churchill, 18.3.42; Strang 158. *Allied suspicions*: see above, ns. 3, 5, 8, 9, 11; Roosevelt 163; *CT* 376.

13 *US 'out-gunned'*: Bryant i. 447, citing Sir Ian Jacob, Diary, 13.1.43. *Marshall's character and abilities*: Pogue, op. cit. and *Ordeal and Hope* (New York, 1963) *passim*. Cf. Stimson 436–8; Leahy 128; Sherwood i. 165–6; Burns 85, 415. *Br. view of Marshall*: Moran 36, 56, 86, 132, 590; Churchill v. 278, 370; Cunningham 466; Ismay 251–2; Bryant i. 295–6, 300–1, ii. 87. *King*: Leahy 86, 128–9; Churchill iv. 396; Sherwood i. 165; Burns 183, 316–17; Bryant i. 289, 299, 449–50, 458, 505; Ismay 253; Cunningham 465–6; Pogue, *Ordeal and Hope* 84–6; Bryant ii. 119; Pogue, *Organizer of Victory* 7. *Arnold*: Ismay 253–4; Pogue, op. cit. 7, 71–6. *Leahy*: Pogue 7–8; Bryant i. 446, ii. 76; Sherwood ii. 615, 832–4. *Stilwell and Chennault*: Pogue 285–7, 478–9; Terraine 135; de Wiart 186–7; Stimson 530–40; *FRUS (1943): China* 130–1, 135–6; M. Stilwell, *The Stilwell Papers passim*; Thorne *passim*; Arnold 215. *Hurley*: Hull ii. 1506–7, 1513–14; Roosevelt 192–3, 197; Thorne 103, 551, 573–4, 580, 692. For Wedemeyer, his own book *Wedemeyer Reports* reveals the man very fully.

14 *Hopkins*: Sherwood's two volumes give a full picture of the man: also Stimson 333; Ismay 213–16; Pogue 433–4; Churchill iii. 20–2; Harriman 10–14; Roosevelt 231–2; Leahy 166–7; Moran 20, 32–3, 152–3, 155–7, 164; Leahy 167.

15 *Cadogan*: Barker, *Eden* 24–5, 27, 111, 143, 266–7; Moran 78–82; Cadogan, *Diaries passim*, esp. 3–23. *Mountbatten*: Bryant i. 266–7, 309, 330, 569–70, 583–4; Leahy 210–11; Pogue 258–9, 281, 396; Leasor 125–31; Eisenhower 75, 258; Terraine *passim*. For de Wiart, see his *Happy Odyssey passim*. Cunningham also published memoirs (*A Sailor's Odyssey*) in which he acknowledges his lack of experience in grand strategy (p. 178). He was however much respected by the Americans (Eisenhower 99; Leahy 130; Pogue 258; cf. Bryant ii. 56). *Portal*: Arnold 140; King 128; Bryant i. 456 n., quoting Jacob Diaries; Pogue 6, 27–9; Leahy 195–6. Brooke reveals himself fully in his diaries, which often show degree of strain he lived with. Sir D. Fraser's biography also gives full and balanced picture. See also: Field Marshall Viscount Montgomery, *Memoirs* (London, 1958) 59, 543–5; Sir J. Grigg, *Prejudice and Judgment* (London, 1947) 417–20; Leahy 195; Ismay 317–18; Pogue, *Ordeal and Hope* (see above, n. 13) 272, 284, 308–10; Sherwood ii. 528. *Dill*: Kennedy 179, 284; Bryant i. 71, 233, 345; Ismay 244; Pogue, *Organizer of Victory* 30, 32, 337, 481–3.

16 *Chiangs*: see above, n. 8. *Chinese at Cairo*: Stilwell 273; Bryant ii. 68–70.

17 *C.o.S. mtgs., 9–10 Nov.*: Bryant ii. 57–9; Ehrman 109–11; *C.o.S. proposals*: *CT* 409–11; Br. records CAB 80/76, CCS 409. *Churchill's anxieties*: WM(43) 150. Churchill v. 220–1, 267–8, 277–8, 291–4; *CT* 34, 38–9. *Churchill on 'overall cd.'*: Churchill v. 271–2. *Landing-craft*: Matloff 264, citing CCS 126 mtg., CCS memo 397/5, US ref. ABC 384, Mediterranean. *Unified Mediterranean Cd.*: CCS memo 387 (CAB 88); *CT* 248, 251–3; Bryant ii. 57.

18 *'Set-to'*: Bryant ii. 60.

19 *US Chiefs' views:* CT 203–5, 210–13, 227–9; Matloff 338–41, 343–4.

20 *Dill as commander:* CT 209–10, 248–52; Pogue 318. *SE Asia ops.*: CT 234–41 (CCS 390/1—Br. CAB 88). *China capability:* CT 242–3 (CCS 300/2). *Doubts on CBI theatre:* Matloff 326; Wedemeyer 251. *Chiang's demands:* Matloff 324–5, citing US records, CM-IN 11139, 12040, 12672, 15127. *Marshall:* Pogue 305; Matloff 349–50. *Roosevelt:* Sherwood ii. 736; Burns 201–5, 378, 445; Matloff 342–3, 350. *Chiang Agenda:* CT 245–6, 257–9.

21 *Churchill Agenda:* CT 246–7. *COSSAC plan for Germany ('Rankin'):* CT 253–6, 423; Matloff 341–2; Sir F. Morgan, *Overture to Overlord* (London, 1950), Ch. V.

22 *US wish to avoid European involvement, and suspicion of UK:* see above, n. 21. *Roosevelt–Hull mtgs., 4 and 5 Oct.*: Hull ii. 1265–6, cf. 1584, 1596.

CHAPTER VII

1 *Cairo arrangements:* Churchill v. 289. Burns 403; Matloff 345; Bryant ii. 65; CT 293–4. *Algiers, Malta:* Churchill v. 287–9; Butcher 378–81; Eisenhower 213–14; Bryant ii. 62–5; Ismay 332–4; CoS mtg. 18.11.43 (CAB 99/25, pp. 4–5). CAB 99/25 contains a record of all British and Combined military mtgs. at Cairo and Teheran, together with relevant papers. It is referred to hereafter as UK.

2 *Brooke's 'anti-Americanism':* Ambrose 45–6. *Dill:* Bryant ii. 65 (Alanbrooke files, Dill to Brooke, 16.10.43). *Brooke on Alexander:* Bryant, *Triumph in the West* 99–101; Fraser 381. *On Montgomery:* Bryant ii. 114, 133, 156, 132. *Eisenhower on strategy:* CT 360; UK, p. 15; Eisenhower 214.

3 *Tunis and 'Overlord' cd.*: Butcher 381–5; Roosevelt 132–9; Eisenhower 214–17; Arnold 221; Pogue 267–73. *Burma campaign:* Bryant ii. 41–3, 91; Ehrman 128–34, 137; Terraine 138–40.

4 *Iowa recommendations:* CT 210–43.

5 *November 22:* CT 301–8; UK, pp. 5–6, 142–4. *Roosevelt agendas:* CT 245–7. *Churchill on Roosevelt:* Avon 424. *C.o.S. mtg.*: UK, pp. 5 – 6; Bryant ii. 66. *US documents on SE Asia:* CT 243. *US agenda:* CT 305, 368 (CCS 404). *Br. agenda:* CoS 'Sextant 3 (UK); CT, 369, CCS 404/1. *Churchill* aide-mémoire: CoS Sextant 1 (UK, pp. 29–30); Churchill v. 291–3. *JCS:* CT 301–3. *Soviet pressures:* Harriman 251; Deane 31–5; Butcher 384–5; Ehrman 156; Matloff, 285–6, 303.

6 *Roosevelt–Stalin:* CT 373–4. *Chiang:* Churchill v. 290; CT 307. *CCS:* CT 304–7; UK, pp. 142–4. *Stilwell proposals:* CT 370–1; UK, pp. 143–4 (ref. CCS 405, CCS 319/2). One joint meeting with the Soviet representative, Voroshilov, was held at Teheran.

7 *Roosevelt dinner*: CT 307–8; Leahy 236; Bryant ii. 66; Arnold 461. *Mountbatten plans*: CoS Sextant, 12, UK, p. 36. CT log gives Chiang as present, as does Arnold, but this seems unlikely from Roosevelt's opening remarks the next day (CT 312). Leahy and Brooke do not mention Chiang in their references. Future status Hong Kong may have been discussed at this mtg. (cf. CT 887–8; Avon 374, 426).

8 *23 November*: CT 309–26; UK, pp. 6–8, 133–5, 145–6. *C.o.S.*: UK, pp. 6–8; Bryant ii. 66. *JCS Far East ops.*: CT 232, 243, 370. *Mountbatten memos*: SEACOS 19 and 30, JS Sextant, 3, JS Folder, UK; cf. also MB memo, (CoS Sextant, 11, UK, p. 36). *JCS proposal VLR airfields*: CCS 401 and Davies memo (UK, p. 52; CT 371, 377). *Conflicting F. East aims*: FRUS (1943): China 558; Sherwood ii. 768; Thorne 718–30 and *passim*.

9 *Plenary mtg.*: CT 311–15; UK, pp. 133–4; Churchill v. 294; Leahy 236; Pogue 305; Bryant ii. 66; Arnold 220. *Vyshinsky*: CT 309–10; Matloff 348–9.

10 *Hong Kong*: see above, n. 7. *CCS*: CT 317–22; UK, pp. 145–6; Ehrman 163; Matloff 348–52; Bryant ii. 67–9; Stilwell 230; Arnold 220–1; Churchill v. 294; Leahy 236–7; ref. CCS 397, 405, 300/2, 390/1 (SE Asia). *'United Chiefs'*: CT 379; UK, p. 210, ref. CCS 406.

11 *Churchill–Marshall mtg.*: CT 326, 331; Pogue 306. *Roosevelt–Chiang mtg.*: CT 323–5, 367, 485, 864, 868–9; E. R. Stettinius, *Roosevelt and the Russians* (New York, 1950) 237–8; Burns 404; Sherwood ii. 791–2; Roosevelt 142, 155–6, 164–6. Main source is Chinese memo, which, however, does not seem to cover everything discussed. Cf. FRUS (1943): China 558. *Iowa discussions*: CT 257–8. Roosevelt's free disposal of French colonial territory seems even today somewhat off-hand. But one cannot deny that his Indo-China plan, if carried out, might have averted much suffering. *Hopkins memo*: CT 376; Harriman 261–2. There seems some doubt as to exact contribution of these two men to memo, which discounts Chinese fears of Soviet intentions. *Roosevelt on Chinese 'democracy'*: Roosevelt 164.

12 *24 November*: CT 326–45; UK, pp. 9–10; Harriman 258–61; Leahy 237; Roosevelt 147–9, 151, 153; Stilwell 232; Bryant ii. 72. *Landing-craft*: Matloff 362, 382, 398–401, 425–6, and *passim*; Ehrman 33–8, 157–9, 166–7, 181–9, 191–2, 210; C. Wilmot, *Struggle for Europe* 138–9, 142, 175–80 (citing King, *US Navy at War* (New York, 1952) 137). Tables given by Matloff (p. 398) and Wilmot (p. 180) relate to different periods. Even allowing for this, there seems little relation between them. Different nomenclature also makes comparisons difficult. *'Cart before horse'*: Bryant ii. 66, 68, 70. *Chennault*: Harriman 260–1.

13 *JCS*: CT 326–9; Harriman 258–9.

14 *C.o.S.*: UK, pp. 9–10; Bryant ii. 71. *Mediterranean ops.*: CoS/JPS, Sextant, 6 (UK, p. 32). *United Chiefs*: CCS 406 (CT 379–80), CoS 406. *Enemy situation*: CCS 300/3 (CT 214–28); UK, pp. 179–83.

15 *Plenary CCS*: CT 329–34; UK, pp. 146–50; Churchill v. 294; Bryant ii. 70; Matloff 352–3; Leahy 237; Sherwood ii. 770; Pogue 306. *Sumatra*:

SEACOS, Sextant, 12 (UK, p. 36). *US Chiefs' reactions*: Sherwood ii. 770; Moran 151–2; Roosevelt 144.

16 *Marshall–Chiang mtg.*: *CT* 388; Stilwell 232; Pogue 305–6. *Roosevelt talks*: *CT* 345; Leahy 200; Sir H. M. Wilson, *Eight Years Overseas* 187; Roosevelt 150–1.

17 *CCS*: *CT* 336–45; UK, pp. 147–50; Matloff 350; Bryant ii. 71–2; Pogue 306; Stilwell 232. *United Chiefs*: *CT* 379, 390; ref. CCS 406 and 406/1; cf. Chiang memo, *CT* 388. *SEAC boundaries*: CCS 308/7 (*CT* 391; CoS Sextant, 11, UK, p. 36). *Roosevelt–Hull–Steinhardt*: *CT* 386. *Turkish supplies*: Roosevelt 149.

18 *Mountbatten–Chiang–Churchill*: Romanus 63. Churchill memoirs ignore this mtg. and indeed pass over whole conference cursorily, as over unpleasant memory. *Chiang memo*: *CT* 387–9.

19 *25 November*: *CT* 346–51; UK, pp. 10–12; *Cadogan–Hopkins*: Cadogan 577; Thorne 312, citing PREM 4/74/2; *CT* 401–2, 408, 448; cf. Avon 425. *JCS*: Matloff 350–1. *C.o.S.*: UK, pp. 10–12; Bryant, ii. 72. *Aide-mémoire*: UK, p. 215, CoS(43) 7080, later CCS 409 (*CT* 409–11). This memo begins ominously 'For some time it has been clear disagreement exists between us' (over Mediterranean ops.). Howard (pp. 49–51) and Fraser (p. 384) both feel Brooke exaggerates differences. Cf. Bryant ii. 57–9; also JCS 611, November 26.

20 *Churchill–Chiang*: Avon 424; Bryant ii. 72. *Roosevelt–Stalin*: *CT* 373, 385, 413, 438–40.

21 *CCS*: *CT* 346–9; UK, pp. 151–2; Bryant ii. 72; Leahy 237. *SEAC ops.*: Arnold 535; Romanus 63. *'Hump' tonnage*: *CT* 413; Ehrman 164. *Mountbatten memo*: UK, p. 36, CoS Sextant, 12; Ehrman 165–6; Moran 151–2.

22 *Roosevelt–Stilwell–Chiang*: Romanus 64–5; Stilwell 231–2, 246, 251–2; *CT* 349–50, 366, 484, 567, 784, 868–9; 889–91; Sherwood ii. 767–9, 791; Matloff 350; Churchill v. 290. It is clear Churchill never agreed with Roosevelt's promise. This is somewhat blurred in accounts by King (pp. 314–17), Leahy (p. 239), and Sherwood (ii. 767–9). Romanus (p. 65) quotes Stilwell that Chiang reversed previous acceptance of Churchill/Mountbatten arguments (*CT* 430; UK, p. 217; CCS 411/2), no doubt thinking he could get more from Roosevelt. *Chiang–Roosevelt*: *CT* 874. *Dairen*: H. Tong, Chinese delegate, subsequently stated Chiang agreed to consider it, if Chinese retained sovereignty. *Thanksgiving dinner*: Roosevelt 159–60; *CT* 350; Churchill v. 300–1. *Poland*: Avon 424; *CT* 381–5.

23 *26 November*: *CT* 351–67; UK, pp. 12–14. *Roosevelt–Mountbatten–Chiang–Arnold*: *CT* 351–4; Romanus 65; Roosevelt 166; Stilwell 232; Matloff 352.

24 *JCS*: Matloff 351–4. *Changing US Chiefs' attitude*: Pogue 308. *C.o.S.*: UK, pp. 12–14. *JCS memo*: *CT* 426; UK, p. 211 (cf. Deane to JCS, JCS 606, *CT* 373). *'Overall Command'*: CCS 408, 408/1 (*CT* 405–7, 424; UK, pp. 213–15); Churchill v. 297–8; Ehrman 167; Bryant ii. 73. *Strategic Air*

Cd.: CoS Sextant, 8 (UK, pp. 34, 199); CCS 400, 400/1, 400/2 (*CT* 228–9, 432, 787). *Mountbatten memo*: see above, n. 22. *Turkey*: JPS Sextant 2, 4, 8, 9 (UK, JPS Folder); CoS Sextant 13 (UK, p. 37); cf. Roosevelt 149.

25 *CCS*: *CT* 359–65; UK, pp. 152–4; Leahy 235; Bryant ii. 72. *Mediterranean ops.*: Eisenhower 219; Arnold 214; Pogue 307–8; Matloff 354–5. In a memo, Churchill described Andamans as 'trivial prize' compared with Aegean (CoS Sextant, 6, UK, p. 32). *Teheran Agenda*: *CT* 426–8; UK, pp. 211–13 (CCS 407, 407–1).

26 *Eden–McCloy*: *CT* 351–4; Avon 425; see also *CT* 423 442–4.

27 *Roosevelt–Churchill–Chiang*: *CT* 366–7; Leahy 235; Roosevelt 166; Romanus 65; also above, n. 11 for other possible topics of conversation. *Churchill memo (29 Nov.) on 'Buccaneer'*: PREM 3/136/12; Churchill v. 290.

28 *Communiqué*: *CT* 356–7, 366, 399–40, 448–55, 618, 848; also above, n. 19 and Appendix B. *Hopkins–Chiang*. *CT* 367.

29 *Br. attitudes to conference*: Bryant ii. 72–5; Avon 425–6; Churchill v. 289–90; Ismay 334–7; Cadogan 548. *US attitudes*: Sherwood ii. 766; Leahy 238–9; Pogue 309; Matloff 355; Hull ii. 1317; Harriman 260; Burns 404–5.

CHAPTER VIII

Note: Soviet record is in *The Teheran, Yalta, and Potsdam Conferences*, hereinafter referred to as *RUSS*.

1 *Kuriles, etc.*: *CT* 257; Avon 378. *Eden, Harriman, Roosevelt, and Poland*: Avon 371–3, 403; *CT* 154. *Roosevelt on Germany*: Avon 373, 378; Hull ii. 1265. *USSR and Chinese Communists*: *FRUS (1944): China* 97, 253; cf. Thorne 690; Roosevelt 172.

2 *27 November*: *CT* 459–61, 475–6; PREM 3/136/1, pp. 4–9. *Roosevelt's residence*: *CT* 310–11, 397, 439–40, 463, 475–6, 867; Harriman 262–5.

3 *Agenda*: Harriman 263; Cadogan 578–9.

4 *28 November*: *CT* 476–514; UK, pp. 14ff.; PREM 3/136/11. *Br. attitudes after Cairo*: Moran 154; Bryant ii. 74–5. *C.o.S.*: UK, p. 14; Bryant, loc. cit.; ref. UK, JPS folder, JPS Sextant 9; CoS Sextant, 15 (UK, p. 39); PREM 3/13/12, pp. 20–3; CoS Sextant 14 (UK, p. 38). *Churchill's rebuff*: Harriman 265; Churchill v. 306, 320 suggests this rebuff occurred 29th, not 28th. *JCS*: *CT* 476–82; Pogue 309–10; Matloff 358–9; see also US Sextant Conference Bk. and Appendix C for this and other JCS mtgs. Discussion at previous JCS mtg. revolved round similar pts., particularly question of Sov. wishes *re* Mediterranean ops. Advice on time taken to open Dardanelles route came from Somervell. 'Political motivation' of Br.-sponsored Med. ops. was common ground among US Chiefs (cf. Leahy 237, 247; *CT* 481). As Matloff points out (p. 359) Br. Chiefs

thought this equally true of Roosevelt's sponsoring of 'Buccaneer' and King's desire to focus on US-controlled Pacific ops.

5 *Marshall's absence from plenary*: Pogue 310; *CT* 464. Pogue seems to be mistaken in thinking Big Three lunched together. Harriman (pp. 267–8) says after this he took personal responsibility for arrangements. *Roosevelt–Stalin mtg.*: *CT* 485; Roosevelt 175–6; Sherwood ii. 771; Moran 155; Harriman 265–6. *Free French*: USSR had made overtures to de Gaulle. Its recognition formula had been more liberal than that of US and UK: de Gaulle ii. 192–3; Macmillan 390; Woodward ii. 460. *Brooke on Stalin*: Bryant ii. 77. *Djilas*: op. cit. 61.

6 *1st plenary*: *CT* 487–508; PREM 3/136/11, pp. 117–27; *RUSS* 7–14; Churchill v. 306–16; Bryant ii. 76–8; Sherwood ii. 772–6; Leahy 241–2; King 515–17; Ehrman 173–7; Matloff 360–2; Deane 42–4. All versions agree Roosevelt did not mention Southern France op. in opening remarks, nor Churchill until Stalin had spoken. Yet *CT* and *RUSS* give Stalin as immediately mentioning such a possibility. This suggests degree of familiarity with Western strategic debates, however obtained. On the other hand, possibility had been mentioned at Moscow. Stalin may have remembered this. His interest in S. France 'took western delegates by surprise' (Matloff 361). Stalin's apparent familiarity with details of Western strategic debate (of which this is first example) together with tendency of Sov./US delegates to re-echo each other's arguments, has led some Br. historians to suspect collusion (e.g. Fraser 387–8). Leahy or Roosevelt himself seem most likely culprits: but if US quarters had concealed microphones, this would also explain it. However at this early stage there had been no opportunity for 'listening-in' as presidential party had only just moved in. *Roosevelt on 'Overlord'*: Bohlen gives most emphatic version 'Cross-Channel op. should not be delayed by secondary ops.'. CCS has 'must avoid delaying O/L beyond May/June'; Br. and *RUSS* omit reference. *Soviet entry, Japanese war*: US/Br. records agree Stalin promised future Soviet participation; *RUSS* omits this. There is no doubt pledge was given—all later Western discussion took it as datum. Possibly Stalin ordered its exclusion from record from excess of caution; and Sov. editors much later printed what they found (cf. Sherwood ii. 779; Churchill v. 308). *Size of western divisions*: Churchill referred to these as 'twice as strong as German divisions', for which Stalin had previously given figure of 13,000 men (8–9,000 front line). The 35 divs. allotted to 'Overlord' would then have amounted to about ¾ m. men. Churchill refers to 'a million men being placed in France'. This presumably includes HQ and ancillary troops—or Churchill may have included later period, after reinforcement. *Adriatic*: Churchill emphasized Roosevelt had *first* mentioned this (cf. *CT* 493, 503; Sherwood ii. 780). Roosevelt was probably still thinking of forestalling Turkish/E. Med. ops. *'Decisive thrust'*: foll. passage closely duplicates US arguments. *Turkey*: Churchill later implied Bulgaria, Rumania, Hungary might all surrender (*CT* 537; Churchill v. 369). Br. record reports Stalin as advocating coercion of Turkey. *CT* and

RUSS do not support this. *Voroshilov*: Br./Bohlen (*CT*) give this patronizing remark. CCS minutes have 'Voroshilov will be available'. *RUSS* has 'V and I can arrange something'. Harriman (p. 266) thought it strange Stalin only brought V.—'one of Stalin's old stooges, incompetent, not dangerous'. Cunningham has 'stolid and woodenheaded'. Leahy, however, surprisingly describes V. as 'young and vigorous'. V. was about sixty at this time.

7 *US reactions*: Pogue 310; Leahy 242; Ehrman 176; Matloff 361–2. *Br. reactions*: Moran 154, 156, 162; Bryant ii. 76–8; Ismay 339; Churchill v. 305–6. Churchill thought 'he could have gained Stalin'. There seems little ground for this. *Previous Soviet Mediterranean demands*: Harriman 251; Deane 31–5.

8 *Hopkins on Roosevelt*: Burns 409. *Dinner mtg.*: *CT* 509–14 (Bohlen); PREM 3/136/11, pp. 31–3; Harriman 268–9; no Sov. record; Sherwood ii. 776–7; Churchill v. 317–20; Avon 427; Moran 161. *Kiel Canal*: Stalin reacted strongly to Roosevelt's first reference to 'Baltic', mistakenly imagining reference to Sov. territorial claims. Baltic States had 'voted to join USSR' (*CT* 510). *Danubian fedn.*: For earlier Br. formulation of this idea, see WP(41) 287; cf. J. Wheeler-Bennett, *Action This Day* 83; Churchill iii. 472–3, 586–90. *Poland*: At one point Stalin asked 'Do you think I am going to swallow Poland?', going on to imply no intention of annexing Poland, but 'might have a bite at Germany' (PREM 3/136/11, p. 33).

9 *29 November*: *CT* 514–55; PREM 3/136/11, pp. 96–129; UK, p. 15; *RUSS* 16–37. *Military staffs mtg.*: PREM 3/136/11, pp. 83–129; UK, pp. 128–31; *CT* 515–28; *RUSS* 16–25; Bryant ii. 78–80; Ismay 338; Pogue 311; Leahy 244–5; Cadogan 580; Matloff 362–3; Ehrman 177–9. There are variations in records, but all seem to give fairly accurate account of gist of arguments. *RUSS* (p. 17) omits Brooke's statement that 21 German divs. were in Balkans and (p. 18) that Allied bomber offensive kept million Germans occupied. *RUSS* (p. 20) omits parts of Marshall–Voroshilov exchange which underline necessity of taking landing-craft from 'Overlord' if major amphibious ops. launched in Med. (*CT* 521–2; PREM 3/136/11, p. 105). Br/US records (*CT* 525; PREM 3/136/11, pp. 111–12) report Voroshilov saying Stalin 'did not insist on southern France op., only on "Overlord"' *RUSS* (p. 23) has it 'Stalin did not insist on *prior* southern France landing' but did regard it as mandatory some time. Br. record omits Brooke's brusque statement that not enough discussion had taken place (p. 116). *CT* includes but softens it (p. 528). At following plenary mtg. it was decided not to hold further tripartite staff mtg. (*CT* 539).

10 *C.o.S. mtg.*: UK, p. 15. *Earlier stages of discussion of Southern France*: Ehrman 104–5; Matloff 124, 163, 175, 213, 229, 243, 252, citing CCS 303 (9 Aug. 43) and CCS 319/5 (24 Aug. 43). For somewhat confusing accounts of how this plan (JPS 249), dating from 9 Aug., was produced and modified at Teheran, see Matloff 365–6, esp. ns. 43, 44, citing ABC 384, Europe,

9-A. Eisenhower's later appreciation had been 'cautious and not entirely favourable' (Ehrman 104; Matloff 255; cf. NAF 492, 29 Oct. 43, UK, p. 16). At that time he favoured gaining Po valley first before launching 'Anvil'. His perspective then was of course 'Mediterranean'. Bryant ii. 79: '"Anvil" was a suggestion of Eisenhower's never seriously considered by CCS' is slightly misleading. CCS had agreed at Quebec some such ops. should probably be launched: there had been much discussion at planning level, and between CCS and Eisenhower's AFHQ (Matloff, loc. cit.). *'Stripping of Italy'*: Marshall later corrected false Br. impression that majority of troops would be taken from Italy for 'Anvil'.

11 *Roosevelt and JCS*: Sherwood ii. 779; *CT* 529, 617–19; Deane 45. *Roosevelt–Stalin 2nd mtg.*: *CT* 529–33; Harriman 270; Roosevelt 177–80; Sherwood ii. 779–82; Matloff 366–7; Churchill v. 320–1; no Sov. record. It is not clear if Molotov was present: log includes him but record does not record his participation in talk. Strangely, Roosevelt apparently allowed his son to be present. Churchill memoirs comment 'Stalin more realistic than Roosevelt on China' and also complain Roosevelt did not make it clear to Stalin that he, Churchill, also contemplated world council as well as regional councils. E. Roosevelt states Manchuria, Chinese Communists, free elections discussed (p. 183). This is not in *CT*. Manchurian railway system would carry Soviet goods to Dairen and Port Arthur (cf. *CT* 869).

12 *Stalingrad Sword*: *CT* 466; Bryant ii. 78; Churchill v. 321. *2nd plenary*: *CT* 533–52; PREM 3/136/11, pp. 83–95; UK, pp. 123–7; *RUSS* 25–37; Harriman 271–3; Bryant ii. 78–80; Ismay 338; Leahy 245; Churchill v. 321–9; Moran 158–60; Pogue 312–13; Matloff 363–5; Ehrman 179–81. Stalin's point that 'Overlord' cdr. shd. be appointed as soon as possible, since the latter might want to change 'Cossac' plan was valid. It is what happened (Eisenhower 238; Montgomery, *Memoirs* (London, 1958) 218–21). Difficulty over Marshall's appointment is fully discussed by Pogue, Sherwood, and Matloff. *Balkans*: estimated number of Axis divs. in that area varied widely. Ehrman (p. 82) puts number Oct. '43 as 15, compared with Bryant's 18 (p. 28) and Churchill's 21 (p. 324). *CT* and *RUSS* quote Churchill as using figure of 42 in discussion, which seems like a mishearing, unless Churchill by mistake gave the wrong figure. *RUSS* (p. 33) has Stalin telling Churchill his figures are 'wrong' and giving figure of 12–13 divs. JCS, when subsequently queried, gave figure as 25. Much depends, of course, on precise month referred to. *Turkey*: Br, US, and Sov. texts agree Churchill undertook to threaten Turkey with loss of Western support over Straits. Churchill memoirs (p. 324), written in early 1950s when Western support for Turkey was unequivocal, perhaps deliberately softens this remark. *RUSS* similarly (p. 31) omits Stalin's conditional promise to declare war on Bulgaria, given in both US and Br. texts. *Overlord date*: Bohlen (*CT* 538) has Roosevelt saying 'I'm in favour of Quebec date'. *RUSS* has similar wording. Br. has 'there are obvious dangers in delay to O/L'. Only CCS minutes (*CT* 551) has Stalin's angry

remark: 'General Brooke cannot force our opinions.' *E. Roosevelt*: op. cit. 183. *Ref. back to military staffs*: Leahy (p. 245) suggests Churchill was 'playing for time'. Bohlen (*CT* 539) has Stalin describing last question to Churchill as 'indiscreet'; Br. text has 'very direct'. *Churchill's 'Moscow conditions'*: *FRUS (1943): General* 776–7 and FO 371/37031/N 6921, 20 Oct. mtg.

13 *Dinner mtg.*: *CT* 552–5 (Bohlen, from subsequent notes); Churchill v. 329–30; Roosevelt 186–9; Harriman 272–3; Moran 159–60; Sherwood ii. 784–5. Churchill and E. Roosevelt give very different accounts of this; Bohlen tactfully omits whole episode. *Br. reactions*: Bryant ii. 78–80; Moran 160–2. *Hopkins's visit to Churchill*: Bohlen 148.

14 *30 November*: *CT* 555–85; PREM 3/136/11, pp. 25–7, 33–6, 78–2; UK, pp. 16, 127, 154–7. *Aegean/Italy*: Brooke's biographer (Fraser, pp. 372–3) accepts Kennedy's contemporary view that only a major Balkan campaign could have produced results Brooke's diary entries imply could have been achieved in that area. This would have meant 'no Overlord in 44' (Kennedy 305). Professor Howard rightly (pp. 47–8) says Brooke's more heated entries (Bryant ii. 51–3) are difficult to justify. Perhaps one can attach too much importance to diary entries written in the heat of the moment, but Brooke repeated his views in post-war comments (Bryant, loc. cit.); while other diary entries (Bryant ii. 47) show he sometimes doubted possibility of reconciling Aegean ops. with Italy which he regarded as more important. *C.o.S.*: UK, p. 16; Bryant ii. 80–1; *CCS*: CT 555–64.

15 *CCS*: *CT* 555–64; UK, p. 129; Bryant, loc. cit.; Leahy 247; Pogue 313; Matloff (p. 365) says 'CCS agreed O/L would be launched during May'. *CT*, however, (p. 564) and Churchill (v. 336) make it clear CCS wording was 'by June 1st', which Roosevelt altered. Leahy's query to Brooke again re-echoes Sov. arguments, which has caused suspicion of 'collusion'. '*So ended*': argument flared up again briefly over 'Anvil' date in '44 (Ehrman 230–47). During CCS discussion Brooke pointed out planned 'Overlord' lift was less than Salerno, a near-disaster (*CT* 562).

16 *Overlord date*: Roosevelt (p. 19) slightly misrepresents decision. *Iran*: CT 564–5, 646–51; Roosevelt 192; Hull ii. 151–9; Hurley, Dreyfus, and Elliott Roosevelt were present.

17 *Churchill–Stalin*: PREM 3/136/11, pp. 25–7; Churchill v. 331–6; no *RUSS* record. Mtg. lasted ¾hr. *Big Three lunch mtg.*: *CT* 565–8; PREM 3/136/11, pp. 36–7; no *RUSS* record; Churchill v. 336–7. Br. record omits report of military decisions. In response to Churchill's pertinent question to Stalin if he approved Cairo communiqué (which *inter alia* promised restoration of Manchuria to China), *CT* (p. 566) and Churchill agree Stalin's answer was slightly evasive. *CT* (p. 567) says Churchill first mentioned warm-water ports, Br. record (p. 36) says Stalin did so. *Dairen*: Sherwood (ii. 786) says he was told subject discussed at Cairo and Chiang agreed to free port. Both Chinese record (*CT* 324) and Hopkins's note (p. 367) cast doubt on this. Br. record omits reference.

18 *Eden–Molotov–Hopkins*:   *CT*   568–75;   PREM   3/136/11, pp.   31–6;
Harriman 275; Sherwood ii. 786–7; no *RUSS* record. *'Strong points.*:
Hopkins (*CT* 569) dissented from Eden's remark that UK had been glad
to accept US bases in W. Indies, presumably implying concession had
been prompted by dire need; therefore France would be equally reluctant,
but Chinese would do so because they wanted US alliance. *Turkish entry*:
PREM 3/136/11 (p. 35) has Hopkins say this would be 'psychologically
tremendously advantageous'. *CT* omits. PREM 3 much condenses discussion of French bases, but includes Eden's remark that UK wished
France 'to be strong again' which *CT* omits. PREM omits Eden's statement 'that consequences would follow' Turkish refusal (*CT* 571). PREM
has Molotov reiterate (p. 11) 'Turkey should declare war this year' which
CT omits. *Stalin's demands*: *CT* (p. 574) omits Hopkins' assurance (PREM,
p. 35) that Big Three would agree on these demands. Foreign Ministers
did not meet again separately but joined heads of government next day for
lunch.

19 *3rd plenary*: *CT* 576–81; PREM 3/136/11, pp. 78–81; *RUSS* 38–40;
Churchill v. 337–9; King 311; Bryant 81–2; Leahy 247–8. *CT* and *RUSS*
omit Churchill reference to Italy, Yugoslavia, Turkey. Churchill's hope
they would spend two more days on political questions was vain—another
instance of Sov.–US wishes prevailing. *Military communiqué*: *CT* 652;
RUSS 51–2; PREM 3/136/11, p. 82 prints only portion of mil. agreements
later incorporated in public statement: CT has full text, including aid to
Yugoslavia, action on Turkish entry, O/L in May, S/France op.,
simultaneous Sov. offensive. Anglo-American agreement on advance to
Pisa–Rimini line was excluded as not being part of tripartite agreements
(UK, p. 42, Ismay memo, CoS Sextant 19, Dec. 3).

20 *Dinner mtg.*: *CT* 582–5; Churchill 339–43; Bryant 82–5; Leahy 250;
Bohlen 149–50; Harriman 276–8. Bohlen was present, but minutes are by
Boettiger, Roosevelt's son-in-law. *Brooke–Stalin*: Churchill says Stalin had
already complained to him of Brooke's dislike of Russians. Boettiger
implies Stalin spoke half-humorously. Brooke did not think so. Roosevelt
(p. 196) mentions Brooke's reply but characteristically omits attack which
provoked it, thus making it seem unpleasantness was Brooke's fault.
Bohlen memoir says Brooke specifically referred to previous Nazi–Soviet
association: one wonders whether even Brooke would have been quite so
blunt. Presumably Stalin's anger was prompted by Brooke's opposition to
Soviet military demands.

21 *1 December*: *CT* 585–605; PREM 3/136/11, pp. 37–50; *RUSS* 40–50.
Tripartite lunch mtg.: *CT* 585–93; PREM, pp. 37–42; *RUSS* 40–4;
Churchill v. 344–8; Avon 428; Bohlen 150–2; Sherwood 787–8. Different
records of this mtg. which began at 12 noon are confusing. *CT* says lunch
talk covered Turkey and Finland; was followed 3.20 by private
Roosevelt–Stalin mtg., Churchill rejoining them at 6 p.m. for discussion
of Italian shipping, Poland, and Germany. PREM includes Italy in lunch
talk and implies Poland discussed before Finland; *RUSS* has only Turkey

as subject at lunch, omits Finland altogether, and has second session on Poland/Germany lasting from 4 p.m. till 7.40 p.m. *RUSS* omits Roosevelt–Stalin mtg. Other sources clearly follow national records. Roosevelt later told a Cabinet colleague he had teased Churchill in front of Stalin to put the latter in better humour (F. Perkins, The Roosevelt I Knew 84). This probably cut no ice with Stalin and was little appreciated by Churchill. *Inönü: CT* 632–4. According to *RUSS* (p. 41) Stalin asked about 2 Br. divs. allotted to Aegean ops.: Churchill said this would only be if Rhodes op. took place. Sherwood (pp. 787–8) says Hopkins edited minutes, inserting statement of US belief there were no landing-craft available for Rhodes: and even if some did become available, a better use for them might emerge (i.e. 'Buccaneer'). Therefore no promise should be made to Inönü. (Not in PREM or *RUSS*.)

22 *Finland: CT* 590–3; PREM 3/136/11, pp. 45–8. PREM has Stalin saying that 'some frontier corrections in favour of USSR' (as Finns suggested) was not enough. In general, Stalin's tone in Br. record is less accommodating than in *CT*. *CT* also tones down Roosevelt's apparent suggestion that Finns should surrender Karelia. *Hangö, Petsamo*: PREM has Roosevelt calling this 'a fair exchange' which *CT* omits. PREM/*CT* agree Stalin outlined Sov. demands as (1) 1940 frontiers, with Petsamo annexed to USSR; (2) compensation in kind for 50% of war damage; (3) breach with and expulsion of Germans; (4) Finnish demobilization (*CT* 'reorganization' seems probable misprint). Roosevelt/Churchill queried reparations, appeared willing to accept other points.

23 *Italian shipping: CT* 586–7; PREM 3/136/11, pp. 41–2; *RUSS* 44–6; Churchill v. 347–8.

24 *Roosevelt–Stalin: CT* 594–6; Harriman 278–80; Bohlen 151; Avon 428. No *RUSS* record. Eden/Churchill did not apparently learn details of talk till much later. Russians interpreted Roosevelt's acceptance of 'westward shift' of Polish–Sov. frontier as in effect Curzon Line (*CT* 885); *FRUS: Conferences at Malta and Yalta* 202–5, 667; Harriman 359; Churchill vi. 209. It is not clear if there had been any prior Churchill–Roosevelt discussion of accelerated date of departure. Presumably there had.

25 *Poland: CT* 597–601; PREM 3/136/11, pp. 42–5; *RUSS* 46–50; Churchill v. 348–51; Harriman 280; Bohlen 152; Avon 428. *Polish government*: Bohlen is mistaken in saying subject did not 'come up' at all, also that Roosevelt took absolutely no part in discussion (cf. *CT* record and Harriman 280). Eden and Cadogan (p. 381) agree they got little concession from Stalin, in spite of frontier offer. *CT* omits Stalin's complaint that frontier proposals had not previously been linked with resumption of Sov.–Polish relations; in general *CT* gives v. brief summary of discussion. *Frontiers: RUSS* has Churchill saying Poland should be satisfied at expense of Germany, which *CT*/PREM attribute to Stalin. *RUSS* omits ref. to Molotov–Ribbentrop Line. Map used with Stalin annotations is in *CT* 601. Stalin asserted map based on Polish statistics (Bohlen 152).

26 *German partition: CT* 600–4; PREM 3/136/11, pp. 48–50; *RUSS* 48–50;

Churchill v. 354–6; Harriman 280–2. PREM makes it clear Churchill wished to continue discussing Poland, which *CT/RUSS* omit, also Stalin's jibe that Churchill did not want to discuss G. partition. PREM implies, but *CT* does not, that Roosevelt offered his plan tentatively; both *CT* and PREM agree Stalin spoke strongly in favour of partition, while *RUSS* gives impression S. did not commit himself strongly, merely saying 'this can be examined'. All agree S. opposed 'Danubian federation'. *Churchill's 'formula'*: *RUSS*/PREM agree C. mentioned Curzon Line, *CT* is vaguer, perhaps deliberately. *RUSS* attributes suggestion of exchange of populations to Churchill; *CT/PREM* give it as Roosevelt question. *CT/RUSS* omit Churchill statement that discussion represented only 'preliminary survey'. *CT* has no record of Churchill's full proposals on frontiers.

27 *Communiqué*: *CT* 659–41; *RUSS* 51–2. *Iran Declaration*: *CT* 646–9; *RUSS* 52–3. Negotiations had been conducted by Hurley on Roosevelt's orders. Roosevelt had to intervene personally to secure Stalin's assent.

CHAPTER IX

1 *C.o.S.*: UK, pp. 19–20; ref. Ismay memo CoS Sextant, 19 (UK, p. 42). Teheran military communiqué embodied only tripartite military agreement. It did not include separate Anglo-American decision to mount 'Shingle' and advance to Pisa–Rimini line; cf. Bryant ii. 87. Brooke complained Churchill already weakening (in Inönü talks) on Rhodes operation. Brooke was also annoyed that 2nd Cairo conference scheduled to end 6 Dec. *CCS, 3 Dec.*: *CT* 668–74; UK, pp. 157–9; ref. CCS Memo 423/2 (military conclusions); *CT* 796–7, UK, pp. 239–40. *Turkey in War*: CCS 418/1; *CT* 782; UK, pp. 229–30. *Overall plan for defeat of Japan*: *CT* 765–73; UK, pp. 225–9. Agreed military agenda, Cairo II, also included still unsettled question of integrated US air cd., 'Rankin', and final report. *Churchill–Roosevelt mtg., 3 Dec.*: *CT* 674; Churchill v. 361–7; Leahy 251–2; Pogue 316–17; Ehrman 183–202; Matloff 378–87.

2 *C.o.S.*: UK, pp. 23–4 (4 Dec.). *Plenary*: *CT* 675–81; UK, pp. 137–9. *CCS* CT 681–90; UK, pp. 159–62. *Andamans*: Marshall questioned Portal's view of potential size of airstrips. *Mountbatten*: Churchill v. 363–6; Terraine 139. For these mtgs. see also Bryant ii. 87–8, Churchill v. 362–4. Pogue 316–22, Ehrman, loc. cit., Matloff, loc. cit.

3 *C.o.S.*: UK, pp. 20–2. *CCS*: *CT* 699–705; UK, pp. 162–4. *Plenary*: *CT* 705–11, UK, pp. 139–41. *Second CCS mtg.*: *CT* 719–25; UK, pp. 164–6. Telex to Mountbatten included in both accounts. *Roosevelt's decision*: *CT* 725–6; cf. Churchill v. 364; Stilwell 251. *Roosevelt to Chiang*: *CT* 803–4. For above mtgs. see also Pogue 316–17; Ehrman 183–202; Bryant ii. 98–9; Roosevelt 207–8.

4 *Turkish talks*: *CT* 690–9, 711–18, 726–34, 739–47, 751–6; PREM

3/136/11, pp. 51–77; Churchill v. 367–9; Avon 429; ref. CCS 418/1 (*CT* 782; UK, pp. 229–30); Roosevelt 207–8; Leahy 253; Matloff 378–87; Ehrman 183–202.

5 *Mediterranean Cd.*: CCS 426/1—final Report of CCS to PM and President (*CT* 810–15; UK, p. 242). CCS 387/3—Eisenhower directive (*CT* 794–6; UK, p. 25). *US Strategic Air CD.*: CCS 400/2 (*CT* 757; UK, pp. 201–2); cf. Arnold 218 for his 'second thoughts' on the question. *'United Chiefs'*: *CT* 815; UK, p. 242. *'Overlord' appointment*: Pogue 318–22; *CT* 819; Sherwood ii. 793–4; Roosevelt 209–10. According to latter, President blamed Churchill for Marshall's disappointment; which was true only in sense of Br. opposition to idea of 'Overall Cdr.'. Churchill had always been willing for Marshall to cd. 'Overlord' and Pogue (p. 262) had it on Stimson's authority that Churchill suggested Marshall at Quebec. Brooke, however, thought Eisenhower more suitable, purely because of greater cd. experience (Bryant ii. 89).

6 *'Percentages Agreement'*: Churchill vi. 197–9; see also M. F. Herz, *Beginnings of Cold War*, Ch. V. It is interesting that some historians have suggested that even before this period Br. FO had reconciled itself to absolute Soviet predominance post-war in Eastern Europe (e.g. Howard 52), and it is of course true that Eden and FO were already looking ahead to possible 'worst case' in E. Europe. On the other hand Eden took a full package of proposals on E. Europe to Moscow conference; even in first six months of '44 FO minutes suggest (Woodward iii. 109–12) govt. not completely reconciled to (as Churchill put it) 'Communization of E. Europe'. This view is confirmed by senior officials of that period (Lord Gladwyn, Sir Frank Roberts, and Lord Sherfield to the author). *Roosevelt and Greece*: Avon 430–1; Barker, *Eden* 186–8, citing PREM 3/211/5; *CT* (pp. 740, 844), published before Avon, makes only minimal reference. Roosevelt's action was as inexplicable as it was indefensible. *Final Cairo mtgs.*: *CT* 756–64; UK, pp. 25–6; Arnold 474; Churchill v. 370–1.

7 *Roosevelt on post-war Soviet power*: Roosevelt 185; cf. also Quebec report, Sherwood ii. 744. Roosevelt had already said that 'Eastern Europe would have to get used to Soviet domination'.

8 *Marshall and Teheran*: Pogue 317. *'Buccaneer'*: Pogue 316. *Roosevelt comments*: Stimson 443; *CT* 785. *Roosevelt broadcast*: S. I. Rosenman (ed.), *Public Papers and Addresses of F. D. Roosevelt* (New York, 1950) 553–62. *Harriman–Bohlen comments*: Harriman 289; Bohlen 153–4. Bohlen's judgement, however, 'Teheran did not decide the issues' (ibid.) seems true only in part. The combination of political and military understandings, in present writer's opinion, helped to prejudge some at least of issues. The reader must judge this for himself or herself.

9 *Eden's report*: WM(43) 169, 13 Dec. *Brooke's report*: WM(43) 174, 22 Dec. *Poland*: cf. WP (43) 528. 22 Nov.; WM(44) 8, 18 Jan.; Avon 434–6. *Eden's later judgment*; op. cit. 428–9. *Churchill*: Churchill v. 358, Chs. XXV, XXVII; Bryant ii. 88–9, 93–6; Moran 160–2, 165–6, 168–71, 181–2, 191. Churchill's comment to War Cab. at time (6 Dec.) was 'we

have reached very sound conclusions all along the line' (PREM 3/136/12, p. 34). It is fair to say that Churchill memoirs say nothing about 'political motives' which may or may not have influenced his support for 'Shingle'; but to have done so, even after the war, would have been to concede what he denied at the time. Professor Howard (p. 52) and others have argued convincingly that before Teheran there is little evidence for anything other than 'strategic opportunism' in Churchill's Mediterranean strategy. In a communication to the author, Professor Howard points out that Churchill's frenetic activity over the Anzio operation was characteristic of his tendency to become obsessed with an operation he had decided to support. It would have been strange, however, if Churchill's outlook had been unaffected by Soviet–American axis at Teheran and its consequences. To discuss matter fully wd. require another chapter. When Churchill papers are fully open, they may settle matter finally. M. Stoler (*The Politics of the Second Front* 155–7) is probably not too far from truth. What Stoler says also of Roosevelt's tendency to conceal thoughts from advisers, and 'to distort record for sake of his future reputation' is not entirely inapplicable to Churchill. Documents do not always tell the full story: military and political considerations intermingle and overlap. A 'Ljubijana gap' strategy was probably impracticable by June 1944, or possibly earlier. Churchill's views in any case were often not shared, or not fully, by Br. Chiefs of Staff. *'Retribution' in Germany*: Churchill v. 359, 621.

10 *Stalin's views*: Djilas 61–2. *Poland*: quotation is from Barker, *Eden* 251.

11 Quotations are from Feis (pp. 277–8) and Deane (pp. 43–4). *Roosevelt doubts on Germany*: Hull ii. 1265; *US* 542. *Stalin on Churchill motives*: CT 553–4, 837; PREM 3/136/8, p. 24. On politics 'input' into US strategic thinking, see Stoler 135–6ff. citing JCS 533 series, Nov. 43 MM, CCS 381, Secs 1 and 4; *CT* 210–13; MM, OPD Exec. 9, Item 13, Paper 112. Quotation on Turkey is from Wheeler-Bennett and Nicholls 169; cf. Kennedy 305.

12 On the connexion between Teheran and Yalta there is an interesting but little-known article by the editor of *CT*, W. M. Franklin: 'Yalta, viewed from Teheran', in *Some Pathways in Twentieth-Century History* (New York, 1960) 254–301.

BIBLIOGRAPHY

A. DOCUMENTARY SOURCES

British Documents

The following documents are available in the Public Record Office, Kew, London:

1. War Cabinet Minutes and Memoranda (WM and WP series), filed under CAB 65, 66, 68 on open shelves.
2. Defence Committee Minutes and Memoranda (D.O. series), filed under CAB 69.
3. Prime Minister's Papers, filed under PREM, especially PREM 3.
4. Chiefs of Staff Committee Minutes and Memoranda (CoS series), filed under CAB 79, and CAB 99.
5. Combined Chiefs of Staff Committee Minutes and Memoranda (CCS series) filed under CAB 88.
6. SEXTANT Conference Book (Cairo and Teheran Conferences), filed under CAB 99/25.
7. Papers of the Earl of Avon, filed under FO 954.
8. Papers of Lord Inverchapel, (Sir A. Clark Kerr) filed under FO 800.
9. Foreign Office Papers, filed under FO 371. Especially FO 371/37031 – Foreign Ministers' Conference.

Private Papers

I have had access to those private papers of A. V. Alexander, C. R. Attlee, Ernest Bevin, P. J. Grigg, Lord Halifax, Lord Hankey, and Lord Strang which are available at Churchill College, Cambridge: also to those of Lord Cherwell at Nuffield College, Oxford. None of these contained anything of major interest for this book. The diaries of Sir Andrew Cunningham (British Museum), Lord Ismay, Sir Alan Brooke (both at King's College, London), and Hugh Dalton (London School of Economics and Political Science) are of interest to all students of the Second World War.

United States Documents

The main diplomatic documents for this book were available in published form in *Foreign Relations of the United States, 1943* (Washington, Department of State), particularly Vol. I (General), which includes Moscow Conference documents; and volumes on China and Cairo–Teheran.

I have had only limited access to the US Archives. Those most frequently cited by official US historians and other sources include the following:

1. Papers of Franklin Roosevelt and Harry Hopkins (Roosevelt Library, Hyde Park, New York State).
2. Papers of General H. Arnold, Cordell Hull, Frank Knox, and Admiral W. D. Leahy (Manuscript Division, Library of Congress, Washington).
3. State Department Records (National Archives, Washington) particularly Decimal files 740.0011 (Moscow); 740.0011 (European War); 111.11 (Cordell Hull).
4. US Army Records, Washington, especially Chief of Staff records (WDCSA); Operations Division, War Department (OPD) records; and US Joint Chiefs of Staff minutes and memoranda (JCS).

Through University Microfilms, Ann Arbor, Michigan, I have had access to two interesting unpublished doctoral theses: C. J. Marion, 'Ministers in Moscow', Indiana University, 1970 and L. E. Hoska, Jnr., 'Summit Diplomacy during World War II', University of Maryland, 1966.

B. BOOKS

Alexander of Tunis, Earl: *Memoirs*, London, Cassell, 1962.

Ambrose, S. E.: *The Supreme Commander*, London, Cassell, 1971.

Arnold, H. H.: *Global Mission*, New York, Harper, 1949.

Auty, P. and Cloggs, R.: *British Policy towards Wartime Resistance in Yugoslavia and Greece*, London, Macmillan, 1975.

Avon, Earl of: *The Reckoning*, London, Cassell, 1965.

Barker, E.: *British Policy in South-East Europe in the Second World War*, London, Macmillan, 1976.

—— *Churchill and Eden at War*, London, Macmillan, 1978.

Beitzell, R.: *The Uneasy Alliance*, New York, A. Knopf, 1972.

Benes, E.: *Memoirs*, London, Houghton, 1954.

Berezhkov, V.: *Teheran, 1943*, Moskow, Izdatel 'stvo agentsva pechati novosti, 1968.

Birse, A. H.: *Memoirs of an Interpreter*, New York, Coward-McCann, 1967, and London, M. Joseph, 1967.

Blum, J. M.: *From the Morgenthau Diaries* (3 vols.), Boston, Mass., Houghton Mifflin, 1963 – 7.

Bohlen, C. E.: *Witness to History*, London, Weidenfeld, 1973.

Boyle, J. H.: *China and Japan at War, 1937 – 45*, Stanford, Calif., Stanford UP, 1972.

Bryant, Sir A. (ed.): *The Alanbrooke War Diaries* (2 vols.), London, Collins, 1957 and Fontana (paperback), 1965.

Buhite, R. D.: *Patrick Hurley and American Foreign Policy*, Ithaca, NY, Cornell UP, 1973.

Burns, J. M.: *Roosevelt, The Soldier of Freedom*, New York, H. Brace, 1970.

Butcher, H.: *My Three Years with Eisenhower*, London, Heinemann, 1946.

Calvocoressi, P. and Wint, G.: *Total War*, London, Allen Lane, 1972.

Carlton, D.: *Anthony Eden*, London, Allen Lane 1982.

Castellano, G.: *La Guerra Continua: La Vera Storia dell' 8 Septembre con Documenti Inediti*, Milan, 1963.

Ciechanowsky, J.: *Defeat in Victory*, New York, Doubleday, 1947.

Chandler, A. D., Jnr. (ed.): *The Papers of Dwight David Eisenhower* (5 vols.), Baltimore, Md., John Hopkins, 1970.

Chiang-Kai-Shek: *China's Destiny*, ed. P. Jaffer, New York, 1947.

Churchill, W. S.: *The Second World War* (6 vols.), London, Cassell, 1948 – 54.

Cunningham, Viscount: *A Sailor's Odyssey*, London, Hutchinson, 1951.

Deakin, F. W.: *The Brutal Friendship*, New York, Harper and Row, 1962.

Deane, J. R., *The Strange Alliance*, London, Murray, 1947.

De Gaulle, C.: *War Memoirs* (3 vols. and documents), London, Weidenfeld and Nicolson, 1955 – 60.

Deutscher, I.: *Stalin, a Political Biography*, London, Oxford UP, 1949, and London, Penguin (paperback), 1951.

Dilks, D. (ed.): *The Diaries of Sir Alexander Cadogan*, London, Cassell, 1971.

Divine, R.: *Roosevelt and World War II*, Baltimore, Md., John Hopkins, 1969.

Djilas, M.: *Conversations with Stalin*, New York, Harcourt Brace, 1962, and London, Penguin (paperback), 1963.

Ehrman, J.: *Grand Strategy,* Vol. v, London, HMSO, 1956.

Eisenhower, D. D.: *Crusade in Europe*, New York, Doubleday, and London, Heinemann, 1948.

Eubank, K.: *The Summit Conferences, 1919 – 60*, Norman, Okla., Oklahoma UP, 1966.

Feis, H.: *Churchill, Roosevelt, Stalin*, Princeton UP, 1957.

Fischer, L.: *The Road to Yalta: Soviet Foreign Relations, 1941 – 5*, New York, Harper, 1972.

Foreign Relations of the United States: The Conferences at Cairo and Teheran, Washington, DC, Department of State, 1961.

Foreign Relations of the United States, 1943 (6 vols.), Washington, DC, Department of State, 1962.

Forrestal, J.: *The Forrestal Diaries* (ed. W. Millis), New York, Viking Press, 1951.

Fraser, Sir D.: *Alanbrooke*, London, Collins, 1982.

Fuller, J. F. C.: *The Second World War*, London, Eyre and Spottiswoode, 1948.

Gaddis, J. L.: *The United States and the Origins of the Cold War*, New York, Columbia, 1972.

Gladwyn, Lord: *Memoirs*, London, Weidenfeld, 1972.

Greenfield, K. R.: *American Strategy in World War II*, Baltimore, Md., John Hopkins, 1963.

Harriman, W. A. and Abel, E.: *Special Envoy to Churchill and Stalin*, London, Hutchinson, 1976.

Harvey, J. (ed.): *The Diplomatic Diaries of Oliver Harvey, 1937 – 40*, London, Collins, 1970.

Herz, M. F.: *The Beginnings of the Cold War*, New York and London, McGraw-Hill, 1969.

Howard, M.: *The Mediterranean Strategy in World War II*, London, Weidenfeld and Nicolson, 1968.

Hull, C.: *Memoirs* (2 vols.), London, Hodder & Stoughton, 1948.

Ismay, Lord: *Memoirs*, London, Heinemann, 1960.

Kennedy, Sir J.: *The Business of War*, London, Hutchinson, 1957.

King, E. J. and Whitehill, W. M.: *Fleet Admiral King*, New York, Norton, 1952.

Kuklick, B.: *American Policy and the Division of Germany*, Ithaca, NY, Cornell UP, 1972.

Leahy, W. D.: *I Was There*, New York, McGraw-Hill, 1950.

Leasor, J.: *War at the Top*, London, M. Joseph, 1959.

Lewin, R.: *Churchill as Warlord*, London, Batsford, 1973.

Liddell-Hart, B.: *History of the Second World War*, Cassell, 1970.

Loewenheim, F. L. *et. al.*: *Roosevelt and Churchill, Their Secret Wartime Correspondence*, London, Barrie and Jenkins, 1975.

Long, Brekinridge: *The War Diary of Breckinridge Long* (ed. F. Israel), Lincoln, Nebr., Nebraska UP, 1966.

Macmillan, H.: *The Blast of War*, London, Macmillan, 1967.

Maisky, I. M.: *Memoirs of a Soviet Ambassador*, London, Hutchinson, 1967.

Marion, C. J.: see Sect. A of this Bibliography, p. 360 above.

Matloff, M.: *Strategic Planning for Coalition Warfare, 1943 – 44*, Washington, DC, Office of the Chief of Military History, 1959.

Mcneill, W. H.: *America, Britain and Russia: Their Cooperation and Conflict, 1941 – 46*, London, Oxford UP, 1953.

Micolajczyk, S.: *The Pattern of Soviet Domination*, London, Sampson Low, 1948, published as *The Rape of Poland*, New York, McGraw, 1948.

Moran, Lord: *Winston Churchill, The Struggle for Survival*, London, Constable, 1966, and Sphere (paperback), 1968.

Moscow Conference of Foreign Ministers of the USSR, USA and Great Britain, 1943, Moscow, Publishing-House of Political Literature, 1978. (In Russian)

Moseley, P.: *The Kremlin and World Politics*, New York, Random House, 1960.

Murphy, R.: *Diplomat among Warriors*, New York, Doubleday, 1964, and London, Collins, 1964.

Nicolson, N.: *Alex*, London, Weidenfeld & Nicolson, 1973.

North, R. C.: *Moscow and the Chinese Communists*, Stanford, Calif., Stanford UP, 1953.

Notter, H.: *Postwar Foreign Policy Preparation, 1939 – 45*, Department of State Publication 3580, Washington, DC, US Government Printing Office, 1950.

Payne, R.: *Chiang-Kai Shek*, New York, Weybright and Tolley, 1969.

Pelling, H.: *Winston Churchill*, London, Macmillan, 1974.

Perkins, F.: *The Roosevelt I Knew*, New York, Viking Press, 1946.

Pogue, F. C.: *The Organizer of Victory*, New York, Viking Press, 1973.

Pratt, J. W.: *Cordell Hull*, New York, Cooper Square, 1964.

Raczynski, E.: *In Allied London*, London, Weidenfeld, 1962.

Range, W.: *Franklin D. Roosevelt's World Order*, Athens, Ga., Georgia UP, 1959.

Reilly, M. F.: *Reilly of the White House*, New York, Simon and Schuster, 1947.

Richards, D.: *Portal of Hungerford*, London, Heinemann, 1977.

Romanus, C. F. and Sutherland, R.: *Stilwell's Command Problems*, Washington, DC, Office of the Chief of Military History, 1953.

Roosevelt, Elliott: *As He Saw It*, New York, Duell, Sloan, and Pearce, 1946.

Rothwell, V. *Britain and the Cold War*, London, Cape, 1982.

Russell, R. B.: *A History of the United Nations Charter*, Washington, DC, Brookings, 1958, and London, Faber, 1958.

Sherwood, R. S.: *The White House Papers of Harry L. Hopkins* (2 vols.), London, Eyre & Spottiswoode, 1948.

Smith, Gaddis: *American Diplomacy During the Second World War*, New York, J. Wiley, 1965.

Snell, J.: *Wartime Origins of the Dilemma over Germany*, New Orleans, La., Hauser, 1959.

Soviet Commission on Foreign Diplomatic Documents: *Correspondence between the Chairman of the Council of Ministers of the USSR and the Presidents of the USA and the Prime Ministers of Britain*, Moscow, Foreign Languages Publishing House, 1957.

Standley, W. H.: *Admiral Ambassador to Russia*, Chicago, Regnery, 1955.

Stilwell, J.: *The Stilwell Papers*, New York, W. Sloane, 1948.

Stimson, H. L. and Bundy, McG.: *On Active Service in Peace and War*, New York, Harper, 1947.

Stoler, M.: *The Politics of the Second Front*, Westport, Conn., and London, Greenwood, 1977.

Strang, Lord: *At Home and Abroad*, London, Deutsch, 1956.

Teheran, Yalta and Potsdam Conferences, Moscow, Progress, 1969.

Terraine, J.: *The Life and Times of Lord Mountbatten*, London, Hutchinson, 1968, and Arrow (paperback), 1969.

Thorne, C.: *Allies of a Kind*, London, H. Hamilton, 1978.

Trukhanovsky, L.: *British Foreign Policy in the Second World War*, Moscow, Progress, 1969.

Tsou, T.: *America's Failure in China, 1941–50* (2 vols.), Chicago, University of Chicago Press, 1963.

Viorst, M.: *Hostile Allies: F.D.R. and de Gaulle*, New York, Doubleday, 1975.

Wedemeyer, A. C.: *Wedemeyer Reports*, New York, H. Holt, 1958.

Werth, A.: *Russia at War*, London, Barrie & Rockliffe, 1964, and Pan (paperback), 1965.

Wheeler-Bennett, J. (ed.): *Action this Day*, London, Macmillan, 1968.

—— and Nicholls, A.: *The Semblance of Peace*, London, Macmillan, 1972.

de Wiart, C.: *Happy Odyssey*, London, Cape, 1950, and Pan (paperback) 1955.

Wilmot, C.: *The Struggle for Europe*, London, Collins, 1952.

Wilson, Sir H. M.: *Eight Years Overseas*, London, Hutchinson, 1950.

Woodward, Sir L.: *British Foreign Policy in the Second World War* (5 vols.), London, HMSO, 1970–5.

INDEX

033588

940.532 Sainsbury, Keith.
SAI
                The turning point
                    24.95

DATE		

© THE BAKER & TAYLOR CO.